On the Barricades

On the Barricades

RELIGION AND FREE INQUIRY IN CONFLICT

WITH

Sidney Hook	Martin Gardner
Steve Allen	Daniel Boorstin
E. O. Wilson	B. F. Skinner
James Randi	Isaac Asimov
Paul Kurtz	Rita Swan
Albert Ellis	Thomas Szasz
L. Sprague de Camp	

. . . AND MANY MORE

EDITED BY

ROBERT BASIL • MARY BETH GEHRMAN • TIM MADIGAN

Prometheus Books
700 East Amherst St. • Buffalo, New York 14215

for Doris Doyle and Jean Millholland
who kept it going

Library of Congress Card Catalog Number 89-63454
ISBN 0-87975-563-6

Table of Contents

I.

INTRODUCTION

T he premiere issue of *Free Inquiry* was put together in between the time Ronald Reagan was elected president in November 1980 and when he was inaugurated the following January. Reagan's victory was hailed by a confident and vocal coalition of fundamentalist Christians. Their support for the new president was not based so much on his own religious practices. (Indeed, by all accounts Reagan was a rather lax churchgoer; it was Jimmy Carter who was powered by born-again zeal.) What the religious right saw in Reagan was a savior of sorts: Here was a man who upheld "traditional Judeo-Christian values," who loathed feminism, who wanted the children of America to open their school days with prayer. And, just as important, Reagan knew who the enemies were: *nonbelievers*. In an interview with *Time,* Reagan said, "Some of the exponents of atheism . . . do not realize that, in effect, they have created almost a religion of their own in that belief and are demanding things for their religion that they would deny others."

Conservative wags saw the conspiracy, too. Patrick J. Buchanan (a Catholic who has never recovered from the reforms of Vatican II) wrote that "the religion of which Reagan spoke is secular humanism." Phyllis Schlafly chimed in: "To replace the tenets of traditional religion, humanism proclaims its own set of self-serving, unproved dogmas." Examples: "Humanism works for the establishment of a 'secular society,' a 'socialized economic order,' world government, military disarmament, and population control by government. . . . The reason humanism has become something reporters need to be informed about is that alert parents have discovered that Secular Humanism has become the established religion of the U.S. public school system. Many parents believe that the humanist manifestos, like the Rosetta Stone, provide the key to decipher the code languages of progressive education, values clarification, sexuality curricula, situation ethics, and the various rationales that have caused the public schools to eliminate prayer, moral training, and the teaching of basics."

In the face of this kind of misinformation, and amid the growth of religious fundamentalism around the world, *Free Inquiry* was founded by Paul Kurtz. The first issue published "A Secular Humanist Declaration." Endorsed by Sidney Hook, Betty Friedan, Sir A. J. Ayer, B. F. Skinner, Isaac Asimov, Milovan Djilas, W. V. Quine, Walter Kaufmann, and dozens of other scientists, philosophers, and writers, the Declaration tried to set things straight:

> Secular humanism is a vital force in the contemporary world. It is now under unwarranted and intemperate attack from various quarters. This declaration defends only that form of secular humanism which is explicitly committed to democracy. It is opposed to all varieties of belief that seek supernatural sanction for their values or espouse rule by dictatorship. . . .
>
> Countless millions of thoughtful persons have espoused secular humanist ideals, have lived significant lives, and have contributed to the building of a more humane and democratic world. The modern secular humanist outlook has led to the application of science and technology to the improvement of the human condition. This has had a positive effect on reducing poverty, suffering, and disease in various parts of the world, in extending longevity, on improving transportation and communication, and in making the good life possible for more and more people. It has led to the emancipation of hundreds of millions of people from the exercise of blind faith and fears of superstition and has contributed to their education and the enrichment of their lives. Secular humanism has provided an impetus for humans to solve their problems with intelligence and perserverance, to conquer geographic and social frontiers, and to extend the range of human exploration and adventure.

As we said, the Declaration *tried*—but, for an enormous portion of American society, it didn't quite convince. Secular humanism was, simply, dangerous blasphemy. The claims religion has made over the ages to exclusive (and often mutually exclusive) moral authority are not easily countered in the hearts of the faithful.

But with the founding of *Free Inquiry,* secular humanists and other "unchurched" citizens finally had an intelligent, even combative voice. It has been disconcerting that, in a nation wholly pervaded by the media, criticism of religion remains taboo, and that until *Free Inquiry* nonbelievers could be subjected to malicious criticism with impunity. It is not surprising, then, that the magazine quickly developed a large, singularly devoted readership.

The 1980s frequently saw *Free Inquiry* set off sparks in the public forum: taking a number of church/state cases to court; launching wide-ranging investigations into the faith-healing rackets; and subjecting the claims of traditional religions, as well as some New Age ones, to the methods of free, scientific inquiry. As important as these critiques have been, perhaps the magazine's boldest ambition is this: to argue persuasively that science, reason, tolerance, and a flexible ethics can replace humankind's age-old reliance on religious dogma and revelation.

Within the covers of this book, *Free Inquiry* makes its best case.

Robert Basil,
Mary Beth Gehrman,
and Tim Madigan

II.

A SECULAR HUMANIST DECLARATION

Drafted by Paul Kurtz

Secular humanism is a vital force in the contemporary world. It is now under unwarranted and intemperate attack from various quarters. This declaration defends only that form of secular humanism that is explicitly committed to democracy. It is opposed to all varieties of belief that seek supernatural sanction for their values or espouse rule by dictatorship.

Democratic secular humanism has been a powerful force in world culture. Its ideals can be traced to the philosophers, scientists, and poets of classical Greece and Rome, to ancient Chinese Confucian society, to the Carvaka movement of India, and to other distinguished intellectual and moral traditions. Secularism and humanism were eclipsed in Europe during the Dark Ages, when religious piety eroded humankind's confidence in its own powers to solve human problems. They reappeared in force during the Renaissance with the reassertion of secular and humanist values in literature and the arts, again in the sixteenth and seventeenth centuries with the development of modern science and a naturalistic view of the universe, and their influence can be found in the eighteenth century in the Age of Reason and the Enlightenment. Democratic secular humanism has creatively flowered in modern times with the growth of freedom and democracy.

Countless millions of thoughtful persons have espoused secular humanist ideals, have lived significant lives, and have contributed to the building of a more humane and democratic world. The modern secular humanist outlook has led to the application of science and technology to the improvement of the human condition. This has had a positive effect on reducing poverty, suffering, and disease in various parts of the world, in extending longevity, on improving transportation and communication, and in making the good life possible for more and more people. It has led to the emancipation of hundreds of millions of people from the exercise of blind faith and fears of superstititon and has contributed to their education and the enrichment of their lives. Secular humanism has provided an impetus for humans to solve their problems with intelligence and perseverance, to conquer geographic and social frontiers, and to extend the range of human exploration and adventure.

Regrettably, we are today faced with a variety of anti-secularist trends: the reappearance of dogmatic authoritarian religions; fundamentalist, literalist, and doctrinaire Christianity; a rapidly growing and uncompromising Muslim clericalism in the Middle East and Asia; the reassertion of orthodox authority by the Roman Catholic papal hierarchy; nationalistic religious Judaism; and the reversion to obscurantist religions in Asia. New cults of unreason as well as bizarre paranormal and occult beliefs, such as belief in astrology, reincarnation, and the mysterious power of alleged psychics, are growing in many Western societies. These disturbing developments follow in the wake of the emergence in the earlier part of the twentieth century of intolerant messianic and totalitarian quasi-religious movements, such as fascism and communism. These religious activists not only are responsible for much of the terror and violence in the world today but stand in the way of solutions to the world's most serious problems.

Paradoxically, some of the critics of secular humanism maintain that it is a dangerous philosophy. Some assert that it is "morally corrupting" because it is committed to individual freedom, others that it condones "injustice" because it defends democratic due process. We who support democratic secular humanism deny such charges, which are based upon misunderstanding and misinterpretation, and we seek to outline a set of principles that most of us share. Secular humanism is not a dogma or a creed. There are wide differences of opinion among secular humanists on many issues. Nevertheless, there is a loose consensus with respect to several propositions. We are apprehensive that modern civilization is threatened by forces antithetical to reason, democracy, and freedom. Many religious believers will no doubt share with us a belief in many secular humanist and democratic values, and we welcome their joining with us in the defense of these ideals.

1. *Free Inquiry.* The first principle of democratic secular humanism is its commitment to free inquiry. We oppose any tyranny over the mind of man, any efforts by ecclesiastical, political, ideological, or social institutions to shackle free thought. In the past, such tyrannies have been directed by churches and states attempting

to enforce the edicts of religious bigots. In the long struggle in the history of ideas, established institutions, both public and private, have attempted to censor inquiry, to impose orthodoxy on beliefs and values, and to excommunicate heretics and extirpate unbelievers. Today, the struggle for free inquiry has assumed new forms. Sectarian ideologies have become the new theologies that use political parties and governments in their mission to crush dissident opinion.

Free inquiry entails recognition of civil liberties as integral to its pursuit, that is, a free press, freedom of communication, the right to organize opposition parties and to join voluntary associations, and freedom to cultivate and publish the fruits of scientific, philosophical, artistic, literary, moral and religious freedom. Free inquiry requires that we tolerate diversity of opinion and that we respect the right of individuals to express their beliefs, however unpopular they may be, without social or legal prohibition or fear of sanctions. Though we may tolerate contrasting points of view, this does not mean that they are immune to critical scrutiny. The guiding premise of those who believe in free inquiry is that truth is more likely to be discovered if the opportunity exists for the free exchange of opposing opinions; the process of interchange is frequently as important as the result. This applies not only to science and to everyday life, but to politics, economics, morality, and religion.

2. *Separation of Church and State.* Because of their commitment to freedom, secular humanists believe in the principle of the separation of church and state. The lessons of history are clear: wherever one religion or ideology is established and given a dominant position in the state, minority opinions are in jeopardy. A pluralistic, open democratic society allows all points of view to be heard. Any effort to impose an exclusive conception of Truth, Piety, Virtue, or Justice upon the whole of society is a violation of free inquiry. Clerical authorities should not be permitted to legislate their own parochial views—whether moral, philosophical, political, educational, or social—for the rest of society.

Nor should tax revenues be exacted for the benefit or support of sectarian religious institutions. Individuals and voluntary associations should be free to accept or not to accept any belief and to support these convictions with whatever resources they may have, without being compelled by taxation of contribute to those religious faiths with which they do not agree. Similarly, church properties should share in the burden of public revenues and should not be exempt from taxation. Compulsory religious oaths and prayers in public institutions (political or educational) are also a violation of the separation principle.

Today, nontheistic as well as theistic religions compete for attention. Regrettably, in communist countries, the power of the state is being used to impose an ideological doctrine on the society, without tolerating the expression of dissenting or heretical views. Here we see a modern secular version of the violation of the separation principle.

3. *The Ideal of Freedom.* There are many forms of totalitarianism in the modern world—secular and nonsecular—all of which we vigorously oppose. As democratic secularists, we consistently defend the ideal of freedom, not only freedom of conscience and belief from those ecclesiastical, political, and economic interests that seek to repress them, but genuine political liberty, democratic decision-making based upon majority rule, and respect for minority rights and the rule of law. We stand not only for freedom from religious control but for freedom from jingoistic government control as well. We are for the defense of basic human rights, including the right to protect life, liberty, and the pursuit of happiness. In our view, a free society should also encourage some measure of economic freedom, subject only to such restrictions as are necessary in the public interest. This means that individuals and groups should be able to compete in the marketplace, organize free trade unions, and carry on their occupations and careers without undue interference by central-ized political control. The right to private property is a human right without which other rights are nugatory. Where it is necessary to limit any of these rights in a democracy, the limitation should be justified in terms of its consequences in strengthening the entire structure of human rights.

4. *Ethics Based on Critical Intelligence.* The moral views of secular humanism have been subjected to criticism by religious fundamentalist theists. The secular humanist recognizes the central role of morality in human life. Indeed, ethics was developed as a branch of human knowledge long before religionists proclaimed their moral systems based upon divine authority. The field of ethics has had a distinguished list of thinkers contributing to its development: from Socrates, Democritus, Aristotle, Epicurus, and Epictetus, to Spinoza, Erasmus, Hume, Voltaire, Kant, Bentham, Mill, G. E. Moore, Bertrand Russell, John Dewey, and others, There is an influential philosophical tradition that maintains that ethics is an autonomous field of inquiry, that ethical judgments can be formulated independently of revealed religion, and that human beings can cultivate practical reason and wisdom and, by their application, achieve lives of virtue and excellence. Moreover, philosophers have emphasized the need to cultivate an appreciation for the requirements of social justice and for an individual's obligations and responsibilities toward others. Thus secularists deny that morality needs to be deduced from religious belief or that those who do not espouse a religious doctrine are immoral.

For secular humanists, ethical conduct is, or should be, judged by critical reason, and their goal is to develop autonomous and responsible individuals, capable of making their own choices in life based upon an understanding of human behavior. Morality that is not God-based need not be anti-social, subjective, or promiscuous, nor need it lead to the breakdown of moral standards. Although we believe in tolerating diverse lifestyles and social manners, we do not think they are immune to criticism. Nor do we believe that any one church should impose its views of moral virtue and sin, sexual conduct, marriage, divorce, birth control, or abortion, or legislate them for the rest of society.

As secular humanists we believe in the central importance of the value of human happiness here and now. We are opposed to Absolutist morality, yet we maintain that objective standards emerge, and ethical values and principles may be discovered, in the course of ethical deliberation.

Secular humanist ethics maintains that it is possible for human beings to lead meaningful and wholesome lives for themselves and in service to their fellow human beings without the need of religious commandments or the benefit of clergy. There have been any number of distinguished secularists and humanists who have demonstrated moral principles in their personal lives and works: Protagoras, Lucretius, Epicurus, Spinoza, Hume, Thomas Paine, Diderot, Mark Twain, George Eliot, John Stuart Mill, Ernest Renan, Charles Darwin, Thomas Edison, Clarence Darrow, Robert Ingersoll, Gilbert Murray, Albert Schweitzer, Albert Einstein, Max Born, Margaret Sanger, and Bertrand Russell, among others.

5. *Moral Education.* We believe that moral development should be cultivated in children and young adults. We do not believe that any particular sect can claim important values as their exclusive property; hence it is the duty of public education to deal with these values. Accordingly, we support moral education in the schools that is designed to develop an appreciation for moral virtues, intelligence, and the building of character. We wish to encourage wherever possible the growth of moral awareness and the capacity for free choice and an understanding of the consequences thereof. We do not think it is moral to baptize infants, to confirm adolescents, or to impose a religious creed on young people before they are able to consent. Although children should learn about the history of religious moral practices, these young minds should not be indoctrinated in a faith before they are mature enough to evaluate the merits for themselves. It should be noted that secular humanism is not so much a specific morality as it is a method for the explanation and discovery of rational moral principles.

6. *Religious Skepticism.* As secular humanists, we are generally skeptical about supernatural claims. We recognize the importance of religious experience: that experience that redirects and gives meaning to the lives of human beings. We deny, however, that such experiences have anything to do with the supernatural. We are doubtful of traditional views of God and divinity. Symbolic and mythological interpretations of religion often serve as rationalizations for a sophisticated minority, leaving the bulk of mankind to flounder in theological confusion. We consider the universe to be a dynamic scene of natural forces that are most effectively understood by scientific inquiry. We are always open to the discovery of new possibilities and phenomena in nature. However, we find that traditional views of the existence of God either are meaningless, have not yet been demonstrated to be true, or are

tyrannically exploitative. Secular humanists may be agnostics, atheists, rationalists, or skeptics, but they find insufficient evidence for the claim that some divine purpose exists for the universe. They reject the idea that God has intervened miraculously in history or revealed himself to a chosen few, or that he can save or redeem sinners. They believe that men and women are free and are responsible for their own destinies and that they cannot look toward some transcendent Being for salvation. We reject the divinity of Jesus, the divine mission of Moses, Muhammad, and other latter-day prophets and saints of the various sects and denominations. We do not accept as true the literal interprettion of the Old and New Testaments, the Koran, or other allegedly sacred religous documents, however important they may be as literature. Religions are pervasive sociological phenomena, and religious myths have long persisted in human history. In spite of the fact that human beings have found religions to be uplifting and a source of solace, we do not find their theological claims to be true. Religions have made negative as well as positive contributions toward the development of human civilization. Although they have helped to build hospitals and schools and, at their best, have encouraged the spirit of love and charity, many have also caused human suffering by being intolerant of those who did not accept their dogmas or creeds. Some religions have been fanatical and repressive, narrowing human hopes, limiting aspirations, and precipitating religious wars and violence. While religions have no doubt offered comfort to the bereaved and dying by holding forth the promise of an immortal life, they have also aroused morbid fear and dread. We have found no convincing evidence that there is a separable "soul" or that it exists before birth or survives death. We must therefore conclude that the ethical life can be lived without the illusions of immortality or reincarnation. Human beings *can* develop the self-confidence necessary to ameliorate the human condition and to lead meaningful, productive lives.

7. *Reason.* We view with concern the current attack by nonsecularists on reason and science. We are committed to the use of the rational methods of inquiry, logic, and evidence in developing knowledge and testing claims to truth. Since human beings are prone to err, we are open to the modification of all principles, including those governing inquiry, believing that they may be in need of constant correction. Although not so naive as to believe that reason and science can easily solve all human problems, we nonetheless contend that they can make a major contribution to human knowledge and can be of benefit to humankind. We know of no better substitute for the cultivation of human intelligence.

8. *Science and Technology.* We believe the scientific method, though imperfect, is still the most reliable way of understanding the world. Hence, we look to the natural, biological, social, and behavioral sciences for knowledge of the universe and man's place within it. Modern astronomy and physics have opened up exciting new dimensions of the universe: they have enabled humankind to explore the universe

by means of space travel. Biology and the social and behavioral sciences have expanded our understanding of human behavior. We are thus opposed in principle to any efforts to censor or limit scientific research without an overriding reason to do so.

While we are aware of, and oppose, the abuses of misapplied technology and its possible harmful consequences for the natural ecology of the human environment, we urge resistance to unthinking efforts to limit technological or scientific advances. We appreciate the great benefits that science and technology (especially basic and applied research) can bring to humankind, but we also recognize the need to balance scientific and technological advances with cultural esplorations in art, music, and literature.

9. *Evolution.* Today the theory of evolution is again under heavy attack by religious fundamentalists. Although the theory of evolution cannot be said to have reached its final formulation, or to be an infallible principle of science, it is nonetheless supported impressively by the findings of many sciences. There may be some significant differences among scientists concerning the mechanics of evolution; yet the evolution of the species is supported so strongly by the weight of evidence that it is difficult to reject it. Accordingly, we deplore the efforts by fundamentalists (especially in the United States) to invade the science classrooms, requiring that creationist theory be taught to students and requiring that it be included in biology textbooks. This is a serious threat both to academic freedom and to the integrity of the educational process. We believe that creationists surely should have the freedom to express their viewpoint in society. Moreover, we do not deny the value of examining theories of creation in educational courses on religion and the history of ideas; but it is a sham to mask an article of religious faith as a scientific truth and to inflict that doctrine on the scientific curriculum. If successful, creationists may seriously undermine the credibility of science itself.

10. *Education.* In our view, education should be the essential method of building humane, free, and democratic societies. The aims of education are many: the trans-mission of knowledge; training for occupations, careers, and democratic citizenship; and the encouragement of moral growth. Among its vital purposes should also be an attempt to develop the capacity for critical intelligence in both the individual and the community. Unfortunately, the schools are today being increasingly replaced by the mass media as the primary institutions of public information and education. Although the electronic media provided unparalleled opportunities for extending cultural enrichment and enjoyment, and powerful learning opportunities, there has been a serious misdirection of their purposes. In totalitarian societies, the media serve as the vehicle of propaganda and indoctrination. In democratic societies television, radio, films, and mass publishing too often cater to the lowest common denominator and have become banal wastelands. There is a pressing need to elevate standards of taste and appreciation. Of special concern to secularists is the fact that the media

(particularly in the United States) are inordinately dominated by a pro-religious bias. The views of preachers, faith-healers, and religious hucksters go largely unchallenged, and the secular outlook is not given an opportunity for a fair hearing. We believe that television directors and producers have an obligation to redress the balance and revise their programming.

Indeed, there is a broader task that all those who believe in democratic secular humanist values will recognize, namely, the need to embark upon a long-term program of public education and enlightenment concerning the relevance of the secular outlook to the human condition.

Conclusion

Democratic secular humanism is too important for human civilization to abandon. Reasonable persons will surely recognize its profound contributions to human welfare. We are nevertheless surrounded by doomsday prophets of disaster, always wishing to turn the clock back—they are anti-science, anti-freedom, anti-human. In contrast, the secular humanistic outlook is basically melioristic, looking forward with hope rather than backward with despair. We are committed to extending the ideals of reason, freedom, individual and collective opportunity, and democracy throughout the world community. The problems that humankind will face in the future, as in the past, will no doubt be complex and difficult. However, if it is to prevail, it can only do so by enlisting resourcefulness and courage. Secular humanism places trust in human intelligence rather than in divine guidance. Skeptical of theories of redemption, damnation, and reincarnation, secular humanists attempt to approach the human situation in realistic terms: human beings are responsible for their own destinies.

We believe that it is possible to bring about a more humane world, one based upon the methods of reason and the principles of tolerance, compromise, and the negotiations of difference. We recognize the need for intellectual modesty and the willingness to revise beliefs in the light of criticism. Thus consensus is sometimes attainable. While emotions are important, we need not resort to the panaceas of salvation, to escape through illusion, or to some desperate leap toward passion and violence. We deplore the growth of intolerant sectarian creeds that foster hatred. In a world engulfed by obscurantism and irrationalism it is vital that the ideals of of the secular city not be lost.

(Winter 1980/81)

III.

HUMANISM

The term *secular humanism* is one that many people have heard but few can define. For those who are curious to find out what it means, there is no better place to turn to than *Free Inquiry* magazine, the only unabashedly secular humanist magazine in the country.

Sidney Hook, a frequent contributor to the magazine, can rightly be considered the most prominent secular humanist of recent times. A lifelong fighter for human freedom and intellectual honesty, a noted philosopher and scholar, and a friend of such leading figures as Bertrand Russell and John Dewey, Hook embodied what is best about the humanist life stance. His article "The Ground We Stand On" appeared in the premiere issue of *Free Inquiry*. Reprinted here, it forcefully spells out the humanist commitment to democratic principles. Democracy is one of the key principles of "The Affirmations of Humanism: A Statement of Principles and Values," which is found on the back cover of the magazine. These say in part that:

- We are committed to the application of reason and science to the understanding of the universe and to the solving of human problems.
- We deplore efforts to denigrate human intelligence, to seek to explain the world in supernatural terms, and to look outside nature for salvation.
- We believe that scientific discovery and technology can contribute to the betterment of human life.
- We believe in an open and pluralistic society and that democracy is the best guarantee of protecting human rights from authoritarian elites and repressive majorities.

- We are committed to the principle of the separation of church and state.
- We attempt to transcend divisive parochial loyalties based on race, religion, gender, nationality, creed, class, or ethnicity, and strive to work together for the common good of humanity.
- We believe in enjoying life here and now and in developing our creative talents to their fullest.

Secular humanism has much in common with the movement known historically as "Freethought." Gordon Stein, who is considered the leading scholar in this field, gives a lively presentation of "Freethought Past and Present."

A claim often leveled against secular humanism is that it is a form of religion, with its own creed, shrines, doctrines, and saints. Paul Kurtz and the other editors of *Free Inquiry* have strenuously objected to this view. A debate ensued in the pages of *Free Inquiry* between the late Paul Beattie, a prominent Unitarian minister who felt that secular humanism should rightly be categorized as a religion, and Hook, Kurtz, and Joseph Fletcher, the noted medical ethicist, who held that it is a misuse of language to equate the two.

Although not a religion, secular humanism has had a major impact on American social thought. Adolf Grünbaum shows the positive effect humanism has had on this country's history, especially in regard to its emphasis on pluralism, reasoned debate, and the toleration of differing belief systems.

Humanism is a serious philosophy, but humanists are not a grim bunch. While they have a predilection for laughing at the foibles of organized religion, they are just as willing to laugh at themselves. Included here is a piece by the famous humorist Art Buchwald, and my own, "Humanists and Humor."

Paul Kurtz ends this section with a thoughtful examination of "The Future of Humanism"—a future sure to be charted in upcoming issues of *Free Inquiry*.

—*T.M.*

The Ground We Stand On: Democratic Humanism

Sidney Hook

That the forces and institutions of intelligence are on the defensive throughout the world can be demonstrated by the headlines and news stories of the daily press. They were never in the ascendancy in any country. But there was some legitimate basis for hope that, with the defeat of fascism after World War II, efforts would be made to establish genuine welfare states throughout the world, based on the recognition of the inviolability of human rights. Unfortunately, because World War II was fought, not on the basis of the four freedoms proclaimed by the leading statesmen of the West, but from the point of view of a narrow military perspective, those who put freedom first confronted on a global scale the threats of aggressive communist totalitarianism, terroristic nationalism, and militant religious fanaticism—all contemptuous of democratic processes, the values of a rational humanism, and the integrity of free inquiry.

Despite all the limitations of its current foreign and domestic policies, the United States still remains the bastion of a free society. Not the U.N. as it is presently organized, but the preservation and extension of its philosophy of human rights and welfare is the last best hope of mankind. Integral to that philosophy is the commitment to free inquiry and reliance upon the methods and resources of scientific intelligence.

These methods and resources are under attack by recent developments on the American scene. Although manifestations of religious fundamentalism are a recurrent phenomenon in American life, during the last few years a union of powerful evangelical movements has emerged as a strong political force. Its obscurantist philosophy is based upon outspoken hostility to scientific inquiry and its denial that the findings of such inquiry are in any way relevant to the resolution of problems of life and death. Although of an entirely different order, there has been a revival of religious faith in certain sophisticated intellectual quarters. It is argued by some that in the last analysis—as if there ever is a last analysis!— all fundamental explanatory paradigms, whether scientific, metaphysical, or theological, are of equal validity; a rigorously consistent set of superstitions is thought to be as intellectually acceptable as any critically tested scientific hypothesis.

Of greater relevance to the concerns of rational humanists is the contention that without commitment to transcendent religious beliefs or values no programs of social reform can be justified or implemented. Even some neo-conservative thinkers who are resolute in their defense of human freedom hold this view. Let us examine it and its various ramifications.

By religion I mean faith in the existence of some supernatural power that governs human destiny and serves as a cosmic support of human ideals. Insofar as religion functions purely as a consolation to the individual for the irremediable evils and tragedies of existence, it is too personal a matter to be anyone else's concern, and I shall not discuss it further. But the consolatory function of religious beliefs must not be proclaimed as valid evidence for their truth, since it is obvious that myths as well as truths may be consoling.

In recent years many large claims have been made for religious faith. It has been celebrated as the taproot of democracy, indeed of all morality. Its revival has been hailed as the best ground for reasonable hope of an enduring world peace. It has been urged as a specific for industrial strife, crime, poverty, and all other impediments to a just society. It has been widely asserted that we must choose between a renewed faith in religion and a faith in some totalitarian ideology which is certain to blossom wherever religion withers. A whole chorus of voices insists that the crisis of our age must ultimately be defined in these terms.

I believe all of these claims are false. The validity of democracy as a moral and political ideal does not rest upon religious doctrines. Despite the resurgence of religion during the past decade, the world is not noticeably a better place to live in. In many respects it is worse. The alternative to religion is not necessarily the brutalitarian nihilism of Hitlerism or the dictatorial, secret police-state of Stalinism or any other variety of totalitarianism that embraces what is morally best in religion, fortified by reliance not on supernatural dogmas but on the instruments of enlightened, scientific intelligence. Religion has had thousands of years to unify the world into a semblance of a just and cooperative world order. It has failed. Democratic humanism may fail, too. That depends, in part, upon whether the ardor and devotion that have been expended on transcendental objects of faith can be transferred to the democratic heritage as a pattern for the reconstruction of social life.

It is an open question whether the revival of religious beliefs and institutions may not lead to the exacerbation of differences among men. For most religions make claims to being the exclusive repositories of God's truth, acceptance of which is a necessary condition of salvation. Were these claims to be abandoned, the justification for *separate* religious organizations would largely disappear. But to a militant believer religion means *the* religion—his own. When he looks to the future of religion to liberate mankind from its burden of evils, he looks primarily to his own church and its teachings.

It is hard to find a doctrine common to all religious faiths and of sufficient importance to override doctrinal differences. Belief in the Brotherhood of Man under the Fatherhood of God comes closest perhaps to being the common article of faith of all religious groups in the Western and Near Eastern worlds. It is this belief, we are told, on which the democratic philosophy rests. To accept the latter and reject the former is to be guilty of inconsistency, of sentimental and unintelligent belief in democracy.

Logically, the derivation of democracy from this belief is a complete *non sequitur*. The proposition that all men are brothers, whether taken theologically or biologically, does not entail any proposition essential to the democratic faith. No matter what the origin of man is, supernatural or natural, we cannot legitimately infer from his equality of opportunity or equality of citizenship. These democratic beliefs are compatible with many different alleged "presuppositions." Our reasons for accepting democracy rather than its ethical and political alternatives are not only independent of our reasons for accepting the theological or biological brotherhood of man; they are far more warranted in the light of experience. This is true for any moral ideal. Our grounds for belief in honesty and kindness do not depend upon belief in supernatural dogma or other "presuppositions." We would be horrified by anyone who told us that, if he surrendered his belief in the existence of God or the second law of thermodynamics or whatnot, he would no longer regard dishonesty and cruelty as morally wrong. The same logic holds for the belief in the democratic ideal. It is in terms of its fruits and consequences in human experience that we accept or reject it, not in terms of supernatural belief, whether taken literally or metaphorically.

Historically, there is little warrant for the assertion that religious dogmas are the prime source of modern democracy. The most religious countries are notoriously not the most democratic ones. The historical record shows that organized religion has accommodated itself to all social systems and forms of government, no matter how tyrannical, which have tolerated its existence. In some countries it has actively supported social iniquities. Undeniably there have been religious movements, and still more often great religious personalities, that have aided the cause of freedom. What moved them in the main were moral insights and a complex of historical interests, shared by secular movements, too, and not special theological dogmas. For these dogmas served as identical premises in the thinking of those who opposed progressive movements. We know that Judaism countenanced slavery, while Christianity never condemned it in principle. Organized religion was one of the mainstays of feudalism. In Spain it supported Franco. In Russia it supported Stalin—when he let it.

The organizational structure of institutions based on supernatural dogmas and of the social systems they actively support tends toward theocracy, not democracy. Recognition of the rights of individual conscience, toleration of religious minorities, freedom of scientific inquiry, abolition of child labor, birth control, the use of anesthetics, secular education, separation of church and state, and other liberal and humane practices have made their way in the face of opposition of organized religion.

It is sometimes maintained that nonreligious protagonists for a better world have drawn their inspiration and fire from the dying embers of a religious faith which, despite their denials, still glow within them. This is obviously question-begging, for it assumes that no validation of moral ideals is possible except in terms of supernatural belief—precisely the point at issue. It would be truer to say that religious believers who have supported the cause of social justice have been moved by the evidence of experience and not by the compelling force of theological doctrine. The evidence that men share a common lot and destiny in a world of atomic power is far stronger than the evidence that they share a common origin, and a supernatural one at that.

Those who see promise in the revival of religion overlook the significance of the fact that supernatural faith is marked by the sharpest dualism in its conception of the place of man in nature. This dualism is the root source of ambiguity in the application of religious dogmas. It denies that man is a child of nature. It endows him with an immortal soul which is essentially independent of his body and his culture. Man's soul is the most precious thing about him. He can and must keep it pure, no matter what the world, his transitory home, is like. It is as immortal souls that all men are equal before God. And this equality is essentially unaffected by any kind of social and political inequality. Consequently, it is always possible to square supernatural dogmas with societies in which democracy is absent—or present. It is never clear on religious grounds alone how its dogmas are being applied. That is why they are compatible with social policies that are mutually contradictory to each other. More important still, it is impossible within the framework of religious thought to find a *method* that will enable us to judge and negotiate conflicting interests in empirical situations. A common supernatural faith therefore provides no principle of direction for the intelligent control of social change.

Religion is sometimes understood, not as involving belief in the supernatural or acceptance of doctrine, but as an attitude of ultimate concern or, in William James's phrase, "a man's total reaction upon life." In this sense everyone who is passionately alive to something exciting in the world, or to some possibility struggling to be born, is religious; the irreligious, apparently, are those who are dead but still unburied. We possess a number of perfectly good words to designate this activity of vital emotional interest, and I prefer not to be converted to religion by definition. But if we use the term in this sense, there is a certain danger in equating religion with any large faith and then welcoming a general revival of religion. For it underestimates, when it does not ignore, the quality, content, and fruits of faith, which should be of infinitely greater concern to us than the bare act of faith, no matter how intense. Better a man of little faith in good than of great faith in evil.

Many years ago it was quite fashionable to speak of fascism as a great faith that integrated the personality of its believers, elicited a passionate devotion to objects greater than themselves, and brought a firm discipline into their emotional life. The fruits of that faith were evident even in the past to all who wished to know the truth. But in the moment of its triumph, many bowed down in vulgar worship of power, blinded by its nimbus of glory. Similarly, there are today some who believe that the communist faith is the only basis upon which the civilized tradition can be rebuilt. Its total reign of terror, which has grown in intensity over the years, is callously written off as a part of the costs of "progress," although the costs of Christianity, the industrial revolution, capitalism, and democracy are computed with great care and indignation. In the case of both fascism and communism, we observe a sharp dissociation between ends and means, and substitution of unlimited faith in the future for the exercise of intelligence and humanity in the present. These faiths should be judged, not by the intensity with which they are held, but by their consequences on the lives of the human beings who accept them, on the lives of their victims, and on the lives of those on whom they are *imposed.* For in countries where such faiths are official, they are not freely selected among alternatives. In short, religious faith cannot be separated from doctrines, and from the practices to which doctrines lead or which they justify.

Some who deplore totalitarian faiths because of their degrading effects express the wish that the fanaticism with which their adherents are imbued could be harnessed to faith in democracy. This disregards the ways in which what is most typical in totalitarian faith is indissolubly bound up with its creed and practices— a union that is happily no longer true in present-day religion. A democrat cannot be fanatical in the same way as a fascist or communist, for whom an unanalyzed end justifies the use of *any* means. But it does not follow that because he is humane and intelligent a democrat cannot be passionate and active in his faith, that he must be a political Hamlet, irresolute before the combination of toughness and chicanery with which his totalitarian opponents confront him.

Instead of a revival of religious faith in general, we should work specifically toward a revival, or a new birth, of faith in democracy. Such a faith is the only one that can unify society without imposing uniformity upon it. It is a faith that can embrace believers and nonbelievers in a vast number of different "presuppositions"—theological, metaphysical, naturalistic. For these are all compatible with democracy. Required of those who profess them is only that they sincerely accept the democratic practices by which equality of concern for all individuals, collective participation, and freely given consent of the governed— the cardinal doctrine of democratic faith—are implemented. It excludes none but avowed totalitarians and the secret totalitarians who redefine democracy to make it synonymous with its opposite. Such a democratic faith has many fronts on which to fight: race relations; education; social, political, and economic organization. It does not fear to use power; otherwise it is at the mercy of nondemocratic faiths. It seeks to tame power by making it intelligent and responsible; that is, it is designed to achieve morally inclusive ends through institutions that provide for wide participation and open criticism.

As a social philosophy, the democratic faith accepts that measure of social control that would liberate the productive forces of modern technology without curtailing the freedoms enshrined in the Bill of Rights, which would remove the blight of poverty and the threat of insecurity without making a fetish of efficiency and centralization, which would provide, as far as possible, those objective conditions of social and cultural life in whose absence "equality of opportunity for all" is a hollow phrase. It may be a tautology to say that such a form of social democracy can exist only where political democracy exists. But a tautology is important when contraposed to an absurdity—such as the view that a humanist society can be achieved by the political dictatorship of a minority party.

The democratic faith is not only a social philosophy but a personal philosophy as well. It calls for a mode of behavior in our daily interchanges with each other that makes the inescapable occasions of differences and dispute opportunities for cooperative discussion in which all interests receive a fair hearing. It recognizes that no profound social change is possible that does not involve a change in institutions, in the impersonal relationships that govern men. But is also recognizes that institutions are even less capable than machines of running according to blueprints and plans alone. No matter how generous the declared purposes of an institution may be, unless it is operated by men and women dedicated in their own lives to these purposes, it can easily be transformed into an agency of human oppression.

There is nothing promised by a revival of religious faith, considered in terms of doctrine, that is not promised by a new growth of faith in democracy. But there are some things threatened by the revival of the first that are not threatened by the growth of the second.

How to inspire, extend, and strengthen faith in democracy, and build a mass movement of men and women personally dedicated to it, is the great issue of our time. But it is clear that, although devotees of the democratic faith may be found the world over, the most practical opportunities exist where democratic traditions have until now, despite all their imperfections, been strongest. In countries in which political democracy still exists, we have something to go on, a certain pattern of democratic life, and an area of freedom in which it can be enriched and deepened. If the destinies of these countries can be linked together in a common resolve not merely to preserve political democracy but to build democracy as a way of life into the very fabric of their social institutions, they will conquer the world not by force of arms but by force of example. For democracy is like love in this: it cannot be brought to life in others by command. Shared experience, sympathetic understanding, and good works are ultimately the best nourishment for democratic convictions.

(Winter 1980/81)

Freethought: Past and Present

Gordon Stein

The colorful history of freethought (atheism, rationalism, humanism, secularism, and skepticism) is not widely known. Although there have been a number of books written on the subject, none has been widely read by the educated public, and a knowledge of the history of freethought has been restricted to a few specialists.[1] Freethought has been defined in a number of different ways. In the present case, I am using the term as a world outlook that rejects the appeal to authority of any dogmas, especially religious dogmas. Freethought is thought that is free of the assumptions of religious dogmas. The freethought movement had several historical peaks in popularity (as measured by activities and membership), and also went through periods of virtual dormancy and decline. The purpose of this article is to highlight the historical facts, and to explore some of the possible reasons for the decline in the movement, a decline that extends into the present.

Although there were atheistic schools of philosophy among the ancient Indians (Cārvāka) and atheism was far from unknown in ancient Greece, we can identify the first organized (or rather concerted) attempt at a freethought movement— the publication of Anthony Collins's *A Discourse of Free Thought* in 1713. This book was one of the most popular influences in facilitating the spread of deism. Deism, a precursor of freethought, may be defined as "atheism *with* God." By that it is meant that, although the deists believed that a god had created the universe, they held that he then had no further contact with it, so that for all practical purposes there was no God in men's lives. It was only later, with the growth of the science of astronomy, that the need for a god in the creation of the universe was no longer felt. Deism flourished from about 1700 to 1750 in England, and from about 1730 to 1800 in the United States. It went into a swift decline in both places, probably because there was nothing left to say about its doctrines that had not already been said.

The book that revived the freethought movement in both the United States and England was, strangely enough, written as a deist work. I am referring to Thomas Paine's *The Age of Reason,* first published in 1794–1796 in two parts. Paine states quite clearly in this book that he believes in God, yet it was condemned as atheistic from the very beginning. Rather, the book was the first work critical of the Bible that was written simply enough to be read by the average workingman. As such, it had an enormous influence upon the hold that religion had on the workingman's life. Most of the freethought movements of the later part of the nineteenth century looked upon the artisan and the informed workman as the major source of their support. *The Age of Reason* was responsible for making more people into "infidels" than any other book except the Bible.

In France, unbelief was greatly aided by Voltaire, who can be called a deist in his outlook, and by such outright atheists as D'Holbach and Diderot. The publication of the *Encyclopédie* in the late 1700s was a milestone in the development of the use of reason to explain the world.

Organized freethought developed slowly. Richard Carlile helped spread the idea of unorthodoxy by bravely republishing all of Paine's works, along with those of most of the earlier freethinkers, in spite of a government prohibition against doing so. Carlile spent more than nine years in jail upon conviction for blasphemy and several other offenses related to his religious and political opinions.

The first actual freethought organizations, which went back to Carlile's day, were the Zetetic Societies. They were found largely in Scotland. During the 1840s, there were other freethought societies in existence, such as the Anti-Persecution Union, the London Atheistical Society, and the Halls of Science. The latter were originally a part of Robert Owen's Socialist movement, but eventually were associated with the freethinkers. In the United States, the first freethought groups were called the Free Enquirers. Frances Wright and Robert Dale Owen were their original organizers. A short-lived group of Thomas Paine admirers had preceded this. They were called the Theophilanthropists. In the 1830s, attempts at national organization of freethinkers were made in the United States. They were not very successful. In 1845, there was a meeting held in New York City at which the Infidel Society for the Promotion of Mental Liberty was formed. It was also not very successful. The Infidel Association of the United States was formed at a meeting in Philadelphia in 1857. Again, the group only lasted a short while.

Freethought reached one of its peaks of popularity and notoriety in the 1842–1843 period. At that time, most of the important figures then active in a leadership role in England were being prosecuted for blasphemy. George Jacob Holyoake (who coined the word *secularism*), Charles Southwell (publisher of the first openly atheistic magazine in England, *The Oracle of Reason)* and Henry Hetherington (an early freethought publisher) were all prosecuted, convicted, and jailed. In the United States, the blasphemy trial of Abner Kneeland (the founder of the rationalist paper *The Boston Investigator)* ran through the 1836–1838 period, including the appeals. Kneeland also served time in jail upon his conviction.

The next peak of freethought activity, in both England and the United States, was the 1865–1900 period, which has been called "the golden age of freethought." Charles Bradlaugh began his career in the British freethought cause at about this time, while in the United States, D. M. Bennett started his freethought magazine, *The Truth Seeker,* in 1873, and Robert G. Ingersoll began lecturing on freethought subjects in the early 1870s. Ingersoll's later immense popularity as a lecturer was largely responsible for the development of the "golden age" of freethought in the last quarter of the nineteenth century. Bradlaugh can share in the responsibility for helping produce a "golden age" of freethought in England at the same time by means of his lecturing, writing, and parliamentary struggles.

From this time until about 1900 in the United States, and until about 1915 in the United Kingdom, freethought was at its all-time peak. Freethought periodicals, such as *The Freethinker* and *The National Reformer* in England and *The Freethinker's Magazine* in the United States, were founded and prospered by today's standards. Charles Bradlaugh was joined in the leadership of the British freethought movement by Annie Besant, George W. Foote, Charles Watts, George Jacob Holyoake, and "Saladin" (W. S. Ross). Although there was a rivalry among these leaders, most of the time they were on speaking terms. Occasionally, an issue such as birth control would bitterly divide the leadership and the movement itself. In the United States, the main leaders besides Ingersoll and Bennett at this time were J. R. Monroe, Charles C. Moore, Eugene Macdonald, Samuel P. Putnam, B. F. Underwood, and H. L. Green. Ingersoll became the best-known orator in the United States and was friendly with virtually everyone of importance. His lectures were widely reported in the regular press and were presented to large and enthusiastic audiences.

Annie Besant defected to Theosophy in 1890. Bradlaugh died in 1891 and Ingersoll in 1899. Watts and Holyoake died in 1906. After 1906, freethought was on the decline. G. W. Foote carried on until his death in 1915. Although Chapman Cohen in England was able to hold together the remnants of the movement through the Second World War, there was no similar leader in the United States who could single-handedly maintain the movement. Charles Smith tried for a while during the late 1920s and 1930s, but the "Great Depression" dealt a financial death blow to his highly publicized American Association for the Advancement of Atheism.

In the twentieth century, we have seen the development of the humanist movement. The same sort of people who may have joined the secularists or rationalists in the late 1800s now find the humanist groups more accessible to them. The rhetoric of these groups has been toned down considerably from its outspokenness of the pre-1900 period. Humanism has become almost "respectable."

In England, the Rationalist Press Association reached its peak in membership at the time of the Second World War. After that, it showed some rises and falls in membership, but the overall trend was downward. The National Secular Society also had an overall downward trend in membership after World War II.

The reasons for the fall in membership and interest in freethought organizations in the last fifty years are rather complex. Basically, it can be stated without too much fear of contradiction that the more repressive a society is seen to be (with regard to religious liberty), the stronger will be the organizing ability and the larger the membership of freethought groups. However if belonging to a freethought group is illegal and dangerous, many people will not join, but the number of freethinkers in the populace will be high in such a society.

Modern Western society has seen an increasing amount of secularization occur. This has removed, to an extent, the immediate pressure for rebellion against the inequities of religion. When religion is weak, not too much reason to oppose it is seen. Examples of this peculiar relationship between the pervasiveness of religion in a society and the strength of organized freethought in that society can best be seen in Spain and Italy. There, freethought has always existed in modern times, but it has increased (along with the anti-clerical elements) at times of particular piety.

Freethought has always had three strikes against it. It could not obtain newspaper or magazine space in which to advertise or publish things that the public would see. It was denied access to fund-raising methods open to religion. Finally, because of this lack of finances, the freethought movement was unable to publicize itself and unable to produce much impact on society with its own limited periodicals and speakers. Therefore, the movement has always been receptive to the presence of a charismatic leader. When such a leader arose, the freethought movement usually revived and entered a period of rapid growth. On the other hand, the deaths of these leaders rapidly reduced freethought to a state of dormancy.

We are now seeing in the United States a growth of the so-called pentecostal types of Christianity. Unfortunately, history has shown that these groups are the very ones that have the least respect for the religious liberty of any group other than themselves. They yell and scream very loudly when any infringement of *their* religious liberty occurs, or is perceived to occur. An example is the millions of letters to the Federal Communications Commission that were received when the totally erroneous idea was spread in fundamentalist publications that Madalyn Murray O'Hair had started a suit that would have forced religious programs off the air. In fact there was never any such suit. At the same time, many members of these fundamentalist groups are also supporters of conservative political movements. They use these movements to make their religious feelings known to the government and to the public.

All of this relates rather directly to the future of the freethought movement in the United States in the following way: As the strength of pentecostal or evangelical Christianity grows, history would tell us that the reaction to this growth will also produce a growth in the freethought movement. Of course there really is only an increased *potential* for the growth of freethought. If new leaders do not arise, with the dedication to advance the freethought cause, the potential may not be realized. It is a sad commentary that there must be a growth in organized superstition and mental tyranny, in the form of evangelical Christianity, with its loss of mental liberty, in order for freethought to be strengthened, but that may well be the current state of affairs.

Notes

1. See John M. Robertson's *History of Freethought in the Nineteenth Century*, and his *History of Freethought, Ancient and Modern, to the Period of the French Revolution.* There is also Edward Royle's *Victorian Infidels* and his *Radicals, Secularists and Republicans,* as well as Marshall Brown and Gordon Stein's *Freethought in the United States,* and Sidney Warren's *American Freethought, 1860–1914.* David Tribe's *100 Years of Freethought* is also worth consulting. Most of the other, more difficult to obtain freethought histories are mentioned in these books.

(Winter 1980/81)

The Religion of Secular Humanism
Paul H. Beattie

As far back as we go into the history of Western culture, to the beginnings of Greek, Hebrew, and Christian thought, we find two tendencies in interpreting religion: One is assimilationist, and the second represents the categorical rejection of religion or of some aspects of religion. In the prophet Elijah, who challenged all of Baal on Mount Carmel, we see both tendencies. On the one hand, Elijah was against idolatry, and so he had the prophets of Baal killed; on the other hand, he asserted that Yahweh, who was originally a nomadic god, had assimilated the agricultural and rain-making functions of the Baals, who were agricultural deities.

In Greek philosophy, beginning with the pre-Socratic thinkers, we see the same two tendencies at work. Philosophy can be used to criticize religion in order to stop being religious, or philosophy can be used to purify religious concepts so as to make them more acceptable and useful. When Protagoras said that "Man is the measure," he was abandoning all supernatural standards, and his book on the gods apparently took an agnostic stance that claimed it was impossible to know whether the gods existed or not. Protagoras was interested in freeing people from dependence upon the gods. In different ways, both Plato and Aristotle tried to purify and exalt human thinking about god or gods, making god into the basis for absolute idealism in Plato's system or into the unmoved mover in Aristotle's system. Epistemologically speaking, Aristotle was a humanist, yet he, like the eighteenth-century deists, used the word *God* in his system of thought.

Jesus, as presented in the New Testament, represents both tendencies; he rejects some aspects of religion and reinterprets others. He said he came not to destroy the law but to fulfill it, but he also insisted that one could not put new wine into old wineskins, or patch an old garment with new (unshrunk) cloth. In some places in the New Testament, Jesus insists that he comes only to the house of Israel and that his teaching, when presented to gentiles, is like casting pearls before swine; in other places he seems to indicate that his mission is to all of humanity. He said that the Sabbath was made for man, not man for the Sabbath, a very humanistic approach to religion; however, his summary of religion as love to God and love to man is in conformity with the best Jewish religious thought of his day and with the Old Testament scriptures.

A sophisticated view of religion, it seems to me, has to recognize the value and validity of both of these tendencies of religious thought. Religion has always needed to be criticized for its excesses, its follies, its foibles, its imperfections, and its untruths. Every religion constantly needs to be examined critically and improved by those who try to practice it. Unfortunately, self-criticism and self-correction have not been the strong suits of religion and religious functionaries. At the same time, every culture seems to need to reinterpret, to adapt traditional religious views to new situations as cultural change occurs. It is not impossible, but probably doubtful, that human beings will ever develop a culture that is so secular and so successful that religion will wither away or be totally repressed and disappear. The existence of religion seems to be based on human need; this is the insight of one of the early and most articulate humanists, Ludwig Feuerbach.

Some years ago I was fortunate to be able to secure the great cultural historian William H. McNeil of the University of Chicago as a speaker for the annual meeting of the Fellowship of Religious Humanists. In his address he likened religious humanists, Unitarians and Universalists, Ethical Society members, and members of the American Humanist Association to the ancient Stoics, much to be admired but doomed never to make a great impact on the mass of human beings who need something more mystical and emotional than the rationalism stoics prefer. If he is right, and I suspect that he is, critical thought about religion will always involve both rejection of some aspects of religion and reinterpretation of others.

Some people, especially some humanists and freethinkers, may reject religion and religious concepts and choose to live without any positive connection with religion. In today's cosmopolitan world it is possible for some individuals to live with no connection to a religious community. In my view this is a mistake, because it deprives such individuals and their families of a staying power that is much needed and deprives religion of meaningful dialogue with some of the most enlightened people in our society. If this had been the practice of all humanists in the past, a great many classic works on religion by authors like A. Eustace Haydon, John Dewey, Julian Huxley, and Bertrand Russell would never have been written.

*   *   *

As a "religious humanist" I am under attack from the Right and the Left. The Right includes a whole coterie of fundamentalists who claim that secular humanism is the most dangerous religion in the world today. Their understanding of what *religion* is and of what *humanism* is, and of what *secularism* is, constitutes a massive and irremediable confusion of the mind. They tend to think that anything they see as bad or wrong in the modern world is due to the machinations of secular humanists. Fundamentalists feel their tenets are threatened by a great conspiracy of secular humanists who are controlling the modern world. My view of their fears is that their critique of humanism is so intellectually deficient that it will fall of its own weight. They have had some success on some political issues by combining with other groups, as in joining Roman Catholics in opposing abortion, but they have had little success in influencing the general public to make humanism the scapegoat for the anxieties of modernity. The forces that have created the modern world have also created humanism; to annul humanism, the fundamentalists would have to abolish modernity. This they cannot do; for them to succeed in such a goal would mean a new dark age, like that initiated by Ayatollah Khomeini in Iran. The modern world is here to stay; and, painful as it is, the fundamentalists are going to have to get used to that fact.

The attack from the Left against my religious humanism is exemplified by some of my humanistic colleagues, in particular two noted humanists whom I consider to be long-time close friends. Joseph Fletcher and Paul Kurtz represent the anti-religious tradition of modern secular humanism. In 1933, with the signing of the first Humanist Manifesto, humanism came to national attention as a choice one could make in developing a philosophical life stance or a religious stance. Right from the beginning there were humanists who eschewed any contact with religion and those who thought of humanism as their religion. Thirteen of the original thirty-four signers of Manifesto I were Unitarian ministers, one was a Universalist minister, two others were Ethical leaders, and one a liberal rabbi. Thus half of the original signers were liberal clergymen. The author of the statement, Roy Wood Sellars, thought of himself as a religious humanists and was a member of the Unitarian church in Ann Arbor, Michigan. Two others were Unitarian laymen. Thus, Unitarian Universalists alone accounted for seventeen signatures, again half of the original signers. While proclaiming that religion was under pressure from the changes of the modern world, the Manifesto insisted that ". . . through all its changes religion itself remains constant in its quest for abiding values, an inseparable feature of human life." It uses the phrase "religious humanism" and "religion" in a positive way in eight of its fifteen propositions.

Since the founding of the American Humanist Association in 1941, there has been continuing tension between those who see humanism as a religion and those who would eschew religion. When the Fellowship of Religious Humanists was founded in 1967, it organized outside the AHA, even though it had originally been conceived as a programmatic development to be connected with the AHA. Many, though not all, who have been connected over the years with the AHA have wanted to distance themselves from religion. On the other hand, to secure draft exemption for humanist conscientious objectors, the AHA allowed itself to be classified as a religion—and rightly so.

Back in 1963, when I was a minister to the Unitarian church in Concord, New Hampshire, I took part in planning, and then got my church to host, a conference on population problems, which was unique because it brought all the key experts on the subject to a single platform for the first time. Alan Gutmacher, Curtis Wood,

John Rock, and many others participated. One of the most impressive performances was by Joseph Fletcher, who at the time was an Episcopalian priest and teacher of ethics at the Episcopal Theological Seminary. In a day when even Dr. Gutmacher would not publicly endorse abortion on demand and even denounced the new Yugoslav vacuum machine, Dr. Fletcher gave a beautifully reasoned, gently persuasive talk in favor of abortion. We got on well and much later became good friends. At the time, he was a Christian and I was a religious humanist.

I sent Dr. Fletcher a sermon I had written called "Religion Without God Is Possible; Life Without Religion Is Difficult." He wrote back that, as a theologian, he felt obliged to keep God, but had long ago abandoned religion and would have no truck with it at all! "Churchianity" at its worst can be quite disillusioning (and I would add also unreligious), and it was such "churchianity," I suspect, that made Fletcher abandon organized religion—or even the use of the word. Years later, when Dr. Fletcher and I met again, he had also abandoned God and had become a full-fledged secular humanist. Fletcher rejects all definitions of the word *religion* that would make it compatible with humanism. He told his story in an article titled "An Odyssey: From Theology to Humanism," which appeared in the Fall 1979 *Religious Humanism.* "My story is not one of changing religions, or of going somehow from theistic to humanistic religion. I have no wish to use the word religion at all. . . . The humanism I have embraced—or perhaps it has embraced me—is secular, not religious."[1] Fletcher's personal example, and point of view, is a strong argument against linking humanism with religion; his secular humanism is so gracious, intelligent, and independent. However, I can't help wondering if Fletcher would be the fine person he is without his many years as a member of a very high quality religious community. He admits as much himself in his article.[2]

* * *

While Fletcher's example on behalf of humanism without religion is effective, it is my good friend Paul Kurtz who has given the most damaging and sustained critique aimed at separating humanism from religion. In recent years Kurtz has increasingly moved from a stance that was largely neutral to religion or mildly critical of religion to a secular humanism that is anti-religious. His most complete statement on this matter occurred in an article he wrote for the Fall 1983 *Free Inquiry,* "The Future of the Humanist Movement." It was later reprinted in his book *In Defense of Secular Humanism* (Prometheus Books, 1984).

Kurtz's objection to connecting humanism and religion has two sources: first, his linking of the failures of explicitly humanist groups to their religious connections; and second, his analysis of religion. Concerning the failure of humanism, Kurtz argues that organized humanism has been weak and ineffective, first, because it has not developed any inspiring and sufficiently clear message; and, second, because it has lacked charismatic leadership of sufficient skill and dedication; and, third, because humanist organizations have ". . . mistakenly sought to become another denomination or sect competing with other denominations and sects, when humanism should have become a broad-based educational movement." He deduces a number of other reasons for the weakness of organized humanism in our day, most of them true, including his statement that humanism "has at times become narrowly political and strident, [and] identified [itself] with only one part of the political spectrum."[3] With this last criticism I entirely agree: humanism is a frame of orientation, a ground for dialogue—not a package of accepted political nostrums. But I do not agree that connection with religion or the attempt to copy religious models has hurt humanism. Quite the contrary. I argue that a broad-based educational movement, while necessary and important, will have less influence and staying power than a humanism that is held as a religion of the individual.

The major thrust of Kurtz's objection to the religious model for humanism grows out of his analysis of religion. He sees Judaism, Christianity, and Islam as having the same basis. Historically speaking, they each accept a divine message; they each had a charismatic founder: Moses, Jesus, Muhammad; they each developed institutions, rules, and clergy; they each utilized ethnic allegiances; they each had a common linguistic and cultural heritage associated with their religion. And, in addition, each of these religions has four seemingly essential rules by which they maintain themselves. They each have impulses to convert nonbelievers; they each insist that children be brought up within the faith; they each discourage marriage outside the faith; they each have ways to stamp out dissent and excommunicate heretics.

Presented in this way, religion seems obviously incompatible with humanistic ideals. But not as much as one might think. For example, consider Kurtz's four rules. I think a good humanist has impulses to spread his or her point of view and will be apt to bring up children so that they know and will accept the humanistic perspective. Most of us hope that our children will marry people who are philosophically compatible. I would be appalled if my son or daughter married a fundamentalist. If my children's humanism has any depth at all, such a marriage would be highly unlikely. Thus, I am comfortable with three of the four rules that Kurtz says are part of most religions. The fourth, the idea of excommunication for heresy, I explicitly reject; but this is a tendency in most human groups. Even humanists have to be careful that they do not excommunicate other humanists for "political heresy." In other words, Kurtz does not deal with the question of to what extent historic religions can be modified and reinterpreted to make them more relevant in the modern world.

Consider his first five points and my response as a religious humanist. We do not have a divine message, but we have the classics of humanism. We do not have a single charismatic founder, but we have humanist heroes and heroines of the past and present. We cannot utilize ethnic allegiances the way traditional religion has done, nor would we want to; but such ethnic allegiances occurred late in the history of Christianity, which originally had universalistic impulses—reaching out for Greek, barbarian, Roman, Jew. Our humanism does have a common linguistic and cultural heritage; it is the heritage of the Western world—

and, more broadly, of the whole epic of humanity. The Roman poet Terence spoke for all humanists when he said, "Nothing human is foreign to me."

Not only has Kurtz failed to show that the religious tradition is incompatible with humanism, but he has also failed to recognize that there are millions of people who are both actively engaged in their religious traditions and furthering and endorsing humanistic values. In other words, the values humanists cherish and most espouse are supported by millions who do not call themselves humanists and who, in fact, are members of Judaism, Christianity, or Islam. Of course there are many exponents of these religions who are narrow-minded, but millions of believers are not. In his book Kurtz presents a list of thirteen humanist values and principles, and every one is supported by millions of people who do not call themselves humanists.

These humanist values and principles are (1) a commitment to free inquiry and the open mind; (2) a belief in the courage to live without fear or trembling; (3) a confidence in the power of human creativeness, inventiveness, achievement; (4) (a commitment to make) constant efforts to improve the human condition, mitigate suffering, and eliminate disease, conflict, war, and cruelty; (5) respect for the rights of others; (6) a dedication to the preciousness and dignity of the individual, his or her creativity and growth; (7) cultivation of happiness and the full life; (8) an emphasis on love, shared experience, human joy; (9) tolerance of other points of view and styles of life; (10) a commitment to social justice and humanitarian help; (11) a universal focus transcending national, ethnic, sexual, and racial barriers—the ideal of a world community; (12) an emphasis on compromise and negotiation of differences; (13) belief in a free, open, pluralistic, and democratic society.[4] If these values, right now, were not being supported by more than just the organized communities of humanists and those who say they are explicitly humanistic in their thinking, our world would be in deep trouble. These values are crucial in the lives of millions of traditional believers and non-believers; they are the result of the secularization of the entire world, with input from traditional religions and cultures.

These values that Kurtz has listed have been mainline thought in America since the Enlightenment. People do not live in logic-tight worlds. For example, it does not matter to the average Christian that the Bible is essentially undemocratic, that it stresses the concept of theocracy, rather than democracy. This does not faze the average Methodist or Presbyterian; he or she is still a democrat. Indeed, it is possible to show that both Methodism and Presbyterianism have made major contributions to democratic theory and practice in spite of the undemocratic nature of the Christian tradition and scripture. While Kurtz has asserted an incompatibility between humanist values and religious organizational models, he has not proven his case; in the practice of millions of Americans, and of other people throughout the world, the exact opposite of his case is demonstrated every day.

I will turn his argument around and argue that it is best if some humanists attempt to use some of the traditional aspects of religion in the service of humanism. First, however, I want to make one more point about the thirteen humanistic values Kurtz listed. Humanists do not have any magic way of coming to agreement among themselves as to how best to implement humanistic values. We all want a peaceful world, but who best interprets Soviet intentions and how to meet them, Sidney Hook or Corliss Lamont? We all want to use psychology to improve human life, but who should we follow, B. F. Skinner or Carl Rogers? We all want economic abundance for as many people as possible, but who is right, the socialist Eric Fromm or the free-enterprise advocate Milton Friedman? Humanist values transcend the humanist community, and humanists have no easy answers to how best to implement those values—it will take intelligence and dialogue without and within the humanistic community. Drawing the sharp line that Kurtz does between humanism and religion is counterproductive, because it removes humanists from the wider dialogue.

*   *   *

Whether a humanist is religious or not depends upon one's definition of religion. My definition makes it possible for me to gladly call myself a "religious humanist." When I ask myself about the content of my religious humanism I realize that much of it comes from the secular perspective in Western history. Thus I can comfortably say that my religion is the religion of (secular) humanism!

Let me attempt to define humanism. Humanism is a "man centered" or "human centered" life stance, reminiscent of Protagoras's statement that man is the measure. Humans are the only beings that we know of who make value judgments. Our concept of humanism grew out of the Renaissance. The term *humanista,* from which humanism was derived, originally meant "teacher of Latin," which was the language in which Roman and, for a time, Greek cultures were studied.[5] The word *humanism* was popularized by mid-nineteenth-century cultural historians, and first seems to have come into usage about 1832. It is interesting to note that the very forces that were creating Renaissance humanism were also beginning the process of secularizing the Western world, a process that has been a central defining characteristic of Western history and culture for most of modern history.

> The term *secular* is [appropriate] to describe humanism and humanists because humanism was the product of a secularized society. Indeed, *studia humanitatis* referred in the Renaissance to the study of secular as opposed to divine literature. *The Oxford English Dictionary* preserves this distinction in its first definition of humanist; "A student of human affairs, or of human nature; formerly sometimes a secular writer (as distinguished from a divine)."[6]

Today most humanists are agnostic, atheistic, or ignostic. Most humanists are Hellenophiles, most accept the scientific method as the most trustworthy way of knowing, most view the evolutionary hypothesis as the central metaphor for self-understanding and for best understanding how to direct human destiny, and most humanists believe in the democratic process and the ideals of the Enlightenment as interpreted in the Bill of Rights of the American Constitution.

Now let's define the word *religion*, a most difficult task. I remember reading years ago somewhere that a scholar by the name of Leuba had collected more than two hundred definitions of religion that were not compatible with each other, and none of which adequately fit all existing religions. *The Encyclopedia of Philosophy*, edited by Paul Edwards, takes the fascinating tactic of listing nine characteristics of religion, some specific (belief in gods and supernatural) and others general (religion involves the total organization of one's life based on a world view). After listing the nine characteristics, the encyclopedia suggests that being religious is a matter of degree, concluding: "We . . . encounter less and less obvious cases of religion as we move from, for example, Roman Catholicism through Unitarianism, humanism, and Hinayana Buddhism to communism."[7] Definitions and examples of religion differ greatly. In effect, a person or a religion can create a unique definition that can be put into perspective by contrasting it with other religions and definitions of religion. There can be no absolute standard (culturally or definitionally) as to what is or is not a religion.

Here is my definition, in two parts. First, a religion is an individual's response to life. It is the core of attitudes and values out of which a person lives. Second, a religion possesses an institutional and community aspect. As my friend Rabbi Sherwin Wine has pointed out, you don't have a religion until you have a religious community, a religious community that marks the important life passages—birth, puberty, marriage, death—and that celebrates the seasons of the year. A religious community is a primary group that assembles regularly, and hence provides us with a community by which we measure ourselves, and a way of conditioning and maintaining one's life. In such an assembly one is renewed in one's sense of commitment to truth and justice and one's dedication to love. This is the great secret of Western religion: the synagogue, the church, and the mosque are primary group communities that allow individuals to live in artificially extended families or tribal groupings in the midst of a cosmopolitan, secular civilization. More than anything else, it is the sociological format of Judaism and Christianity that has triumphed, not the particular dogmas of Judaism and Christianity. For most people nothing is so supportive and reinforcing, outside the family, as the church or synagogue experience. There are many individuals, like Freud and Darwin, who have no need of religious community, and many ordinary people, too, who do quite well without religious membership. But for a large portion of the human population, religious community is helpful in living.

*   *   *

There is no better way to spread a set of ideas about how best to live, or to intensify commitment to such ideas, than by means of religious community. Not only were fourteen signers of Humanist Manifesto I Unitarian Universalist ministers, but since then Unitarianism has created more humanists than any other movement in America.[8] Back in 1967, a scientific study showed that 52 percent of Unitarians and Universalists felt *closer to a distinctive humanist religion* (as opposed to liberalism, Protestantism, the ecumenical movement within Christianity, or to an emerging universal religion).[9] The percentage of Unitarian Universalists who feel this is probably higher today. But leaving the percentage constant, we can say that about 67,000 Unitarians and Universalists feel that their point of view in religion is closest to a distinctive humanist religion than to any other option. In other words, Unitarian Universalists, using the religious model, have led more people to humanism than has the American Humanist Association, Ethical Culture, and the Fellowship of Religious Humanists combined. The AHA has perhaps 4,000 members, the FRH about 500, the Ethical Union in America about 3,000—combined they have about 7,000 or 8,000 members, while the Unitarians have about 67,000 humanists.

Obviously the university movement in Western society and free public education spread humanistic tendencies throughout the population, but this has not led many people to join organized humanist groups. I conclude that the religious model is a model that humanists should adopt, not only to spread their ideas and ideals, but also to reinforce their own humanistic values. We should always remember that humanists who think of their humanism as compatible with religion, and those who do not, are natural allies and can cooperate and reinforce one another in many ways.[10]

Having explained in what sense I use the word *religion* when I say that I am a religious humanist, let me now describe the content of my religious humanism. I believe that we can learn much from the study of all religions, and especially those of our own cultural tradition. However, in the end, I have to admit that most of my ideas and values come from the secular tradition of the Western world. Secularism occurred in medieval Europe. In the beginning the church had almost total control of every aspect of life, and gradually more and more of the life of Western men and women was emancipated from church control. The period in which secularism began started with the church asserting that the purpose of life was to find heaven in the next life, and it ended with the widespread acceptance of the idea that the purpose of life is to prosper intellectually, spiritually, and materially *in this life.*

During the medieval period the word *saecularis* meant "the present era"; however, it also applied to clergymen who did not take monastic vows because they worked in the world rather than isolating themselves in monasteries. Since their morality often did not conform to the absolute purity of the Christian ideal, these secular religionists were often looked down on by the church. Secularism has always had a negative connotation to those with a traditional religious perspective. It is interesting that religious functionaries helped to pioneer the concept.

Beginning in the Renaissance, the story of the Western world has been a story of increasing secularization. As one of the best dictionaries puts it simply: Secularism is "the view that consideration of the present well-being of mankind should predominate over religious considerations." Our modern usage of the word *secular* was coined by George Jacob Holyoake, a working-class reformer and lecturer in the English Owenite movement. In 1841 he was the last person jailed in England for public blasphemy, and he served a sentence of six months in the Gloucester jail. In those days one could be imprisoned for advocating atheism! Upon his release, he wrote a book in which he coined the term *secularism,* which he thought less offensive than atheism. In effect, he wanted the good of the working class to be based on a calculation of their earthly condition and not on the basis of reasoning derived from an otherworldly, theistic perspective.

*   *   *

Secularism is a good thing; without it the modern world as we know it would be impossible. The Secular Humanist Declaration in 1980 listed ten concepts of secularism, all of which have come to us from the secularization of the Western world: (1) the right to free inquiry; (2) separation of Church and State; (3) the ideal of individual and democratic freedom; (4) ethics based on critical intelligence instead of supernatural pronouncement; (5) moral education can and should be cultivated in children apart from religion, for example, in the public schools. Good citizenship does not necessarily depend on religion; (6) the cultivation of religious skepticism—and, indeed, skepticism toward any unproven assertions; (7) the commitment to giving priority to reason and truth arrived at rationally; (8) the recognition of the scientific method as the most trustworthy way of knowing; (9) the acceptance of the evolutionary hypothesis and its constant testing and refinement; and (10) a commitment to universal education and literacy.

As I look at these ten principles, which have to be elaborated to a greater extent to be fully appreciated in terms of their power to aid human beings, I find that *these* are the core of attitudes and values out of which I want to live my life. These represent my religion. The secularism of the Western world has given me the values, the content of my religion. So it is not a contradiction, as one might think, to talk about "the religion of secular humanism." My religion is the religion of secular humanism. I will defend my religion against the fundamentalist who tries to hold that both my humanism and my secularism are evil— the power and vitality that can grow out of religious community when religious community is rightly understood and constructively used to further the best goals and aspirations of human life.

Residual Religion
Joseph Fletcher

Another way to state or express Paul Beattie's "religion of secular humanism" would be to call it "the religion of the humanism that dispenses with religion." This rephrasing helps us to see into the heart of the issue he raises. If we went through the roster of contemporary secular humanists—Hook, Flew, Skinner,

Djilas, Ayer, Quine, Popper, Wilson, Crick, Sagan, just as a sampling—and asked them if they pray and lead hymns on Sundays, they would say, "Certainly not."

Professor Kurtz and I say we are agnostics or atheists, one or the other. Being a religious humanist and the minister of a church, Beattie could not intelligibly, and does not, call himself by such plainly secular names. The simple fact is that to speak of religious secularity is a contradiction of terms. People who use the English language "as she is spoke" will have no trouble seeing the contradiction.

Webster's, aside from the medieval uses of the term ecclesiastically, defines *secularism* as "indifference to or rejection or exclusion of religion." It says of religion, first, that it means "the service and worship of God or the supernatural." This is what the term ordinarily connotes. Then it adds, as the broadest and least specifying definition, "a personal or institutional system of religious attitudes, beliefs, and practices." Beattie, as we all know, is religious not in the first or common sense but in the second indeterminate sense.

To speak, therefore, as Beattie does, of religious secularism or secular religion is, to say the least, surprising. He does this by means of what some logicians call the "fallacy of indefinition." He cites Kurtz's list of the traits to be found in most secular humanists (many of which fit Beattie as an individual), he never explains how he would himself define either "secular" or "religion," leaving the rest of us open to considerable surprise as well as bewilderment.

The surprise is twofold. It comes not just on the score of his lexical contradiction. Far more seriously, at least in my book, Beattie has also given aid and comfort to the politicians and courts who are also trying these days, like him, to include secular humanism among the religions. They do this, of course, because they want to ban it from school curricula as an illegal subject of study—one which thus defined or redefined would fall under the Supreme Court's ban on any or all religious teaching in the public school system.

Jerry Falwell and the Religious Right constantly rail against the Supreme Court's separation of church and state in the schools and hope someday to see their propaganda become legal. But in the meantime their strategy is to pretend that secular humanism is a religion, just as religious humanism is, and should therefore be as illegal as any other religion. Senators Orrin Hatch and Jesse Helms are the congressional sachems pushing this strategy of suppression by redefinition.

*   *   *

And now, alas, comes Paul Beattie—an old ally in the humanist fold—to bolster up the reactionaries. Informed people have known all along that some humanists are religious and some are secular, but now comes Beattie to say that the difference is really nonexistent and the distinction between religious and secular humanism is a mistake. On this logic the secular Darwinian version of evolution is just as religious as the creationist biblical version, and therefore (this, of course, is what they are after) if one can be banned from the schools as religious so can the other—and both for the same reason!

Secular humanists have no desire to deny the right of other humanists to be religious, if they freely choose to be. Even so, agnostics and atheists think religious humanists are still embroiled in the religiosity of prescientific discourse. Residual religion. Religion that has lost its intellectual specificity and therefore any recognizable shape.

One more point is worth making. Not content with trying to argue that secular humanism is by redefinition a religion, Beattie in so arguing also claims that Kurtz's values (note: his values, not what he thinks) are "mainline thought in America." It may well be, I suppose, that many of Kurtz's ideals of open-mindedness, freedom of thought and speech, and the like, are commonly professed in our native land, but Beattie then suggests that Kurtz's thinking, his judgments and conclusions, are also mainline American.

This is simply not true. Kurtz's rejection of religious ideas and his secular views are (like mine) not at all mainline American. Surely I cannot be so completely mistaken about my own country as to suppose that Kurtz's (and my) repudiation of religious faith is a mainline position for Americans. We wish it were so, of course, but it isn't.

I charge Paul Beattie with indefinition, and I urge him further to recognize that definition is essentially negative, not positive. Defining and describing should make clear what something is not as well as what it is.

The issue his article raises falters because he fails to explain what a secular humanist is not. I put it to him that the proper answer is "not religious." The adjective "religious" is what we are discussing, not the noun "humanism." Some adherents among the Christian, Jewish, Muslim, and all the other religious traditions can be and are humanists when the noun is defined only positively—as in Terence's phrase, "Nothing human is alien to me."

We can be sure, for example, that most of the modern popes beginning with Leo XIII would like to have been known as Christian humanists. To be a *secular* humanist, to thus qualify the noun, means to be a certain kind of humanist; to think, that is, about men and their problems and prospects without God or heaven or any other religious ideas and aspirations entering in. No prayers or hymns or church services. Not only detheologized, but dereligionized. No residual wonderings about the "transcendental" or searching for the "ultimate." No more worship of either God or man.

Pluralistic Humanism
Sidney Hook

Unfortunately, the English language "as she is spoke" is not a guide to formulating wise policy in combating the onslaughts of fundamentalists against the teaching of science and the cultivation of critical, scientific thinking in our public schools. For one thing, English "as she is spoke" is a developing thing, the norms of correct usage are historical, and sensible people infer meaning from and in context. Even oxymoron has its appropriate usage, which cannot be outlawed out of hand by declaring it merely "a contradiction in terms." For another thing, English is not the only language of human discourse, and what cannot be rightfully said according to its current rules of grammar and correct usage may find appropriate expression in another language. The furniture of heaven and earth is discovered by scientific inquiry. It is not created by semantic legislation.

In the interest of religious freedom, I am eager to protect Paul Beattie's right to speak of the religion of humanism. I believe that the prospects of religious freedom improves with the multiplication of religions, especially religions that are free of the dogma of supernaturalism. The watchdogs of fundamentalism are not going to be quieted even if humanists, Ethical Culturists, and other holders of nontheistic world-views forswear the use of the terms *religion* and *religious*. Their goal is to limit, where they cannot bar, the study of science and the development of rational, scientific habits of thought in our schools.

So far as I know, secular humanists and religious humanists (except for Christian humanists) do not teach their distinctive beliefs as such in public schools any more than Ethical Culturists do. The fundamentalists assume that the absence of instruction in their own particular faith is tantamount to a commitment to *the teaching* of a non-religious or irreligious faith. This assumption is mistaken both in logic and in fact. Of course moral or character education is integral to the education of children, but the case for the teaching of the moral, intellectual, and social virtues can easily be made without reference to supernaturalism or revelation.

Anyone who reads Homer Duncan's *Secular Humanism: The Most Dangerous Religion in America* will see that what irks him and his supporters is that the Christian gospel is not a part of the curriculum of the public school, that the scientific theory of evolution is considered appropriate but not the biblical story of the divine creation of species. Personally, I would have no objection to stating the Anstatilian notion that species have existed from eternity and the biblical story of species creation as alternative views to the theory of evolution and considering all of them critically, but Homer Duncan would have an apoplectic fit at the prospect of any such approach. Anyone who has corresponded with him on these issues will be convinced of his helplessness in the face of reasonable objections to the dogmas he would teach by fiat.

*   *   *

I am less concerned by the indeterminate meaning of religion than I am by the reference to the existence of God by individuals who no more believe in his existence than I do. Although I have never considered myself a religious person, I am accustomed to being called "religious" by writers inspired by William James or Niebuhr or Tillich, who define religion in terms of ultimate concern. To be sure, we understand what is meant when one says that money or music or love is one's religion and that he or she worships Mammon or Apollo or Priopus. But we can understand what is being said very well without the use of the term *religion*. Feuerbach once observed that atheism is his religion, and I suppose other atheists have said something similar to indicate that they can live a full, contented, and moral life without the crutch of supernatural myths.

I find the use of the term *God* more objectionable because in the Western world, especially, it is almost invariably identified with the God of Judeo-Christianity. I recall questioning John Dewey when I read the manuscript of his *A Common Faith*—in which he defined God as the union of the ideal and real—about the wisdom of the use of the term. He justified it by saying that no one had patented a meaning of it, that the God of Abraham, Isaac, and Joseph was not the God of the New Testament, nor the God of Plato or Aristotle or Spinoza or Hegel or Whitehead. He wasn't a "theist," but there was a connotation of a small-town, small-minded negativism about the term *atheism* that he disliked. His "God" was a positive ideal that stressed the worthiness of striving to make the world a better place for mankind, and most of the people who believed in God, according to him, were making a moral commitment. I confess I was taken by surprise at the warmth of his statement, but predicted that sooner or later some clergyman was going to try to establish a connection between Dewey's God and the anthropomorphic God of the Bible. My prediction turned out to be accurate. The Reverend Wieman did claim Dewey for some kind of Christianity, and I believe Dewey had several exchanges with him in an attempt to be freed from his fraternal embrace.

Regardless of whether secular humanism is called a "religion," the members of the Ethical Culture Society will call their group a religion. The strategy of combating the thrust of fundamentalism and supernaturalism—and a religion can still be supernatural even if it is not theistic—should not rely on surrendering the use of the term *religion* by those naturalists who wish to regard themselves as religious. We are dealing with a *historical* situation in the United States in which officially there has never been a separation of church and state from the time the First Amendment was adopted to the present. So long as church property is exempt from taxation there can be no absolute separation. On the other hand, in some countries like England, Scandinavia, and Israel, where church and state are not separated, the state of religious freedom is as healthy as it is in the United States. Were we founding a society from scratch, secular humanists could reasonably propose policies that might not be realistic when we have to take our point of departure from historical situations that reflect the great influence of the religious past. It is the *direction* in which the community is moving, toward or away from secular humanism, that should be our primary concern.

On the Misuse of Language:
A Response to Paul Beattie
Paul Kurtz

When I first read Paul Beattie's paper "Is Secular Humanism a Religion?" I was dismayed at his flagrant misuse of language at a particularly inopportune time. Right-wing and fundamentalist religious forces have been insisting for several years that secular humanism is a religion and that in order to preserve the principle of separation of church and state, it must be extirpated from the schools and from other areas of public life—the media, the universities, the courts, etc. Secular humanists, as other good citizens, are committed to upholding the First Amendment, and their opposition to the establishment of religion is well known.

I have argued for many years that *secular* humanism is a nonreligious humanism and that it has an appropriate role to play in public schools and in our civic life. Paul Beattie, a good friend and colleague with whom I share many beliefs and values, argues that secular humanism is a religion. This seems to me to violate the ethics of language. Like Humpty Dumpty in *Alice's Adventures in Wonderland*, he makes words mean their opposites. I have been the leading proponent of the term *secular* humanism in order to distinguish it from *religious* humanism. Clearly religious humanism exists, and it has many adherents, especially among members of the Unitarian church. Paul Beattie is a dedicated leader of the Ethical Culture societies, the Fellowship of Religious Humanists, and the Society for Humanistic Judaism. I have no objection to these groups adopting the label "religious humanism." Nor do I want to engage in definition-mongering and insist on only one meaning of the term *humanism*. Nevertheless, words have meanings, and there is an ethic concerning the use and abuse of language. I think that Paul Beattie has violated this ethic. Why seek to impose a religious definition on all forms of humanism? In particular, to misuse the word *secular* as to call secular humanism a "religion"?

*   *   *

There is some sense in which the term *religious* as distinct from *religion* is meaningful when applied to some forms of humanism. John Dewey used the term *religious* to refer to the quality of experience in which we express our commitment to ends and values. Dewey was even willing to use the term *God* in his controversial book *A Common Faith* (1934) in a naturalistic way to refer to our devotion to ideal ends. I might add that at that time two leading humanist thinkers, Sidney Hook and Corliss Lamont, objected to Dewey's use of these terms. They argued that, if these definitions were consistently applied, in one sense practically everything could function religiously. Paul Tillich, the influential Protestant theologian, introduced the term *ultimate concern* to refer to this form of religiosity; and he found that both Christianity and atheistic humanism displayed the same religious characteristics.

Here he was referring to the human qualities of experiences and claimed that as religious Christians, Jews, and Muslims may be devoted to their religious faith or creed, so atheists, Marxists, and naturalists may have an equal devotion and dedication to theirs. This commitment may be called "religious" if it expresses one's "whole response" to life—"core attitudes and values," to use Beattie's terminology.

But this is where the issue becomes complicated. Does this mean that *any* intense commitment to a set of beliefs and practices, if it has deep roots in the personality, should be designated as "religious"? If one is a vegetarian and believes firmly that "Thou shalt not eat meat," would this be a religious commitment? Perhaps it makes some sense to stretch the term to cover such cases, but how far do we go? If one is a committed member of a political party, believes deeply in the party's aims and goals, works hard during and between election campaigns to further its influence, should we say that this, too, is a *religious* commitment? Similarly, if one is a devoted fan of the New York Jets or the San Diego Chargers, goes to all the football games, and roots passionately for the victory of his or her team, is it stretching the term to say that this is "religious" behavior? Is a member of the Wine-Tasters Society also "religious" if he or she is a connoisseur of wines and visits the French wine country annually to sample its delightful products? If one is willing to use the term *religious* indiscriminately, it would boomerang; whatever people deem important in their lives could be considered "religious."

But there is a difference between being *religious* and adhering to a *religion*. Even if some of the above-mentioned examples of dedicated interest may be said to be *religious*," in a metaphorical sense, they surely are not examples of *religions*. A *religion* refers to a set of practices and beliefs, a creed or code (however liberally applied), a ministry, rites, and rituals, churches or other centers of worship or prayer, and an organized community of believers. Unitarianism though generally noncreedal and individualistic, nevertheless roughly fits this definition. *Secular* nontheistic, atheistic, agnostic, or naturalistic humanisms cannot be said to be religions in this sense. They do not have a clergy or a priesthood, they have no established churches or temples, there are no codes or creeds; nor do they provide for common worship, prayer, or other services. Indeed, usually there is no fixed institutional framework to espouse a set of core values or to maintain a creed. However, these forms of secular humanism do have a set of ethical values, which they consider of prime significance (e.g., freedom of the individual, autonomy, tolerance, etc.); they are committed to the use of reason in evaluating claims to truth; and they believe that science best approximates our knowledge of the universe at any one time in history. These forms of secular humanism explicitly hold, however, that human beings can live good lives without clergy or churches, i.e., without a *religion* as the term is commonly understood. Millions of secular humanists are even indifferent to religion, and they may accept secular humanism only nominally. Most secular humanists do not even belong to a humanist organization per se. They are neither religious nor members of a religious institution. They are *nonreligious* secular humanists.

Now some secular humanists may be passionately devoted to their beliefs and values. They (a relatively small number) may even be members of humanist organizations, and may publicly advocate the values and methods of secular and scientific humanism. Perhaps they are religious in Dewey's sense; that is, they may have a deeply rooted psychological and sociological commitment. As freethinkers they may be outspoken critics of certain excesses of religion, especially those that are authoritarian, dogmatic, or sectarian. They are nonreligious and anti-religious—*religiously* so, Paul Beattie might say—but here we are referring to the intensity or sincerity of conviction in a secular humanist's psychological framework, and nothing beyond that; it is like being a committed vegetarian, a strong Republican, or an avid sports fan.

Although there may be some similarities between these various positions there are still genuine differences between the theistic and the nontheistic use of the term *religious,* and this should not be fudged. Indeed, there is a substantial difference in kind between a pious, believing Christian, Jew, or Muslim and a nonbelieving atheist, agnostic, or skeptic. The former claims to have a sense of the presence of a divine being, who is worshiped, loved, or feared, and to whom is attributed powers that affect one's life and the universe. There is a kind of awe about the noumenal character of reality, a belief in some transcending force—and there is a creed—a confession of faith— that is often recited publicly. Nontheists, too, may be inspired by the majesty and mystery of the universe but they can find no evidence for a divine being or purpose. They have no feelings of theistic piety. Thus viewed from *within* the experience, the phenomenological character of the theistic believer is markedly different from that of the nonbeliever, however much the latter may (or may not, as the case may be) be devoted to his or her ideals. Theists deny that nontheists have the same religious qualities of experience they do, and they often attack secularists on this score. They claim a special mystical, noumenal awareness that nontheists do not believe in. Thus it is a cardinal mistake to say that *all* experiences that represent "ultimate concern" are synonymous and hence religious. They differ fundamentally. The theist believes that there is some external divine source or ground for his belief, but the nontheist denies that his concern is ultimate in that sense. (Both are only *human,* says the humanist.) The term *religious* thus has different meanings and cannot be applied in the same way to all endeavors in which there is intensity, dedication, or commitment to a cause.

If we approach the problem from the standpoint of the term *religion,* the differences are even clearer. Secular humanism is not a religion. Beattie's definition of a religion is so broad that it includes any community of association or fellowship of individuals who hold the same set of core values. The skeptic, atheist, or secular humanist can form an organization to achieve certain common goals without being thereby designated as having a religion—much the same as educators, doctors, lawyers, and others who voluntarily join professional associations or special interest groups. But they do not include common worship or prayer and the other paraphernalia and trappings of religion.

*   *   *

A person can live a good life, have a set of core values, and possess a sense of belonging to a particular community, and yet *not* be said (a) to be religious or (b) to have a religion. One can live with an intense commitment to a wide range of ideals—which may express one's core values—and not be religious in the usual sense of having piety, a creed, or a sense of transcendence. Moreover, one can participate in various communities—moral, social, economic, intellectual—but they need not all be reduced to religion. One may even commemorate rites of passage—birth, graduation, marriage or divorce, retirement, even death—in a purely secularized fashion without invoking any transcendent being or religious sense. To insist that this implies a religion is to read far more into it than what is intended.

Beattie is obfuscating language. Secular humanism is distinct from religious humanism. Is there not a right to freedom of conscience and freedom *from* religion for those who insist upon it, without being accused of being covertly religious? Surely one who is indifferent to or neutral about religion, or nonreligious or even anti-religious should not be labeled "religious." To deny this would mean that something is what it is as well as its opposite—a clear contradiction. There are many other institutions other than religious ones that can fulfill human needs, express core values, and satisfy psychological and sociological needs. The fact that Beattie shares most of the values, methods, and outlook of secular humanism does not mean that it is religious. He also accepts the rules of arithmetic and grammar, but this does not mean that they too are religious. Secular humanism is *secular,* not religious. The term should not be turned upside down.

Notes

1. Joseph Fletcher, "An Odyssey: From Theology to Humanism," *Religious Humanism,* vol. 13, no. 4 (Autumn 1979), p. 146.

2. Ibid., p. 157.

3. Paul Kurtz, *In Defense of Secular Humanism,* Prometheus Books, p. 178.

4. Ibid., p. 185.

5. Bernard K. Duffy, "A New Meaning for Secular Humanism," *Religious Humanism,* vol. 18, no. 4 (Summer 1984), p. 128.

6. Ibid.

7. William P. Alston, "Religion," *The Encyclopedia of Philosophy,* ed. Paul Edwards. Macmillan, 1967, vol. 7, p. 142.

8. Edwin H. Wilson, "Historical Note: A Humanist Manifesto (1933)," *The Free Mind,* vol. 27, no. 2 (March/April 1985), p. 2.

9. Robert B. Tapp, *Religion Among the Unitarian Universalists: Converts in the Stepfather's House,* Seminar Press, 1973, p. 236.

10. Gerald Meyer has recently written a fine article stressing the similarities between secular and religious humanists in which he makes a plea for cooperation between the two groups. See *The Churchman,* vol. CXCIX, no. 3 (March 1985), pp. 14–15.

(Winter 1985–86)

Secular Humanism in
American Political Culture

Adolf Grünbaum

All of us have heard it said that a liberal college education widens our intellectual horizons and makes a valuable contribution to good citizenship in our country. Alas, recently the coin of public discourse has been debased by attacks on liberal education, featuring ideological demagoguery and coercive political attempts at philosophical intimidation. We are told that much of our educational system instills the doctrine of secular humanism—and that this outlook on the world is responsible for evils ranging from drug addiction and smut in the media to the repressiveness of Soviet society.

The strident voices that level this demonstrably untutored and shallow moral indictment of secular humanism are not confined to the televangelists, whose judgmental penchant for moral self-righteousness has recently boomeranged. Regrettably, the sloganeering detractors also include high public officials like the fundamentalist Senator Jesse Helms. And, yes, they can claim support from the president of the United States, who decries godlessness more vaguely but who has seen fit to say misleadingly that the theory of evolution, in contrast to the Book of Genesis, is "just" a theory. Chiming in with Reagan, William J. Bennett, his Secretary of Education, opined last year that "religion promotes tolerance" and that, in the public schools, "neutrality to religion turned out to bring with it a neutrality to those values that issue from religion."[1] Others maintain that secular humanism is *itself* a religion after all, but one that we must shun like the plague.

Just what is it about secular humanism that is so pernicious? Is it justified, or even workable, for our public officials to try to intimidate secular humanists by linking good citizenship to religious belief?

The Core of Secular Humanism

For a concise statement of the core of secular humanism, one can do no better than to turn to Albert Einstein's essay on "Science and Religion," which he delivered in 1941 at a Conference on Science, Philosophy, and Religion.

Speaking of "the actual content of the historical religions," Einstein characterized their "concept of God" this way:

> During the youthful period of mankind's spiritual evolution, human fantasy created gods in man's own image, who, by the operations of their will were supposed to determine, or at any rate to influence, the phenomenal world. Man sought to alter the disposition of these gods in his own favor by means of magic and prayer. The idea of God in the religions taught at present is a sublimation of that old conception of the gods. Its anthropomorphic [wish-inspired] character is shown, for instance, by the fact that men appeal to the Divine Being in prayers and plead for the fulfillment of their wishes.
>
> Nobody, certainly, will deny that the idea of the existence of an omnipotent just and omnibeneficent personal God is able to accord men solace, help, and guidance; also, by virtue of its simplicity the concept is accessible to the most undeveloped mind. But, on the other hand, there are decisive weaknesses attached to this idea in itself, which have been painfully felt since the beginning of history. . . .
>
> The main source of the present-day conflicts between the spheres of religion and science lies in this concept of a personal God.[2]

In Einstein's view, one of the decisive weaknesses of the concept of God is that a supposedly omnibenevolent God permits the existence of a vast amount of cruelty and evil in this world. Let me point out that much of this evil is *not* man-made at all; its existence cannot be explained away as being the result of human abuse of God's gift of free will. For example, thousands of animals die slow, agonizing, and painful deaths in forests from diseases not induced by humans, and they do not even have palliative relief from our own decisions or actions. Thus, *this* sort of evidence against God's benevolence cannot be neutralized even by the grotesque sort of reasoning used by the ultra-orthodox Rabbi Teitelbaum in his lame effort to reconcile the Nazi Holocaust with divine omnibenevolence.

Einstein goes on to elaborate his objections to the traditional concept of God:

> The more a man is imbued with the ordered regularity of all events, the firmer becomes his conviction that there is no room left by the side of this ordered regularity for causes of a different nature. For him neither the rule of human nor the rule of divine will exists as an independent cause of natural events. To be sure, the doctrine of a personal God interfering with natural events could never be refuted, in the real sense, by science, for this doctrine can always take refuge in those domains in which scientific knowledge has not yet been able to set foot.
>
> But I am persuaded that such behavior on the part of the representatives of

religion would not only be unworthy but also fatal. For a doctrine which is able to maintain itself not in clear light, but only in the dark, will of necessity lose its effect on mankind, with incalculable harm to human progress. In their struggle for the ethical good, teachers of religion must have the stature to give up the doctrine of a personal God, that is, give up that source of fear and hope which in the past placed such vast power in the hands of priests. In their labors they will have to avail themselves of those forces which are capable of cultivating the Good, the True, and the Beautiful in humanity itself. This is, to be sure, a more difficult but an incomparably more worthy task.[3]

Let me illustrate Einstein's *denial* of "divine will . . . as an independent cause of natural events." When President Reagan escaped permanent injury from Hinckley's bullets, Nancy Reagan expressed her conviction that God had been on her husband's shoulder during the shooting, deflecting the bullet from all of his vital organs. But her proposed explanation raises, of course, an urgent question: What was God doing while another bullet devastated the brain of Reagan's poor press secretary, Jim Brady? Is Mrs. Reagan suggesting that Brady got what God thought he deserved? Isn't it more reasonable, and compassionate, to hold that, if there is a God, he had nothing to do with the trajectories of any of Hinckley's bullets?

Einstein concludes his essay by saying:

The further the spiritual evolution of mankind advances, the more certain it seems to me that the path to genuine religiosity does not lie through the fear of life, and the fear of death, and blind faith, but through striving after rational knowledge.[4]

My quotations from Einstein can serve as a kind of secular humanist manifesto in at least three major respects: he takes an explicit stand in the debate between atheism and theism by asserting that man created the idea of God as a figment of his own imagination; he urges us to locate the meaning of our existence within human life itself rather than in the fulfillment of some inscrutable cosmic purpose dictated by divine will; and he declares that man himself has the responsibility for making moral discriminations between good and evil, between right and wrong.

In its traditional form, theism asserts the existence of an omnipotent, omniscient, and omnibenevolent creator who is accessible to personal communion with us. This divine being is to be respected, loved, and feared. In fact, compliance with His purported ethical demands normally holds out the promise of heaven, though there have been theists who did not believe in personal immortality. Clearly, to *deny* the existence-claim made by theism is to assert a theism. Thus understood, Einstein's version of secular humanism, as well as those of the philosophers Nietzsche, Schopenhauer, and Bertrand Russell, for example, are instances of atheism.

It is vital to appreciate that, like any other doctrine, either theism or atheism can be asserted with varying degrees of conviction. Thus, either of them might be held, more or less tentatively, as the best working hypothesis. Alternatively, either may be held dogmatically, with a degree of certainty characteristic of fanaticism. However, scientifically literate secular humanists know all too well that even a hypothesis enjoying much evidential support *may* nonetheless still be false. When secular humanists endorse atheism, they do so in the sense of regarding it as the most reasonable hypothesis in the light of the currently available evidence. As Einstein noted, it is not necessary to produce a knock-down, irrevocably conclusive *disproof* of the existence of God in order to reject belief in theism. Instead, such *disbelief* is reasonable if the evidence *for* theism is weak or poor, and there is impressive evidence against it, such as the problem of evil.

Let me point out that in contexts not related to religion, we can likewise have excellent reasons to disbelieve a certain hypothesis, even when we haven't conclusively disproved it. And we are surely not required to accept a hypothesis merely because it has not been utterly disproved.

Einstein only barely touched on the sources of theism's *psychological* appeal. But other secular humanists—such as Sigmund Freud, who was a self-declared atheist—have eloquently recognized the immensely powerful psychological attraction that many people feel for the consolations and wish-fulfillments provided by belief in God. Freud eloquently describes this appeal:

> . . . the terrifying impression of helplessness in childhood aroused the need for protection—for protection through love—which was provided by the father; and the recognition that this helplessness lasts throughout life made it necessary to cling to the existence of a father, but this time a more powerful one. Thus the benevolent rule of a divine Providence allays our fear of the dangers of life; the establishment of a moral world-order ensures the fulfillment of the demands of justice, which have so often remained unfulfilled in human civilization; and prolongation of earthly existence in a future life provides the local and temporal framework in which these wish-fulfillments shall take place. Answers to the riddles that tempt the curiosity of man, such as how the universe began or what the relation is between body and mind, are developed in conformity with the underlying assumptions of this system.[5]

The protector, creator, *and* lawgiver are all rolled into one. No wonder, then, that religious systems can secure the acquiescence of their believers, if they teach that the will of God is mysterious or inscrutable and that some religious tenets transcend human understanding. In fact, Freud contends repeatedly that theism psychologically *infantilizes* adults by reinforcing the childish residues in their psyches.[6]

Freud sums up as follows:

> Religion is an attempt to master the sensory world in which we are situated by means of the wishful world which we have developed within us as a result of biological and psychological necessities. But religion cannot achieve this. Its doctrines bear the imprint of the times in which they arose, the ignorant times of the childhood of humanity. Its consolations deserve no trust. Experience teaches us that the world is no nursery. The ethical demands on which religion seeks to lay stress need, rather,

to be given another basis; for they are indispensable to human society and it is dangerous to link obedience to them with religious faith.[7]

As we know, the ethical demands of different religious systems tend to contradict each other. Indeed, even within the same denomination there can be clashes over basic moral doctrine. Hence Freud's reference to "the" ethical demands made by religion has to be construed as merely generic. By the same token, in advocating an alternative secular foundation for such demands, he means only that some ethical rules are essential to a civilized society. Freud surely did not intend that the secular humanist will vindicate and incorporate moral directives merely because they had been issued under religious auspices. On the contrary, the secularist would pick and choose among the latter, rejecting a fair number of them, of course.

*   *   *

How can Einstein, Freud, and other secular humanists logically dispense with a theological basis for ethical rules of conduct? This very question, I claim, rests on an unexamined assumption—that an articulated system of rights and wrongs, *specific enough to give us concrete moral guidance for our actions,* can be deduced from divine omnibenevolence and revelation. I *deny* just this assumption. In fact, as I shall try to argue, theism itself is morally sterile.

To make my case, let me first distinguish between the following two very different questions:

1. Do the Ten Commandments, the moral injunctions of the New Testament, or the ethics of the Koran logically follow from the hypothesis that there is an omnibenevolent God who revealed Himself to humans?

2. Can the clergy of some denomination simply tack on particular ethical directives to a given theological hypothesis, with a view to then claiming divine sanction for these injunctions?

The first of these two questions asks about the *logical deducibility* of a concrete ethical system from the pertinent theological existence-claim. But the second query leaves such deducibility wholly aside and pertains to connecting an idea of God to a set of ethical imperatives that is gotten from elsewhere. Obviously, it is feasible to conjoin an independently obtained ethics with theism. Equally obviously, in the event of such mere tacking on, the specific ethical injunctions are not derived from theism, although they are issued under clerical auspices. Thus, as we know, a great variety of radically incompatible moral imperatives can be and have been sanctioned by avowedly theistic religious institutions.

But what of the logical derivability of ethics from theism, which is asserted by those who claim that belief in God and revelation not only yields an ethical system but is even an indispensable foundation for it? Let us grant, just for argument's sake, that the notion of divine omnibenevolence is itself unproblematic. Assuming such omnibenevolence on God's part, it presumably follows that all divinely ordained conduct is morally right. But here is the crucial question: Which particular conduct is divinely ordained? If the reply be that the relevant moral directives are supplied by revelation, then I ask: Within Christendom, or within theism in general, which one of the conflicting purported revelations is supposed to supply us with concrete ethical rules? It emerges that the concepts of divine omnibenevolence and revelation are altogether unhelpful with regard to the *specific* moral issues over which we agonize.

It is no wonder that the Judeo-Christian theology to which many of our public officials claim allegiance has been invoked as a sanction for diverse, and even incompatible, ethical doctrines, such as the divine right of kings; the inalienable rights of life, liberty, and the pursuit of happiness; black slavery; "Deutschland über alles"; the Social Darwinism of Spencer; and socialism. For example, in a very recent issue of the *New Republic,* Crocker Coulson challenged neoconservative Christians like Catholic theologian Michael Novak to explain how they reconcile their free market philosophy with the following New Testament injunctions[8]:

No man can serve two masters: for either he will hate the one, and love the other; or else he will hold to one, and despise the other. Ye cannot serve God and mammon. [Matthew 6:24]

If thou wilt be perfect, go and sell that thou hast, and give it to the poor, and thou shalt have treasure in heaven. [Matthew 19:21]

Woe unto you that are rich! for ye have received your consolation. Woe unto you that are full! for ye shall hunger. [Luke 6:24–25]

Precisely such passages from scripture have been invoked since the 1960s by those Catholic priests in Latin America who espouse the neo-Marxist "liberation theology." As Coulson points out, Latin America is home to almost half of the world's Roman Catholics, and, despite Vatican objections, liberation theology "has become the accepted creed of the Church hierarchy in several countries," having established tens of thousands of communities among the peasantry and urban poor.[9] Launched at the 1968 Bishops Conference in Medellín, Columbia, liberation theology described Latin American capitalism as a "situation of sin" and has been used to justify diverse political activities, ranging from nonviolent protest to agrarian reform and armed revolution.

The enormous moral ambiguity of religious belief can be illustrated by innumerable other examples. Thus, some religious sects in India would have us abstain from the surgical excision of cancerous growths in man, and Christian Scientists in this country reach somewhat similar conclusions from rather different premises. Roman Catholics, on the other hand, endorse the medical prevention of death but condemn interference with nature in the form of artificial birth control, a position not shared by leading Protestant and Jewish clergymen. Perhaps one could reply that this ambiguity of practice is resolved by a uniformity of intention: as long as one tries to serve God, one's act cannot be immoral. But both Mahatma Gandhi and Adolf Hitler saw themselves as serving God. And divine providence was as frequent a feature of Hitler's speeches as it is of Ronald Reagan's. Indeed, Hitler's invocation of divine providence illustrates anew that religion can be the last refuge of the scoundrel. By the same token, belief in God leaves us in the dark whether to share or abhor, for example, the Reverend Jerry Falwell's and Rabbi Meir Kahane's claim that a nuclear Armageddon is part of God's just and loving plan for us. From Rabbi Kahane we learn: "The Messiah will come. There will be a resurrection of the dead—all the things that Jews believed in before they got so damn sophisticated." In a fairly recent "Nightline" program, Jerry Falwell rejected astrophysical findings regarding the formation of the stars' heavier chemical elements because they conflicted with the biblical tenet of man's fall.

To the likes of Falwell and Kahane, as well as to the patrons of their theology in high places, secular humanists reply: "The genie of critical thought is out of the bottle; not even all the president's men and all of his horses will ever succeed in putting it back again! No demagogue will be able to turn the clock back to the dark ages."

When, through history, theology has attempted to find prescriptions, down-to-earth aims and thought were typically every bit as decisive as they have been in the reflections of secular ethicists who deny theism. The perplexity of moral problems is not at all lessened by the theological superstructure, which itself leaves us in an ethical quandary. That this superstructure is at best logically superfluous for ethics, or is simply unavailing, emerges further from the failure of divine omnibenevolence to answer a key question put by Socrates in Plato's *Euthyphro:* is the conduct approved by the gods right because it is *intrinsically* good, or is it right *merely* because it pleases the gods to command it? If God enjoins us to do what is just or good *in its own right,* then ethical rules do not depend for their validity on divine command. But if conduct is good *merely* because God enjoins it, then we are again faced with the cacophony of conflicting revelations—and, within denominations, conflicting interpretations regarding the revelations' ethical meaning.

These difficulties teach a cardinal lesson: Even if a person attempts to defer completely to theological authority on moral matters, he or she has no choice but to decide *which* religious authority will be the ethical guide. Try as they may, people cannot abdicate theiry own responsibility for determining the moral norms of their lives. As Freud stressed, "the world is no nursery." In just this decision-making sense, I contend, man is inescapably the measure of all things, for better or for worse.

Alexander Solzhenitsyn denied this conclusion. Thus, his famous 1978 commencement address at Harvard University contains the following lament, which he addressed to the West no less than to the Soviet Union:

There is a disaster which is already very much with us. I am referring to the calamity of an autonomous [despiritualized] and irreligious, humanistic consciousness. It has made man the measuure of all things on Earth—imperfect man, who is never free of pride, self-interest, envy, vanity, and dozens of other defects. . . . Is it true that man is above everything? Is there no Superior Spirit above him?

This declaration may sound ingratiatingly modest. Alas, it is morally hollow and theologically question-begging. Which revelation, I must ask Solzhenitsyn, is to supplant man as the measure of all things? The Czarist Russian Orthodox church's? The Ayatollah Khomeini's as enforced by his mullahs? The Dutch Reformed church's, which has legitimated apartheid in South Africa? Or the revelation of Pope John Paul II, who—amid starvation in Africa—is getting support from the native episcopate for the prohibition of artificial birth control?

Solzhenitsyn's charge of moral inadequacy against an irreligious humanistic consciousness is of a piece with his rhetorical questions, "Is it true that man is above everything? Is there no Superior Spirit above him?" In our current state of biological evolution, our species may indeed be limited to certain intellectual horizons—much as theoretical physics defies comprehension by dogs. And there just might be extra-solar organisms that do not have to operate within our assumed horizons. But, surely, this assumption that man may not be above everything hardly requires belief in the existence of God. Solzhenitsyn's jeremiad simply replaces secular men with *clergymen,* who become the moral measure of everything. It would seem that his well-justified loathing of Soviet totalitarianism has prompted him to embrace the outmoded ideals of a chauvinistic Russian theocracy. But atheism, which Solzhenitsyn passionately attacks, is no less compatible with belief in free-enterprise capitalism, than with the socioeconomic doctrines of the Swedish welfare state, or with the ideology of Communist China. For instance, the late author Ayn Rand was an advocate of both belligerent atheism *and* unregulated capitalism, scoffing at much of our social welfare legislation as the decadent pampering of the undeserving. Certainly, while all orthodox Marxists are atheists, it does *not* follow that all atheists are Marxists, let alone Soviet-style communists. American politicians who use the phrase "atheistic communism" unscrupulously insinuate that the unacceptable and repugnant features of Soviet governance derive from the atheism of the Politburo.

But, in so doing, they conveniently ignore that the secret police flourished in Russia under the vauntedly theocratic Czarist Romanov dynasty. Indeed, the repressive and egregiously autocratic Empress Alexandra Feodorovna, who was shot by the Bolsheviks, surrendered to extreme theocratic exaltation under the guidance of the notorious monk Rasputin, whom she regarded as God's gift to Russia. One of Rasputin's religious injunctions was "Sin in order that you may obtain forgiveness." This elevating directive was fervently applied at the court. Indeed, it legitimated wanton debauchery and orgies wild enough to make the wife-swapping reportedly practiced by Pentecostal televangelists seem tame indeed.

Yet there are public figures in this country who glibly and reflexively blame the rampancy of pornographic material here on the alleged moral permissiveness of secular humanism and on the absence of prayer in our public schools. In their demagogic fervor, they are not even given pause by the puritanical sexual prudishness of the Soviet government, an institution in which sexual improprieties jeopardize political careers at least as much as avowed religiosity does. Also conveniently ignored is the fact that, in Castro's Cuba, homosexuality—far from being abetted—is inhumanely punished. There are innumerable other facts that refute the purported linkage of secular humanism with various totalitarian evils. We need only recall the warm welcome extended to Hitler in Vienna by the Roman Catholic Cardinal Innitzer, who proclaimed that Austria's incorporation into Nazi Germany was ordained by divine providence. Yet, unencumbered by such evidence, the attacks on secular humanism continue relentlessly.

Coercive political intimidation of secular humanists in this country will neither banish nor invalidate their ideas, any more than Soviet psychiatrists have been able to cow Russian nonconformists into intellectual submission. Nor did Soviet state-sponsored atheism browbeat Mrs. Nikita Krushchev into abandoning her openly declared religious beliefs. Apart from being ineffective, political intimidation of irreligious American citizens can hardly be justified by the fact that President Eisenhower chose to insert the phrase "under God" after the words "one nation" in the Pledge of Allegiance. Have we not all had enough of the shameful history of religious coercion? And are we Americans not sobered by the fact that the rising tide of Islamic fundamentalism is deeply hostile to us, even when President Reagan proclaims us to be a God-fearing people, whose secret emissaries arrived with Bible in hand? Is it not time to stop using the term *secular humanist*— and, yes, also the label *atheist*—as scare or code words for conjuring up a scapegoat, whipping boy, or bugaboo?

All too often, the level of public discourse in our country on philosophical issues of national importance is appallingly low. Our republic and our people deserve much better, if only because the received political and religious pieties have alienated many thoughtful citizens from our political processes. If we are really to cope with our problems in this land, and in the world at large, both religious and irreligious people must forsake smug, self-congratulatory claims of superior moral probity.

Notes

1. Quoted in John B. Judis, "Mr. Ed," *New Republic,* April 27, 1987, p. 18.

2. Reprinted in D. J. Bronstein and H. M. Schulweis, eds., *Approaches to the Philosophy of Religion* (New York: Prentice Hall, 1954), pp. 69-70.

3. Ibid., p. 71.

4. Ibid., p. 72.

5. Sigmund Freud, *Standard Edition of the Complete Psychological Words of Sigmund*

Freud, tr. John Strachey et al. (London: Hogarth Press, 1953–1974), 1927. vol. 21, p. 30.

6. Ibid., 1927, vol. 21, p. 49; 1930, vol. 21, p. 85.

7. Ibid., 1933, vol. 22, p. 168.

8. *New Republic,* May 4, 1987, p. 35.

9. Ibid., p. 32.

(Winter 1987/88)

Secular Humanists: Threat or Menace?

Art Buchwald

The new threat to this country, if you believe the Moral Majority and the television preachers, is not communists or fellow travelers but "secular humanists."

The secular humanists are the ones who are brainwashing our children with books about evolution, sex, race relations, the Equal Rights Amendment, and naughty words.

This means we have to get the books out of the schools and libraries. The book censors are starting to organize, the moral crusade has begun, and the hunt for secular humanists is on.

*   *   *

I am always intimidated by book burners, so I want to get on the bandwagon as soon as possible.

My problem is, unlike the Red-baiting witch-hunts of the McCarthy days, I find it impossible to know who a secular humanist is.

It was easy to tell a Commie or fellow traveler in the fifties because he always carried a *Daily Worker* under his arm and didn't bother to shine his shoes. He never had a nice thing to say about Senator Joe McCarthy or Roy Cohn, and he kept taking the Fifth Amendment when he was called in front of the House Un-American Activities Committee. Also, you could check up on him by finding out if he once belonged to one of the hundreds of subversive organizations listed by the government as being for the violent overthrow of the government.

*   *   *

But a secular humanist is a different breed of cat. From what I can gather, he is much harder to identify unless he openly admits he thinks Darwin's theory of evolution makes sense.

Secular humanists are not joiners. They don't have cells where they plot anti-American and anti-God propaganda. Most of them work alone, doing historical research, writing textbooks and novels, and explaining how babies are born. They pollute children's minds with how the world is rather than how the anti-humanists would like it to be.

What makes them so dangerous is that secular humanists look just like you and me. Some of them could be your best friends without your knowing they are humanists. They could come into your house, play with your children, eat your food, and even watch football on television with you, and you'd never know that they have read *Catcher in the Rye, Brave New World,* and *Huckleberry Finn.*

Of course there are some who flaunt their humanism and will brag they are for abortion and against prayers in public schools. You can throw them out of the house.

But for every secular humanist who will tell where he or she stands on a fundamentalist issue there are ten who keep their thoughts to themselves and are working to destroy the American family.

No one is safe until Congress sets up an Anti-Secular Humanism Committee to get at the rot. Witnesses have to be called, and they have to name names of other secular humanists they know.

Librarians and teachers must be made to answer for the books they have on their shelves. Publishers have to be held accountable for what they print. Writers must be punished for what they write.

*   *   *

The secular humanists should be put on notice that they can no longer hide behind the First Amendment.

If we're going to go back to the old moral values that made this country great, we're going to have to do it with search-and-destroy methods. First, we must burn the books—and if that isn't enough, then we must burn the people.

(Fall 1981)

Of Humanists and Humor

Tim Madigan

The philosopher Henri Bergson said of laughter that "it is a social sanction against rigid behavior." I must shamefacedly admit that I know of his definition not through reading his works but from hearing it spoken during a television interview by the comedian John Cleese, of "Monty Python" fame—surely an impeccable source. Regardless of where it is found, Bergson's point is an important one, especially in regard to humanism. The ability to see the humor in human situations is crucial. It is laughter that can bring down the walls of intolerance and cause us to reexamine our doctrinaire positions. In fact, one could add the following to the "Affirmations of Humanism": *We humanists are able to laugh at ourselves.* And, as we enter the twenty-first century, this is an ability that needs to be cultivated.

As national coordinator for the local *Free Inquiry* groups, I have had the opportunity to meet many professed secular humanists. What particularly strikes me is the great sense of humor most of them possess; meetings of humanists have more than their fair share of mirth. When you think of it, this is not surprising. Because humanism has no dogma, we don't have to get upset over "sacrilegious" remarks. Because it has no absolutes, we don't have to worry about breaching taboo subjects. Because it doesn't claim to have all the answers, we don't have to get perturbed when its principles are called into question.

Irreverence is an important humanist trait. We don't *venerate* anything, in the sense of feeling awe mingled with fear. Veneration impedes questioning, and humanists are, if nothing else, inquisitive beings. We wish to understand the world we find ourselves in, which means that no subject is off-limits to us. Why *did* the chicken cross that road?

Above all else, we humanists recognize the foibles of all rational beings. For this reason we can never make gods out of humans, as our opponents claim we do. How can one worship so silly a race? We can respect, but we cannot *revere* anyone (with the possible exception of the guy who yelled out, "The British are coming, the British are coming!").

I do not claim that *all* humanists are laugh-riots. I've met a few sourpusses in my travels, too (*you* know who you are), who act as if a good belly-laugh would split them asunder. Nor do I claim that only humanists can laugh at themselves. One of my best friends, and the wittiest person I know, is a devout born-again Christian. Still, he can chuckle over the vagaries of the world, and even over his own church's creeds (although this has been known to get him into hot water with his fellow parishioners).

Humor is essential to our well-being. We live in a world with many problems and much adversity, both natural and man-made. Of course I don't advocate laughing at everything at all times (for example, I do not find anything amusing in the *Police Academy* films, truly a tragic waste of valuable celluloid). Some things are, indeed, deadly serious. But one should note that to laugh at a subject is not necessarily to denigrate or ridicule it. Laughter at its best puts things into human perspective. How much better it would have been if Abraham slapped his knee and chortled: "You want me to do *what* to my first-born son? What a sense of humor you've got, Big Guy!" Friedrich Nietzsche wrote "I would believe only in a god who could dance." I would amend that to "I would believe only in a god who could take a joke."

The righteous ask, "Is nothing sacred?" We humanists reply "Precisely!" It is the people whose hearts have been hardened by certainty who find it most difficult to let loose and guffaw. They are unwilling to challenge their own convictions, and they detest anyone who pokes fun at their beliefs. But one can be philosophical about life without being grim. Lest we forget, Charles Dodgson, the noted logician, was also the author of such hilarious works as *The Hunting of the Snark* and *Alice In Wonderland* (under the nom-de-plume Lewis Carroll). And it is a little-known fact that Morey Amsterdam once held the Chair of Moral Philosophy at Cambridge—until someone made him let go of it.

Steve Allen, the famous entertainer and social critic, says in the introduction to his book *Funny People:* "Without laughter life on our planet would be intolerable." I heartily concur. It is the duty of humanists to slay sacred cows with the sword of laughter. As we head toward the next century, we should be ever mindful of the importance of humor as a self-corrective method of keeping us from becoming stern absolutists. Or, in the stirring words of Henri "Shecky" Bergson: "Take my dogma, please!"

(Summer 1988)

The Future of Humanism

Paul Kurtz

I

Humanism is a major force in the United States and the world, according to our critics, who claim that humanists dominate the schools and universities, the media, literature, the sciences and arts, the courts and other institutions of modern society. Certainly humanist ideas and values have had a powerful and continuing impact on the modern world. Yet those of us who have been involved in the organized humanist movement are dismayed to hear of the influence our critics attribute to us. We are perplexed by our *failure* to build viable humanist organizations, despite our alleged "success."

Indeed, some believe that this is a time for deep soul-searching and hard decisions. The truth is as we all know that humanist associations are very weak institutions. I am referring here principally to humanist organizations in North America: the American Humanist Association, the American Ethical Union, the Fellowship of Religious Humanists, the Society for Humanistic Judaism, the Council for Democratic and Secular Humanism, and the Canadian Humanist Association. My analysis, I believe, also applies to most other humanist organizations worldwide. They have pitifully small budgets, woefully small memberships, and relatively low circulations of their publications. The average local church in almost any city has more members and resources than any of the major humanist groups, yet we claim to be a national movement. And so we naturally ask, what can we do to increase our effectiveness?

I think we should recognize that humanist organizations are not the epitome of humanism; indeed, at times I think they have betrayed its ideals. We sometimes exaggerate their importance. These groups are certainly not coextensive with humanism as a movement. Humanism is broader in scope and will continue long after they are gone. There are many humanistic personalities, organizations, and publications in the world—perhaps hundreds—who do not call themselves "humanist." Humanism, in this broad sense, is one of the deepest currents of thought and feeling in the world. It will not be easily swept aside. Nevertheless, historical trends are not predetermined, and humanist ideas and values may be overwhelmed by forces of unreason and intolerance. This happened in the fourth century when Hellenic and Roman civilization was subverted by an obscure mystery cult (Christianty) from Asia. It may happen again. If it does we may have to recreate humanism. Meanwhile we must treasure, defend, and expand it wherever we can.

By every comparative standard, we have failed in our mission. There are two questions to be answered: Why have we failed? What should we do about it?

From a perspective of intimate involvement in the humanist movement and in the spirit of constructive and responsible criticism, I propose to make an in-depth analysis of organized humanism and raise some basic questions about its future, at least in North America.

II

Why has humanism failed to develop strong and viable organizations? In my view, they have never been sufficiently clear about their goals and to whom they were addressing their message. They have also lacked a clear strategy of growth and development. There are various reasons for this. First, the organized humanist movement has failed because it *lacks an inspiring message* of sufficient clarity and drama to command public attention. The humanist message has been couched in a way that has made it seem boring and redundant. To many younger men and women it sounded outworn, outdated, based on nostalgic hunger for spiritual pabulum inappropriate to the deeper needs of contemporary society. Second, organized humanism *lacks charismatic leadership* of sufficient skill and dedication. Third, each of these organizations has mistakenly sought to become another denomination or sect to compete with other denominations and sects, when the effort should have been made to make humanism a broad-ased educational movement. These are the reasons the movement has not been able to build or sustain institutions strong or viable enough to function effectively.

Other factors are pertinent, and I shall enumerate them briefly and without discussion. Although the following seem to be less important, they may prevent us from coming to terms with the main difficulties:

- The humanist movement is for the most part dominated by individuals who lack sufficient national stature or impact.
- It has not been able to develop a broad base of financial support independent of a small power elite.
- It tends to attract cantankerous individuals from other movements.
- It often bickers itself to exhaustion in petty internal squabbles.
- It has at times become narrowly political and strident, identified with only

one part of the political spectrum.

- It has been infiltrated by its opponents, whose aim is to keep it off balance and destabilize it.
- It has been badly mismanaged and has lacked efficient business procedures.

It is obvious that I do not consider the lack of finances as the main problem. I do not deny, of course, that sound financing is important; but it is not necessarily the secret of virtue or success.

If the humanist movement does not have a charismatic leadership and viable ideas to communicate, we cannot hope to attract financial support. To blame the failure of our growth on the lack of money is irresponsible, a self-deceiving extenuation. We in the humanist movement have no one to blame for our failure but ourselves.

III

The first question to be asked is: What is it that we want the humanist movement to accomplish?

In looking at contemporary humanism, many humanists often compare it with religious institutions and churches around us that may wax and wane but never disappear. Humanism, some say, should be a strong alternative to them and should attract adherents as they have. I question the premise that humanism will ever become or should become another religion. Is membership in a humanist organization analogous to membership in a church? I think not and I will explain why.

But first let us focus on three religions and the charismatic individuals who helped (at least indirectly) to found them: Judaism and Moses, Christianity and Jesus, Islam and Muhammad:

Judaism is one of the oldest religions; it has survived for more than three thousand years. Moses, its alleged founder, was a tongue-tied savior who led the children of Israel out of Egypt to the Promised Land. He communicated with God on Mt. Sinai and proclaimed his message with all of the authority of divine sanction: the Hebrews were God's "chosen people" and had to follow his law obediently. There were seven million Jews in the Roman Empire at the time of Christ; there are twelve million today. They have suffered persecution at the hands of the gentiles, and tens of millions of Jews over the centuries converted or intermarried, became Christians or pagans. Yet a hard core has survived the destruction of the Temple in 70 C.E., the period of the Diaspora, and the Holocaust of World War II.

What is the Jewish religion? It involves (1) a message of divine power and the promise of a Messiah to restore the children of Israel to the homeland; (2) charismatic figures (Moses and the prophets) to interpret it; (3) institutions, a strict legal code (circumcision, dietary laws, the Talmud, etc.), synagogues, and a rabbinate.

At least two other ingredients were essential to its long survival and provided continuity: (1) *ethnicity*—strong prohibitions against intermarriage (though it constantly occurred) and (2) *a common cultural heritage,* including the Hebrew language, understood only by Jews. Anti-Semitism, in my judgment, has its roots in part in the Old Testment and the synagogue, both of which advanced the view that the Jews were the exclusive "chosen people." This could only engender hatred. But it also helped solidify the resistant inner core, leading to a ghetto mentality that fostered survival.

Christianity, unlike Judaism, intended its message to be universal. Whether Jesus existed is still open to dispute; but assuming that he did, he was either mad (his relatives believed he was) or a magician. The ancient Jews and pagans thought that he was a fraud, that his father was Panthera, a Roman soldier, that he performed magical tricks like others of his day, and that he did not die on the cross but was spirited out of his tomb by his disciples, and that he then fled in fear. It was Paul of Tarsus who converted the simple moral message of the Sermon on the Mount into a mystery religion, by making Jesus Christ the mediator between God and suffering humanity and promising eternal life to those who accepted the new faith. One didn't have to be circumcised, abstain from pork, or follow the Mosaic laws. The mythology of Christianity was far more wondrous than that of the Old Testament prophets, and it promised more to all human souls—the poor, the sick, the enslaved, as well as the wealthy—who were converted and thereby "saved."

Today there are about one billion Christians, nominal or genuine. (1) They have accepted the dramatic and incredible message of a dead and risen deity, a God who took on human form and can save all who believe in him. (2) Christianity involves a central *charismatic figure,* Jesus, a man of great appeal; and it attracted charismatic disciples and martyrs, Paul, Peter, and a host of saints, who gladly sacrificed everything to bring the gospel to the world. (3) From the early years there developed *church communities* (quite unlike our humanist chapters or ethical societies) and rules and dogmas that were eventually codified by the Council Nicaea in the fourth century. The church developed as an institution, with a priesthood and political leadership. (4) Although Christianity is missionary in its initial impulse (unlike Judaism), once it is accepted in a territory or by a people, it also has *ethnic roots,* and one is born into a particular denomination or sect. Children are Irish, Polish, Italian Catholics, German Lutherans, English Anglicans, Southern Baptists, etc. (5) A *common cultural and linguistic heritage* preserves the religious faith that is woven almost without question into the social fabric and because part of a person's being.

It is interesting how the basic Christian message has had a charismatic appeal in generation after generation; new sects and denominations are still being founded. In the nineteenth century, the Seventh-Day Adventist church (followers of Ellen G. White) was founded; there are now over 600,000 members. The Mormons' Church of Jesus Christ of Latter-Day Saints, founded by Joseph Smith, now has over five million members. And Mary Baker Eddy's Christian Science church is still growing. Today there is Reverend Moon of the Unification church and

Reverend Armstrong of the Worldwide Church of God.

A similar analysis may be applied to *Islam.* Like Christianity (1) it has a *message* from God as revealed in the Koran; (2) it has a *charismatic founder,* Muhammad; (3) it has established *institutions* of mosques and clergy and strict rules that regulate conduct; (4) it has an *ethnic basis*—non-Western, Arab, black, and Asian; and (5) it has a rich *cultural heritage.* The point is that once a religion is implanted—in the case of Islam, conquered by the sword at first—it becomes the way of life of a people and grows by osmosis and heritage. Eventually it becomes intertwined with nationality and even with race.

For a classical type of religion to grow, at least four rules seem vital. (1) One should try to convert the heathen; both Christianity and Islam did that. (2) One must insist that those in the fold bring up their children in the faith. (3) One cannot permit marriage outside the faith. (4) One must stamp out dissent and excommunicate heretics. These implicit rules, especially the last three, have been more or less utilized and explain the persistence of the major religions, which generally have been more or less utilized and explain the persistence of the major religions, which generally have an ethnic or geographic domain. The problem for classical religions in the modern world is that, with mobility, rapid communication, and the growth of secularism, there are pluralistic sets of competing religions, so that it becomes difficult for the established religions to enforce their hegemony.

IV

As humanists, surely we do not wish to develop according to the model of the classical religions. Though these religions have provided a social structure, a moral framework, and psychological comfort for their adherents, humanism is not and should not be a denomination or sect competing with others. We reject the notion of *ethnic* identification; we have none. We are committed to a universal ideal. We do not have an exclusive cultural heritage but consider ourselves part of world culture. We are opposed to and have not built churches and accredited clergy, although Ethical Cultural societies and Unitarian-Universalist churches have done so. We are ethnically pluralistic. We do not enforce strict rules of conduct or require a creed or dogma. More important, we do not pretend to have an "inspiring message," nor a charismatic leader.

Our model is not Moses, Jesus, or Muhammad, but Socrates. And for many secular humanists in the twentieth century, there is also Karl Marx—but Marx the fighter for human freedom, not the mummified god of Moscow, Peking, and Havana. I mention these two individuals because they expressed humanist ideals and values; they provide sharply contrasting models, however, for fulfilling humanism. Socrates, like Jesus, was martyred, dying at the hands of the Athenians. He never founded a church but instead inspired a literature of philosophy and ethics, beginning with Plato, who was so enamored of Socrates that he dedicated his Dialogues to him and founded the first great university, the Academy. Socrates was a curious figure. He was condemned by what amounted to an "Un-Athenian

Affairs Committee" for "making the better appear the worse," "denying the gods of Athens," and "corrupting youth." As a result he was forced by the Athenian democratic party to drink the hemlock. Was he a charismatic figure? Plato thought so, but his contemporary Aristophanes did not; in the comedy *The Clouds* Aristophanes depicted Socrates as an uncouth figure and a buffoon. More over, Socrates had no clear message. Although he believed that we ought to practice virtue, said he was inspired by the legendary priestess Diotima, and had intimations of immortality, he never claimed divine revelation. Indeed, he insisted in Plato's *Euthyphro,* that ethics was independent of the traditional religious pieties. He was committed to free inquiry. He did not know what truth, beauty, or goodness were. He was the wisest of men, he said, because he knew how ignorant he was. Yet, although Socrates talked about absolute ideas and even a utopian society in which justice prevailed, it was his devotion to the life of the mind that became his lasting contribution. Plato's pupil Aristotle went on to found the Lyceum, and his successors ever since have fulfilled the basic principle of humanism: a commitment to free inquiry and rationalism.

An average city in the United States has several hundred churches and synagogues, but only a few have a college or university, or an art, history, or science museum. These, in a sense, are the legacy of Socrates. There is no cult that reveres his name, yet Western civilization (in spite of its indelible Judeo-Christian influences) can draw on the heritage of the Socratic quest for truth. Perhaps that is why the disciples of the Socratic mission have failed to build institutions, for we are dealing with the realm of ideas. It is the difference between philosophy and science on the one hand (which are committed to the open mind and open society) and religion on the other (which, in its original Latin sense, means "to be bound" to a set of beliefs and practices). Religion, when given sufficient political power, shows a marked preference for the closed society.

Karl Marx, for a large part of the world, has been the most influential humanist of the twentieth century, even though his followers have taken a different approach. Marx was a disciple of the Enlightenment. He, too, rejected traditional religion and was committed to reason. But he thought that in order to bring humanism into reality we had to go *beyond* atheism, and build a "classless society." This could best be accomplished, he believed, by revolutionary means. He argued that mankind needs to destroy class oppression and thus liberate human potentialities. Both Socrates and Marx pictured a utopia, but the followers of Marx, inspired by his *millennial message,* became Marxists and were resolved to put it into practice. In my view, most forms of Marxism have betrayed Marx and the ideals of humanism. Implicit in Marx's writings, I submit, are anti-humanistic elements; for instance, the dialectical process is at work, leading to the allegedly inevitable achievement of socialism. In this view the ultimately beneficent laws of history take the place of providence.

I am not talking about democratic socialists, who wish to use Marx's dialectic only as a method of analysis or a guide, and who (despite Marx's jeers about justice) have been influenced by Marx's indictment of the injustices of capitalist society. Rather, I am thinking of the committed communist idealogue, who has developed a new religion, albeit a secular one. For these disciples Marxism has its *charismatic figures.* However, Marx was not one of them. He was a poor scholar supported by the surplus value his wealthy friend Engels sweated out of the proletariat of Manchester, a man who spent a good part of his life in the library of the British Museum, was afflicted with boils, and, unlike Job, had a fairly nasty temper. I am referring rather to political-ideological figures such as Lenin, Mao, Castro, and Ho Chi Minh, who led national revolutions. Following Leninism–Stalinism, there rapidly developed a strict structure and code, *bureaucratic commissars* replaced priests, and the party replaced Mother Church as the infallible source of truth. Moreover, obedience to party authority became the ultimate moral code and the test of loyalty; and heretics who dissented could be liquidated. In the place of ethnicity emerged new bonds, those of *class identity* and nationality. It was national liberation from colonial oppression, particularly in the third world, that became the wellspring of communist devotion.

This new ideology has abandoned freedom and democracy, a central principle of humanism. Willing to use any means (even terror) to achieve its ends, totalitarian regimes have emerged as terrible as any the world has seen. Would Christ be a Christian or Marx a Marxist if they could return? Marx disclaimed being a Marxist at one point. Both inspired—in spite of themselves—dogmatic religions in their names. Humanists surely do not wish to follow that direction. In regard to Marxism, a new *egalitarian world culture,* burdened with Marxist symbols, is beginning to emerge virtually everywhere except in the United States. This may swamp democratic culture and, like Christianity, eventually dominate world culture. Only time will tell whether it will succeed. Interestingly, Marxism has enlisted vast numbers of ordinary people, intellectuals, and students under its banner, not where it already rules but only where it is promised. Once it is implemented, however, disillusionment sets in.

V

What is the humanist message? What do we wish to accomplish?

I interpret the message of contemporary humanism as having four major components: (1) it is a method of inquiry; (2) it presents a scientific world-view ("cosmic humanism"); (3) it offers a set of moral values to provide meaning and direction for life; and (4) it provides a rich storehouse of artistic, poetic, and literary forms of expression.

(1) Our first principle is a commitment to free inquiry. That is, we maintain that our beliefs should be grounded as far as possible upon rational methods of inquiry, not faith, mysticism, revelation, authority, or custom. This entails a commitment to evidence as the test of truth claims, and it means that we wish to extend the methods of scientific inquiry. Although rationalism has its roots in Greek philosophy, it came to fruition with the development of modern science in the sixteenth and seventeenth centuries and the ensuing Copernican, Darwinian,

and behavioral revolutions. Concomitant with the use of critical intelligence is the need to cultivate skepticism about beliefs that transcend experience. That is why we are dubious about claims of divine revelation or a transcendent deity, though we are always open to new discoveries. To be committed to science does not mean that we ignore art, poetry, morality, passion, or other aspects of human experience, which we seek to cultivate and enjoy. It means that we will apply reason, science,and technology to the solution of social and moral problems.

(2) Humanism is also committed to a scientific view of nature. This world-view is constantly changing and expanding. Basically, it is the model of astronomy and physics: the universe is probably fifteen billion years old and life has evolved over an extended period of time. Social institutions can also be explained by this historical process. Thus naturalistic evolutionary hypotheses compete with a theistic view of the universe. As far as we can tell, man does not have a privileged place in the scheme of things, nor is immortality promised.

A challenge for humanism is to compete with traditional religion in the sphere of the imagination. I believe that within the sciences there are tremendous opportunities for exciting the imagination. The sense of mystery and awe that we develop from studying astronomy can be far more breath-taking than religious piety. The possibility that life—indeed, perhaps even intelligent life—exists in outer space is among the most exciting possibilites of our times. We live in an age in which, through scientific technology, we are able to escape from our solar system and explore the universe. That is why it seems to me that we need to defend a *cosmic humanism*, not an earthbound humanism. The tremendous growth of interest in the paranormal, UFOlogy, and science fiction points to the emergence of new cosmic religions. However untested their claims, we must admit that they are inspired by the vast splendor of the boundless universe. Carl Sagan, Isaac Asimov, and George Abell are secular humanists and fellows of the Committee for the Scientific Investigation of Claims of the Paranormal, but they are also interested in possible interplanetary communication. Here is the great new frontier for a humanist adventure in ideas.

(3) Humanism is also an ethical philosophy. Indeed, many people consider this aspect crucial to its message: we offer an alternative sense of the meaning of life. "No deity will save us," says Humanist Manifesto II, "we must save ourselves." We are responsible for our own destinies on this planet, as individuals, as a society, and as a species. This is our great battle in America today with fundamentalist critics. We believe that their moral codes are archaic insofar as they are based upon theological foundations.

What are our humanist values and principles? There is a long list, but I shall mention only thirteen here, without elaboration. Ethical humanism involves:

- a commitment to free inquiry and the open mind;
- a belief in the courage to live without fear or trembling;
- a confidence in the power of human creativeness, inventiveness, achievement;
- constant efforts to improve the human condition, mitigate suffering, and

eliminate disease, conflict, war, and cruelty;
- respect for the rights of others;
- dedication to the preciousness and dignity of the individual, his or her creativity and growth;
- cultivation of happiness and the full life;
- emphasis on love, shared experience, human joy;
- tolerance of other points of view and styles of life;
- social justice and humanitarian help;
- a universal focus transcending national, ethnic, sexual, and racial barriers— the ideal of a world community;
- an emphasis on compromise and negotiation of differences;
- belief in a free, open, pluralistic, and democratic society.

Humanistic morality is not fixed or final. Although the ethical humanist draws upon the collective wisdom of experience and a body of tested moral principles, he is nonetheless willing to develop moral growth. He should always be willing to use intelligence to revise principles and values in the light of altered conditions and to bring into being new forms of morality.

(4) Humanism not only has an intellectual and moral component; it can also arouse the deepest forms of aesthetic appreciation. If the theist seeks to render his visions and aspirations in aesthetic symbols and metaphors—magnificent cathedrals and mosques, music and literature, sculpture and painting—so too can the humanist artist express in art form his deepest insights and values. The heroic art of classical Greece and Rome—its architectural and sculptural spelndor, the power of its literature and philosophy—can still inspire us today, as can great Renaissance cities like Florence and Venice and great artists and authors like Leonardo and Michelangelo, Shakespeare, and Montaigne. Much of modern art, the novel, drama, poetry, music—from Beethoven and Picasso to Frank Lloyd Wright and Hemingway—also expresses humanist values and outlook. Some products of modern society and technology likewise exemplify the highest ranges of human creativity, as Promethean men and women have sought to tame nature to suit human interests and needs and fulfill human aspirations. Thus, the fine and the practical arts are eloquent witnesses to the highest forms of creative aesthetic expression, and they constantly provide us with instruction and inspiration.

Now, if we examine the preceding statement of the humanist point of view, it seems to me there are three points we need to make clear. First, it is vital that we offer strong negative criticism of false religions and ideologies. All the great religions have grown by attacking those about them. As secular humanists, we need to defend skepticism, nontheism, agnosticism, and we need to question the false doctrines found in Judaism, Christianity, Islam, and Marxist ideology, as well as the new cults of unreason. Moreover, we need to guard against the intrusion of religion into our secular institutions. Second, we need to enunciate the positive thrust of humanism. That is why humanism is not synonymous with atheism, for humanism is committed to an alternative set of ethical values. We are not simply naysayers; we have a constructive alternative perspective full of meaning and significance. Third, we should not clothe our message solely in rational terms but must make it eloquent and dramatic, appealing to the whole person, including his emotions, and expressing both the tragic and humorous elements of the human condition. This means we are committed to the expansion of the creative dimensions of humanism.

VI

The vital and practical questions I now wish to raise are: (1) To whom should we direct our message? (2) Do we have charismatic leaders to enunciate it? (3) How shall we deliver it?

Clearly, we are interested in the widest possible dissemination of the humanist outlook to the general public throughout the world. However, we face several obstacles. Gulllibility is very deep in human nature. Our message has been somewhat esoteric. At the very least it presupposes some degree of sophistication and education. Although people demand certainties, we only offer them probabilities. When they seek absolutes, we say that they should examine situations and be aware of possible exceptions. When they hunger for easy solutions, we point to complexities. They thirst for spiritual bread and wine, and we serve them skeptical doubts. Is it possible to develop in the wider population an appreciation of the methods of critical intelligence, the open mind, the suspension of belief, and skepticism? Can we, along with this, arouse joy in choosing how to live and an aesthetic appreciation for the humanist stance? Because humanists are skeptical it does not mean that we do not have strong beliefs and commitments. Is it possible to cultivate a sense of tolerance and the willingness to negotiate differences in values? If it is hard enough keeping our values alive among humanists, how can we possibly spread them widely? I believe that we can and must.

However, our first task, indeed our primary task in my judgment, is not salvation but *education;* that is how we differ from Judaism, Christianity, Islam, and Marxist ideology. We are not interested in converting souls or gaining disciples, but we do wish to transform lives by keeping alive the free play of intellectual interests, the exploration of values, and aesthetic appreciation. That is what we mean by creative growth and why we are interested in the realization of human potentialities.

I submit that humanist organizations are not and should not be religious organizations and should not attempt to compete at that level. We don't have a "Thus saith the Humanist!" dogma or creed. We are not concerned with indoctrination, but with inquiry; not with blind faith, but with evidence; not with unquestioned trust, but with wide ranges of knowledge. We are secular (not religious) humanists because we believe that it is possible to lead the good life without need of deity or clergy. Many of us believe that religious institutions that grew up before or along with science are no longer necessary for humanity. We believe in morality and the possibility of a genuine ethic relative to human needs, not divine dictate.

As a first task, I submit that our main focus should be the educated public. The battle for humanist ideals still has to be waged on the intellectual level, involving theologians, politicians, educators, scientists, and poets in dialogue and debate. We can expect progress, for upwards of 50 percent of the population goes on to institutions of higher learning in the United States. Hence, much of the spadework has been done. The four principles of humanism that I have defended are now already being widely espoused in society and are accepted—however inconsistently— by wide sectors of the public. Moreover, innumerable institutions that further these humanist ideals exist. The most important are our schools—primary and secondary, private and public—and our colleges and universities. The latter in particular are secular institutions that keep alive the basic themes of modern humanism: the quest for truth, free inquiry, the scientific outlook, the exploration of values, and aesthetic creativity. There are three million schoolteachers and half a million college and university faculty. Moreover, millions of scientists, professionals, lawyers, and doctors are concerned with many or most of the ideas and values we espouse. What is Harvard University, the Smithsonian Institution, California Institute of Technology, the American Civil Liberties Union, the Philadelphia Symphony Orchestra, the American Museum of Natural History? Our society is rich in humanist institutions performing all the functions we wish to fulfill.

What then can *we* do, inasmuch as the humanist revolution—modernism— is well under way? We can deal with those areas of the modern humanist outlook that are not being properly addressed: (1) the defense of the rational method wherever it is under attack; (2) promotion of the scientific-naturalistic outlook; (3) strengthening of the humanist ethical stance as an alternative to the cults of unreason, the ideologies of despair, the churches of dogma; and (4) a cultivation of humanist artistic expression. In other words, our present mission, as I see it, is to keep alive free thought, criticize theological and ideological nonsense, and present the meaning of life from a humanist perspective. Our message has been watered down, distorted, and deflected. Instead of dealing with the deeper truths of the human condition as an alternative to messianic theology and ideology, we have become bogged down in trivia and banality; we have become fixated on the political battles and slogans of the day, rather than the more profound issues.

If I could present a scenario for a future humanistic society, perhaps every city would have "Humanist Centers for the Meaning of Life" to supplement the other schools. I am not talking about humanist chapters or ethical societies, which have failed to gain support, but creative centers for renewal, creative opportunities to explore naturalistic ideals. Existing alongside art galleries and symphonies, these centers would be places for creative dialogue and stimulus. But I am going to put that scenario aside; there is too much else to do before we go that far. Since the task is so great, it seems to me that we must move on to another urgent scenario, one that is achievable.

Humanist organizations, I suggest, should be at this stage leadership organizations, generating new ideas, keeping alive alternative possibilities, stimulating provocative discussion. Our primary audience at first should be educators, movers of public opinion and the media, professionals, doctors, psychiatrists, lawyers, scientists, ministers, and theologians. If we cannot convince them of our position, at least perhaps we can influence them to moderate, liberalize, and humanize their beliefs and make them tolerant of dissenters. Many in the humanist movement have agreed with this aim. Unfortunately, we have never succeeded in achieving it. Our basic problem is that we have an uninspiring message and we lack the leadership to enunciate a new one. The trouble with humanism as it is currently organized is that it is too often an intellectual and moral embarrassment, particularly for the most sophisticated and educated part of our society, and for that reason it lacks support. It fluctuates between two extremes, strident noise and warmed-over porridge, neither of which will inspire the educated world. To put it bluntly, I'm afraid we turn off more than we attract.

However, those who are dedicated to humanist ideals should not give up. We have an urgent role to play in society, especially in light of the massive attacks on humanism now coming from many quarters. This is a time to move ahead, not retreat into a humanism of nostalgia. All humanists who share the conviction that our most important task is *educational*—at least at this stage of our development—need to work together to fulfill that noble aim. The humanist movement can still attract new support, but this will require a shift in emphasis.

This analysis, I should add, applies to existing humanist groups. Although the American Humanist Association has only 3,500 members after forty years of effort, other groups have not done any better. The American Ethical Union has only 3,500 members after a hundred years, the Society of Humanistic Judaism 4,000 adherents, and the Fellowship of Religious Humanists 300—and these figures may be on the generous side. Within the Unitarian church, which is declining in members, humanism is beleaguered and is losing its influence.

My suggestions would not necessarily mean supplanting existing humanist organizations. Rather they should move in a new direction, away from the model of a church to that of an educational institution. Our eventual goal is to reach the broader public—students and men and women from all walks of life—but we must first address ourselves to their educators.

I have not suggested practical methods to implement our educational goals; that is the task of another analysis. I have merely suggested that the building of local societies, chapters, churches, or temples—on the model of existing religious institutions—is a wrong direction; if we are to have any lasting effect on the larger issues of the day or the public imagination, we need to alter both our strategy and our ends. We need to be clear about what it is we wish to achieve and why. To think that we can found a new religion to compete with the ancient or ideological religions of the day is to betray and contradict humanist ideals. Let us turn our attention in a positive direction, one in which we can succeed.

(Summer 1984)

IV.

CRITIQUING THE RELIGIOUS MIND

everend Barney Lee is the director of the Center Road Christian Academy, an independent fundamentalist school in New York State that begins each morning with the "Pledge of Allegiance to the Christian Flag": *I pledge allegiance to the Christian Flag, and to the Saviour for Whose kingdom it stands, one Saviour, crucified, risen, and coming again with life and liberty for all who believe.*

Then the children turn to their books, which spin tales of creationism and Lucifer-inspired revolution. According to the widely used Accelerated Christian Education, Inc., texts, the Spanish Armada was defeated by England's inferior fleet because God didn't want England Catholic again. "Surely the Lord desired America to become a home base for Protestant settlers and a nation from which missionaries could one day be sent to the rest of the world." As Mary Beth Gehrman reports in "Reading, Writing, and Religion," there are thousands of such schools in this country, and the number is quickly growing, as fundamentalists and Pentecostals flee from public school systems, which they believe are contaminated by the godless values of secular humanism.

None of the authors presented in this section blames the new evangelical zeal in America on the poor Spanish Armada. What drives the mind of the Bible believer, then? And what are we to expect from it next—in political and cultural terms?

William Sims Bainbridge and Albert Ellis look closely at religious thinking. One sees it as an emotional necessity, the other as an emotional disturbance. According to Bainbridge, himself a nonbeliever, the level of religiosity in American society has remained constant over the years. Most of us simply need the "supernatural compensators" it provides for our always tragic lives. Ellis, in turn, argues that the insistent clinging to faith in the supernatural promotes mental illness; skepticism, he argues, helps establish mental health.

A contradiction? No—though perhaps a paradox, one testified to with painful eloquence in the autobiographical pieces by Rita Swan, an ex-Christian Scientist whose fifteen-month-old son, Matthew, died, untreated, of meningitis, and "Laura Lage" (a pseudonym), whose family was ripped apart by the fury and fervor of the Jehovah's Witnesses.

George Smith's piece is a fascinating examination of the birth of our nation's largest native religion, the Church of the Latter-Day Saints, and the composition of its Book of Mormon. "The membership of the Mormon church," Smith writes, "is taught not to 'question the mysteries': 'When the Prophet speaks, the thinking has been done.' Feeling is placed over evidence, spirit over science, and faith over history. Feeling, spirit, and faith reflect instruction from church leaders, confirmed by personal prayer and study. The message is obedience."

The section closes with two short looks at our nation's most quickly growing religious movements: Thomas Szasz reflects on Islamic zeal, and I try to pull some sense out of the New Age movement.

—R.B.

Reading, Writing, and Religion

Mary Beth Gehrman

In recent decades America's public-school system has been blamed for virtually every one of society's ills. While government agencies and public-school administrators have been busy initiating various reform programs, however, a veritable holy war has been going on in education.

The soldiers in this new crusade are fundamentalist Christians. Their weapons, what U.S. Secretary of Education William Bennett calls "those values all Americans share." Their enemy, secular encroachment on the public-school system.

Most trace the first battle to 1962 and 1963 Supreme Court decisions to ban from the public schools state-sponsored prayer and devotional readings. Since that time, enrollment has climbed steadily in independent, mainly Baptist-affiliated Christian day schools. Today new schools open at a rate of one every seven hours, and their total enrollment tops one million.

Uniform rejection of the liberal social policies of the 1960s and 1970s, backed by a sense of religious mission, has given these schools a base upon which to build. However, the surge of growth that has occurred in this decade is obviously correlated to the rise of fundamentalism in general and the country's swing toward conservatism. Many nonfundamentalist parents are also dissatisfied with the allegedly liberal and irreligious bias of instructors, teachers unions, and school bureaucracy; the declining standards of progressive education; and the general intellectual and moral climate of public schools. They favor the "back to basics" philosophy that Christian schools espouse and are prepared to do whatever is necessary to get their children the education they think best.

Ironically, while most educators consider the Christian-school movement a radical departure from the mass-education system once almost universally supported by conservative Protestants, fundamentalist Christians see it as a return to the country's religious roots. America's cornerstones, they say, are God and the Bible:

the house of God and the schoolhouse of colonial times were one, and the separation of church and state represents the separation of this nation from its very foundation. Secular encroachment is perceived as the vehicle of a godless humanistic philosophy that is considered the "basic cause" of declining skills and morals. The state, at one time seen as the bulwark of nondenominational Protestantism, is now regarded as the enemy responsible for undermining traditional values. James Carper, coauthor of *Religious Schooling in America,* has said that this disillusionment is not only with public schools but with "the society which sustains the educational enterprise."[1]

*   *   *

Many Christians believe that there is a conscious attempt by secular humanists to control young minds, and they frequently note in this context that Hitler's minister of propaganda said, "Let me control the textbooks and I will control Germany." This analogy is all too real in the minds of fundamentalists, many of whom believe that secular humanists are in control of the public schools. Humanist philosophy, according to disgruntled Christian parents, is responsible for declining academic standards, rebellion against parental authority, sexual permissiveness and perversion, drug and alcohol addiction, divorce, abortion, pornography, child abuse, murder, euthanasia, vandalism, suicide, mind control, unwanted pregnancy, telepathy, witchcraft, idolatry, socialism, communism, Satanism, and the decline in U.S. power. According to an NBC News report, one Christian school pamphlet even blames humanism for causing "stomach- and head-aches, nightmares, and other inexplicable maladies among elementary and secondary school children."

This alarmist view of humanism stems from the judgment of most Christian-school administrators that no subject can be taught objectively. According to the Reverend Thomas A. Cline, principal of Maranatha Christian Academy in Mayville, New York, "The Bible says, 'Learn not the ways of the pagan.' We can't believe a curriculum is neutral. . . . We don't believe there is any neutral ground." All subjects therefore must be taught from one of two perspectives— Christian, which in this case maintains that the Bible is the absolute, literal word of God; or humanistic, which from a Christian point of view categorically denies the existence of God in order to enthrone man as the center of the universe.

"Why a Christian School?" asks a pamphlet published by the First Baptist Christian School of North Tonawanda, New York. "Because the fear of the Lord, which is the beginning of wisdom and knowledge, is rejected in secular schools. Because the secular philosophy of life creates a conflict in the lives of young people which surfaces in the form of rebellion during the teenage years. Because all truths are related to God which can only be taught in a Christian school. Because God never intended ungodly men to teach our children." There are financial incentives as well: Sending your child to a Christian school is "cheaper than lawyer's fees to get him out of jail, or sending him to a Christian school and teaching him how to live might be cheaper than raising his children from a broken home."[2]

Many fundamentalists believe that public-school texts not only fail to refer to the Protestant religion but actively attack Christian values. Some even maintain that teachers verbally attack children who express belief in Jesus.[3]

The goal of Christian schools, on the other hand, is to produce young people who will go to heaven by virtue of their solid Christian character, which embodies love of God and country, self-discipline and responsibility, the ability to distinguish moral truth from error, and a respect for parents, teachers, and national leaders. Says the executive director of the Association of Christian Schools International, Paul A. Kienel,

> Christian schools are Christian institutions where Jesus Christ and the Bible are central in the school curriculum and in the lives of teachers and administrators. This distinction removes us from direct competition with public schools. Although we often compare ourselves academically, we are educational institutions operating on separate philosophical tracks. Ours is Christ-centered education presented in the Christian context. Theirs is man-centered presented within the context of the supremacy of man as opposed to the supremacy of God. Their position is known as secular humanism.[4]

The "Statement of Faith" of the Grand Island Christian School in Western New York explains it this way: "We believe that heaven and hell are definite places . . . that the true church is composed of all those who have been born again . . . [and that] the Bible teaches separation from the world and from unbelief." The school's objectives are typical: "To teach the necessity of being born again . . . the application of Biblical principles to every part of daily life . . . the need for separation from the world and its deceptive allurements [and] to integrate subjects with the Bible."

The standardized fundamentalist curriculum offered by the Basic Education Institutional Product Catalogue, printed by Reform Publications of Texas, states: "It is impossible to educate without a philosophical and theological base. . . . You cannot build charactered, responsible young people without a positive foundation of life-building, character-building presuppositions and values: (1) God created all things, (2) God has communicated to man through . . . the Bible [and] Jesus Christ, (3) The fear of the Lord is the beginning of Knowledge, Understanding [and] Wisdom, (4) A relationship with God must be established by the individual, (5) Salvation is through the atonement of Jesus Christ by the grace of God."

The more than three thousand products outlined in this catalogue form the basis of one of the two main vehicles of this "right-thinking" philosophy. One is the Accelerated Christian Education (ACE) program, a sort of franchise of evangelical thought developed in 1970 in a small church in Texas by Donald Howard, a Ph.D. in Christian Education. Along with the slightly more traditional A Beca Book Publishing Company of Pensacola, Florida, ACE is the main supplier of Christian schools throughout the country, with a mailing list of more than six thousand. It is also one of the driving forces behind the growth of the Christian school movement, since for less than a thousand dollars any pastor or group of parents with the space and inclination to do so can acquire the materials to begin a school.

The program is a combination of the Bible and the so-called basics, delivered mainly through workbooks called Packets of Accelerated Christian Education (PACEs). During the school year, the student progresses at his or her own rate through about twelve of these workbooks in each of four subjects—math, social studies, language arts, and science—and supplements this work with rote exercises and readings from Scripture and other approved literature.

Each student is assigned a small cubicle or "office" in which to work. He is not allowed to communicate with other students, get up, or turn around without permission. If he is having difficulty with a lesson, he raises a small American or Christian flag to signal the supervisor that he needs help. Lectures, homework, and traditional teachers are virtually eliminated, and students are motivated through inspirational tapes, daily goal charts, privileges, rewards, and fields trips. A student must receive a minimum of 80 percent on each test before progressing to the next level of workbooks.

The ACE curriculum differs not only in the structure of the learning environment but in the content of the course material. Fundamentalist philosophy is woven into every aspect of the Christian-school curriculum, and the Bible is an integral part of each subject.

Mathematics, for example, is seen as a manifestation of God's orderly universe. Bible-inspired equations, such as the calculation of the dimensions of Noah's Ark or Solomon's Temple, are a common type of math problem.

English is taught as the way to properly articulate and spread God's word. The high-school reading list overlooks such classics as *Romeo and Juliet, The Great Gatsby,* and *Huckleberry Finn* in favor of books like *Pilgrim's Progress, Did Man Just Happen?, The Celestial City,* and *In His Steps.* Typical of the elementary level multiple-choice questions are "Jesus died for (your, you're) sins" and "God (is, are) good."

Science is chiefly concerned with natural science, biology, comparison of "the facts of creation with the fallacies of the many theories of evolution," and "a Scriptural view of the earth's past, present and future condition."

Fundamentalists believe that evolution directly contradicts the Word of God and that children behave badly when they are taught that they have descended from apes. In 1975 the *Louisville Courier-Journal* quoted Christian school activist John Thoburn as saying, "We believe public schools are immoral. . . . [They] breed criminals. They teach [children] they're animals, that they evolved from animals."

Because God created the universe, all truth is God's truth. If there is a question about the accuracy of a textbook, the Bible is always the final arbiter. *Biology for Christian Schools* states, "The people who have prepared this book have tried consistently to put the word of God first and science second."

Christian-school texts invariably contain editorial comment. For instance, *Physical Science for Christian Schools* tells its student readers:

> The categories [of elements] are a reflection of the kinds of people we find in the
> world. On the two extremes are the saved and unsaved people. . . . Unfortunately
> there is an intermediate group, the metalloid Christian—the worldly or carnal
> Christian. This type of person says he is saved but acts like an unsaved person
> at times. You should not be a metalloid Christian.

Referring to such passages, Dr. Walter Fremont, dean of education at Bob Jones University in South Carolina, says "the public schools teach a subtle humanistic philosophy, and we teach a subtle Christian philosophy. The public school uses sentences that condone dope and a lack of moral standards. We're just fighting fire with fire."

Sex education, perhaps surprisingly, is part of the Christian school curriculum. A booklet published by the Center Road Christian Academy of West Seneca, New York, an ACE school, implies that the only proper way to approach the topic is with heavy reference to moral absolutes. It states that all conduct that stimulates sexual desire (including dancing, hugging, and holding hands) is forbidden to the school's students; all sexual activity should take place only within the confines of matrimony, because premarital sex of any sort is "condemned by God"; masturbation and homosexuality are "not normal and right"; and it is wise to avoid "alluring dress habits, flirting, etc." and "places and activities where Christ would not be welcomed." Perhaps the most telling aspect of Christian sex-education, however, is that for each of the three educational levels described in this booklet (elementary, junior high, and senior high), the first precept to be taught students is "thought control covering all matters of self life."

Social studies provides an especially fertile medium for inculcating fundamentalist philosophy. History is presented as the unfolding of "God's plan," beginning with the seven days of creation and early Bible stories and concluding with selective discussions of foreign and domestic policy of the 1970s. The history of the world focuses on the Middle East, Greece, Rome, the Renaissance, and the Church. The history of America is designed to give the student an "appreciation for the Christian elements" of his country's past, particularly in relation to territorial expansion, the American Revolution, the Civil War, and the growth of industrialism. Controversial current and historical events and figures are studiously avoided.

Social studies also includes economic systems of the Bible, "biblical principles of handling credit," biblical precepts in relation to proposed government spending, and "biblical perspectives on employer-employee relations."

Morals are taught most comprehensively in social studies courses. Many fundamentalists believe that public school "values clarification" courses, in which students are asked to debate a wide range of subjects without condemning or prejudging the opinions of others, have caused grave social problems among teenagers and young adults. Permissive attitudes in the schools, they feel, have spawned several million "morally confused" baby-boomers who don't know the difference between right and wrong. According to the Reverend Barney R. Lee of the Center Road Christian Academy, "The permissiveness of parents and teachers has reared a society of thoughtless, ungrateful, rude, loud-mouthed brats. . . . There is no one that likes a loud mouth, disloyal, arrogant, self-centered, irresponsible, ungrateful, unfaithful, inconsiderate, bullish, proud, busy-body, with a superior boastful, hateful attitude. But this is the product of today's philosophy of 'do your own thing.' "

The only way to counter this trend, say Christian-school administrators, is to teach morals as absolute; there is no room for gray in an area that the Bible states is black and white. Lee and others like him believe that the "situation ethics" taught in the public schools is dangerous. Only by learning that God is in total control of our world and that right and wrong are not contextual but absolute can a child "learn how to live before [he] can get out in society," Lee says. "We teach them right, and the wrong will usually take care of itself. You don't have to teach a child to lie. They lie from the time they're babies. They cry when they're not wet, but just want to be picked up." His school's introductory pamphlet states: "Humanism, Progressivism, Situation Ethics, and the New Morality are refuted and replaced by the absolutes for standards of right and wrong."

"God's career for your life" is, in many ways, wholly determined. The roles of men and women are "traditional" and Bible-defined:

> Men are often better at math and science because of the way their minds work. . . . To fulfill their duties as protectors and providers, men usually have stronger, heavier muscles. . . . Men usually enjoy work outside the home, while women usually find great enjoyment working within the home. . . . Some vocations are distinctly for men, while others are distinctly for women.

Social studies also repeatedly discusses, on all educational levels, the United Nations' role in Satan's plan to install a socialistic one-world government before the Second Coming: "Many supporters of the United Nations sincerely desire a one-world government. They see national sovereignty as a major threat to the World peace they so much desire. Such a super-government, however, is quite undesirable to most evangelical, Bible-believing Christians."

The righteousness of United States supremacy is one of the basic tenets of Christian schools. The Center Road Christian Academy booklet states that "Christian Americanism places emphasis on the greatness of America's heritage and the sacrifices of its heroes. America is a republic which guarantees liberties to educate and preserve its freedom. We unabashedly teach the Biblical doctrines of self-discipline, respect for those in authority, obedience to law, and love for flag and country." As NBC News put it, these schools are "based on a lie that God and America are the same"—that we as a nation made a covenant with

God and thus are the true chosen people. This presents an interesting dichotomy in fundamentalist thought. On one hand, obedience to all forms of authority is of paramount importance, and questioning or challenging God, the Bible, America, elected officials, fundamentalist leaders, pastors, teachers, or parents is not permitted. On the other hand, state encroachment, the authority that promotes godless humanistic doctrine in the schools, must be fought at every turn. Accreditation is an especially controversial issue, because in many areas nonpublic schools are not subject to state or local educational regulations and have only to meet fire, health, and safety laws to remain in operation.

Fundamentalists believe that church, home, and school form an indivisible triune, that parental control is of primary importance, and that any state-mandated guidelines are an attempt to limit religious freedom. In the Spring 1985 issue of *Educational Theory,* William J. Reese noted that to the minds of many Christian-school administrators "God and the Bible are the ultimate standards . . . [and] state licensing opens the door to state control, which means slavery to humanism." The booklet of the Center Road Christian Academy bears out this observation: "State curriculum is totally unacceptable in philosophy and goals . . . [because it is] developed by secular educational administrators who may not be Christians."

Fundamentalists do not see a need to justify the apparent contradiction between their promotion of "Christian Americanism" and their opposition to local, state, and federal regulations. They choose instead to focus on the need for total compliance with the forms of leadership they deem proper and holy. At the Dade Christian School in Miami, for example, students must pledge not to "draw, wear, or display in any way the 'peace' symbol." At the Center Road Christian Academy, only language and music that "glorify the Lord" are permitted. "Books and magazines must be approved in writing by parents and approved by supervisors upon arrival at school." And a dress code is strictly enforced. After-school jobs, too, must be approved by the school. The thoughts and actions of students must comply unwaveringly with those of their parents and teachers.

The Grand Island Christian School, near Niagara Falls, New York, states that its aim is to "teach the student to think for himself and to stand up for his personal convictions provided they do not contradict the Word of God and the Code of Conduct of our school." The Center Road Christian Academy booklet is less circumspect, "Daily lessons in the Scripture are designed for programming the mind to enable the child to see life from God's point of view. . . . Teaching is training."

Parents are also expected to conform. Most schools require that they regularly attend a fundamentalist church and parent-teacher meetings. At least one ACE school even states that the children of parents who do not attend these meetings will be expelled.

Criticism of the school is not tolerated: "Should it be necessary to withdraw a student, it is critical that the student be warned against any negative behavior toward the school, either while the student is still in attendance or after. A critical attitude spreads among the students, undermining much of what would have been accomplished."

Although corporal punishment is said to be seldom used to encourage conformity, teachers are "given the liberty to enforce classroom regulations in the manner which is in accordance with Christian principles and the discipline as set forth in the Scriptures." For parents who might be inclined to spare the rod, in "Why a Christian School—Principles in Character Building," the Reverend Lee devotes eight of the booklet's twelve pages to expounding on scriptural verses like this one: "Thou shalt beat him with the rod and shalt deliver his soul from hell" (Proverbs 23:14). Lee stresses that to show their obedience to God, parents must be consistent in requiring obedience from their children:

> This is the blessing of the rod. Once it is used, we can completely forget the incident and fellowship is restored between parent and child. . . . Grounding, nagging, scolding and threatening is very cruel. . . . When the rod is used consistently for the slightest disobedience, it is never associated with anger, displeasure or rejection, because the parent is never driven to that point. . . . You can't improve on God's way and when you try, the harm you do is everlasting. . . . When the child is too young to use a switch, paddle or belt, a couple of swift swats with the hand on the thigh or bare bottom, laying the child down and hastily walking out of the room, showing total rejection is effective if you are sure the baby is dry and not hungry or sick. . . . The cradle is the place to lick the teenage problem. . . . If the child will murder, steal, be immoral, lie, be unthankful, domineering and unholy with no respect for self, man, or God, this is 85% settled by the age of five. . . . If these principles are new to you and you already have untrained children, know that God will be very gracious to recover. It is not too late.

*   *   *

Although Jerry Falwell considers Christian schools "the hope of the Republic," many secular educators believe that they are part of a growing anti-intellectualism. Some maintain that by legislating morality and censoring materials, Christian schools deprive children of their right to learn and their ability to reason. Students at these schools, they charge, will never know of the diversity of America's cultural, religious, and political heritage.

The prevailing attitude among nonfundamentalist educators is that public-school teachers and curricula are being unjustly attacked. Few educators, for example, would frown on including in the curriculum a discussion of religion in historical or literary contexts. Dorothy Olsen, a public-school teacher and a member of the Elim Baptist Church in Anoka, Minnesota, writes, "One area in which I am guilty is teaching my students not to blindly accept anyone's values. I teach them to be responsible and to accept consequences of their behavior. . . . I cannot see that as a threat to parental values. . . . What will the Christians use after their school experience to escape from the reality of life?"[5]

Indeed, the children who attend these schools are purposely sheltered, raised in a "hothouse" environment in which fundamentalist ideas and attitudes are strenuously reinforced in church, home, and school. The movement's supporters feel that this helps keep young people from experimenting with drugs or getting into other trouble: "People say you're brainwashing your kids. We're not brainwashing them. If you're convinced that loving God is the highest commandment, you're going to want your child to love God."[6]

In an article called "What's a Parent to Do?" Sharon Sheppard adds,

> Obviously, Christian schools are not for everyone. Some kids apparently thrive in public schools. They have a strong Christian base from their home and church, and the spiritual vigor to maintain a firm witness and to withstand peer pressure to conform to ungodly standards. They have the analytical skills to sort out the underlying philosophy on critical issues in light of scriptural principles.
>
> For such youngsters, the public school offers a variety of opportunities, both for testing their faith and for developing their varied interests.
>
> On the other hand, there are some who are not strong enough to withstand peer pressure and to sort out questionable philosophies, and who quickly become saturated with subtle, ungodly attitudes that color their thinking for a lifetime. For them, the Christian school offers a haven where they can grow and develop, where they can establish wholesome friendships, build self-esteem, and find acceptance in classrooms that are generally less crowded and less threatening.[7]

*   *   *

Moral issues aside, parents and educators want to know whether a Christian-school education is basically a quality education. Though diplomas from these schools were only recently accepted by the military and are still challenged at most state colleges and universities, fundamentalist educators claim numerous success stories. ACE claims that it has made A students out of many who could barely read and write in public school, and that their children generally score well above the national norms on standardized achievement tests.

Statistics don't always bear this latter claim out. The *Miami News* reported that a sampling of students graduating in from 1983 to 1985 from the Freedom Christian Academy in Miami shows that the students actually "scored 'well below' the national average on college entrance SAT exams, averaging a combined 726 on math and verbal, almost 170 points below the national average."

Many charge that the ACE curriculum is frustratingly inaccurate, dotted with errors, and was hastily prepared, and that the "supervisors" who help students through the program often may not be qualified. Though nonpublic schools need not be accredited, most of the larger ACE schools do claim to employ state-certified "supervisors" and to exceed minimum educational requirements set forth by the government. Some educators question the validity of this claim and speculate that state accreditation may be merely a "gentleman's agreement."

Bruce Cooper, an associate professor at Fordham University who has studied Christian schools, says, "The problem with ACE is the higher order learning. Sure, in math two plus four is always six. That's the only answer. But in other subjects at the higher end, where you're asking a child to synthesize facts into thoughts and interpret materials and render an analysis, ACE falls down. It doesn't prepare a child to think."⁸

Notes

1. James C. Carper, "The Christian Day Schools," in *Religious Schooling in America,* edited by James C. Carper and Thomas C. Hunt (Religious Education Press, 1984), p. 116.

2. A. C. Janney, "Christian Education Doesn't Cost, It Pays," American Association of Christian Schools, (Fairfax, Va.: n.d.).

3. Tim LaHaye, in a televised debate with Paul Kurtz, "The Larry King Show," July 14, 1986.

4. Paul A. Kienel, "The Forces Behind the Christian School Movement," *Christian School Movement* (1977), p. 1.

5. Dorothy M. Olsen, "Rising Tide of Pride," *Standard* (Arlington Heights, Ill.), October 1986, p. 55.

6. Pastor Greg Edwards, quoted in the Jamestown, New York, *Post Journal,* "Christian Schools Base Curriculum on Religious Beliefs," September 27, 1985.

7. Sharon Sheppard, "What's a Parent to Do?" *Standard* (Arlington Heights, Ill.) August/September 1986, p. 12.

8. Bruce Cooper, quoted in "Fundamentalist Revival," by John Doussard, *Miami News,* September 28, 1985.

(Fall 1987)

Is Belief in the Supernatural Inevitable?

William Sims Bainbridge

In a pair of books, *The Future of Religion* and *A Theory of Religion,* Rodney Stark and I have tried to demonstrate that religion is the inevitable human response to the conditions of life. Hemmed by drastic limitations to our desires and faced with the ultimate loss of everything we hold dear, humans have no choice but to postulate beings and forces that exist beyond the natural world and to seek their aid. *A Theory of Religion* deduces the necessity of religion from a few, simple propositions about humans and the world we inhabit, while *The Future of Religion* offers empirical data to support our theoretical analysis. We are not so naive or conceited, however, as to imagine that our arguments and data will convince those who dislike our conclusions.

Social science has given religion a very low priority for more than half a century. Not since Emile Durkheim's *Elementary Forms of the Religious Life* (1915) or the several short books on religion by Sigmund Freud has there been a general theory of religion—a systematic attempt to explain it and to understand the human qualities that give it birth—not until our pair of books. Scientists tend to be irreligious, and the career of a university scholar rewards skepticism today far more than faith. Indeed, it can appear rather perverse for two contemporary social scientists to propose the inevitability of belief in the supernatural, all the more so when both of them personally admit they lack this belief.

Yet scientists are trained to pay attention to the evidence and to ask penetrating questions. And in the social sciences it is quite common for the facts to lead in directions uncomfortable for the researchers. So, rather than press my views upon you, let me invite you to ask a set of three simple questions. In return, I will offer you evidence and explanations that Stark and I have gathered. If you find them insufficient as answers, then you will be left to struggle with three very serious questions:

1. Why have humans traditionally possessed religion?
2. What is the condition of religion in America today?
3. How viable are the alternatives to religion?

Why Have Humans Traditionally Possessed Religion?

Many answers have been offered, from Durkheim's claim that religion expressed social solidarity to the calumny of Marx that religion was a tool of oppression by the ruling class. Yet the answer that I seem to find most often coming from intellectuals is that religion is a primitive way of understanding the world, a veil of primitive myths woven when our species was immature, ignorant, and superstitious.

While Marx might hope for an end to class oppression, and Durkheim might wonder how solidarity might be expressed in a wholly secular world, neither of their theories predicts the inevitable end of religion. Class struggle, or the consensual solidarity that is its opposite, might continue forever, perpetuating into all eternity the conditions that Marx and Durkheim believed gave rise to religion. But the view that religion is primarily a primitive way of thinking clearly points the way to its extinction, when science banishes the spooks of ignorance from the popular mind—as many scientists and scholars smugly believe it already has from their own.

What else could faith be? One possibility is that faith is the sister of hope, and that both are children of desire. The human mind did not evolve in order to create a race of philosophers and scientists. Rather, in the long course of biological evolution, greater mental capacity proved valuable in meeting life's practical tasks. Ages before *Homo* became *sapiens,* our ancestors sought rewards and tried to avoid punishments. Pleasure and pain were mechanisms that guided the organism toward survival and reproduction. As increased brain size and a high level of sociability produced the phenomenon we call "intelligence," these animal instincts were served in far more refined ways. Philosophers and scientists exist today because they serve very particular functions in the contemporary division of labor. But their mental habits are quite atypical, and the dominant function of the mind remains the hunt for material or social gain.

Probably more than any other creature, humans are aware of time. Within limitations, we can know and interpret the past, but we can never influence it. The future, however, can be influenced for our benefit, on the basis of knowledge derived from the past. Thus, humans seek what they have learned to perceive as rewards and avoid what they have learned to perceive as costs. The ultimate definition of reward must be in terms of our animal desires for survival, nourishment, activity, social interaction, and the like. But, with our complex brains and the socially created tool of language, we discover many instrumental rewards, leading ultimately to satisfaction of instinctual drives by very roundabout routes.

Daily, humans face some of the same problems, again and again. Situations recur, requiring investments of particular kinds to obtain rewards. In solving our problems we imagine possible means of achieving the desired reward, and we select the one with the greatest likelihood of success in the light of available information. Then we pursue action along the chosen line until the reward has been achieved or our solution to the problem has proved unsatisfactory. In solving problems, then, the human mind must seek explanations. *Explanations* are statements about how and why rewards may be obtained and costs are incurred.

But the search for explanations that provide desired rewards is often fruitless. Some desired rewards are limited in supply, including some that simply do not exist. It is tragic that humans can conceive of a dead child coming back to life yet have no natural means to accomplish this. The list of our unsatisfiable desires is very long, but at the head of the list is eternal life itself.

Most rewards sought by humans are destroyed when they are used. This is obvious in the case of food. But the principle also holds for many far less material rewards. Our species must do all the work of love-making afresh each time, unable to hold its erotic pleasures long, before losing them. Even honor and respect must be continually replenished through significant efforts to keep them alive.

In pursuit of desired rewards, humans will exchange rewards with other humans. This can profit both parties of the exchange, because they need not value equally the things they trade. Because many rewards are consumed when used, we are drawn into continuing relationships with particular other humans who can keep providing them to us. If the exchanges continue to provide rewards, we come to value the exchange partner highly, and to trust him. Among the rewards most highly desired are good explanations concerning how to obtain other rewards. We are apt to develop some trust in the explanations we receive from the people who have given us the most valuable rewards, including explanations, in the past.

Some explanations are very hard to evaluate, particularly when a reward is highly desired and difficult to obtain. In the absence of a desired reward, explanations often will be accepted that posit its attainment in the distant future or in some other nonverifiable context. Stark and I call these explanations "compensators." When the value of the reward promised is very great, we refer to "general compensators."

A compensator is like an I.O.U. or any other kind of promise that, if certain things are done—certain investments are made—a reward will return. Of course, people prefer to get a reward immediately, and they will not often turn to mere compensators when the reward is available to them. But when the reward is highly desired and practically unobtainable, humans will accept general compensators instead.

A *religion* is a system of general compensators based on supernatural assumptions. *Supernatural* refers to forces beyond or outside nature that can suspend, alter, or ignore physical forces. The reason religion is so successful as a purveyor of general compensators is that it is, in principle, impossible to examine the supernatural and prove whether or not it really can deliver the desired rewards. Politics also demands considerable faith of its adherents, but in relatively short order a political program must deliver the goods or be discredited. Religion, in contrast, can require a person to await delivery in the afterlife or in some higher plane of consciousness unattainable by the unfaithful.

This, in a nutshell, is the Stark-Bainbridge theory of religion. The fact that we took the better part of a thousand pages to communicate it in our two books suggests that the above is a very sketchy outline, requiring much greater specificity to be precise enough for scientific test. But the central ideas should be clear enough.

Religion is not the residue of the crudest human thoughts, but a reaching out for the most sublime, the natural extension of our intelligence beyond the limitations set by our environment and our physical natures. Born in the tragedy of the human condition, religion is the rational response of a courageous species never willing to accept defeat. What we cannot have here and now we work collectively to achieve in the future. If the combined effort to help each other and to benefit from each other that we call "civilization" cannot succeed this side of death, then it must continue beyond.

Note that this theory does not merely say that an individual will postulate the supernatural as wish-fulfillment for unrealized desires. Ours is a social theory that derives religion from social interaction between exchange-partners, and it is an historical theory that requires long periods of time for major religious changes. In social history there are many forces that may modify religion, and the kind of religion we know today is not the only variety that has existed or could exist. But whatever varies in human life, the terrible limitations of the human condition will continue, and these are the roots of religion.

What Is the Condition of Religion in America Today?

Religion today has some influence on public affairs, but the church has little power over other institutions or over many individuals. One might deduce from this that religion is on the decline, because our image of previous centuries is one in which religion had great coercive power, and such a decline is commonly called "secularization." However, this picture of a near-theocratic past is a myth. Stark has recently shown that, by some measures, such as the rate of church membership, religion has steadily gained over American history.

The process of secularization is quite real, but Stark and I think it has been misunderstood. In every age of history when there was a free market of religion, the dominant religious organizations were under social pressure to moderate their beliefs and practices to fit those of secular elites. Often, this means that the elite religious denominations are in decline, and thus there is the appearance that religion in general is on the wane. But simultaneously, other organizations in the same religious tradition will be growing, fundamentalist denominations and the schismatic groups we call "sects."

As the churches of the elite accommodate to secular culture, their grip on the supernatural weakens. Like liberal churches today, they may have little to promise members and little to demand of them. The ticket to heaven becomes

Table 1
Estimated Membership of
Some Major Denominations in America

Denomination	1971	1980	Change
Catholics	44,863,492	47,502,152	+ 6%
Liberal Protestants			
Episcopal	3,032,197	2,823,399	− 7%
United Church of Christ	2,271,432	2,096,014	− 8%
United Presbyterian Church	3,546,941	2,974,186	−16%
Unitarian-Universalists	194,733	156,286	−20%
Moderate Protestants			
American (Northern) Baptist	1,693,423	1,922,467	+14%
American Lutheran	2,490,537	2,361,845	− 5%
Disciples of Christ	1,158,855	1,212,977	+ 5%
Lutheran Church in America	3,010,150	2,911,817	− 3%
Lutheran Church—Missouri Synod	2,772,996	2,622,847	− 5%
Presbyterian Church in the U.S.	1,147,499	1,038,649	− 9%
United Methodist	11,511,709	11,552,111	0%
Conservative Protestants			
Church of God (Anderson)	389,989	535,647	+37%
Church of God (Cleveland)	369,989	474,315	+28%
Church of the Nazarene	869,831	885,749	+ 2%
Churches of Christ	994,926	1,600,177	+61%
Seventh-Day Adventists	536,082	668,611	+25%
Southern Baptist	14,488,635	16,281,692	+12%
Mormons			
Latter-Day Saints	2,133,072	2,684,744	+26%

Sources: *Churches and Church Membership in the United States—1971,* by Douglas W. Johnson, Paul R. Picard, and Bernard Quinn (Washington, D.C.: Glenmary Research Center, 1974); *Churches and Church Membership in the United States—1980,* by Bernard Quinn, Herman Anderson, Martin Bradley, Paul Goetting, and Peggy Shriver (Atlanta, Ga.: Glenmary Research Center, 1982).

cheap, but the route map is lost. Existing conservative denominations and new sects will expand to fill the gap. Originally finding their social base in disadvantaged groups, they can grow into the mainstream of the society and eventually possess many elite members. At this point they become vulnerable to the same forces that weakened the earlier elite denominations, and more conservative rivals will arise to take their places. Secularization is a self-limiting process, a cycle of religious expansion, liberalization, decline, and fresh expansion.

This model fits the current situation in America. The liberal churches are declining, but this is not destroying religion in general. The conservative churches are growing, but this does not mean future religion will be extremely conservative. The historical record indicates that the American cycle of religious decline and replenishment is well balanced. These points deserve detailed, scientific study. But simple data on membership in some of the main denominations, given here in Table 1, sketch the big picture.

The data are taken from a pair of massive surveys of denominational membership, published by the Glenmary Research Center, dating from 1971 and 1980. The Catholics appear to be holding their own, and within their tradition liberal and conservative tendencies probably balance out. Protestant denominations differ greatly in their acceptance of secular standards versus assertion of supernatural absolutes. Despite its huge financial and cultural capital, the Episcopal church is losing members, as are other liberal denominations. The Unitarian-Universalists, who never believed Christ was divine and now doubt that even God is, are quickly declining.

Moderate Protestant denominations are holding their own, while the conservative groups are expanding rapidly. This table is not designed to illustrate the liberalization of many successful denominations, which in the long run offsets conservative gains; but at least one of the moderate groups, the Missouri Synod Lutherans, might have been considered conservative a few years ago. At the bottom of the table we see evidence of the success of Mormonism, a group that is not a mere fundamentalist Protestant sect but a whole new religious tradition.

A dynamic theory of secularization is not complete until it can encompass the emergence of wholly new religions. While rooted in Christianity, as Christianity was in Judaism, Mormonism possesses a considerable set of new teachings, complete with holy books, and a powerful religious community well adapted to success in the modern world. Stark and I believe that we have entered into one of those exciting periods of history when new religious traditions arise.

Without meaning any disparagement, we call novel religious groups that represent new religious traditions "cults." While sects arise within a religious tradition to replace declining denominations, cults expand to fill the gap when an entire tradition declines. For the past decade, Stark and I have searched for every possible way of testing our proposition that cults will thrive when conventional religion fails to serve people's needs.

We have seen relatively high rates of acceptance of occult and pseudoscientific ideas among respondents to surveys who report no religious affiliation or who are members of the highly secularized liberal denominations. It appears that traditional religion inoculates believers against novel superstitions. However, critics may always raise doubts about the way we phrased questions in our surveys or how we recruited our respondents. Therefore it is of great importance that we have been able to test our theory using data based not on responses to our questionnaires but on the actual religious behavior of vast numbers of American citizens.

The statistics on church membership for 1971 and 1980 by the Glenmary Research Center, from which I drew the data in Table 1, made it possible to estimate overall church membership rates for American cities, with data on Jews coming from the annual Jewish Yearbook. These were official data from the denominations themselves, and some groups either did not have such information or refused to participate. However, the coverage was quite good, and we were able to develop unbiased methods for estimating the total number of people who formally belonged to congregations in each city outside New England. The trouble with New England is purely technical. The smallest geographic unit in the religion statistics, and the smallest for many government statistics, is the county. But in New England, unlike the rest of the nation, the county boundaries and the official boundaries for metropolitan areas do not coincide.

My complete analysis is based on 289 metropolitan areas outside New England, but for sake of simplicity I will report here on just the seventy-five metropolitan areas having populations of a half million or more in 1980. Conveniently, we can divide these seventy-five into three groups of twenty-five each, in terms of their rates of church membership. As Table 2 shows, on average 67.7 percent of the population of a city are members of religious groups in the group of twenty-five with the highest rates. The average church membership rate for the twenty-five cities in the middle is 53.8 percent, still a majority. But on average only 38.5 percent are church members in the lower twenty-five cities.

Where are the most religious cities? Are they in the Bible Belt? Among the top twenty-five are New Orleans, Birmingham, Greenville, Memphis, Charlotte, Louisville, and Richmond. So far, it looks like the South. But the cities with the highest rates of church membership also include Pittsburgh, Buffalo, Cleveland, Chicago, Milwaukee, Philadelphia, Albany, Jersey City, Newark, and New York City. In all of these, more than 60 percent of residents belong to churches.

Cities with high rates can be found throughout the East, South, and Midwest. The cities with the lowest rates are mainly concentrated in the West. About 40 percent of the residents of Tampa are church members. The cities that fall between 40 and 35 percent are: Tucson, Phoenix, San Francisco, Portland, Denver, and Oxnard. Below 35 percent are: Riverside, Anaheim, Sacramento, San Diego, Honolulu, Seattle, and San Jose.

The best explanation we have found yet is the simple fact that rates of geographic mobility are especially high in these same cities. While about 75 percent of people in the twenty-five cities with high church-member rates were born in the state where they now reside, only 50 percent of people in the twenty-five cities of low church membership were. While 42 percent of people in the highest twenty-five cities changed homes in the past five years, 55 percent of those in low cities did so. When people move, they lose membership in their old congregation, and it often takes a complex process of developing friendships with several members of a particular church in the new town to establish membership again. This is more

Table 2
Church Members and Cults in 75 American Cities

Group of 25 Cities	Percent Church Members	*Fate* Letter Writers	Scientology Clears	Spirit Community	Christian Science	Transcendental Meditation
High	67.7%	0.69	1.34	0.72	0.77	344.3
Medium	53.8%	0.77	2.54	0.92	1.01	435.8
Low	38.5%	1.35	9.09	1.90	2.01	598.4

difficult in the mobile West, and thus rates of church membership are much lower.

But people do not lose the need for hope, comfort, and the feeling that life has meaning, merely because they travel west. Large pools of potential converts to some kind of religion are found near the shores of the Pacific, and even the strangest cults can have some success dipping into them. Table 2 reports information on five different cults or aspects of the occult milieu about which I was able to develop good data. For each I have calculated rates per 100,000 population.

Fate magazine is the central publication of the American occult, established in 1948 and giving its readers a monthly dose of astrology, ancient mysteries, religious cults, pseudoscience, and advertisements for a dizzying array of cultic businesses. Among the standard features are three columns of letters from readers, two of which report readers' mystic experiences and contacts with the dead. I tabulated the addresses of all such letters published in the 120 issues from 1975 through 1984, calculating rates for each metropolitan area.

Cults rise and fall, but perhaps the most consistently influential and fascinating novel religion for the past thirty-five years has been Scientology, the creation of science-fiction author L. Ron Hubbard. Believers who have attained a high level of spiritual enlightenment are called "clears." David Aden of Scientology of Boston was kind enough to obtain for me a tabulation of Scientology clears in all postal zip areas in 1985, which I was then able to assign to the right metropolitan areas for the calculation of rates.

Since the early 1970s, a New Age cult in San Rafael, California, has published *Spiritual Community Guide,* a traveler's directory of groups and businesses somehow connected with the occult or New Age counterculture. The largest number of listings is found in the 1974 edition, partly because the group began charging an advertising fee after that issue. Again, it was a straightforward task to calculate rates of listings for all metropolitan areas.

Christian Science is one of the most solidly established cults in America, more than a century old and well known throughout the world. Despite having its headquarters in Boston, Christian Science has always been most popular in newly developing areas, like the far West. In journal articles about the 1920s and about Canadian cults, I have been able to analyze actual membership statistics for Christian Science, but new American data are not available. However, the church publishes a monthly guide to the professional practitioners of its healing methods, so I could tabulate rates of Christian Science healers for each city from its December 1984 issue.

More than a million Americans have tried Transcendental Meditation, the spiritual technique of guru Maharishi Mahesh Yogi. The "TM" organization provided me with a huge computer printout listing the number of people initiated into this mild cult in each of 3,200 urban areas from 1970 to 1977, which I was able to combine into the appropriate metropolitan areas. Only the TM rates look really big, but it should be realized that statistics for the other cults do not report membership totals. Those who write letters to *Fate* magazine are a small minority of its total readers. Scientology clears and Christian Science practitioners are leaders in their respective churches, while each *Spiritual Community Guide* listing represents a number of individual cult members or occult customers.

Thus new religions do arise where old ones decline. To be sure, the cults of America have not filled the gap, and western cities continue to have low rates of religious participation—but these are low rates only when compared to the rest of the country, not historically low rates. The example of the Mormons shows that an occasional new religion can rise to great strength, even in the industrial age. We have to predict that other novel religions, suited especially well to society in the third millennium of Christianity, will arise to fill any gap left by any decline of this ancient tradition.

How Viable Are the Alternatives to Religion?

Speaking in terms of major social institutions, the chief alternatives to religion are science and politics. Each of these has its own social causes and consequences, of course, and here we speak only of their aspects that challenge religion and might substitute for it. The modern world cannot do without these two, but do they offer viable alternatives to supernaturally based compensators?

If religion is nothing but a primitive explanation of nature, then science has some chance of supplanting it. Yet as a scientist I am shocked at how little the typical citizen really understands about science. My university students are woefully ignorant not only of the facts of science, but also of its methodologies and—most important for the present discussion—of the general theories of nature advanced by science. With luck, a bright college student will have some idea that biological evolution involves natural selection, but typically students think of evolution as something that individual organisms accomplish, if they think of it all. They know the phrase "Einstein's Theory of Relativity," but few of them have any concept to go with it. While quantum theory is complex and counterintuitive, some of its basic ideas are both simple and fascinating. One would have thought that fifty years was quite enough time for them to make their way into the minds of most educated nonspecialists. But, no.

One concept, widely used throughout the sciences, does seem to have become popular and directly challenges religion: the concept of mechanical or impersonal causes. The fact that we are surrounded by machines that operate without constant supervision—the clocks that have been ticking away for centuries—reinforces this concept. However, humans are quite capable of being dualists, and if people have need of supernatural beliefs, they can easily coexist with mechanism.

Until it has completed its task and established a unified and empirically supported theory of nature, science will not be able to answer the big questions for which humans most strongly desire answers. Extrapolating from current perspectives in several of the sciences, I would have to guess that we will not find science's ultimate answers very pleasing. They are not likely to give the human individual a central role in the scheme of things, nor to offer him a solution to all his problems.

The rapid growth of science obscures the possibility that science will not be able to complete its task. As James Blish pointed out years ago, the crucial experiments may turn out to be too expensive to perform, a possibility nuclear physicists may have to face when the currently planned "supercollider" has completed its research program. Whether science ends in complete wisdom or financial bankruptcy, an era of stability in scientific knowledge would be one in which new religions could adapt to the world-view bequeathed by science, exploiting it in their rise to dominance rather than being challenged by it as old religions might be. Furthermore, the prestige of scientists, and of the secularism they promote, could end soon after they have completed their main labors, simply because their profession was no longer needed.

One's analysis of politics, I need hardly mention, is conditioned by one's political ideology. Yet perhaps even the most diehard ideologue would have to admit in the privacy of his own thoughts that these are tough times for ideology. Developing nations still have the chance to discover afresh the fantastic ideologies that have exhausted the utopianism of industrial societies. And so long as an ideology is not put to the severe test that political power imposes upon it, it may serve as an alternative to religion. But the industrial nations have seen the more radical parties inflict vast pain on humanity when they had a chance, and the more moderate or liberal ideologies do not offer an alternative to religion.

Much has been made of the fact that secularism is far advanced in a number of European nations, although it takes some doing to convince an American that this is proof of the advancement of Europe over the apparently more religious United States. The fact is that Europe has been going through a transition stage in the relationship of religion to the state, one that has temporarily discredited the church with many citizens but has also prepared the way for a new era of revival and religious innovation, signs of which can already be seen. In the early stages of the development of democracy, state churches were controlled by traditional elites, and so in opposing the elites the new political movements of the Left often became anti-religious. But, as the church has been progressively disestablished in Europe, it is free again to serve all the people, and the new range of denominations, sects, and cults offers forms of religion attractive to many previously unchurched groups.

While a purely political ideology cannot offer a solution to human mortality, it may claim to solve most other problems. Certainly, every modern political ideology pretends to know how justice can be achieved, and most promise social peace and progress as well. But only extremely radical movements can make promises that rival the general compensators of religion, and both wings of the political spectrum have been discredited in the miseries of our century. While there will always be fire-breathing revolutionaries, experience teaches reasonable people to fear political radicalism of any kind. And, while we can hope that good government will result from a healthy competition between moderate parties, salvation is not a credible outcome of the political process.

Unable to supplant religion, modern science and politics nonetheless have transformed the world in which religion exists. Religion is forced to adapt to them. This accelerates the secularization of the liberal denominations, whose clergy often attend the same universities as the scientists. And it places the entire ancient religious traditions, created as they were under radically different social and cultural conditions, under increasing pressure. These aspects of secularization, resulting from rapid developments in science and politics, are bad for existing denominations. But in the short run they stimulate the emergence of radical sects in the ancient traditions, and in the long run they stimulate the birth of cults, the most successful of which will be the major denominations of the distant future. The old order changes, giving place to the new, and religion fulfills itself in many ways.

(Spring 1988)

Is Religiosity Pathological?

Albert Ellis

This article will try to make a succinct and cogent case for the proposition that unbelief, humanism, skepticism, and even thoroughgoing atheism not only abet but are practically synonymous with mental health; and that devout belief, dogmatism, and religiosity distinctly contribute to, and in some ways are equal to, mental or emotional disturbance. The case against religiosity that I am about to make is, of course, hardly unassailable and is only presented as a firm (and undevout!) hypothesis that I believe has validity but that (like all scientific hypotheses) is tentative and revisable in the light of later substantiating or nonsubstantiating evidence. I shall try to state it so that, as Karl Popper has advocated, it is as falsifiable and therefore scientific.

Before I attempt to write about the advantages and disadvantages of devout religion (or religiosity), let me try to define these terms clearly. Traditionally, the term *religion* has meant some kind of belief in the supernatural. Thus, *Webster's New World Dictionary* defines religion as: "(1) belief in a divine or superhuman power or powers to be obeyed and worshipped as the creator(s) and ruler(s) of the universe; (2) expression of this belief in conduct and ritual." However, in recent years religion has also come to be defined in broader terms than this, so that the same dictionary continues: "(3) Any specific system of belief, worship, conduct, etc., often involving a code of ethics and a philosophy: as, the Christian religion, the Buddhist religion, etc. Loosely, any system of beliefs, practices, ethical values, etc., resembling, suggestive of, or likened to such a system: as, humanism is his religion."

In the following article, I shall mainly discuss two particular forms of devout religion or religiosity. The first of these is a devout or orthodox belief in some kind of supernatural religion, such as Judaism, Christianity, or Muhammadism—the pious adherence to the kind of religion mentioned in *Webster's* first two definitions. The second form of religiosity I shall discuss is a devout or rigid belief in some kind of secular ideology (like Libertarianism, Marxism, or Freudianism)—that is, a dogmatic, absolutistic view is sacrosanct, provides ultimate answers to virtually all important questions, and is to be piously subscribed to and followed by everyone who wishes to lead a good life.

I shall not, then, particularly discuss *Webster's* third definition of religion, because I do not think that this kind of "religion" leads to any special individual or social harm. Stated a little differently: I shall now attempt to relate absolutistic *religiosity* rather than mild *religion* to the existence of mental and emotional health.

Although no group of authorities fully agrees on a definition of the term *mental health,* it seems to include several traits and behaviors that are frequently endorsed by leading theorists and therapists. I have outlined the desirability of these "healthy" traits in several of my writings on rational-emotive theraphy (RET),[1] and they have also been generally endorsed by many other therapists, including Sigmund Freud, Carl Jung, Alfred Adler, Karen Horney, Erich Fromm, Rudolf Dreikurs, Fritz Perls, Abraham Maslow, Marie Jahoda, Carl Rogers, and Rollo May. These include such traits as self-interest, self-direction, social interest, tolerance, acceptance of ambiguity, acceptance of reality, commitment, risk-taking, self-acceptance, rationality, and scientific thinking. Not all mentally healthy individuals possess the highest degree of these traits at all times. But, when people seriously lack them or when they have extreme opposing behaviors, we often consider them to be at least somewhat emotionally disturbed.

Assuming that the above criteria for mental health and a few other related criteria are reasonably valid, how are they sabotaged by a system of devout religious belief or religiosity? And how are they abetted by adherence to the principles of unbelief, humanism, skepticism, and atheism? Let us now consider these questions.

1. *Self-interest.* Emotionally healthy people are true to themselves and do not masochistically subjugate themselves to or unduly sacrifice themselves for others. They tend to put themselves first—realizing that, if they do not take care of themselves, no one else will—a few selected others a close second, and the rest of the world not too far behind.

Rather than be primarily self-interested, devout deity-oriented religionists put their hypothesized god(s) first and themselves second—or last. They are so overconcerned whether their god loves them, and whether they are doing the right thing to continue in this god's good graces, that they sacrifice some of their most cherished and enjoyable interests to supposedly appease this god. If, moreover, they are a member of any orthodox church or organization, they feel forced to choose their god's precepts first, those of their church or organization second, and their own views and preferences third.

Masochistic self-sacrifice is an integral part of most major organized religions— as shown, for example, in the ritualistic self-deprivation that Jews, Christians, and Muslims must continually bear if they are to keep their faith. Orthodox religions deliberately instill guilt (self-damnation) in their adherents and then give these adherents guilt-soothing rituals to (temporarily) allay this self-damning feeling.

Pious secular religionists, instead of bowing to supernatural gods, create semi-divine dictators (like Stalin and Hitler) and absolutistic entities (like the U.S.S.R. and Third Reich) and masochistically demean themselves before these "noble" powers again to the detriment of their own self-interest.

2. *Self-direction.* Mentally healthy people largely assume responsibility for their own lives, enjoy the independence of working out their own problems; and, while at times wanting or preferring the help of others, do not think that they absolutely must have such support for their effectiveness and well-being.

Devout religionists (both secular and divine) are almost necessarily dependent and other-directed rather than self-sufficient. To be true to orthodoxies, they first must immolate themselves to their god or godlike hero; second, to the religious hierarchy that runs their church or organization; and third, to all the other members of their religious sect, who are watching them with eagle-eyes to see if they defect an iota from the conduct that their god and their church leadership define as proper.

If devout religiosity, therefore, is often masochism, it is even more often dependency. For humans to be true believers and also to be strong and independent is well-nigh impossible. Religiosity and self-sufficiency are contradictory terms.

3. *Social interest.* Emotionally and mentally healthy people are normally gregarious and decide to try to live happily in a social group. Because they want to live successfully with others, and usually to relate intimately to a few of these selected others, they work at feeling and displaying a considerable degree of social interest and interpersonal competence. While they still are primarily interested in their personal survival and enjoyment, they also tend to be considerate and fair to others, to avoid needlessly harming these others, to engage in collaborative and cooperative endeavors, and to distinctly enjoy some measure of interpersonal and group relationships.

Devout deity-inspired religionists tend to sacrifice human love for godly love (*agape*) and to withdraw into monastic and holy affairs at the expense of intimate interpersonal relationships. They frequently are deficient in social competence. They spend immense amounts of time, effort, and money on establishing and maintaining churchly establishments rather than on social welfare. They foment religious fights, feuds, wars, and terrorism, in the course of which orthodox believers literally batter and kill rather than cooperatively help each other. They encourage charity that is highly parochial and that is linked to god's glory more than to the alleviation of human suffering. Their altruism is highly alloyed with egotistically proving to god how great and glorious they can be as human benefactors.

Devout secular religionists are often much more interested in the propagation of absolutistic creeds (e.g., Maoism) than they are in intimately relating to and in collaboratively helping humans. Like the god-inspired religionists, their charity is exceptionally parochial and is often given only to members of their own religious group while it discriminates against members of groups with opposing credos.

4. *Tolerance.* Emotionally healthy people tend to give other humans the right

to be wrong. While disliking or abhorring others' *behavior,* they refuse to condemn *them,* as total *persons,* for performing their poor behavior. They fully accept the fact that all humans seem to be remarkably fallible; and they refrain from unrealistically demanding and commanding that any of them be perfect; and they desist from damning people in toto when they err.

Tolerance is anathema to devout divinity-centered religionists, since they believe that their particular god is absolutely right and that all opposing deities and humans are positively and utterly false and wrong. According to orthodox religious *shalts* and *shalt nots,* you become not only a *wrongdoer* but an arrant *sinner* when you commit ethical and religious misdeeds; and, as a sinner, you become worthless, undeserving of any human happiness, and deserving of being forever damned (excommunicated) on Earth and perhaps roasted eternally in hell.

The pious secular religionist, without invoking god or hell, believes that the rules and regulations of his/her group or community (e.g., the orthodox religious faction in Iran) are completely right and that, at the very least, social ostracism, political banishment, and perhaps torture and death should be the lot of any dissenter. Religiosity, then, by setting up absolute standards of godly or proper conduct, makes you intolerant of yourself and others when you or they dishonor these standards. Born of this kind of piety-inspired intolerance of self and others come some of the most serious of emotional disorders—such as extreme anxiety, depression, self-hatred, and rage.

5. *Acceptance of ambiguity and uncertainty.* Emotionally mature individuals accept this fact that, as far as has yet been discovered, we live in a world of probability and chance, where there are not, nor probably ever will be, absolute necessities or complete certainties. Living in such a world is not only tolerable but, in terms of adventure, learning, and striving, very exciting and pleasurable.

If one of the requisites for emotional health is acceptance of ambiguity and uncertainty, then divinity-oriented religiosity is the unhealthiest state imaginable— since its prime reason for being is to enable the religionist to believe in god-commanded certainty. Just because life is so uncertain and ambiguous, and because millions of people think that they cannot bear its vicissitudes, they invent absolutistic gods and thereby pretend that there is some final, invariant answer to human problems. Patently, these people are fooling themselves—and instead of healthfully admitting that they do not need certainty, but can live comfortably in this often disorderly world, they stubbornly protect their neurotic beliefs by insisting that there must be the kind of certainty that they wrongly believe they need.

This is like a young boy's believing that he must have a kindly father in order to survive; and then, when his father is unkind, or perhaps has died, the boy dreams up a father (who may be a neighbor, a movie star, or a pure figment of his imagination) and insists that this dream-father actually exists.

Devout secular religionists invent the "certainty" of unequivocally knowing that their special political, economic, social, or other creed is indubitably true and cannot be falsified. Like the superhuman-oriented religionists, they also pigheadedly refuse to accept ambiguity and uncertainty—and thereby render and keep themselves neurotically defensive and immature.

6. *Flexibility.* Emotionally sound people are intellectually flexible, tend to be open to change at all times, and are prone to take an unbigoted (or, at least, less bigoted) view of the infinitely varied people, ideas, and things in the world around them. They are not namby-pamby but can be firm and passionate in their thoughts and feelings; but they comfortably look at new evidence and often revise their notions of "reality" to conform to this evidence.

The trait of flexibility, which is so essential to effective emotional functioning, is frequently blocked and sabotaged by profound religiosity. For the person who dogmatically believes in a god, and who sustains this belief with a strong faith unfounded on fact—which a pious religionist of course does— clearly is not open to many aspects of change and, instead, sees things narrowly and bigotedly.

If, for example, a man's scriptures tell him that he shalt not even covet his neighbor's wife—let alone have actual adulterous relations with her—he cannot ask himself, "Why should I not lust after this woman, as long as I don't intend to do anything about my desire for her? What is really wrong about that?" For his god and his church have spoken; and there is no appeal from this arbitrary authority once he has brought himself to unconditionally accept it.

Any time, in fact, that people unempirically establish a god or a set of religious postulates that supposedly have a superhuman origin, they can thereafter use no empirical evidence to question the dictates of this god or those postulates, since they are (by definition) beyond scientific validation. Rigid secular religionists, too, cannot change the rules that their pious creeds establish. Thus, devout Nazis cannot accept any goodness of Jews or of Gypsies, even when it can be incontrovertibly shown that such individuals performed good acts.

The best that devout religionists can do, if they want to change any of the rules that stem from their doctrines, is to change their religion itself. Otherwise, they are stuck with its absolutistic axioms, as well as their logical corollaries, that the religionists themselves have initially accepted on faith. We may therefore note again that, just as devout religion embraces masochism, other-directedness, intolerance, and the refusal to accept uncertainty, it also seems to be synonymous with mental and emotional inflexibility.

7. *Scientific thinking.* Emotionally stable people are reasonably (not totally!) objective, rational, and scientific. They not only construct reasonable and empirically substantiated theories relating to what goes on in the surrounding world (and with their fellow creatures who inhabit this world) but they also are able to apply the rules of logic and of the scientific method to their own lives and to their interpersonal relationships.

In regard to scientific thinking, it practically goes without saying that this kind of cerebration is antithetical to religiosity. The main requisites of the scientific method—as Bertrand Russell, Ludwig Wittgenstein, Hans Reichenbach, Herbert Feigl, Karl Popper, W. W. Bartley, Michael Mahoney, and a host of other philosophers of science have pointed out—include: (1) At least in some final analysis, or in principle, all scientific theories are to be stated in such a manner that they are confirmable by some form of human experience, by some empirical referents. (2) Scientific theories are those that can in some way be falsified. But deity-oriented religionists contend that the superhuman entities that they posit cannot be seen, heard, smelled, tasted, felt, or otherwise humanly experienced and that their gods and their principles are therefore beyond the realm of science. Pious deists and theists believe that the gods or spirits they construct are transcendent—which means, in theology or religion, that they are separate or beyond experience; that they exist apart from the material universe; that, whatever science says, they are indubitably true and real.

To believe devoutly in any of the usual religions, therefore, is to be unscientific; and we could well contend that the more devout one is, the less scientific one tends to be. Although a pious religionist need not be entirely unscientific (as, for that matter, neither need be a raving maniac), it is difficult to see how such a person could be consistently scientific.

While people may be both scientific and vaguely or generally religious (as, for example, many liberal Protestants and Reform Jews tend to be), it is doubtful whether they may simultaneously be thoroughly devout and objective. Devout secular religionists (such as fanatical believers in phrenology or reincarnation) are not necessarily driven to believe in superhuman and supernatural concepts. But they almost inevitably favor absolutistic convictions about certain other issues; and absolutism and dogma are the antitheses of science. Just about all absolutists, secular and godly, tend to flout some of the basic postulates of the scientific method.

8. *Commitment.* As I have noted on several occasions in my writing on RET, emotionally healthy and happy people are usually absorbed in something outside of themselves, whether this be people, things, or ideas. They seem to lead better lives when they have at least one major creative interest, as well as some outstanding human involvement that they make very important to themselves and around which they structure a good part of their lives.

In regard to the trait of commitment, devoutly religious people may—for once!—have some advantages. For if they are truly religious, and therefore seriously committed to their god, church, or creed, to some extent they acquire a major interest in life. Pious religious commitment, however, frequently has its disadvantages, since it tends to be obsessive-compulsive and it may well interfere with other kinds of healthy commitments—such as deep involvements in sex-love relationships, in scientific pursuits, and even in artistic endeavors (because these may interfere with or contradict the religious commitments). Moreover, religious commitment is an absorption that is often motivated by guilt or hostility and that may consequently serve as a frenzied covering-up mechanism that masks, but that does not really eliminate, these underlying disturbed feelings. Pious god-inspired commitment, moreover, is frequently the kind of commitment that is based on falsehoods and illusions and that therefore can easily be shattered, thus plunging the previously committed individual into the depths of disillusionment and despair.

Not all forms of commitment, in other words, are equally healthy or beneficial. The grand inquisitors of the medieval Catholic church were utterly dedicated to their "holy" work, and Hitler and many of his associates were fanatically committed to their Nazi doctrines. But this hardly proves that they were emotionally stable humans. In fact, a good case can be made for the proposition that, although involvement in or passionate commitment to some cause or ideal is normally healthy and happiness-producing, devout, pious, or fanatic commitment to the same kind of cause or ideal is potentially pernicious and frequently (though not always) does much more harm than good.

9. *Risk-taking.* Emotionally sound people are able to take risks, to ask themselves what they would really like to do in life, and then to try to do this, even though they have to risk defeat or failure. They are reasonably adventurous (though not foolhardy); they are willing to try almost anything once, if only to see how they like it; and they look forward to some different or unusualy breaks in their usual routines.

In regard to risk-taking, I think it is fairly obvious that pious theists are highly determined to avoid adventure and to refuse to take many of life's normal risks. They strongly believe in rigid and unvalidatable assumptions precisely because they are often afraid to follow their own preferences and aims. They demand a guarantee that they will be safe and secure, come what may; and, since the real world does not provide them with any such guarantee, they invent some god or other higher power that will presumably give it to them. Their invention of this deity, and their piously subjugating themselves to it, thereby confirms their view that the world is too risky and gives them a further excuse for sticking to inhibiting, straight-and-narrow (and often joyless) paths of existence.

Devout nontheistic religionists mainly substitute dogmatic belief in some philosophy or cause for a fanatical belief in god; and they use this sacralized cause to inhibit themselves against adventure and risk-taking. Thus, pious nutritionists will under no conditions risk eating white bread or sugar, even when it might do them some good. And devout adherents of cognitive therapy (including devout RETers) may not tolerate the idea that *any* feeling can be free of thought and will insist that *all* dysfunctional behaviors (like headaches and feelings of depression) *must* be of purely ideological origin.

Enormously fearing failure and rejection, and falsely defining their own worth as humans in terms of achievement and approval, devout religionists sacrifice time, energy, and material goods and pleasures to the worship of their assumed gods or godlike philosophies, so that they can be sure that at least their god loves and supports them or that an inherent rightness is on their side. All devout religions seem to be distinctly inhibiting—which means, in effect, that piously religious individuals sell their soul, surrender their own basic urges and pleasures, in order to feel comfortable with the heavenly helper or the indubitably correct creed that they have invented or adopted. Religiosity, then, consists of needless, self-defeating inhibition.

10. *Self-acceptance.* People who are emotionally healthy are usually glad to

be alive and accept themselves as "deserving" of continued life and happiness just because they exist and because they have some present or future potential to enjoy themselves. In accordance with the principles of RET, they *fully* or *unconditionally* accept themselves (or give themselves what Carl Rogers calls "unconditional positive regard"). They try to perform adequately or competently in their affairs and to win the approval and love of others; but they do so for enjoyment and not for ego-gratification or for self-deification. They consequently try to rate only their acts, deeds, and traits in the light of the goals, values, and purposes they choose (like the goals of graduating from school or of having an enjoyable sex-love relationship); and they rigorously try to avoid rating their *self,* their *being,* their *essence,* or their *totality.*

Healthy people, in other words, unconditionally accept themselves because they *choose* to do so, regardless of how well or badly they perform and regardless of how much approval they receive from others. They distinctly *prefer* to act competently and to win others' favor; and they accordingly assess and criticize their own *behaviors* when they fail in these respects. But they don't hold that they absolutely *must* do well or be loved; and they therefore don't conclude that they, in toto, are good people when they succeed and are rotten individuals when they fail.

In regard to self-acceptance, it seems clear that devout religionists cannot accept themselves just because they are alive and because they have some power to enjoy life. Rather, orthodox theists make their self-acceptance contingent on their being accepted by the god, the church, the clergy, and the other members of the religious denomination in which they believe. If all these extrinsic persons and things accept them, then and only then are they able to accept themselves— which means that these religionists define themselves only through the reflected appraisals of God and of other humans. Fanatical religion, for such individuals, almost necessarily winds up with lack of unconditional self-acceptance and, instead, with a considerable degree of self-abasement and self-abnegation—as virtually all the saints and mystics have found.

What about theistic religions, like Christianity, that presumably give grace to all people who accept their tenets and thereby allow all humans to accept themselves unconditionally? As far as I know, there are no theistic creeds that actually do this. The best of them—like Science of Mind—state that God (or Jesus) is all-loving and that s/he therefore always gives everyone grace or unconditional acceptance. But these theistic religions still require their adherents to believe (1) that a god (or son of god) must exist; (2) that s/he personally gives you unconditional acceptance or grace; and (3) that, consequently, you must believe in this religion and its god to receive this "unconditional" grace. Unless you accept these three conditions of grace, you will presumably never be fully be self-accepting. And these conditions, of course, make your acceptance of yourself conditional rather than *un*conditional. Nonreligious philosophies, like RET, teach that you can always choose to accept yourself just *because* you decide to do so, and that you require no conditions or redundant beliefs in God or religion to help you do this choosing.

Ironically, when you do decide to adopt a religious view and choose to accept yourself conditionally (because you believe in a grace-giving god or son of god), *you* choose to believe in this religion and *you* consequently create the grace-giver who "makes" you self-acceptable. All religious-inspired forms of self-acceptance, therefore, in the final analysis depend on *your* belief system; and they are consequently actually *self*-inspired! Even when a religion supposedly "gives" you grace, you really *choose* it yourself, and the religious trappings in which you frame your self-acceptance consist of a redundant hypothesis (that God exists and that s/he gives you grace) that is utterly unprovable and unfalsifiable and that really adds nothing to your *own* decision to be self-accepting.

Although liberal religionists (like the followers of Science of Mind) may be largely self-accepting, devout religionists have much more trouble in gaining any measure of unconditional acceptance. This goes for devout secular as well as pious theistic believers, for the former cannot unconditionally accept themselves because they invariably seem to make self-acceptance (or, worse yet, ego-inflation or self-esteem) depend on rigid adherence to the tenets of their particular creed. Thus, fanatical Nazis only see themselves (and others) as good people if they are good Nazis; and if they perform non-Nazi or anti-Nazi acts (e.g., espouse internationalism or help Jews or Gypsies) they damn themselves as rotten individuals, who presumably deserve to suffer and die. Ku Klux Klanners, along with attacking blacks, Jews, Catholics, and others, excoriate *themselves* as worthless when they fail to live up to ideal KKK standards.

A special way in which devout religiosity sabotages unconditional self-acceptance is its strong tendency to encourage ego-aggrandizement or grandiosity. It is clearly self-defeating to tell yourself, "I am a good person because I have good character" or "I can esteem myself because I am highly competent." If you give yourself this kind of ego-bolstering you make yourself highly liable to self-downing as soon as it can be shown that your character is not so good or that you are beginning, in some important way, to act incompetently.

You will do even worse if you make such self-statements as, "I am a great or noble person because I do outstandingly well at work or at art" or "Because I subscribe to this particular fine philosophy or cause I am better than you are and am indeed a superior individual!" This kind of holier-than-thou self-rating, or arrant grandiosity, assumes that you and other people can be truly superior and godlike—and that you and they are thoroughly ordinary or worthless when not looking down from some kind of heavenly perch.

Devout religiosity particularly foments ego-bolstering and grandiosity. Where mild religionists think of themselves as good people because they are members in good standing of their own religious group, pious ones frequently think of themselves as utterly noble and great because of their religious convictions. Thus, pious Christians, Jews, facists, and communists tend to deify themselves for their beliefs and allegiances; and probably devout atheists also tend to feel somewhat godlike and holy! Grandiosity is one of the most common of human disturbed feelings; and it often compensates for underlying feelings of slobhood. In fact, as Camilla Anderson, a notably sane psychiatrist, has shown, few of us would ever wind up feeling like turds if we did not start off with the grandiose assumptions that we must—yes, *must*—be noble and great.

Anyway, devout religionists are frequently attracted and bound to their piety largely because it presumably offers them holier-than-thouness and oneupsmanship over nonreligionists. And by its appeal to such disturbed individuals, devout religious creeds encourage some of the craziest kinds of thoughts, emotions, and behaviors and favor severe manifestations of neurosis, borderline personality states, and sometimes even psychosis.

11. Emotionally healthy people, it almost goes without saying, accept what is going on in the world. This means several important things: (1) They have a reasonably good perception of reality and do not see things that do not exist and do not refuse to see things that do. (2) They find various aspects of reality, in accordance with their own goals and inclinations, "good" and certain aspects "bad"—but they accept both of these aspects, without exaggerating the "good" realities and without denying or whining about the "bad" ones. (3) They do their best to work at changing those aspects of reality that they view as "bad," to accept those that they cannot change, and to acknowledge the difference between the two.

Devout theistic religionists frequently refuse to accept reality in all three of the ways just listed: (1) They are sure that they see things—gods, angels, devils, and absolute laws of the universe—for which there is no confirmatory empirical data. And they refuse to see some obvious things—such as the ubiquity of human fallibility and the overwhelming unlikelihood that any humans will ever be perfect—that almost certainly do exist. (2) They often whine and scream—and even have their gods whine and scream (as Jehovah presumably did when he turned Lot's wife into a pillar of salt for looking back at Sodom and Gomorrah) when they see something "bad." They especially indulge in childish whining and in temper tantrums when other religionists or nonbelievers refuse to see the virtues of the devout theists' favored religious dogmas. (3) Instead of working hard to change grim reality, they often pray to their god(s) to bring about such changes while they impotently sit on their rumps waiting for their prayers to be answered. When certain obnoxious things are unchangeable— such as the propensity of humans to become ill and to die— they refuse to accept these realities and often invent utopian heavens where humans presumably live forever in perfect bliss.

Devout nontheistic religionists rarely seem to deny reality as much as do devout theists. But because they dogmatically and absolutistically follow narrow creeds, they frequently distort reality in their effort to understand it according to their utopian or teleological systems.

I don't wish to deny that for some people—some of the time—religious notions, even when they are devoutly and rigidly held, have some benefits. Of course they do. Devout adherence to a theistic or secular form of religion can at times motivate people to help others who are needy, to give up unhealthy addictions (to cigarettes or to alcohol, for example), to follow valuable disciplines (dieting or exercising), to go for psychotherapy, to strive for world peace, to follow long-range instead of short-range hedonism, and to work for many other kinds of valuable goals. Historical and biographical data abound to show this good side of religiosity. But I would still contend that on the whole the beneficent behaviors that religious piety sometimes abets would most likely be more frequent and profound without its influence.

Unquestionably, many devout religionists (St. Francis and St. Theresa, for example) have led notably unangry and loving existences themselves, and many others (Pope John Paul II, for example) have helped in the creation of world peace. So pious religion and surcease from human aggression are hardly completely incompatible. The fact remains, however, that fanaticism of any kind, especially religious fanaticism, has clearly produced, and in all probability will continue to produce, enormous amounts of bickering, fighting, violence, bloodshed, homicide, feuds, wars, and genocide. For all its peace-inviting potential, therefore, arrant (not to mention arrogant) religiosity has led to immense individual and social harm by fomenting an incredible amount of ant-ihuman and anti-humane aggression. It can therefore be concluded that anger-attacking and peace-loving religious views that are held undevoutly and unrigidly, as well as similar views that are held by nonreligionists and anti-religionists, probably serve humankind far better than religiosity-inspired peace efforts.

*   *   *

If religiosity is so inimical to mental health and happiness, what are the chances of unbelief, humanism, skepticism, and thoroughgoing atheism helping humans in this important aspect of their lives? I would say excellent. My own view—based on more than forty-five years of research and clinical work in the field of psychology and psychotherapy, but still admittedly prejudiced by my personal predilections and feelings—is that, if people were thoroughly unbelieving of any dogmas, if they were highly skeptical of all hypotheses and theories that they formulated, if they believed in no kinds of gods, devils, or other supernatural beings, and if they subscribed to no forms of absolutistic thinking, they would be minimally emotionally disturbed and maximally healthy. Stated a little differently: if you, I, and everyone else in the world were thoroughly scientific, and if we consistently used the scientific method in our own lives and in our relationships with others, we would rarely seriously upset ourselves about anything—and I mean *anything*.

In sum, it is my contention that both pietistic theists and secular religionists—like virtually all people imbued with intense religiosity and fanaticism—are emotionally disturbed: usually neurotic but sometimes psychotic. For they strongly and rigidly believe in the same kinds of profound irrationalities, absolutistic musts, and unconditional necessities in which seriously disturbed people powerfully believe. When, however, they employ the logico-empirical methods of science, and when they fully accept (while often distinctly disliking and actively trying to change) reality, they are able to surrender their devoutness and become significantly less disturbed. Indeed, I hypothesize, the more scientific, open-minded, and straight-thinking about themselves, about others, and about the world people are the less neurotically they will think, feel, and behave. This is my major hypothesis about the relationship between absolutistic religious belief (religiosity) and mental health. The evidence that I have found, clinically and experimentally, in support of this hypothesis (as well as the evidence falsifying the hypothesis that devout religiosity is significantly correlated with and probably causative of good mental health) seems to be most impressive. But much more investigation of this issue had better be done, since it is up to me and others to bolster or disconfirm these hypotheses empirically.

Note

1. See my "Two Forms of Humanistic Psychology," published in *Free Inquiry*, Fall 1985.

(Spring 1988)

Christian Science, Faith-Healing, and the Law

Rita Swan

In June 1977, our fifteen-month-old son, Matthew, suddenly developed his fourth raging fever. As lifelong Christian Scientists, my husband and I telephoned the most prominent Christian Science teacher in Detroit for treatment. Matthew never walked, sat, crawled, or smiled again.

For two weeks, his practitioners reassured us that they were healing him and demanded more faith and gratitude from us. They claimed that our "false parental thought," in other words, fear, was hampering their treatments. When we wanted to report his unknown disease to the public health department, a practitioner said we were "too concerned about what the community thinks." When Matthew gnashed his teeth deliriously, a practitioner enjoined us to "take the positive interpretation of the evidence" because our baby might be "planning some great achievement" while "gritting his teeth."

Finally, a practitioner suggested that Matthew's convulsions and incoherent moaning might be caused by a broken bone in his neck and pointed out that Christian Scientists are allowed to have broken bones set by an M.D. We immediately went to a hospital. Doctors found advanced meningitis, and with this news the practitioner's biggest concern was that her church would accuse her of recommending medical care. She said we could have taken Matthew to an X-ray clinic and not told "them about the fever and all this other" and she refused to pray for our son any longer. Matthew died after a week of intensive care. We left Christian Science as fast as church officials would let us, and today we are Methodists.

Who are these Christian Science practitioners and what does this church teach about illness? Practitioners take two weeks of religious instruction and can then apply for church accreditation as professional healers. They charge between $7 and $25 a day for spiritual "treatments," usually given without seeing the "patient" or knowing the nature of the illness. The church gives them no limits on what diseases they may treat or any duty to refer cases to other health care providers. It tells them not to report diseases to health departments. The church does tell parents to obey state laws on reporting "suspected" communicable diseases, but few would have the knowledge to "suspect" such diseases when their church tells them that disease is an illusion and that they should get exemptions, won by church lobbyists in many states, from studying about disease in school. If the patient voluntarily chooses medical treatment, the church directs the practitioner not to treat him, thus impressing on its members that God and a doctor are mutually exclusive alternatives. The church is opposed to medical diagnoses, testing, and treatment for children and adults alike. It opposes drugs, hygiene, immunizations, therapeutic diets, chiropractic, chest X-rays, fever thermometers, and taking pulses. Even the simplest human measures for the relief of pain, such as heat, ice packs, enemas, and backrubs are forbidden in Christian Science nursing homes. Their church-trained "nurses" give "no material application" except "normal measures of cleanliness"[1] and are, like the practitioners, unqualified to identify the reportable diseases.

Tied to its charismatic nineteenth-century prophetess, Mary Baker Eddy (1821–1910), the church accepts everything in her published writings as valid, from statements that medicine and hygiene attempt to delude reason and dethrone God to warnings against bathing babies every day. The religion has no way of evolving beyond her. She ruled that the bylaws cannot be changed without her signature; members cling to her every word as divinely inspired final revelation.

Despite this hard line against medicine, church members are allowed to have medical attention under certain circumstances. They can have glasses fitted by optometrists—Mrs. Eddy wore glasses. They can have their teeth filled or extracted by a dentist—Mrs. Eddy was caught by a reporter doing just that. They can have a "hypodermic" to relieve extreme pain—Mrs. Eddy did. They can have their babies delivered by a doctor—one of Mrs. Eddy's students was charged with murder when she attempted to deliver a baby, so Mrs. Eddy changed her rules on childbirth.[2] They can also have broken bones set by a "surgeon." (On this point, W. A. Purrington, in *Christian Science, an Exposition,* suggests the motive was fear of prosecution. Administering drugs was such an inexact science then that internists were rarely charged in the courts, while surgeons had to take more legal responsibility for their actions. Thus, Christian Science practitioners could substitute for doctors by giving drugs with impunity, but not for surgeons.[3])

Many detached observers would expect this religion to have credibility problems in the twentieth century. Who can agree with Mrs. Eddy that "the less we known or think about hygiene, the less we are predisposed to sickness"?[4] who believes that a newborn baby is closer to God because his parents deprive him of a blood test that detects phenylketonuria (PKU) and other treatable disorders? Who believes that doctors "are flooding the world with diseases, because they are ignorant that the human mind and body are myths"?[5]

Yet, the Christian Science church today has astonishing wealth, prestige, and political power. Some Christian Scientists in government include Senator Charles Percy, Congressman David Dreier, former Congressman John Rousselot, Edwin Harper (Reagan's domestic policy advisor until recently), Federal Bureau of

Investigation Director William Webster, and former Central Intelligence Agency head Admiral Stansfield Turner. The church maintains a salaried lobbyist in every state. All the branch churches appoint assistants for the lobbyists. The lobbying network is managed by "The Mother Church" in Boston, with the help of many staff attorneys.

The church has testified in Congress that it has a "system of health care" that is a "recognized alternative to medicine" and is "without legal restriction."[6] Well of course something that parades as a system of health care ought to have legal restrictions, but let's look at the events that gave it recognition. The church persuaded the Internal Revenue Service that sums paid to their practitioners, nurses, and sanatoria are deductible medical expenses. Hundreds of insurance companies, including Blue Cross/Blue Shield in many states, reimburse for the fees charged by church practitioners and nurses. I can't resist interjecting the defense of Massachusetts Blue Cross for such reimbursements: Christian Science treatment goes under a category similar to psychiatric care "where treatment and the success or failure are nebulous."[7] Besides insulting psychiatrists, this explanation ignores the fact that Christian Science practitioners represent themselves as qualified to heal all diseases. There is nothing nebulous about the death of my son.

Medicare law authorizes payment to church sanatoria (in Section 1861 (e) (y) of the Social Security Act). The United States Health Care Financing Administration (HFCA), which administers Medicare, concedes that these sanatoria render "unique" services " not analogous to those provided in a hospital or a nursing home."[8] The law ties the federal government to a church by requiring that these sanatoria "be operated or listed and certified by the First Church of Christ, Scientist, Boston, Massachusetts . . . in order to participate in the hospital insurance program both as a 'hospital' and 'skilled nursing facility.' "[9] An HCFA program analyst told me that his agency had no idea what "skilled nursing care" means in a Christian Science sanatorium and requires no minimum number of nurses to be employed in such sanatoria, although it makes staffing requirements for other institutions receiving Medicare funds. HCFA has recently released Christian Science sanatoria from the obligation to provide a Medicare beneficiary with at least one hour of "skilled nursing care in a 24-hour period."[10] In his view, Congress told them to give Medicare funds to Christian Science institutions and "look the other way."

Church practitioners are authorized to certify sick leave and disability claims for both government and private employees. You might wonder how people with no knowledge of the body or disease can certify sick leave and disability claims, so I reproduce one of their forms below:

I hereby certify that _____ was under my professional care from _____ through _____ due to a physical illness. From what I was told by the patient and from my experience, it was considered inadvisable for the above-named person to report for work or attend to his/her regular duties during this period.
    Signed _____ C.S.

The church suggests that its practitioners say that "the condition seems(ed) to be _____" on disability forms, since they cannot make a medical diagnosis.[11]

In forty-eight states the church has won religious exemptions from immunizations. In the majority of states they have recently won exemptions from metabolic testing of newborn babies. In many states they have religious exemptions from silver nitrate drops, premarital and prenatal blood tests, and from studying about disease in the public schools.

Far more sweeping are the "rights" it has recently claimed to withhold all medical treatment from children. These rights have never been upheld in a definitive court judgment, but they are nonetheless the basis of the church's advice to parents. In 1967 a Massachusetts mother, Dorothy Sheridan, was convicted of manslaughter for the death of her daughter after three weeks of Christian Science treatment. Rather than changing their beliefs or practices, the church decided instead to change the law.

Church lobbyists approached both the United States House Subcommittee on Select Education (which deals with child protection) and the Department of Health, Education, and Welfare (HEW), now Health and Human Services (HHS). Some top HEW officials at that time were members of the church. Soon, HEW put the "religious immunity" provision into the Code of Federal Regulations:

> A parent or guardian legitimately practicing his religious beliefs who thereby does not provide specified medical treatment for a child, for that reason alone shall not be considered a negligent parent or guardian; however, such an exception shall not preclude a court from ordering that medical services be provided to the child, where his health requires it. [45CFR.1340.1-2(b)(1)]

The provision became an eligibility requirement for federal funding for the states' child protection programs. Given this federal pressure and massive, coordinated lobbying by the church, nearly all states have a version of it in either their juvenile or criminal codes or both. States such as Illinois, Connecticut, and Washington mention only Christian Science in these laws. Many other states (and the House subcommittee) have tried to restrict relgious immunity to the Christian Science church with language about "tenets" or a "well-recognized church" and "treatment" by a "duly accredited practitioner thereof." In blatant violation of our Constitution's prohibition against establishment of religion, government has been put in the business of promoting faith-healing, especially Christian Science, and evaluating the social respectability of churches. It is entangled in determinations of whether a church is well enough "recognized" and whether the child's "treatment" is in accordance with the "tenets" of such a church. By granting "duly accredited practitioners" special status in law, government is tied to the Christian Science church's standards for determining the qualifications of its practitioners to treat all diseases of helpless children.

Many believe that court orders provide adequate protection for these children. I want to emphasize in the strongest possible terms that they do not, as dozens of recent deaths prove. While blood transfusions are commonly obtained through court order for children of Jehovah's Witnesses, the courts have no reliable way of discovering sick children in sects that object to all medical treatment and diagnosis. The only ways in which we may hope to protect these children are for the state to retain rights to prosecute parents regardless of religious belief or to develop ironclad reporting requirements for faith-healers.

Interpretations of the religious immunity laws vary. Some scholars believe that the "for that reason alone" phrase makes them virtually meaningless. But the Christian Science church tells its members that they mean that Christian Science treatment is legal health care for children.[12] A test case of their new "rights" came in Alaska in 1969 when Kimberly Sortore died of meningitis with no medical treatment. Manslaughter charges were filed, but the manager of the Christian Science lobbyists flew up from Boston and arranged a deal with the prosecutor: the father would not contest the charges, but the conviction would be overturned if and when the Alaska legislature passed a religious immunity law. Within two years, the legislature had obliged the church: Sortore's conviction was overturned, and all records of the case were ordered expunged.

Religious-immunity laws have definitely deterred prosecution in many faith-related deaths, most notably in Indiana, where several dozen children have died because of Faith Assembly practices, and the prosecutor claims such a law prevents him from filing any charges.

In January 1983, the U.S. Department of Health and Human Services released its new child-protection regulations. HHS made a good-faith effort to respond to my laborious correspondence over many years on this issue. They removed religious immunity from the code, no longer requiring or recommending that states have such laws. They disclaimed intention either to require or prohibit prosecution in cases of religiously motivated medical neglect. They also added "failure to provide medical care" to the states' definitions of child neglect, thus making it a reportable condition regardless of religious belief.[13]

The church was furious and circulated demands on Capitol Hill for a "Christian Science amendment" to the Child Abuse Prevention and Treatment Act. Despite the fact that the state laws had been dictated by Washington and a lobbying network managed in Boston, the church now became the champion of states' rights:

In various parts of the country religious beliefs and practices differ. The states are better equipped to balance and protect these important interests in a country so vast and diversified as the United States . . . These sensitive matters are best addressed at the local level without distant regulatory pressures.

Without our amendment Congres will have taken an irrvocable step toward singling out a religious group by name and severely limiting the religious rights of that group for the first time in a distinguished hundred-year history of faith and contribution to this country.[14]

(The only reason they were mentioned "by name" in the new regulations was that HHS was obligated to summarize the letters that the church itself asked Edward Kennedy and Tip O'Neill to write in support of its "right" to deny children medical care.)

Congressman John Erlinborn, a leader on legislation to guarantee medical care for handicapped infants, submitted a statement for the church at the reauthorization hearings. The House committee accepted it without one word of comment. The next week, Senator Orrin Hatch presented the Christian Science amendment, exactly as the church had drafted it, to his Labor and Human Resources Committee, which added it to the child protection bill, again with no discussion. The amendment states; "However, nothing in this Act shall be construed to limit the right of a state to determine the health care and treatment a parent may provide his child in the exercise of the parent's freedom of religion."

It is hypocritical for the church and Congress to defend "states' rights" on this issue, considering how the states got their laws. It is horrible to have Congress labeling Christian Science treatment and other religious practices as "health care" for children and talking of "freedom of religion" to provide such "health care," when there has never been a definitive court ruling that parents have religious freedom to deny children medical care. Such characterizations of faith-healing and the Constitution will discourage states from changing their laws imposed by Washington. While determined that all other children should be guaranteed medical care, Congress has declared children in faith-healing sects to be pariahs about whom the federal government must say nothing. The amendment has not yet been voted on by the full Senate.

Should the government recognize religious practices as legal health care for children? I feel strongly that such recognition should be given only to state-licensed, secular health care. A child's right to live supersedes a parent's right to practice religion.

Today a wide variety of religions may cause injury to children. Many children have recently been beaten to death because of a belief that beatings promote obedience to divine will. Children have been maimed and killed because of belief in demon-possession. There is no question that the state will file charges in such cases, sometimes even against the church leaders who counsel the parents. So why should our laws suggest that it is all right to deprive children of lifesaving medical care in the name of religion?

Recently in Ohio, for example, parents have been convicted for beating and starving their children on religious grounds, while simultaneously Ohio laws are among this country's most cynical in abandoning Christian Science children. Its juvenile code states that "no report shall be required" on sick children under treatment of a "well-recognized religion,"[15] while its criminal code flatly declares that "it is not a violation of a duty of care, protection, or support" when a parent treats his child's "physical or mental illness or defect . . . by spiritual means through prayer alone, in accordance with the tenets of a recognized religious body."[16] Among the many ghastly Ohio cases that could be cited is that of Christian

Science child Ronald Rowan, who died near Akron in 1979 by strangling in his own vomit because he was too weak to expel it. His body was 30 to 40 percent dehydrated by the time he died—without any medical attention—but the state, of course, did nothing about it.

Or let's look at California's criminal code:

> If a parent provides a minor with treatment by spiritual means through prayer alone in accordance with the tenets and practices of a recognized church or religious denomination, by a duly accredited practitioner thereof, such treatment shall constitute "other remedial care," as used in this section. [Penal Code. Section 270]

In 1973, California convicted parents of manslaughter whose fundamentalist beliefs directed them to withhold insulin from their son, while simultaneously recognizing the spiritual "treatment" of Christian Science practititoners as legal health care for children.

Most bizarre of all are state laws that have allowed courts to order Christian Science treatment for "any child whose health requires it." Maine and Florida had such laws until a few years ago.[17] They are a logical final consequence of state recognition for Christian Science treatment.

Religious exemption laws put the state in the position of establishing special privileges on the basis of religion, in violation of constitutional prohibitions against the government establishing religion. Furthermore, the Constitution has a fourteenth amendment mandating equal protection under the laws. In 1979, the State of Mississippi overturned religious exemptions from immunizations because they deprived children of equal protection from deadly diseases.[18] Let's hope that many other states follow Mississippi's example.

In summarizing the legal status of faith-healing for children, it is an area where we urgently need a Supreme Court ruling. The Mississippi court ruling suggests that all of these religious exemptions may be unconstitutional, yet legislatures continue giving laws to Christian Science lobbyists that suggest that denial of medical care is legal. Before these religious immunity laws came into the states in the 1970s, it was fairly much agreed upon that religion could not be raised as a defense to manslaughter charges. Since then, no charges of child abuse, neglect, or manslaughter were filed in cases involving faith-healing until 1982, when at least six such charges were brought and convictions were won where religious immunity was only in the juvenile code and not the criminal code. These convictions are being appealed. Also they all involved small fundamentalist groups—not the powerful Christian Science church.

Most likely, the religious immunity laws will be changed only over the decades as children die in state after state and their deaths are well publicized. Even after they are repealed, other problems remain. One is the problem of proving that a child's illness could have been treated successfully by medicine. Court opinions have sometimes reflected the assumption that a child may be subjected to any amount of pain unless medicine can guarantee a cure. Another problem is proving that parents whose religion demands ignorance of disease knew that their child's life was in danger. In the Philadelphia area, a Faith Tabernacle family has lost five children to untreated pneumonia over nine years. The prosecutors do not file charges because they say it is possible for the symptoms of pneumonia to develop so rapidly that an untrained parent might not comprehend that the child was dying. It is hard to understand how the same tragedy could happen five times to the same parents and the prosecutors could still conclude that ignorance was a valid excuse, but that was their view.

In 1979, twelve-year-old Michael Schram died of a ruptured appendix. His mother and Christian Science practitioner would not even notify the funeral home for several days. The Seattle area was outraged; both the mother's home and the church were firebombed. But the prosecutor quickly decided not to file charges because the boy's Christian Science beliefs might have discouraged him from expressing pain and therefore his mother might not have known he was seriously ill.

In May 1983, infant Eve Andrews died of diarrhea because the Church of the First Born objects to medical care. Washington state prosecutors declined to press charges because the parents might not have comprehended the danger to their child, even though the parents had also refused to obtain medical care for their first child and had buried his body in their yard.

In October 1983, fifteen-year-old Susan Forslund died in Arkansas after three months of kidney inflammation along with pneumonia. For two and half weeks she was treated by a Christian Science practitioner who never once visited her. She missed a week of school. But again prosecutors decided against filing charges because her parents claimed they were unaware that their daughter was seriously ill, and she never complained of pain. The children in faith-healing sects are trained not to verbalize their pain. Denial is basic to these religions.

The dangers to children associated with faith-healing sects are enormous. They are cared for by people with no medical knowledge, people who are trained to deny disease and its symptoms as illusions, people who demand more faith as the disease gets worse. They have no standard for judging when to give upon on their religion and culture and go to a doctor. Furthermore, the state has no reliable way of discovering these sick children. To my knowledge, no state has a reporting law for sick children that a Christian Science practitioner will obey. Some states have tried to compel reports on sick children from Christian Science practitioners, but have not received any. The reason is that the church tells the practitioners that denial of medical care is not neglect when practiced by Christian Scientists. For example, in Missouri, a state specifically requiring Christian Science practitioners to report suspected child neglect, the church tells its practitioners: "In Missouri, state laws do recognize Christian Science treatment. Therefore providing Christian Science treatment for the child may not be considered as neglect."[19]

Determined that Christian Science treatment is legal health care for children, the church advises parents as follows:

While parents generally are accorded the right to select the type of treatment or care to be rendered for their children when they are ill, nevertheless it should also be recognized that care of children is given very special importance under the juvenile laws. Thus, if a child is being given Christian Science treatment for an illness, inquiries made by school or other public officials as to care of the child should be answered with assurance that such child is being given good care and is having treatment of the illness. Otherwise, such officials may conclude that the child is a neglected child. In talking with such officials, a parent should stay clear of statements such as "belief of illness" or "claim of sickness" which may result in the officials thinking that the illness is being ignored or treated as a fanciful aberration of some kind. Officials must feel the assurance that Christian Scientists love their children and give them effective treatment and responsible nursing care when the nature of the illness indicates the wisdom of having such nursing care.[20]

This semantics game, which I consider deliberate deception, will go on if Senator Hatch's Christian Science amendment, describing religious belief as health care, becomes law.

The prevailing attitude among legislators is to exempt parents and faith-healers from prosecution, while retaining rights to medical treatment by court order. But why do the children associated with faith-healing sects not have the same statutory rights to medical care that other children have? Other parents have a duty to provide medical care, and other children thus have intrinsic rights to medical care. The children in faith-healing sects have no rights until courts accidentally stumble upon their cases and then can prove the children are in imminent danger of dying.

As a former insider, I know that the Christian Science church uses every concession from the state and the insurance industry to persuade its members of its success as a health care system. In a brochure, they say Christian Scientists seek

recognition by law of their right to rely wholly on Christian Science healing for themselves and their children. The widespread legal recognition which this right has already won rests on the proven ability of Chrisitan Science to heal not some but all sorts of disease. Christian Science treatment in lieu of medical treatment has received full recognition by an increasingly large number of insurance companies.[21]

Given his ignorance of the body, the church member will see many healings from the practice of his religion. He sees legislators repeatedly giving the Christian Science church whatever it asks for. Absurd as it may seem, he assumes that objective public officials agree with his church that Christian Science treatment will work just as well as medical care for healing all diseases known to man. He does not comprehend the risks to his children.

Many have asked me if it is possible to draft laws that such isolated people will obey. I can't offer any guarantees, but I think we should try. In many faith-healing sects, members have a posture of passive compliance with the state, of rendering unto Caesar that which is Caesar's. It would relieve many parents of the onus of breaking a religious law if the state would make its standards plain.

We as a society can establish in law that parents have a duty to provide medical care for children without exceptions for religious belief and that something that calls itself a health care system has duties to both the state and its patients.

Notes

1. Christian Science Board of Directors, "Facts about Christian Science" (Boston: C. S. Publishing Society, 1959), p. 9.

2. Robert Merritt and Arthur Corey, *Christian Science and Liberty* (Los Angeles: De Vorss & Co., 1970), pp. 96–100.

3. W. A. Purrington, *Christian Science, an Exposition: A Plea for Children and Other Helpless Sick* (New York: E. B. Treat & Co., 1900), pp. 28–29.

4. Mary Baker Eddy, *Science and Health With Key to the Scriptures* (Boston: Trustees under the Will of Mary Baker Eddy, 1983), p. 389.

5. Ibid., pp. 150–51.

6. Hearings on HR 3394, HR 3411, and HR 3814 before Subcommittee no. 3 of the House Committee on the District of Columbia, 89th Congress, 1st Session, 36 (1965), p. 36.

7. Mitchell Lynch, "A Church in Crisis; Blue Cross Supports Prayer," *Wall Street Journal,* February 27, 1979, pp. 1, 40.

8. Carolyne K. Davis, Health Care Financing Administration, U.S. Department of Health and Human Services, letter to Congressman Berkley Bedell, November 23, 1983, p. 1.

9. "Medicare Christian Science Sanatorium, Hospital Manual Supplement," HHS Health Care Financing Administration publication 32, CS-102 "Conditions of Participation."

10. Ibid., see change in policy CS-200, March 1983.

11. C. S. Committee on Publication for California, *Legal Rights and Obligations of Christian Scientists in California* (Garden Grove and San Francisco, 1980), pp. 68, 70.

12. C.S.C.O.P. for Minnesota, *Legal Rights and Obligations of Christian Scientists in Minnesota* (Minneapolis, 1976), p. 23.

13. U.S. Dept. of Health and Human Services, "Child Abuse and Neglect Prevention and Treatment Program, Final Rule," *Federal Register,* January 26, 1893, pp. 3698–3704.

14. C.S.C.O.P. for Washington, D.C., "Rationale for Christian Science Amendment to HR 1904," Spring 1983.

15. Ohio Revised Code 2151.421.

16. Ohio Revised Code 2919.22.

17. Florida Statutes, Section 827.07, and Maine Statutes 22.3852, definitions.

18. Brown vs. Stone, 378 *Southern Reporter,* 2nd series, pp. 218–24.

19. C.S.C.O.P. for Missouri, *Legal Rights and Obligations of Christian Scientists in Missouri* (March 1976), p. 15.

20. C.S.C.O.P. for Michigan, *Legal Rights and Obligations of Christian Scientists in Michigan* (Detroit, 1978), p. 23.

21. "Facts about Christian Science," pp. 10–11.

The Watchtower: The Truth That Hurts
"Laura Lage"

My marriage problems began the afternoon that my brother Gary appeared at my front door. I hadn't seen Gary for several years and remembered him as a long-haired hippie adorned with love-beads and dressed in casual attire. Now I was startled at his appearance. His hair was trimmed neatly above his white collar, and he looked striking in a smart suit and tie. He carried a brown leather attaché case; his blue eyes sparkled with happiness. Gary's golden hair and fair complexion gave him a look of innocence, but his expression revealed an urgency, as if he were about to unveil a dark truth. I was delighted at his visit and welcomed him into my home, apologizing for the boxes of Christmas ornaments scattered across the green shag carpet. After hugging each other, we settled at the kitchen table to have tea and exchange small talk. Almost immediately, I noticed that Gary seemed to have a negative slant on every subject we touched upon.

"Have you noticed the changing weather patterns, Laurie?" he asked me gravely.

I shook my head and changed the subject. "Are you still involved in art and sculpture, Gary?"

"I have more important things to do now," he said. "People seem to have too much knowledge and nowhere to channel it, no real purpose to anything they do, no hope. The age of increasing knowledge is upon us, and it was all foretold thousands of years ago!"

I was beginning to feel uneasy, sensing that he was leading me somewhere that I was not prepared to go. "Are you aware of the ever-increasing corruption in our government?" he asked. Apparently Gary was deeply troubled by something. While I groped for an explanation, he met my eyes and demanded: "For all your Catholic education, did you ever once hear the true name of God?"

Then, he told me that he had become a minister of the true God, Jehovah. He spoke cautiously, as though he didn't want to reveal too much at once. He was on an important mission, and I was the one in whom he chose to confide. Gary told me he had become a member of the Watchtower Society. He braced himself for a scornful response, or perhaps a chuckle, but receiving no such reaction, he continued: "We're in the last days, Laurie. We're right on the verge of Armageddon, the final battle between God and Satan upon earth. I'm here to warn you, the same way I'd snatch up a man lying on the railroad tracks. There isn't much time." His hand trembling, he opened his briefcase and withdrew several books and magazines. I watched him, still intrigued by his transformation into a concerned man of God. It was a personality foreign to me. I remembered Gary as the militant of the family, the rebel who explored life and lived it to its fullest.

*   *   *

It was getting dark now. My husband, Tom, was due home and would be looking forward to relaxing after a day of urging prospective customers to purchase soft drinks. I turned up the dining-room light and worried about Tom's reaction to Gary's evangelism. My husband was impatient with religion. I was concerned that he would be rude to my brother, who was already winning my heart. My head was throbbing, however, with his abundance of knowledge.

Gary proceeded to proselytize, touching lightly on many subjects while I periodically took leave to tend my children. "The Bible has warned us that in these last days we would be victims of war, famine, earthquakes, and economic strife," Gary said, following me into the children's room. "The government and churches are run by Satan and will be destroyed by Jehovah."

I looked at Gary quizzically, feeling as if a whole new world was being presented to me against my will. My mind wanted to grasp it, but something within me rebelled when I gazed at the two children playing at my feet. I could not help but feel an emptiness, as if someone were about to rob them of childhood and snuff out their lives because they had been born in "the last days." But Gary evoked a sense of shame in me. I felt that somehow I was guilty of standing by without warning people of imminent doom, that perhaps I did need to be more socially responsible.

". . . But our task is not to change governments or tamper with this system in any 'worldly' way," Gary was saying, the inflection in his voice grabbing my wandering attention. "Our responsibility is to warn people and get them out of the churches of Christendom." I was confused, but felt that he must be wiser than I. Gary was ten years older, so he and I had grown up as strangers. In childhood, I had spent years trying to win the approval of the big brother I idolized. But now he was here. He cared about me.

Tom arrived home and welcomed Gary with a smile and a handshake. I briefly explained the nature of his visit, and Tom, to my surprise, appeared to welcome a challenging debate. "I'd love to tell you a thing or two about religion," Tom said laughingly. He quickly washed and, appearing refreshed, sat down at the table stacked with Gary's books. Tom's physical appearance was one of authority and pride; his dark hair was neatly styled and his figure was straight and slender.

I served a platter of spaghetti for dinner, but we ate quickly and cleared the plates to make room for more books. The children were excused and, typically, raised havoc knowing we were preoccupied with our guest.

Tom was usually strongly critical of religion, but this time Gary defused his reaction. By insisting that the "Truth" of the Watchtower Society was *not* a religion but a "way of life," Gary silenced Tom's objections. His steady eyes penetrated Tom's nervous glances. Gradually, I could see that my brother's skill in persuasion was leading Tom to reconsider his firm stand. Time went by unnoticed. For hours we listened. Tom's efforts to argue ceased. Quietly and intently he listened to Gary's version of the Bible. I watched a transformation in my husband that astounded me. Tom, now convinced that Armageddon could occur any time, insisted that we study the Bible at home. Gary assured us that we had nothing to lose and everything to gain. Although I agreed, this strange change in Tom's behavior was puzzling to me.

Having accomplished his mission, Gary left. I looked at Tom's worn face and felt an uneasiness I had to express. "Tom, maybe we shouldn't rush into this. Don't you think that before we get involved we should—"

"If you don't want to do it, then don't!" Tom snapped. "I intend to test it and see where it all leads." I saw determination in his eyes. I sat down in the green living-room chair and gazed out into the blue-black morning sky. I was filled with questions and self-doubt. I wondered if our marriage needed religion. Perhaps we needed to be involved in a cause. The end of the world? Already?

*   *   *

The following afternoon we were introduced to Jeannie, a Jehovah's Witness whom Gary had asked to supervise our studies. Jeannie would become a major factor in our lives, answering questions, soothing our doubts, and paving our road to the Truth. She was lively and beautiful, her middle-aged face glowing beneath the lines of a fretful life. The days she had spent in submission to an abusive husband, rewarded her, she told us, through progress toward the Truth.

Jeannie talked in terms of the "New Order," a "new system" that would prevail on Earth after the destruction of wicked mankind at Armageddon. Before long, we were all waiting anxiously together for the coming New Order that would be populated only with Jehovah's Witnesses.

"He who endures to the end shall be saved." This was a maxim that ruled many consciences. Life in our society, we learned, was miserable and belonged to Satan. Serving Jehovah and enduring our lot would be difficult, but if we proved ourselves worthy, we might be among those who would survive Armageddon.

I wondered was this new way of life actually the Truth that would provide the answers to peace and freedom? How exciting it would be to find myself chosen by God, called out from among the wicked of the world to survive the last great battle on Earth! Yet I faced recurring doubts whenever I glanced ahead in the blue study-book that promised the answers to mankind's woes. "I'll never give up holidays or sell books door-to-door!" I told Jeannie stubbornly. "I would *never* denounce the American flag!" But Jeannie patiently explained that no pressures were being placed on me. "The foundation is built first," she said. I felt reassured. Supposedly, nothing drastic was expected of me.

*   *   *

Six months later, Tom and I decided that the love shown to us by our new "brothers and sisters" was without compare. We were showered with attention by dedicated people who spoke of an ideal society. We became estranged from unbelieving friends and relatives who could not handle our proselytizing; we were warned by the Witnesses of "persecutions" that would come from our loved ones. They said that we must prepare ourselves for the sudden or gradual separation from our family. The congregation of Jehovah's Witnesses became our family. Tom and I grew increasingly aware of every thought, deed, and action that might be contrary to Society teachings. We were afraid that if we "stumbled out of the 'Truth,' " we would be destroyed. Constant encouragement from Jehovah's Witnesses kept our stamina strong enough to endure daily living.

Gradually I began to notice drastic mood changes in Tom and myself. One day I was spiritually high; the next day, deeply depressed. Tom was behaving the same way. "We're suffering persecutions from Satan, Laurie," he told me. "We have a war to fight, a spiritual battle with darkness. Haven't you noticed how everyone we talk to seems to fight the Truth?"

We were often told by society members about the importance of presenting a "good witness" to outsiders. No matter what burdens we were experiencing, we must be good witnesses to others. If we failed in impressing others with our shining example, then we might dissuade them from joining forces with us, thereby causing their destruction.

Days and nights became filled with Watchtower activities, but occasionally we visited with Gary and his wife. My parents joined us for family dinners. Mom and Dad attempted to talk about various subjects, knowing that if the wrong topic was touched upon it would invite Gary's "witnessing." But many times before dinner ended, religion invariably found its way into the conversation.

Gary's attacks were aimed at the small gold cross held by a fine chain around my mother's neck. "It amazes me," he began one night at dinner, how ignorant people are about the origins of their religious traditions. As an example, the cross is a pagan symbol dating back to Babylon!"

Mom was used to Gary's remarks by now. "Don't start in, Gary! You have your faith and I have mine!" she answered. Dad tried unsuccesfully to change the subject to sports, but Gary refused to heed him. Tom attempted to act as mediator between the two opposing family members while Gary's wife and I exchanged glances of concern across the table. Perhaps this would be the night that Mom and Dad would seek the Truth.

"Why can't you face the Truth?" Gary asked calmly with his eyes fixed on Mom's. "If one of your loved ones were killed, would you wear the murder weapon as a constant reminder?"

Mom's voice was loud and trembling as if volume would make up for her lack of knowledge about the Watchtower Society. "The cross represents His victory over death!" she exclaimed.

Gary retorted, "I'm offering the Truth to you! You're in darkness and Satan is blinding you through that weapon around your neck!"

"That does it! I'm leaving!" Mom slammed her fists down on the dining-room table and rose from her chair, tears welling in her eyes. Dad turned to Gary, Tom, and me: "I hope you're all satisfied now. We came fifty miles to enjoy a family dinner and it was all a ploy to preach at your mother and me." With that, they departed.

Gary gave no chance for Tom or me to regret the events of the evening. Taking out his Watchtower Bible, he pointed out scriptures that seemed to explain our mother's "strange" behavior. He pointed out the evil of our parents' ignorance. "Did you see that demonic expression in Mom's eyes? That's how Satan works! He even transforms himself into an Angel of Light, to lead away the chosen!" We listened intently and fervently believed it was our task to rescue Mom from Satan.

In these months, Tom and I approached our relatives, requesting that they no longer give our children Christmas gifts. Christmas, according to the Society, was pagan. There would be no more birthday or Easter celebrations, or other acknowledgments of "worldly" holidays. On Thanksgiving Day that year, we sat solemnly at a local coffee shop, pretending that we were not lonely. We endured for Jehovah.

Because of our intensive studies of Satan's war tactics, my mind was flooded with the fear that I might be next on the devil's list. One night, while Tom slept, I tossed and turned, my eyes kept open by thoughts of the day. Suddenly, a terrific weight pressed firmly against the base of my spine. It felt as though my back was about to snap, although no force was visible. I was terrified. I tried to reach for my husband, but I couldn't move my arms. I tried without success to raise my head. No amount of resistance would fight the force. I attempted to scream, but no sound would come out. In my thoughts I cried out to God, and within seconds the weight was lifted. Finally, I roused Tom, but his efforts to calm me failed. After I'd convinced him that I had not experienced a dream, he reached for the phone and spoke nervously to an elder. We were advised to pray and that such incidents were not uncommon. We were promised that the experience would be explained to us the following morning. Tom's face wore an expression of battle fatigue that night, as if he were faithfully fighting a war with no hope of peace. He questioned how one day we had been so naive and now we were in full combat with the principals of darkness. Yes, he said, we were chosen by Jehovah to fight the good fight.

The next day our elders explained that Satan worked through certain objects detestable to Jehovah. Persecution would come in many forms while Satan tried to break our integrity. If persecution from family members did not work then demonic harassment might, they said. We were told about a woman who battled such influences when demons took control of her car. Later she discovered a "holy card" on the car floor. She was advised of its role in Satan's attempts to destroy her. After intently listening to this counsel, we allowed our house to be swept clean of "pagan" objects such as crosses, pictures of Jesus, and Catholic prayer books. An American flag that was stored in the hall closet was ridiculed by a "brother" as "a rag on a stick" and promptly disposed of. The Society frowns on "flag worship" as a trapping of the evil world.

News of my "attack" traveled quickly through the congregation, and I was given encouragement as if I had visited hell and returned. The experience, it seemed, was my official initiation into the "club," and I was allowed to hear stories of other "demon harassments." Tom and I began to find demon influences in everyday life. Like the other members of our congregation, we refused to attend a Catholic church, would not participate in Christian weddings or funerals, and shunned prayers from "worldly" sources. We never realized that being involved with God could be so painful.

We were informed of Satan's desperate attempts to keep us from making a final commitment to the Truth. To counter these attacks and symbolize our new lives, we were baptized. Tom, the children and I now belonged to the Watchtower Brooklyn Headquarters. We lived cautiously, trying not to make a serious error and thus be cast out of the spiritual "Ark." We never discussed the hardships of our new lifestyle. To do so would be to betray Jehovah and open our minds to satanic influence. We rarely smiled at each other. Memories took on an unreal quality, as if life before the Truth was nothing more than deception.

As full-fledged members of the Society, we were next prepared for the door-to-door distribution of magazines; no more pampering us now! We must work harder than before to recruit new members for the Ark to secure *our* salvation. Canvassing was a task I had been sure I'd never undertake, but the time had come to prove my loyalty to Jehovah. Tom's bold personality and sales experience allowed him to tackle his task with enthusiasm. I strove to overcome a shy nature and ventured forth like a cat poking its paw into water.

Magazine sales were hard on my nerves. I actually prayed that people would not answer their doors. Well prepared for my presentation, I could not help feeling like a religious Fuller brush salesman. It wasn't easy to spurt out a memorized presentation and have the door slammed in my face. But I was educated in the art of talking effectively about the Kingdom, remaining "controlled" or meek in debates, condemning all other religions as pagan, and portraying acceptance of Jehovah as the way to salvation *if* an individual earned it. Although I stumbled and stuttered my way through these encounters, I knew that I must make progress no matter what the cost.

*   *   *

Jehovah's Witnesses hold yearly conventions that draw thousands of faithful delegates from across the United States, a pilgrimage where eager members drew together to receive the latest revelations from the Brooklyn Headquarters. Here, "New Light" was shed upon old false beliefs. Watchtower Society prophecies that had failed to come true were explained and updated away. Hour after hour, the faithful sat in the rain or the sun, concentrating on every word spoken. We were among the faithful who endured this duty; our family life suffered the consequences. One day soaked by rain, the next day sunburned, we returned to a home filled with discontent. We were irritable from harsh weather and endless preaching; our aggressions spilled forth with hot intensity. Tom shouted and I screamed back, both of us releasing long-suppressed anger. We were no longer sensitive to one another. As I reached for Tom, he withdrew.

Several incidents occurred that made me compare our life before with that after our conversion. John, our five-year-old son, began to show signs of rebellion in his kindergarten class. Since Jehovah's Witnesses did not allow the celebration of holidays or birthdays, John was either sent from the classroom or sat withdrawn each time treats were given to other children. He sat apart while classmates saluted the flag or sang patriotic songs. For him to participate would risk his destruction by the hand of Jehovah. I was called by John's teacher and asked if there were problems at home. For the first time in two years, I admitted that the Watchtower religion was destroying my family, and I didn't know how to solve it. We had lost our spiritual sanity; but I had been taught to *endure* to the end! I felt my mind striving to rise above the Watchtower intellect, but at the same time I resisted my natural instincts and fought what I thought was Satan, fearing Jehovah's wrath if I dared to think otherwise. I felt torn, confused, and too frightened to break our ties with the Jehovah's Witnesses. Life became a nightmare. I fought both to hold onto the seed of faith I had found and the pursuit of the freedom I had lost.

On one of the days that followed, Laura, a child in the congregation, died when her parents refused permission to give her a necessary blood-transfusion. The taking of blood is forbidden by Watchtower theology. I was sickened by reports of atrocities committed on Jehovah's Witnesses in Malawi in Central Africa for refusal to carry an identification card issued by the government. These innocent victims were led to believe that identifying with their worldly government would be disobeying Jehovah's word, erroneously referring to "the mark and name of the Beast." Here in the United States, we were warned to prepare ourselves for the persecutions that would soon befall us. I didn't realize that a small committee in Brooklyn, New York, decided the fate of thousands!

The final straw came when Jeannie was institutionalized with a nervous breakdown. She believed herself to be one of the 144,000 described in the Watchtower's version of the Book of Revelation who would help Jehovah battle Satan at Armageddon. She would laugh with joy one moment and shout at Satan the next. She thought she was being "persecuted for Jehovah." When Tom and I visited Jeannie at the hospital she spoke of witnessing with other patients and proudly showed us where she had hidden "Truth books" around the ward. Psychiatrists, she told us, were frowned on by the Society, and she had been advised not to discuss religion with them.

Walking away from the hospital, I looked at Tom to see if he might be showing signs of the concern that I was feeling. "Tom, so many things have happened," I said tearfully. "Jeannie's really sick. I don't know how to help her."

"I know how you feel," Tom said solemnly, casting his eyes downward. "She's not getting the help she needs."

I felt that perhaps Tom, too, was entertaining doubts. "And Laura. She could've lived, Tom. Would you let one of our kids die?"

"It would rip my heart out," he said in a quavering voice. "But Jehovah gave us guidelines to follow."

I became defensive, thinking of one of our children lying on a stretcher in an imaginary hospital, bleeding to death as we stood by enduring for Jehovah. "What kind of god are we serving? What kind of a god would ask us to sacrifice our child on a Watchtower altar?" I demanded an answer, suddenly filled with anger and repulsion.

"Abraham did it, Laurie," Tom answered. "And Jehovah stopped him."

"But he didn't stop Laura from dying, did he?" My voice grew louder, and I was resentful at Tom's stubborn resistance to logic.

About this time, my father started to investigate the Watchtower Society religion, trying to determine what it was we believed that excluded family and friends who would not succumb to our "witnessing." His studies were conducted in our home with Tom and me present to witness another recruit-in-training. I began to see through the elder who cleverly tried to control my father. All of the tactics that had been used on Tom and me were repeated, almost word for word.

After a few weeks, however, Dad approached us with his decision to withdraw from further studies. He had received information concerning the organization from my sister Carol. She had studied with Witnesses but withdrew when she learned from former members of the dangers involved.

Tom reacted angrily to Carol's interference and was fearful of what these "evil" former members might have to say. He quoted several scriptures in the hope of maintaining my father's interest in the Truth. "For a time, I thought maybe you found something to make you happy. I was wrong!" Dad said. "You have to *pretend* you're happy to provide a good witness to me! I found out that members keep *progress reports* on everyone they study with. Which one of you has kept the report on me?"

Tom and I grew silent, as if a dark secret had been discovered. We were taught to think of verbal abuse as Satan's tactics, yet I wanted desperately to interpret my father's words as an expression of his concern. Whom should I believe? Again I faced indecision and the inability to think rationally.

Dad refused to let Tom interrupt him with scripture readings. "I see God in simple ways everyday," he said softly. "In the cloud formations, in the sunrise while I'm driving to work, and in a child's smile. Open your eyes! Look around you!"

"You're misled!" Tom interjected. I looked at my husband and realized that he had changed dramatically. His face revealed how much older he had become. While Dad's face was peaceful and soft as he spoke of his simple faith, Tom looked as though he was an executioner ready to kill. When he spoke of God, he spoke of statistics and mathematical calculations concerning the time of the end. Tom had given up his youth. Where had our lives gone?

My father then left our home. I knew that my freedom was gone. I had been told how to live and how to present myself to others. I wanted more than anything to be a free woman again; free to think, act, dress, and speak as I wished. I wanted to explore life from all sides, to open my mind, and to be rescued from this bondage.

We had been warned by the elders to cut off association with my sister. Curiosity won over fear this time, however, and secretly I agreed to meet the former Jehovah's Witness whom Carol recommended. His name was Brian, and he was as zealous and determined as the most dedicated Watchtower student. But his zeal was channeled into helping frightened Witnesses leave their cultish life. His appearance was that of a Jehovah's Witness—short hair, business suit, tie, and briefcase. He presented a clean-cut image, knowing that I was probably expecting the devil himself. He knew that I needed help, and the first hour was spent convincing me that I was not going to be destroyed for seeking another point of view. My fears somewhat calmed, we proceeded to take the organization's structure apart step by step, scripture after scripture. Within eight hours, I was beginning to feel like the woman I had once been. Watchtower demons were being swept away.

It was as though I had suddenly been allowed to see through eyes that had been blinded. Everything seemed renewed. The winter air was crisp and clean, and the scent of pine branches brought back vivid memories of Christmases past. Men and women carrying armloads of foil-wrapped gift-boxes filled me with a childish joy that I had not known for a long time. Like the resurrection of all living things in spring, I too was brought back from the dormancy of darkness.

My next step was to gather all of the information on the Society that I had been given and attempt to convince Tom of the lie we had been living. I could not remember Tom being so unreachable. I listened to his programmed responses and the repetition of scripture each time I showed him new evidence. "Satan's won a battle over you!" he shouted stubbornly. "The kids and I will never leave the Truth!" My mind went back to the time Tom soothed me through labor pains and watched as the miracle of birth took place. Our innocence had made everything new to us, a miracle of love. I snapped back to the present as Tom scorned me for the "foolishness" of discarding eternal life.

Tom reported my activities to the elders, and I was charged with apostasy—

defection from the faith. The "witch hunt" began, and I felt as though I was waiting to be burned. I felt abandoned and abused, but at the same time willful. I purchased a huge Christmas tree to reinforce my feeling of independence. I brought it into the house, to my husband's horror, and endured the accusations of being "a pig rolling in its mire" and "a dog returning to its vomit," both Watchtower references to backsliders.

*   *   *

That Christmas was my celebration of freedom. I listened to Christmas music, bought the children gifts, and came alive as they laughed like imps again. It took some explaining to convince our son that the tree was not satanic. Now I could see the absurdity of it all. I wondered how adults could be so eager to surrender their minds to people who claimed to know Truth. Our son overcame his timidity and gently touched the tree branches with delight. Tom withdrew to the bedroom with his Bible and persecution complex.

In the disfellowshipping procedure that followed, an elder announced my offense publicly. I was considered to be a member of the "evil servant" class who should be viewed "as one dead." Our friends in the Society could no longer acknowledge me. If they met me on the street, they would bow their heads and ignore me. My brother would not speak with me about scripture, lest he be "tainted" by my "uncleanness." When I approached him, he instructed his son to phone an elder to monitor our conversation. He withdrew his love, and I have not seen Gary since. Tom was supported by the congregation and encouraged to stop communicating with me and guide the children back to Jehovah through constant attendance at meetings. It was hoped that as a result of these measures I would humble myself and return to the Society.

Being shunned by my husband was difficult for me. I finally decided to arrange a deprogramming for Tom without his knowledge. This was accomplished by arranging a "surprise" visit from Brian. Events moved quickly once he entered our home. Tom became defensive and greeted the former Witness with defiance. "What's the matter, Brian?" Tom asked indignantly. "Couldn't make it, huh? So you've dedicated your life to hounding those of us who are stronger than you are?"

Brian replied: "If I were in your shoes, I'd want to know why my wife was being persecuted and defamed by people who claim to love her. Doesn't it seem strange to you that love can be so quickly withdrawn from one who stands up for convictions? Christ sat with sinners, ate with them, and loved them. Are you saying that as a Jehovah's Witness you're better than Christ? It seems to me that Jesus stood up to religious bigots who ruled people with an iron hand."

Tom tightened his lips. His face flushed as he strained to recall a scripture that would bring Brian to his knees. Tom contemplated Brian's coutenance as well as his words as if the power of life and death were within Brian's grasp: was this a man of God or a devil's advocate? I could see the agony etched in deep creases across my husband's forehead.

"Come on, Tom," Brian continued. "Look at life from both sides. Allow me to show you evidence using only Watchtower literature and scripture. I have no other books. See for yourself." Tom was curious now, having grown to rely on Watchtower literature as God's only channel of Truth. Even though speaking with a former Watchtower member was against Society policy, Tom agreed to review the literature at the dining-room table. Slowly and painfully, my husband realized that his freedom of choice had been taken from him in subtle ways. Tom emerged not defeated but liberated from the spiritual trance imposed by the Watchtower Society.

However, I felt that I was walking a tightrope in the days that followed. Tom's resignation was accepted by the Society after he threatened legal action if disfellowshipped. Because he had avoided defamation procedures, "brothers and sisters" would often approach Tom in public without acknowledging my presence. It was nearly impossible to leave the house without experiencing this ordeal, which would reduce me to tears.

As a result of my "witch hunt" and "execution," I was hospitalized for exhaustion and severe abdominal pains. A slow recovery followed, in which I attempted to adopt a nonchalant attitude as self-protection from former friends who once claimed to love me.

*   *   *

Tom and I emerged from our Watchtower experience in the beginning of 1977. By the end of that same year we agreed to divorce. It has taken me almost four years to put the pieces together, to relive the story more than a hundred times in my mind, and to study in depth the psychological battlefield an ex-cultist faces during an overwhelming re-adjustment period.

Tom and I found ourselves seemingly incurable idealists—two young people who wanted desperately to be part of a plan that would initiate peace and dramatically transform the world's population into united, perfect human beings. We had often been asked by the members of the Watchtower Society: "If you were to leave it (the Truth), where else could you go?" Invariably we found that they did not know the Truth, nor did they have "the Answer" to mankind's woes. But we still faced the question: "Where else could we go?"

Ideals and dreams do not fade easily, and we were sure that our idealism could be recycled to fit a new philosophy. How does one toss aside the vision of peace and face head-on the reality of despair without first trying new avenues that offer just as much, if not more, than the old? It is a final attempt to realize a fantasy. It was by now apparent that Tom and I had become two separate individuals—two adamant zealots—but each with a different approach to our new lives of fervor for the Lord's cause.

After our exodus from the Watchtower, Tom and I accepted Jesus as our Savior, a return for both of us to the religion of our childhoods. Through this basic, simple belief, we came together and soothed the wounds of a broken-hearted

family. We felt comfortable with the concept of a God who loved us unconditionally and was not the harsh taskmaster that we had been led to believe.
We were exhausted and in turn exhilarated. Now, on Saturday mornings we
rested in bed, our minds relieved of the pressures of early morning fieldwork.
The children laughed again. The house was once again home. Watchtower demons
were chased away.

Yet we craved something more. As Witnesses of Jehovah, we were offered
warm companionship and the feeling of belonging to "God's family." We had
instant love. The Witnesses thought alike and fought for the same cause. They
could depend on each other for emotional and spiritual support. Having lost
all of our Watchtower friends and having become estranged from friends who
ran from our proselytizing, we were lonely for fellowship, but the punishment
that I had received from the Society stuck in my mind. It reminded me of a
person in the middle of a coliseum who was surrounded by thousands of people
full of hate. How could I ever trust anyone again? I was frightened.

Tom, on the other hand, not having experienced this blow to his self-esteem,
desired to make a commitment to the "born-again" cause which we had been
attracted to while visiting a Christian bookstore. While it was vital to find a
substitute for the belief-system we had abandoned—to keep us from returning
to the Watchtower Society out of fear or loneliness—my needs differed from
Tom's. I felt that *conviction,* a deep personal faith, was all that was necessary.
I was afraid to commit my life to another cause. I needed time to think, to
breathe, to sort things out without the pressures of the end of the world nagging
at my mind. I felt backed against a wall like an arched cat, ready to strike out
at anyone attempting to snatch away my freedom. I was threatened by the born-
again movement and viewed it as another pacifier to wean me away from the
world. My reaction, in Tom's opinion, was radical and rebellious. While I desired
to surround myself with people from all walks of life and envisioned love for
my fellow human beings as something that we chose to do or not to do, and
as something wonderful that begins with the seed of friendship, Tom again narrowed
the realm of the "saved" into one category: the born-again. Anyone without this
status was doomed to hell. Love seemed to be another instantaneous emotion
given freely within the church, but outsiders were "the Enemy."

I repeatedly suffered flashbacks of Watchtower incidents while Tom seemed
to be climbing a spiritual ladder that I felt hesitant to tread upon. I was searching
for a Jesus I had studied nearly all my life. I looked inside cults and churches
but I concluded that God must be strictly within one's being. He could not be
incorporated, advertised, bought, or sold. I began to see a pattern of a lifelong
struggle with prejudice. I realized that the Kingdom was not within the country
clubs and clans I had joined. To me, the Kingdom of God lay within the individual.

Tom and I came to the decision that selling our unhappy home and pursuing
our separate meanings to life—perhaps eventually coming back together—might
save our already damaged relationship. Both of us felt lost inside, desperate, and
sick. Tom sought spiritual commitment, and I wanted spiritual freedom. We had

become like two crusaders fighting on opposite sides. We forfeited our marriage to find new commitments and new convictions. We never reconciled our religious differences, yet we each claim to love God. Who, then, is the saved and who is the damned? God only knows.

*　　*　　*

Many people do not realize that even a group with an immense worldwide following can be categorized as a cult, sharing the same classification as a small sect within only one country. One may argue that the members are respectable, dedicated people. They often are, but that is not the issue. The organizations that *control* these respectable, dedicated people are the concern.

A cult will usually emerge through the mistaken impression that the only means to salvation and the only true way of life is through that particular group. Cult members tend to build up and flatter the ego of a newcomer, and only later reveal a strict, dehumanizing way of life to which the convert must adhere. The religious cult thrives on repetition of scripture or codes of regulations to indoctrinate the new arrival, replacing old thought-patterns with those designed to further the goals of a particular group. Suspicion of outsiders, even loved ones, is encouraged. These are but a few tell-tale signals to be aware of. But what can we do to prevent our own lives or those of our loved ones from being snatched up into spiritual insanity?

It is important to use the power of your own mind. Remember that your greatest power is that of choice; the freedom to take responsibility for decisions and actions. A cult will take away this God-given right. Studying the tactics of cult manipulation will prove beneficial; several books are available on this growing problem. Most people are ignorant about cult activities. By the time a person is inside an organization, it may be difficult to leave freely. If you've had an experience with a cult and have escaped, talk about it, write about it, help others become aware. Be sure that if you desire to study the Bible you do so with an open mind and use your *own* authority and intelligence to draw from it. Cults insist that they are the only authority that can accurately interpret Scripture.

Support groups for ex-cultists are helpful during the months of "rehabilitation." Returning to a world that one has been indoctrinated to think of as satanic is a frightening experience. Keep in mind that there are no quick answers, no rapid changes. Give yourself time to learn and grow. Life is an education. Proverbs 14:15 wisely states, "The simple believeth every word; but the prudent man looketh well to his going."

(Winter 1984/85)

Joseph Smith and the Book of Mormon

George D. Smith

In March 1830, Joseph Smith, a twenty-five-year-old farmer in western New York State, produced the *Book of Mormon,* claiming it to be a record of the Hebrew ancestors of the American Indian that he had translated from "reformed Egyptian" characters engraved on gold plates. He said that these plates had been buried in about 420 C.E. on a hill near his home and that an angel had told him where to find them. On January 4, 1833, "by commandment of God," Joseph Smith described this work to N. E. Seaton, a Rochester, New York, newspaper editor, as recorded in the *History of the Church.*[1]

> The *Book of Mormon* is a record of the forefathers of our western tribes of Indians, having been found through the ministrations of an holy angel, and translated into our language by the gift and power of God, after having been hid up in the earth for the last 1,400 years, containing the word of God which was delivered unto them. . . . By it we learn that our western tribes of Indians are descendants from that Joseph which was sold into Egypt, and that the land of America is a promised land unto them. . . .

Joseph Smith reportedly used a "seer stone" to translate the *Book of Mormon* from the gold plates.[2] Four years earlier, he had attempted to use such a stone to look for buried treasure. At that time, he was brought to trial as a "glass-looker" and an impostor and was convicted of disorderly conduct.[3]

In contrast to his early experience with the seer stone, the *Book of Mormon* brought Joseph Smith international renown and a faithful following that is still increasing, almost 140 years after his murder in 1844. Within nine months of the founding of the church with six friends and family members on April 6, 1830, Joseph Smith took his flock of sixty to Kirtland, Ohio (near Cleveland),

and gained 150 converts from the literalistic Disciples of Christ. In two years, the number of converts totaled about two thousand, and at the time of Joseph Smith's death, about twenty thousand.[4] The Mormon church (Church of Jesus Christ of Latter-day Saints) currently records more than five million members, with adherents on every continent.[5]

Such growth can be attributed to several events and personalities, but the *Book of Mormon* was so important that Joseph Smith termed it "the keystone of our religion."[6] Diaries and letters of early converts to the Church of Christ (as the early Mormon church was called[7]) point to the *Book of Mormon* and to the charisma of Joseph Smith as the primary sources of the conviction that they had found the "restored church."[8] In 1851, Mormon apostle and missionary Orson Pratt wrote:

> The *Book of Mormon* claims to be a divinely inspired record, written by a succession of prophets who inhabited Ancient America. . . .
> This book must be either true or false. If true, it is one of the most important messages ever sent from God to man. . . . If false, it is one of the most cunning, wicked, bold, deep-laid impositions ever palmed upon the world. . . .
> The nature of the message in the *Book of Mormon* is such, that if true, no one can possibly be saved and reject it. . . .[9]

In 1923, LDS general authority and historian B. H. Roberts warned church president Heber J. Grant that "maintenance of the truth of the *Book of Mormon* is absolutely essential to the integrity of the whole Mormon movement, for it is inconceivable that the *Book of Mormon* should be untrue in its origin and character and the Church of Jesus Christ of Latter-day Saints to be a true church."[10] This literalistic true-false dichotomy continues today as Mormon leaders assert both that "This is the only true church" and that the *Book of Mormon* is a literal history.[11]

The Book of Mormon

Written primarily in the style of the King James version of the Bible, the *Book of Mormon* relates the history of two emigrant peoples who leave the Middle East and sail to the New World: the "Jaredites" from the Tower of Babel, and later, the "Nephites" and the "Lamanites" from Jerusalem.[12] The Jaredites came first, after the "Lord confounded the language of the people" when they displeased Him by building the Tower of Babel. The language of Jared's family was not confounded because the brother of Jared was "a man highly favored of the Lord." Instead, the Lord taught the Jaredites how to make boats that were "tight like unto a dish" and led them across the ocean "into a land which is choice above all the other lands of the earth." The Jaredites became numerous and spread out over "all the face of the land." Joseph Smith later wrote that they "covered the

whole continent from sea to sea, with towns and cities."[13] After many generations, they became proud and sinful. According to the *Book of Mormon,* the
Jaredites destroyed one another completely long before the second wave of Hebrew
migration to the Americas around 600 B.C.E.

The *Book of Mormon's* Nephites and Lamanites were descendants of Lehi,
a prophet who was warned by the Lord to flee Jerusalem before it was taken
by Babylon (in 587 B.C.E.). Like the earlier Jaredites, the Nephites and Lamanites
sail to the New World and "cover the whole face of the land, both on the northward
and on the southward, from the sea west to the sea east."[14] However, the Lamanites
"dwindle in unbelief" and "God did cause a skin of blackness to come upon them."
Because of this curse they became "dark and loathsome. . . . an idle people, full
of mischief and subtlety,"[15] and eventually exterminated the light-skinned Nephites,
who were mostly hard-working, pious, and peaceful.

About 421 C.E., one of the last Nephite survivors, Moroni, son of Mormon,
abridger of the plates, "seals up the records of his people." (The Nephites were
inveterate record-keepers, inscribing their important records on gold plates.)

For hundreds of years, the plates lay hidden in the hill where Moroni had
buried them. In 1823, Moroni, by that time an angel, appeared to Joseph Smith
and told him about the plates. In 1827, after yearly conversations with Moroni,
Joseph Smith received the plates and began the work of translation.

The most remarkable event in the *Book of Mormon* is Christ's visit to America
in 34 C.E.. After his resurrection and ascension into heaven, Jesus appears to
the Nephites and repeats several of the miracles depicted in the New Testament.
He also heals the sick, retells (with variations) the Sermon on the Mount, picks
twelve apostles—Nephi, Timothy, Jonas, Mathoni, Mathonihah, Kumen, Ku-
menonhi, Jeremiah, Shemnon, Jonas, Zedekiah, and Isaiah (3 Nephi 19:4)—
administers a sacrament of bread and wine, and recites a version of the "Lord's
Prayer" (3 Nephi 11–28).

As a "new witness" for Christ, the *Book of Mormon* united the New World
with the Old. Ever since the Spanish discovered the Americas in the fifteenth
century, the authority of the Bible had been challenged for making no mention
of the American Indian—or of America. This omission seemed to nullify the
supposedly universal salvation of Christianity as well as the reliability of the creation
accounts in Genesis.[16] The *Book of Mormon* included the American Indian within
the gospel of Christ, and its accounts of Hebrew migrations to the New World
traced Indian lineage back to the creation narratives. Joseph Smith had joined
the battle against the Deists and other skeptics who questioned the validity of
the Bible.

Revivalism and Egyptian Translations

The reasons for acceptance of the *Book of Mormon* may be as many as the number
of converts. However, it is clear that Joseph Smith's story appealed especially to

frontier people who wanted clear and definite answers to their religious questions. The controversies among Protestant groups made people profoundly uneasy. Unitarians rejected the trinitarian view of a three-person God. Deists rejected the biblical portrayal of an arbitrary, vindictive, and cruel God and advocated the study of nature as true theology. To counter the movement of "Rationalism," the churches launched the Second Great Awakening, a wave of revival meetings in search of spiritual conversions. There were claims of divine intervention and warnings of an imminent end to the world. William Miller announced to his Seventh-Day Adventists that Jesus would visit the earth in March 1843 and begin the millennium.[17] In the *History of the Church,* Joseph Smith described the time immediately preceding his first vision as a period of "great confusion and bad feeling" with "no small stir and division amongst the people, some crying 'lo, here!' and others, 'lo, there!' " So intense and prolonged were the religious excitement and contention in western New York (where Joseph Smith lived) at this time that it was called the "burned-over district."[18]

The first part of the nineteenth century was dominated by romanticism, reflected in a high regard for originality and emotional sincerity. Strong feeling was considered a surer guide to truth than reason. Joseph Smith's personal testimony to the truth of his new church swayed many people. To this testimony, the *Book of Mormon* added evidence that the "only true church" of Christ had been restored. His followers were convinced that Joseph Smith must have been directed by God. Their prophet was as unschooled as they were. How could he possibly have created the *Book of Mormon* on his own?

Many nineteenth-century theologians, of course, scoffed at the idea that Christ had visited the Americas, but the more credulous welcomed the news. A strong spirit of nationalism, along with pride in America and its future, was abroad in the land. The idea of an American religion was welcomed by many patriotic citizens.

People were accustomed to looking to the Bible for explanations of any mystery. Discoveries in philology, geology, and anthropology would have a great impact on religion, but at this time people felt there could be no real conflict between science and religion. Because religion was considered "true," scientific discoveries must naturally support biblical explanations. The "Hebrew tribes" explanation of Indian origins supported the Bible and at this time seemed reasonable.

Egyptian theories of Indian origins accompanied Hebrew theories. The discovery of huge burial mounds made by unknown Indian groups who had long since disappeared made people wonder if the American Indian could be related to the ancient pyramid-builders of Egypt (who had, of course, been mentioned several times in the Bible). Stories of the Mayan pyramids in Central America enhanced speculation about the ancient civilization of mound-builders. These mounds dotted the countryside of Ohio and western New York and eight such mounds were located within twelve miles of the Smith farm in Palmyra.[19]

Nineteenth-century interest in the mysterious Egyptian language followed Napoleon's invasion of Egypt in 1799. Egyptian artifacts circulated through the museums of Europe and America, and the puzzling hieroglyphics enchanted both professional linguists and amateurs alike.[20] Indian picture writing was often compared to Egyptian hieroglyphics.[21]

The "Reformed Egyptian" inscriptions upon the *Book of Mormon* plates were carefully concealed. Witnessed "in a vision" and authenticated only by Joseph Smith's close associates, the gold plates were taken away "by an angel" and were never available for scholarly examination.

However, in 1828, Martin Harris, an associate of Joseph Smith, took a facsimile of the *Book of Mormon* inscriptions, prepared by the prophet, to Professor Charles Anthon of Columbia University. In the *History of the Church,* Joseph Smith reported that Anthon said that the characters were "true" Egyptian, Chaldaic, Assyriac, and Arabic and that the translations presented were "correct, more so than any he had before seen translated from the Egyptian." Professor Anthon, on the other hand, declared in a letter of February 17, 1834: "The whole story about having pronounced the Mormonite inscription to be 'reformed Egyptian hieroglyphics' is perfectly false." He described the paper brought by Martin Harris as consisting of "all kinds of crooked characters disposed in columns, and had evidently been prepared by some person who had before him at the time a book containing various alphabets. Greek and Hebrew letters, crosses and flourishes, Roman perpendicular columns, and the whole ended in a rude delineation of a circle divided into various compartments, decked with various strange marks, and evidently copied in such a way as not to betray the source whence it was derived."[22]

Five years after the *Book of Mormon* was published, the Mormon prophet claimed to have made another translation from Egyptian. In 1835, at Kirtland, Ohio, Joseph Smith paid a collector $6,000 for four mummies. From the papyrus scrolls found with the mummies, he translated the "Book of Abraham," including an account of the Creation attributed to the Old Testament patriarch. Subsequently, scholars have identified these papyri as funerary scrolls from the Egyptian Book of Breathings, commonly buried with the dead.[23]

On April 23, 1843, a group of men recovered six bell-shaped brass plates covered with "hieroglyphics" from an old earth-mound outside of Kinderhook, Illinois, near Nauvoo. The "Kinderhook plates" were brought to Joseph Smith, who pronounced them to be genuine and began to translate them. His diary for May 1, 1843, reads: "I have translated a portion of them and find that they contain the history of the person with whom they were found. He was a descendant of Ham through the loins of Pharaoh, King of Egypt, and that he received his kingdom from the Ruler of heaven and earth" (*History of the Church,* vol. 5, p. 372). Photographs of the six plates were included in the *History of the Church* (vol. 5, pp. 374–376).

It was later discovered that the Kinderhook plates were fabricated by Joseph Smith's enemies to entrap him into pretending to translate a writing that was not genuine. On June 30, 1879, Wilbur Fugate, one of the nine men who recovered the plates, confessed in a letter that they were a "humbug" cut out of copper, etched with acid, rusted with nitric oxide, old iron, and lead, and buried under a flat rock eight feet deep in a mound (Wilbur Fugate to James T. Cobb, June 30, 1879, printed in the *Improvement Era,* Sept. 1962, p. 660).

Sophisticated tests have proved that Kinderhook plate No. 5 (recovered from the Chicago Historical Society) is a brass alloy "typical of the mid-nineteenth century" and was etched with acid. Mormon scholar Stanley P. Kimball described the results of the "sophisticated analytical" tests performed by a Northwestern University materials engineer in 1980 and concluded, "The time has come to admit that the Kinderhook plate incident of 1843 was a light-hearted, heavy-handed, frontier-style prank, or 'joke' as the perpetrators themselves called it" (*Mormon History Association Newsletter,* June 1981; tests reported in *The Ensign,* August 1981).

The stories of the *Book of Mormon* gold plates, the "Book of Abraham" papyrus, and the Kinderhook plates form a pattern of claiming to translate divine messages from inscriptions in the unknown Egyptian language. In spite of all the evidence to the contrary, faithful Mormons still accept Joseph Smith's "translations" from the Egyptian as literally "true."[24]

Sources of the Book of Mormon

Joseph Smith's family was easily convinced of his supernatural calling. Perhaps they were only hysterical responses to the revivalistic fervor of the times, but many people in the "burned-over" area had reported seeing visions and hearing voices. Members of the Smith family were no exception. In her *Biographical Sketches of Joseph Smith, the Prophet . . .,* Joseph Smith's mother, Lucy Smith, relates her own visions, and those of her father and her sister Louisa. She describes her brother Jason as a professional faith-healer. Joseph Smith's father apparently also had visions, one of which seems to anticipate his son's story of finding a box of gold plates with the help of an "angel." Lucy Smith describes her husband's "first vision" wherein he was walking with "an attendant spirit" who told him he would discover "on a certain log a box, the contents of which, if you eat thereof, will make you wise, and give you wisdom and understanding." He dropped the box, however, when he came across "all manner of beasts, horned cattle, and roaring animals."[25]

A visitor to the Smith family around 1830 later wrote: "Joseph Smith, Senior, we soon learned, from his own lips, was a firm believer in witchcraft and other supernatural things; and had brought up his family in the same belief."[26] In that same interview, Joseph Smith, Senior, was said to look for buried money using a divining rod, a precursor to his son's digging for hidden treasures using a "seer stone" in a hat. Mormon historian B. H. Roberts acknowledged that some of Joseph Smith's ancestors "believed in fortune telling, in warlocks and witches."[27]

Joseph Smith's occult practices were examined in 1974 by LDS Institute of Religion director, Reed C. Durham. Before the Mormon History Association,

Dr. Durham described the "Jupiter Talisman" that Joseph Smith was wearing at the time of his death. An occult object related to astrology and magic, the Jupiter Talisman contained cabalistic Hebrew letters with numerical equivalents.[28]

Since both Joseph Smith and his brother Hyrum were Masons (Joseph, in 1842, and Hyrum, in about 1827), some Mormon writers have suggested a possible relationship between the story of the *Book of Mormon* and the Masonic legend of the gold plate of Enoch.

As Masonry (and anti-Masonic agitation) spread throughout the early nineteenth century, hard-working, often poverty-stricken frontier people were fascinated by the Masonic legend of a buried treasure, the treasure of Enoch, which was said to have been hidden beneath a sacred hill. A University of Utah English professor, Jack Adamson, wrote, ". . . almost every element of the legend seems to have an analogue of some kind in the history of Joseph Smith or in the scripture which he produced." Considering the possible relationship between Masonic legends and Jewish cabalistic lore, there are many cabalistic undertones in both the *Book of Mormon* and in Joseph Smith's "revelations" to the church (recorded in the *Doctrine and Covenants*).[29]

Some of the *Book of Mormon* resembles Joseph Smith's own personal experiences. Nephi, the nominal author of the first books, begins, "I, Nephi, having been born of goodly parents," just as Joseph Smith begins his autobiography: "I was born in the town of Charon . . . of goodly parents."[30] Like Joseph Smith, Nephi has five brothers, two of them older; two brothers in each family share the same names, Joseph and Samuel. Nephi's unkind older brother, Lemuel, has the same name as a neighbor of the Smiths, Lemuel Durphee, who signed an affidavit in 1833 charging Joseph Smith with immoral character.[31] Nephi even includes a prophecy of Joseph Smith's own coming, calling him "a choice seer" and predicting that his name would be called Joseph, "after the name of his father."[32]

Nephi's father, Lehi, relates a vision that closely resembles a dream that Joseph Smith's father was said to have had in 1811, nineteen years before the *Book of Mormon* was published. His dream was recorded by his wife, Lucy Smith, in her *Biographical Sketches*.[33]

In addition to these specific autobiographical elements in the *Book of Mormon,* Joseph Smith's mother revealed that young Joseph enjoyed telling elaborate stories about ancient Indian civilizations:

> During our evening conversations, Joseph would occasionally give us the most amusing recitals that could be imagined. He would describe the ancient inhabitants of this continent, their dress, mode of traveling, and the animals upon which they rode; their cities, their buildings, with every particular; their mode of warfare; and also their religious worship. This he would do with as much ease, seemingly, as if he had spent his whole life with them.[34]

Stories of the mysterious Indian burial mounds and speculations about the origin of ancient civilizations appeared in local newspapers before the *Book of Mormon* appeared. On January 21, 1818, the *Palmyra Register* referred to the mound-builders as a lost race killed in battle that "had made much greater advances in the arts and civilized life" than any contemporary Indian races. On February 19, 1823, *Palmyra Herald* asserted that the nature of the artifacts "clearly prove them to be the work of some other people," concluding that "what wonderful catastrophe destroyed the first inhabitants is beyond the researches of the best scholar and greatest antiquarian." In the May 26, 1819, *Palmyra Register,* the demise of civilized ancestors is explained: "This country was once inhabited by a race of people, at least, partially civilized, and . . . this race had been exterminated by the forefathers of the present and late tribes of Indians in this country."

The local press also suggested that the undeciphered Egyptian language might be the same as that used on ancient American documents that had been recently discovered. On June 1, 1827, the *Wayne Sentinel* presented an account of a Mexican (Mayan) manuscript written in hieroglyphics that was considered proof that early inhabitants of Mexico and Egypt "had intercourse with each other, and . . . had the same system of mythology." *A View of the Hebrews,* by Ethan Smith (no relation to Joseph), first published about forty miles from Joseph Smith's birthplace in 1823, seven years before the *Book of Mormon,* described some Indian inscriptions as "hieroglyphic records and paintings."[35]

The Hebrew origin of the American Indian had been postulated by writers since the colonial period. Well-known preachers, such as William Penn, Roger Williams, Cotton Mather, and Jonathan Edwards, had all considered the American Indian to be a remnant of the Lost Ten Tribes of Israel. The historian Hubert Howe Bancroft acknowledged that "the theory that the Americans are of Jewish origin has been discussed more minutely and at greater length than any other." Josiah Priest advocated that view in 1825 and later referred to forty-six authors who espoused similar views, adding that "the opinion that the American Indians are descendants of the Lost Ten Tribes is now a popular one and generally believed."[36]

In *A View of the Hebrews,* Ethan Smith quotes the German explorer Baron von Humboldt, who held that: "Israel brought into this new continent a considerable degree of civilization; and the better part of them long laboured to maintain it. But others fell into the hunting and consequent savage state; whose barbarous hordes invaded their more civilized brethren, and eventually annihilated most of them" (p. 184). The story of the Nephites and Lamanites seems to follow this script.

The similarities between the *Book of Mormon* and *A View of the Hebrews* are pervasive. In the opening chapters, both authors wrote of the destruction of Jerusalem and the scattering of Israel, then predict the gathering of Israel in its own land. Isaiah is quoted extensively by both authors in support of this prediction. The *Book of Mromon* incorporates eighteen chapters of Isaiah nearly verbatim.

Whereas Ethan Smith traces the American Indians to "ten tribes of Israel" (p. 85), the *Book of Mormon* describes their Nephite ancestors as coming from maimly two tribes, Ephraim and Manasseh, along with some "Mulekites" from the tribe of Judah. The *Book of Mormon* Jaredites are not unlike Ethan Smith's "lost tribes." The tribes in both stories journeyed northward into a valley and crossed the sea to an uninhabited land—"where there never had man been" (*Book of Mormon,* Ether 2:5) vs. "where man never dwelt" (*A View of the Hebrews,* p. 75).

Both books told of inspired prophets among the ancient Americans, who were a highly civilized people. In each story, savage tribes destroyed their civilized brethren in a final great battle. Here, the *Book of Mormon* seems to follow the error of prevalent folklore, by presuming, like Ethan Smith, the use of iron and steel weapons in a stone age culture.[37] The savage group had been "judged" (*A View of the Hebrews*) or "cursed" (*Book of Mormon* Lamanites) by God and had become idle hunters in the wilderness.

In both accounts, sacred records, handed down from generation to generation, were buried in a hill and then found years later. Ethan Smith related an Indian tradition "that the book which the white people have was once theirs," that "having lost the knowledge of reading it . . . they buried it with an Indian Chief." He tells of some Hebrew parchments "dug up . . . on Indian Hill (near Pittsfield, Massachusetts) . . . probably from an Indian grave" and speculates that this could have been once possessed by a "leading character in Israel" and could have been buried with him when he died.[38] Similar ideas are found in the Nephite figure Mormon's description of burying sacred "records which had been handed down by our father," burying them up "in the Hill Cumorah" (Mormon 6:6).

Both authors identify the American Indians as the "stick of Joseph or Ephraim" (from the northern Ten Tribes of Israel) that is expected to be reunited with the "stick of Judah" (the Jews of the southern kingdom of Judah). See Ezek. 37:16–17.) In 1830, advertising circulars portrayed the *Book of Mormon* as "the stick of Joseph taken from the hand of Ephraim."[39]

Both texts advocated the mission of the American nation in the last days to gather these Indian remnants of the house of Israel and convert them to Christianity, thus fulfilling prophecy and bringing about the millennium.[40]

After examining the numerous similarities between these two nineteenth-century works, Mormon historian and General Authority Brigham H. Roberts wrote:

> Did Ethan Smith's *View of the Hebrews* furnish structural material for Joseph Smith's *Book of Mormon?* It has been pointed out in these pages that there are many things in the former book that might well have suggested many major things in the other. Not a few things merely, one or two, or a half dozen, but many; and it is this fact of many things of similarity and the cumulative forces of them, that makes them so serious a menace to Joseph Smith's story of the *Book of Mormon's* origin.[41]

Biblical Sources for the Book of Mormon

In ways that are problematic, the text of the *Book of Mormon* incorporates numerous passages from the King James version of the Bible. Of the approximately 27,000 words of text taken from the Bible, a significant amount consists of New Testament passages used in stories dated earlier than Jesus.[42] As a result, the *Book of Mormon* presents New Testament language and ideas in an Old Testament time-frame. The biblical source of many *Book of Mormon* passages is confirmed by the inclusion of the italicized English words interpolated in the King James translation from Hebrew to make the Bible read more smoothly.

The *Book of Mormon* also uses Old Testament passages of a time represented as earlier than that of the Hebrew prophets. Here, Nephi, who is supposed to have kept his records 550 years before Christ, apparently quotes Malachi, who lived nearly 150 years later.

> For, behold, the day cometh that shall burn as an oven; and all the proud, yea, and all that do wickedly, shall be stubble; and the day cometh that shall burn them up. [Malachi 4:1]

> . . . shall the Son of righteousness arise with healings in his wings. [Malachi 4:2]

Similar passages from Nephi:

> For behold, said the prophet. . . . the day soon cometh that all the proud and they who do wickedly shall be as stubble; and the day cometh that they must be burned. [1 Nephi 22:15]

> Wherefore, all those who are proud, and that do wickedly, the day that cometh shall burn them up, . . . for they shall be as stubble. [2 Nephi 26:4]

> He shall rise from the dead with healing in his wings. [2 Nephi 25:13]

> But the Son of righteousness shall appear unto them; and he shall heal them. [2 Nephi 26:9]

There are two difficulties with representing Nephi as quoting the later writings of Malachi. First, Malachi's words are quoted prematurely. Second, since Nephi is described as leaving Jerusalem for the New World at about 600 B.C.E., he would not have had access to any Old Testament writings later than that, even if they were quoted in a proper time-frame.

Like Malachi's, some of the Old Testament writings of Isaiah were quoted in the context of a time earlier than that in which they were actually written. Nephi is made to repeat parts of Isaiah written after the Babylonian captivity of Jerusalem in 587 B.C.E., and long after Nephi had allegedly sailed for America.[43]

The Book of Mormon Today

Acceptance of the *Book of Mormon* as the literal history of American Indian progenitors is still a main tenet of the Mormon faith. Twice a year at nationally televised "General Conferences" Mormon General Authorities testify that an angel delivered to Joseph Smith for translation the history of the Hebrew ancestors of the American Indian, a people whom Jesus visited after his resurrection. This message is reinforced in weekly Sunday school lessons, "correlated" to reaffirm these "truths" and to exclude any doubtful material. Seminary and Institute of Religion classes present LDS high school and college students with "faithful history"—putting faith first and using "history" that is edited to strengthen testimonies in the literal truth of Mormon origins, especially in the *Book of Mormon*.[44]

Nevertheless, some Mormons have characterized the *Book of Mormon*, not as literal history, but as inspired allegory—a story to express the inspired communication received by Joseph Smith. Others view it as uninspired allegory.

The Mormon belief-system has survived many assaults from science and history.[45] When discovery of the Bering Strait migrations seemed to invalidate the Indian origin premise of the *Book of Mormon*, some Mormon scholars adopted a "limited region" theory of Nephite occupation of the New World; church authorities, however, preferred Joseph Smith's initial revelation on the subject.[46] In a similar manner, the faith has survived the Anthon statement that Joseph Smith's facsimile of *Book of Mormon* characters was meaningless, and the discrediting of Joseph Smith's "Book of Abraham" translations from papyrus scrolls.

The membership of the Mormon church is taught not to "question the mysteries": "When the Prophet speaks, the thinking has been done." Feeling is placed over evidence, spirit over science, and faith over history. Feeling, spirit, and faith reflect instruction from church leaders, confirmed by personal prayer and study. The message is obedience.[47]

When Mormon General Authority and historian B. H. Roberts addressed the church leadership on "Book of Mormon Problems," they responded with disinterested silence. In a January 9, 1922, letter to church president Heber J. Grant, Roberts complained, "There was so much said that was utterly irrelevant, and so little said, if anything at all, that was helpful in the matters at issue that I came away from the conference quite disappointed . . . I cannot be other than painfully conscious of the fact that our means of defense should we be vigorously attacked along the lines of Mr. Couch's questions [on problems of archaeology, language, and Indian origins], are very inadequate."[48]

Those who make their questions public risk being excommunicated, as were historian and author Fawn Brodie (niece of prophet David O. McKay), and, by their own request, the now anti-Mormon writers Jerald and Sandra Tanner (great-granddaughter of Brigham Young). Mormon scholars who express their questions in a context of faith are sometimes subjected to pressure from church leaders. The *Salt Lake Tribune* recently reported such an "inquisition" of fourteen authors of articles of inquiry about subjects dealing with Mormon origins and history.[49]

Only a small number of LDS students confront the overwhelming evidence of contemporary source material used by Joseph Smith when he translated the *Book of Mormon*. Still, many Mormons continue to look for answers to questions that challenge their faith.

In a letter to church president Heber J. Grant et al. dated December 29, 1921, church historian B. H. Roberts wrote: "I am thoroughly convinced of the necessity of all the brethren herein addressed becoming thoroughly familiar with these Book of Mormon problems, and finding the answer for them, as it is a matter that will concern the faith of the Youth of the Church now as also in the future. . . ."[50]

Notes

1. *History of the Church of Jesus Christ of Latter-Day Saints,* 7 vols., B. H. Roberts, ed. (Salt Lake City: Deseret, 1974), vol. 1, pp. 315, 326, hereafter cited as *History of the Church.*

2. When digging in a well in 1822, Joseph Smith found "a chocolate-colored, somewhat egg-shaped stone," which he used as a "seer-stone," (B. H. Roberts, *Comprehensive History of the Church of Jesus Christ of Latter-Day Saints,* 6 vols. (Salt Lake City: Deseret, 1930), vol. 1, p. 129. He reportedly used the "Urim and Thummin" (two stones in a breastplate found with the gold plates) to translate the first 116 pages, which were then lost. According to his wife, he used the seer stone to translate what became published as the *Book of Mormon.* She wrote: "Now the first that my husband translated, was translated by use of the Urim and Thummin, and that was the part that Martin Harris [Joseph's scribe] lost, after that he used a small stone, not exactly black, but was rather a dark color" (Emma Smith Bidamon to a Mrs. Pilgrim, March 27, 1876, held by the Reorganized Church of Jesus Christ of Latter-Day Saints Library, Independence, Missouri, referred to in Fawn Brodie, *No Man Knows My History,* 2nd ed. [New York: Knopf, 1971], p. 43).

David Whitmer, a scribe of Joseph Smith and one of three witnesses to the *Book of Mormon,* further describes the "translation" process: "I will now give you a description of the manner in which the *Book of Mormon* was translated. Joseph Smith would put the seer stone into a hat, and put his face in the hat, drawing it closely around to exclude the light, and in the darkness the spiritual light would shine. A piece of something resembling parchment would appear, and on that appeared the writing. One character at a time would appear, and under it was the interpretation in English. Brother Joseph would read off the English to Oliver Cowdery, who was his principal scribe, and when it was written down and repeated by Brother Joseph to see if it was correct, then it would disappear, and another character with the interpretation would appear. Thus the *Book of Mormon* was translated by the gift and power of God, and not by any power of man" (David Whitmer, *An Address to All Believers in Christ* [Richmond, Mo., 1887], p. 13, quoted in Richard Van Wagoner and Steven Walker, "Joseph Smith: 'The Gift of Seeing,' " in

Dialogue: A Journal of Mormon Thought 15, no. 2 [Summer 1982], pp. 48–68.

Joseph Smith's wife, Emma, explained that during the translation process the plates were not used but lay close by, wrapped in a tablecloth (interview by her son, Joseph Smith III, in *Saints' Herald,* Oct. 1, 1879, vol. 26, no. 19, pp. 289–90, cited by James E. Lancaster in "The Method of Translation of the Book of Mormon," *John Whitmer Historical Association Journal* (Lamont, Iowa) 3 (1983), p. 52.

3. In October 1825, Josiah Stowell, an established farmer of South Bainbridge, New York, hired Joseph Smith for fourteen dollars a month to discern by means of a seer stone the location of a lost silver mine in the Susquehanna Valley, Pennsylvania. Unsuccessful in his efforts, Joseph Smith was tried for disorderly conduct on March 20, 1826, in Bainbridge, New York, and "by most accounts was convicted" (Donna Hill, *Joseph Smith: The First Mormon* [Garden City, N.Y.: Doubleday, 1977], pp. 61–66.

In 1971, among Chenango County, New York, court documents, the Reverend Wesley P. Walters discovered a bill of court costs for 1826 which, like the published court record, mentioned the trial of "Joseph Smith the Glass Looker" on the same date as recorded in the published account of the trial, and stated the same $2.68 trial fee (Jerald and Sandra Tanner, *The Changing World of Mormonism,* 2nd ed. [Chicago: Moody, 1982), pp. 67–75). Among those who have described Joseph Smith's "money-digging" using a seer stone in a hat were his associates Oliver Cowdery (in *Messenger and Advocate,* October 1835, p. 207) and Martin Harris (in a July 1875 interview with Ole A. Jensen, recorded by Grant Ivins, "Notes on the 1826 Trial of Joseph Smith," LDS Church Archives, cited in Donna Hill, op. cit., p. 66); Brigham Young (*Journal of Discourses,* 26 vols. [Liverpool, 1854–1886], vol. 19 [1878], p. 37); and his mother, Lucy Mack Smith (in *Biographical Sketches of Joseph Smith the Prophet, and His Progenitors for Many Generations* [Liverpool: Published for Orson Pratt by S. W. Richards, 1853], pp. 91–92).

The 1826 trial was recorded in the *Evangelical Magazine and Gospel Advocate* by A. W. Benton, April 9, 1831, p. 120; *Frazer's Magazine, New Series,* vol. 3 (London: Longmans, Green), Feb. 1873, pp. 229–30; Daniel S. Tuttle, "Mormonism," *New Schaff-Herzog Encyclopedia of Religious Knowledge* (New York, 1883), vol. 12, p. 1576.

Joseph Smith's father-in-law, Isaac Hale, at whose Harmony, Pennsylvania, home Joseph stayed when on the digging expedition, equated the process by which his future son-in-law gazed into a hat to find treasure with that by which he translated the *Book of Mormon:* "The manner in which he [Joseph Smith] pretended to read and interpret, was the same as when he looked for money-diggers, with a stone in his hat, and his hat over his face, while the Book of Plates were at the same time hid in the woods" (*Susquehanna Register,* May 1, 1834, cited in Eber D. Howe, *Mormonism Unveiled* [Plainsville, Ohio: Eber D. Howe, 1834], p. 77, quoted in Van Wagoner and Walker, op. cit., p. 52). See also James Lancaster, "The Method of Translation of the Book of Mormon," *John Whitmer Association Journal* 3 (1983), pp. 55–56.

4. Brodie, op. cit., pp. 94–99, 120, 128, 209–10, 362–63.

5. The Mormon church is estimated to have 5.2 million members) 3.5 million in the United States (*Los Angeles Times,* June 26, 1983, p. 1)—and assets conservatively estimated at $2 billion, with an annual income of $1.4 billion, which comes from "tithing" as well as from working assets (*Denver Post,* November 27, 1982, p. 1).

Besides the Mormon church, approximately fifty churches have claimed to represent Joseph Smith's "Restored Gospel" after he died. The second largest church claiming this authority is the Reorganized Church of Jesus Christ of Latter-Day Saints (RLDS, as opposed to LDS), with about 250,000 members. The RLDS church, led by male descendants of Joseph Smith, beginning with his son, Joseph Smith III, is headquartered in Independence, Missouri. (See Stephen L. Shields, *Divergent Paths of the Restoration, A History of the Latter-Day Saints Movement,* 3rd ed. [Bountiful, Utah: Restoration Research, 1982].)

6. Joseph Smith's journal, Nov. 28, 1841, LDS Church Archives, Salt Lake City. Joseph Smith also wrote: "Take away the Book of Mormon and the revelations, and where is our religion? We have none" (Joseph Smith, Ed., *Teachings of the Prophet Joseph Smith* (Salt Lake City: Deseret, 1972), p. 71.

7. On April 6, 1830, six men, Joseph, Hyrum, and Samuel Smith, Oliver Cowdery, and Peter and David Whitmer officially organized the "Church of Christ," which name was indicated by revelation (*Doctrine and Covenants* [*D & C*], Sec. 21). On May 3, 1834, a church conference at Kirtland resolved to change the name to "The Church of the Latter-day Saints." On April 23, 1838, in Far West, Missouri, the name was changed by revelation to "The Church of Jesus Christ of Latter-day Saints" (*D&C,* Sec. 115; see James B. Allen and Glen M. Leonard, *The Story of the Latter-day Saints* [Salt Lake City: Deseret, 1976], p. 47).

8. Mormon historian Donna Hill observed that most of the early converts to Mormonism "had a history of social mobility, economic insecurity, dissatisfaction with contending sects and hope for a millennium." Referring to Oliver Cowdery, Brigham Young, Wilford Woodruff, and others, as examples, she concluded: "To the converts, Joseph's church was not only based upon the *Book of Mormon,* but the book was its reason for having come into existence"(Hill, op. cit., pp. 102, 105).

9. Orson Pratt, "Divine Authenticity of the Book of Mormon," in *Orson Pratt's Works* (Liverpool: Pratt, 1851), p. 1.

10. Cover letter with Roberts's published paper, "A Book of Mormon Study," to church president Heber J. Grant et al., March 15, 1923, in University of Utah Special Collections, Salt Lake City, quoted in George D. Smith, "Defending the Keystone: Book of Mormon Difficulties," *Sunstone* (Salt Lake City), 4, no. 3 (May–June, 1981), p. 45.

11. Joseph Smith claimed that God the Father and his son Jesus Christ visited him in 1820 and told him to join none of the churches, "for they were all wrong" (*Pearl of Great Price,* Joseph Smith 2:18). He then proceeded to restore the "only true church." The reality of Joseph Smith's claim of the "true church" and revealed scriptures was asserted recently in the official *Church News:* "The Angel Moroni did in reality come as a messenger from Almighty God to the boy Joseph Smith. . . . It was an actual visit, not a dream, not a séance of any kind. It was the visitation of one physical being (a resurrected personage) to another physical being, here on this physical earth. And he left a physical reminder of his coming. . . . He revealed the gold plate record of the Book of Mormon . . .that is Moroni's evidence, that is the memento he left of his visit" (*Deseret News,* Church News Section, September 18, 1983, p. 16).

12. Lehi and Ishmael, two descendants of the Hebrew tribes of Manasseh and Ephraim, remained in the Southern Kingdom of Judah, and thereby escaped captivity and dispersal of the "Ten Tribes" by the Assyrians during their invasion of the Northern Kingdom of Israel in 722 B.C.E. These two tribal remnants, plus a small group led by a man named Mulek (from the tribe of Judah) are represented as leaving Jerusalem before the Babylonian captivity of the Southern Kingdom of Judah in 587 B.C.E. These people, collectively referred to in the *Book of Mormon* as Nephites and Lamanites (indicated as ancestors of the American Indian) kept a record that is represented as the "stick" of Joseph or Ephraim,

complementing the "stick" of Judah, the Bible.

13. *Book of Mormon*, Ether 1:33, 34, 42; 2:17; 7:11; *Times and Seasons* 3, no. 22 (Sept. 15, 1842), p. 922.

14. *Book of Mormon*, Helaman 11:20.

15. The curse of the Lamanites with a "skin of blackness" is related in the *Book of Mormon*, 1 Nephi 12:23; 2 Nephi 5:21-24; Jacob 3:5, 9; Alma 3:6-10. Just as the Lamanites once "were white, and exceeding fair and delightsome" (2 Nephi 5:21), for those who were reconverted, "their curse was taken from them, and their skin became white like unto the Nephites" (3 Nephi 2:15).

This association of black skin with God's curse is found in other Mormon scriptures. The "Book of Moses," "as revealed to Joseph Smith the Prophet, in June, 1830," and now published as part of the Mormon scripture *The Pearl of Great Price*, states that "the seed of Cain were black" (Moses 7:22), and when the Lord cursed the land of Canaan, "a blackness came upon all the children of Canaan, that they were despised among all people" (Moses 7:8). In the "Book of Abraham," "translated from the [Egyptian] Papyrus, by Joseph Smith," 1835, also found today in *The Pearl of Great Price*, the Pharaoh was reported to partake of Canaanite blood through Ham, and therefore was cursed "as pertaining to the Priesthood" (Abraham 1:21-27).

Brigham Young explained the practice of withholding the Mormon priesthood from black members." . . . the curse remained upon them because Cain cut off the lives of Abel . . . the Lord had cursed Cain's seed with blackness and prohibited them the priesthood" (manuscript *History of the Church*, Feb. 13, 1849).

On June 9, 1978, Mormon church president Spencer W. Kimball issued a revelation on behalf of the church leaders stating that every worthy male member of the church may now hold the priesthood, effectively reversing the black exclusion doctrine. The church offered no explanation, either for the original doctrine or for the reversal.

16. When the American Indians were discovered, some theologians suggested a separate creation, possibly predating Adam and Eve. Religious skeptics found the omission of the Indians from the Bible narratives a reason to dismiss the Bible as a human fabrication based upon Hebrew legends. An unpublished paper, "An Environmental Approach to the Book of Mormon," by Dan Vogel, examines three centuries of writings, prior to Joseph Smith's *Book of Mormon*, that address these issues.

In 1655, Paul Cabrera recorded a "pre-Adamite" theory voiced shortly after the Spanish conquest: "About the middle of the last century, Isaac Peyrere erected his system of the Preadamites . . . that all the human race are not the descendants of Adam and Eve, and consequently denies original sin and the principles of our holy catholic religion; producing the populations of America as the chief support of this hypothesis, and the ignorance that exists as to the source of its origin" (*A Theological System Upon the Presupposition That Men Were Before Adam* [London, 1655]; quoted in Vogel, p. 93).

In his *American Universal Geography* (2 vol. [Boston, 1793], vol. 1, p. 75) Jedediah Morse argued against multiple creations and that the first peoples of America came from the descendants of Noah.

Vogel reports that Morse's *Geography* went through many editions, was advertised in the *Wayne Sentinel*, Oct. 22, 1823, and was listed in the Manchester, N.Y., rental library (Accession #42). This work would have been available to Joseph Smith.

17. Brodie, op. cit., p. 15.

18. *History of the Church*, vol. 1, pp. 2-3; Whitney R. Cross, *The Burned-Over District:*

The Social and Intellectual History of Enthusiastic Religion in Western New York 1800–1850 (Ithaca, N.Y.: Cornell University Press, 1950).

19. In *A View of the Hebrews* (1825), Ethan Smith describes Indian burial mounds at Marietta, Circleville, Newark, and Chillicothe, Ohio (pp. 188–198), and relates the contemporary speculation as to their origin from Hebrew descendants. (*View* was published in 1823 by Smith & Shute, Poultney, Vermont, the second edition in 1825. In 1964, Utah Lighthouse Ministry [then Modern Microfilm], Salt Lake City, photomechanically reproduced the second edition. In 1977, Arno Press, New York, a subsidiary of the *New York Times*, reprinted the 1823 edition.) Fawn Brodie, op. cit., p. 19, identifies the location of mounds near the Smith farm.

20. See Richard G. Carrott, *The Egyptian Revival: Its Sources, Monuments, and Meaning, 1805–1858* (Berkeley: University of California Press, 1978), pp. 1, 2, 47–50. Carrott wrote: "References to Egypt were common, and even prior to the high point during the 1830's and 1840's of Egyptian Revival architecture, numerous travel books about Egypt had been published . . . But not only could Egypt be read about, it could be seen in the nascent museums of the country . . . In 1835, when the Egyptian Revival was already at flood tide, Joseph Smith, the Mormon prophet, purchased four mummies recently arrived in New York from Paris. In the chest of one was a papyrus which Smith claimed as a part of the *Book of the Dead*. One copy was printed in 1842, another with comments in 1844. It will be remembered that the Prophet had already translated the *Book of Mormon* through the miraculous Spectacles, which had been written in 'hieroglyphics' (1830)" (p. 48).

21. For example, Ethan Smith wrote of "hieroglyphic" books and paintings among the Indians of Mexico (op. cit., pp. 182–85); Vogel (op. cit., p. 155) reports several attributions of Egyptian hieroglyphic writing used by the Indians.

22. See Joseph Smith, Jr., *History of the Church*, vol. 1, pp. 19–20. Roberts quotes part of Anthon's letter on p. 20n; letter is published in its entirety in Eber D. Howe, *Mormonism Unveiled*, op. cit., p. 270–72).

Since Egyptian was not understood in 1828—Champollion, using the Rosetta Stone to decipher hieroglyphics, published his *Egyptian Grammar* in 1836 and his *Egyptian Dictionary* in 1841—Anthon could not have validated the correctness of the transcript. Furthermore, the "Anthon transcript" has not subsequently been authenticated as Egyptian. (See *History of the Church*, vol. 1, p. 71.)

LDS author Donna Hill concludes, "Over the years various attempts have been made to identify these characters as some form of Egyptian, but nothing definite had been established" (*Joseph Smith: The First Mormon*, p. 79). It appears that the characters from the "Anthon transcript" are incompatible with Egyptian.

23. *History of the Church*, vol. 2, p. 236, 238, 245–47; Brodie, op. cit., pp. 170–75, 293, 421–25; Hill, op. cit., pp. 192–94.

24. In semiannual "General Conferences" broadcast across the country on commercial television channels and to some other parts of the world, printed later in the *Church News* and *Ensign*, Mormon General Authorities reassert the literal truth of Mormon origins and the new scriptures translated by Joseph Smith. Two years after professional translations reconfirmed that the Abraham papyri were Egyptian documents, Mormon apostle president N. Eldon Tanner stated: "The First Presidency of the Church of Jesus Christ of Latter-day Saints accepts the '*Book of Abraham*' as 'Scripture given to us through the Prophet [Joseph Smith]' " (*Salt Lake Tribune*, May 4, 1970). Referring to the *Book of Mormon*, Apostle Bruce R. McConkie affirmed that the book was "true and was translated correctly."

Quoting the *Doctrine and Covenants* 17:6, he added, "By revelation [to Joseph], the Lord said of Joseph Smith: 'He has translated the book, even that part which I have commanded him, and as your Lord and your God liveth it is true' " (*Mormon Doctrine*, 2nd ed. [Salt Lake City: Bookcraft, 1966], p. 99).

25. Lucy Smith, *Biographical Sketches of Joseph Smith the Prophet and His Progenitors for Many Generations* (Liverpool, England: 1853), p. 57.

26. Fayette Lapham, *Historical Magazine,* May 1870, p. 306, quoted in Jerald and Sandra Tanner, *Mormonism, Magic and Masonry* (Salt Lake City: Utah Lighthouse Ministry, 1983), p. 18.

27. Brigham H. Roberts, *Comprehensive History,* vol. 1, pp. 26–27.

28. Reed C. Durham, Jr., *Mormon Miscellaneous,* vol. 1, no. 1 (October 1975), pp. 14–15. See discussion in Tanner, op. cit., pp. 2–5.

29. According to Masonic legend, Enoch was taken up in a vision to a hill called Moriah, where he saw a gold plate engraved with an unknown language buried in a cavern. Enoch sought to preserve the gold plate from the Great Flood by placing above the door to the cavern a marble pillar with a hieroglyphic account of the Tower of Babel, and a brass pillar with a history of the creation. On top of the brass pillar was a metal ball that contained maps of the world and that also served as an oracle. Enoch deposited the two engraved pillars in the Hill Moriah along with the gold plate and covered the cavern with a stone lid. He predicted that after the flood an Israelite descendant would discover this sacred buried treasure.

Years later, when King Solomon and his builders, the Masons, were excavating to build the Temple, they discovered the buried records. A Mason (a widow's son) defending the records was killed. His dying words in the legend have since become a Masonic distress call: "Oh Lord, My God, is there no help for the widow's son?" The attacker was slain in his sleep with his own knife. Solomon's Temple then received these treasures, including the marble and brass records, the metal ball, the gold plate, a breastplate, and the Urim and Thummin.

Mormon Institute of Religion director Reed C. Durham, speaking before the Mormon History Association in 1974, spelled out the legend's "remarkable resemblances with Joseph Smith and Mormon history." Joseph Smith identified himself with Enoch in the *Doctrine and Covenants,* Secs. 78, 92, 96, 104. The Mormon record was also buried in a hill by a man who had the initial "M" (Moroni, son of Mormon). There were gold plates containing mysteries of God. The writing on Joseph Smith's gold plates was said to be unknown, like the engraving of Enoch's gold plate, and Egyptian, like the marble record in the Masonic legend. As in the Masonic legend, Joseph Smith claimed to find brass plates with an account of the Creation and also an account of the Tower of Babel. Like the Enoch legend, Joseph Smith at first had a vision of a hill and a cavern covered with a stone lid. Later, he also reported finding other treasures in a stone box beside the engraved records—a breastplate, the Urim and Thummin, and a round metal ball that, like the metal ball atop Enoch's brass pillar, served as a guide and oracle (in the *Book of Mormon,* the Liahona).

In the *Book of Mormon,* a villain was beheaded with his own sword in a dispute over sacred records (the "Brass Plates of Laban"). On June 27, 1844, when Joseph Smith, a Master Mason and a widow's son, was being shot, he reportedly began to call out the Masonic distress signal, "Oh Lord, My God . . . ," unable to complete it with ". . . Is there no help for the widow's son?"

Durham comments that "All of these aspects of the legend seem transformed into the history of Joseph Smith, so much so that it even appears to be a kind of symbolic acting out of Masonic lore."

Jack Adamson, "The Treasure of the Widow's Son" (Salt Lake City, n.d. [c. 1970], and Reed C. Durham, Jr., "Is There No Help for the Widow's Son?" (1974) compiled by Arthuro De Hoyos, *The Masonic Emblem and Parchment of Joseph and Hyrum Smith* (Provo, Utah: De Hoyos, 1982). Masonic sources of the legend of Enoch's gold plate include Thomas S. Webb, *Free-Mason's Monitor* (New York, 1802), and Henry Dana Ward, *Freemasonry* (New York, 1828). Also, see discussion in Tanner, op. cit., *History of the Church*, vol. 4, p. 557.

30. The first (1832) version of Joseph Smith's autobiography is found in Dean C. Jessee, "Early Accounts of the First Vision," *BYU Studies*, vol. 9, pp. 279–94.

31. Ephraim, a seventh brother in Joseph Smith's family, died young. See Brodie, op. cit., p. 43n.

32. *Book of Mormon*, 2 Nephi 3:6, 7, 15. A second prophecy of Joseph Smith's coming may be found in his revision of Genesis. See Brodie, op. cit., pp. 73, 116–17.

33. Lucy Smith, op. cit., pp. 58–59; *Book of Mormon*, 1 Nephi 8, 11. This is one of several dreams Lucy Smith remembered in detail.

34. Lucy Smith, op. cit., p. 85. The reference indicates that these stories were told sometime before the death of her son Alvin in November 1823, possibly about the time Joseph Smith said he was visited by the angel Moroni.

35. Ethan Smith, *A View of the Hebrews*, op. cit., pp. 182–83, 212.

36. Hubert Howe Bancroft, *Native Races* (San Francisco: A. L. Bancroft, 1886), vol. 5, pp. 79–81; Josiah Priest, *Wonders of Nature and Providence Displayed* (Albany, 1825, 1826), and *American Antiquities* (Albany: Hoffman and White, 1833 [eight editions were published between 1833 and 1838]). Other works include James Adair, *The History of the American Indians* (London, 1775); Elias Boudinot, *A Star in the West; or a Humble Attempt to Discover the Long Lost Ten Tribes of Israel* (Trenton, N.J., 1816).

37. B. H. Roberts, *A Book of Mormon Study*, Part 1, Chapter 8: "Could it be that Ethan Smith, influenced and misled by the reported discovery of the evidence of iron and its uses among the native Americans in ancient times, was innocently followed into this error by the author of the *Book of Mormon*? For there is nothing on which the later investigators of our American antiquities are more unanimously agreed upon than the matter of the absence of the knowledge of, and hence the nonuse of, iron or steel among the natives of America."

38. Ethan Smith, op. cit., pp. 115, 217–18, 223.

39. Ethan Smith, op. cit., pp. 52–54, the *Doctrine and Covenants* 27:5. Ethan Smith includes the "Ten Lost Tribes" from the Assyrian capture of the Northern Kingdom in 722 B.C.E. under the stick of Ephraim; the *Book of Mormon* describes three tribes, two from Joseph and one from Judah, who left Jerusalem before the Babylonian captivity of the Southern Kingdom in 587 B.C.E. See Note 12.

40. Further evidence that Joseph Smith may have become familiar with *A View of the Hebrews* is that he quoted from it later in his church newspaper to illustrate the historical accuracy of the Mormon scripture (*Times and Seasons* 3 (June 1, 1842): 813–814). Rather than quoting the 1823/1825 *A View of the Hebrews* directly, he gave a secondary source, Josiah Priest's *American Antiquities* (1833), published three years after the *Book of Mormon*.

41. *A Book of Mormon Study*, Part 1, Chapter 13, pp. 19–24.

42. Word volume estimated from the Bible is found in Brodie, op. cit., p. 58. This represents about 10 percent of the total 275,000-word manuscript dictated to Oliver Cowdery from April 7, 1829, to July. Brodie refers to Francis W. Kirkham's "The Writing of the *Book of Mormon," Improvement Era* June 1941, pp. 341ff. New Testament passages used before Jesus' time found in *Sunstone* 4, no. 3, p. 48.

43. According to modern biblical scholars, Isaiah 40–66 is a sixth-century work. See Peter R. Ackroyd, "The Book of Isaiah," *The Interpreter's Commentary on the Bible,* ed. Charles M. Laymon (Nashville, Tenn.: Abingdon, 1971), p. 329–71; Carroll Stuhlmueller, "Deutero-Isaiah," *Jerome Biblical Commentary,* eds. Raymond E. Brown et al. (Englewood Cliffs, N.J.: Prentice-Hall, 1968), ch. 22. The Mormon "Isaiah problem" and attempts to resolve it by asserting single authorship for this work covering three centuries is found in George D. Smith, "Isaiah Updated." *Dialogue: A Journal of Mormon Thought* (Salt Lake City) 16, no. 2 (Summer 1983), pp. 48–49.

44. In an address to LDS church educators, Elder Boyd K. Packer of the Quorum of Twelve Apostles admonished "selective" writing about the church and the teachings of "faith-promoting history." Elder Packer cautioned seminary and institute teachers that "there is no such thing as an accurate, objective history of the church without consideration of the spiritual powers that attend this work," noting that Brigham Young said not to teach even the times tables without the spirit of the Lord ("The Mantle is Far, Far Greater than the Intellect," 1981, reprinted in *BYU Studies* 21, no. 3 [Summer 1981], p. 259.) In a debate on "the question of faithful history" (February 25, 1982, University of Utah), historian James L. Clayton rejected selective, "faith promoting" history as "intellectually and morally irresponsible," and advocated a simple "willingness to tell the truth." In a talk at BYU, historian D. Michael Quinn responded in a similar way, declaring that if a historian "fails to make reference to pertinent information of which he has knowledge, he is justifiably liable to be criticized for dishonesty" (*Salt Lake Tribune,* February 28, 1982, pp. B1–3).

45. Noted archaeologist of Mesoamerica, Michael Coe, of Yale University, commented upon the evidence for Joseph Smith's translations: "Mormon archeologists over the years have almost unanimously accepted the Book of Mormon as an accurate historical account of the New World peoples between about 2000 B.C. and A.D. 421. They believe that Smith could translate hieroglyphs, whether 'Reformed Egyptian' or ancient American, and that his translation of the Book of Abraham is authentic. Likewise, they accept the Kinderhook Plates as a bona-fide archeological discovery, and the reading of them as correct. Let me now state uncategorically that as far as I know there is not one professionally trained archeologist, who is not a Mormon, who sees any scientific justification for believing the foregoing to be true, and I would like to state that there are quite a few Mormon archeologists who join this group . . . the picture of this hemisphere between 2000 B.C. and A.D. 421 presented in the book has little to do with the early Indian cultures as we know them, in spite of much wishful thinking . . .The bare facts of the matter are that nothing, absolutely nothing, has ever shown up in any New World excavation which would suggest to a dispassionate observer that the Book of Mormon, as claimed by Joseph Smith, is a historical document relating to the history of early migrants to our hemisphere" (*Dialogue* 8, no. 2 [Summer 1973], pp. 41, 42, 46).

46. In an unpublished paper, BYU anthropologist John L. Sorenson argues that the *Book of Mormon* peoples lived within a confined region in Central America, and thus attempts to explain why their history made no mention of the previously arrived migrations from

the Bering Strait ("An Ancient American Setting for the Book of Mormon," 1978). This idea was previously rejected by Mormon historian and apostle Joseph Fielding Smith, later president of the church (*Deseret News,* Church Section, February 27, 1954, pp. 2–3).

In his *Doctrines of Salvation* ([Salt Lake City: Bookcraft, 1954], vol. 1, p. 151), President Smith reaffirmed the traditional Mormon explanation of the origin of the American Indian: "Six hundred years before the birth of Christ another civilization supplanted the previously mentioned (Jaredite) which was destroyed about that time. This second civilization flourished about 1000 years. The people multiplied and spread over the face of the entire continent. Their descendants, the American Indians, were wandering in all their wild savagery when the Pilgrim Fathers made permanent settlement in this land."

Responding to continuing speculation on *Book of Mormon* geography, the church advised against giving the subject further consideration: "The geography of the Book of Mormon has intrigued some readers of that volume ever since its publication. But why worry about it? Why not leave hidden the things the Lord has hidden? If He wants the geography of the Book of Mormon revealed, He will do so through his prophet, and not through some writer who wishes to enlighten the world despite his utter lack of inspiration on the point" (*Deseret News,* Church News Section, July 29, 1978).

47. The LDS *Improvement Era* once carried the cautionary message: "Lucifer . . . wins a great victory when he can get members of the Church to speak against their leaders and 'do their own thinking.' . . . When our leaders speak, the thinking has been done" (June, 1945, p. 354). In a message to "follow the prophet," apostle N. Eldon Tanner updated this admonition: "When the prophet speaks the debate is over." (*The Ensign,* August, 1979, pp. 2–3). Ezra Taft Benson, president of the Twelve, offered to a devotional assembly at BYU "Fourteen Fundamentals in Following the Prophets" (February 26, 1980). He quoted the words of church president Heber J. Grant: "My boy, you always keep your eye on the President of the Church, and if he ever tells you to do anything, and it is wrong, and you do it, the Lord will bless you for it" (*Conference Report,* October 1960, p. 78).

An antecedent to this submission to authority was voiced by Joseph Smith in a letter to Nancy Rigdon in an attempt to justify plural marriage to her after she had refused the prophet's proposal: "Whatever God requires is right, no matter what it is" (*Journal of Mormon History* 5, [1978], p. 32).

48. Special Collections, Marriott Library, University of Utah, Salt Lake City.

49. " 'Inquisition' Reported: Mormon Brethren Silencing Scholars?" *Salt Lake Tribune,* May 26, 1983, p. B4.

50. Special Collections, University of Utah.

Tea and Sympathy on the Way to Mecca

Thomas Szasz

Poking fun at the frauds and follies of religion made Voltaire both famous and infamous. Although it was then risky to do so, it was intellectually respectable—and it made a difference. Today, the situation seems to be just the reverse. Although poking fun at religious frauds and follies is no longer especially risky, it is also no longer intellectually respectable—and, what's more important, it makes no difference. Still, let us imagine what a Voltaire might now be saying about the Muslim pilgrim who killed himself and three hundred other people by brewing his own tea on a jetliner. Or about similar, though perhaps less quickly lethal, American and European religious customs.

He might remark, to begin with, that the essence of religion is not so much reverence for a man-made idol, called "God," but the observance of rituals sanctified by tradition and common usage. The deity is, after all, only a "projection" (he might say, borrowing from Freudian jargon). What really counts are the ritual observances that people perform—ostensibly to honor the idol, but actually to impart significance to their own dreary lives and to make themselves virtuous without having to be nice to anyone.

What a Muslim pilgrim did on a Lockheed Tristar on August 20, 1980, thus qualifies as a genuinely religious piece of behavior. He was brewing tea for himself on a portable gas stove. Unfortunately, the Koran and the Islamic tradition did not anticipate travel by jet plane. As a result, the "good man" incinerated himself and all of his fellow passengers and crew, 301 persons all told.

According to newspaper accounts of this story, pilgrims to the shrine at Mecca often carry gas stoves to make tea in flight 'and on several occasions have touched off fires on airplanes." Presumably the Israelis are working on ground-guidance for passenger aircraft, to enable them to offer Muslims free flights to Mecca—without tea service, of course.

Given the cramped space on airliners, it seems unlikely that a passenger could pull a portable gas stove out of his luggage and light it without his actions being observed. Do some fellow passengers, or most of them, consider this to be normal behavior? How many people on Saudi airliners brew their own tea? No doubt Saudi officials discourage passengers from carrying portable gas stoves onto airplanes. But what, if anything, do they do about devout pilgrims intent on medicating themselves with tea en route to Mecca?

No sooner was this "tragedy" reported in the press (curiously, we don't refer to the consequences of the Christian pilgrims' piety in the Holy Land during the Crusades as a "tragedy," nor do we so refer to the consequences of the Jewish pilgrims' piety today in the Godforsaken land), than King Khaled of Saudi Arabia announced that he was personally giving $15,000 to the families of each of the victims to express his "deep condolences." Tea and sympathy. Surely Voltaire would have called that an insult. Were the responsibility for such a disaster litigated in an American court, the verdict would likely be ten or even a hundred times that amount (at least for some of the passengers). But can one sue the Saudi Arabian airlines? Or does that constitute prima facie evidence of impudence toward a despot who rules in the name of God?

"Regrettably," an official of the Saudi airline is quoted as saying, "some pilgrims traditionally carry with them—secretly—such flammable equipment." But doing so on a jet plane is not merely regrettable, it is criminal. Surely Voltaire would say—and who among us would be so foolish to disagree?—that carrying a portable gas stove onto an airliner and lighting it is an offense rather more grave than serving cocktails aboard it. But then we must remember that when in Rome we must do as the Romans do. En route to Mecca, you may brew your own tea. If you incinerate your fellow passengers and the crew, the Saudi airline directorate will express its regret for the the incident and the king will pay $15,000 for each corpse. (How many seconds does it take for the king to "earn" $15,000?)

Regrets from airline officials. Mini-compensation from the king. What none of the Saudis is talking about is responsibility. But the fact is that the Saudi Arabian airline assumes responsibility toward the Koran by prohibiting serving alcoholic beverages aboard its planes and by enforcing that rule (even though breaking it would not pose any risk of bodily injury or death to anyone). Why, then, does the Saudi airline—that is, its owners and managers (does that include the royal family itself?)—not assume an equally strict responsibility toward its passengers and crew? Why does it not owe them a *duty* to protect them from being set ablaze by pilgrims ritually lighting gas stoves aboard Saudi aircraft?

But enough? It is not quite fair to poke fun only at other people's religious frauds and follies. We have plenty of our own to spoof. In fact, we have our own ceremonial-chemical customs whose victims far outnumber those killed by tea-brewing Muslim pilgrims. A mere hint about what Voltaire might say about this subject must suffice here.

The Saudis don't approve of extramarital sex and punish it severely. We don't approve of extramedical drug-use and punish it almost as severely.

Although the deaths caused by our "tea-brewing" ceremonies do not follow as directly—there are a few intermediate steps—from the acts of those ultimately responsibile for them as do the deaths caused by the literally tea-brewing pilgrim airline passengers, the consequences of our pharmacomythological rituals are no less dangerous and deadly and endanger many more innocent people. How many persons have been robbed, maimed, and murdered in New York City as a result of laws rammed through the legislature in Albany by another oil-spoiled potentate? Perhaps satire could succeed where exposition has failed: people could be shown that the consequences of our ritualized customs, which enshrine our beliefs that licit drugs are good but illicit drugs are bad, are no less real, and not a whit less deadly, than are the consequences of the Muslim belief that drinking alcohol is a grave sin but that the results of brewing one's own tea on a jetliner are only "regrettable."

(Spring 1981)

"New Age" Gurus
Robert Basil

When *Free Inquiry* author Burnham P. Beckwith reported that intelligence and disbelief were positively correlated, he concluded that, as the world's population enlightened itself in terms of education and technology, it would begin to be released from the domination of religious institutions. "Future American and European opinion polls will continue to show almost steady declines in a personal belief in God and in each major dogma of the Christian churches," he wrote. "The amount of religious faith tends to vary inversely and appreciably with intelligence."

Beckwith's conclusions were impressive, although they didn't explain why so many highly educated and intelligent people, even scientific and artistic geniuses, continue to believe. And, more important, his definition of "belief" was so narrow that his results could be misleading. Christian "faith," or "belief," cannot be confused with religious experience. Beckwith focused on beliefs in *Christian* religious dogma (the Creation, a personal God) and the membership in Christian denominations. The incidence of specifically non-Christian religious experiences was never measured.

In a major survey reported in the February issue of *American Health* magazine, belief in reincarnation, clairvoyance, and various out-of-body experiences—important elements of various Eastern and "New Age" philosophies—was measured and was found to be growing. Sociologist and priest Andrew Greeley, working with a team of University of Chicago researchers, discovered that "nearly half of American adults (42 percent) now believe they have been in contact with someone who died"—up from 25 percent eleven years ago. Says Greeley, "If these experiences were signs of mental illness, our numbers would show that the country is going nuts. . . . People who've tasted the paranormal, whether they've accepted it intellectually or not, are anything but religious nuts or psychiatric cases. They are, for the most part, ordinary Americans, somewhat above the norm in education and somewhat less than average in religious involvement."

What we are seeing suggests a kind of neo-Reformation, for these religious concepts are wholly contrary to traditional Christian teachings. Reincarnation, for example, flies in the face of Christianity's "Final Judgment," just as Karma—the doctrine that says you get what you deserve—is in opposition to Christian "grace," which says that sometimes you don't. And, what's most significant, New Age ideas militate against religious institutions and hierarchies *as such*—in the same way Quakerism and other "inner light" Protestant sects did in the past.

In other words, the "reformed" impulse bypasses the approved mediators between the self and religious insight—whether that mediator be the pope, the magesterium, or even sacred texts. Indeed, this impulse is a skeptical one—which we associate with higher education and intelligence—in the sense that it doubts dogmatic authority. New Age precepts tend to be in the American grain, appealing to a sense of individualism and private mystical resources that have been espoused in this country since the time of Emerson and Thoreau. Says J. Z. Knight, who claims to be the "trance channel" for "Ramtha," a 35,000-year-old warrior from the sunken city of Atlantis: "Ramtha teaches about the love of God in us, that we are empowered to make the decisions for ourselves." Shirley MacLaine, an admirer of Knight, whose book and television special, "Out on a Limb," have given New Age philosophies their widest exposure yet, adds, "These are individual approaches to life. There's nobody heading this up" (*USA Weekend,* January 9-11, 1987). MacLaine is heading *something* up, that's for sure, and in an especially American way, founding spiritual seminars around the country—at $300 a person, "$100 for mind, $100 for body, $100 for spirit," she says.

When ABC-TV's newsmagazine, "20/20," did a piece on J. Z. Knight, newsmen Judd Rose and David Doss confirmed Greeley's findings. Most of Knight/Ramtha's followers, they said, were highly educated and financially successful. This point was clearly meant to astonish: From what the ABC clips showed of Ramtha in action, Knight is clearly an actress, or deeply troubled, or some of both. Ramtha's language (how did he learn English?), swollen by portentous constructions and vacuous self-help clichés, makes Knight a dead giveaway.

But why would the highly educated fall for such an obvious fake? The answer that immediately suggests itself is troubling. The technological revolution apparently has failed to invest the lives of those who benefit financially the most from it with an experience of personal meaning. Many, even some at the very highest levels of science and technology, don't feel defined by their success; they feel amorphous, nothing more than a variable in the scientific method. This disillusionment is consistent with Werner Heisenberg's 1932 warning that "every scientific advance" is bought at the price "of renouncing the aim of bringing the phenomena of nature to our thinking in an immediate and living way."

Free Inquiry has made a lot·of hay by criticizing the inadequacies of religious, superstitious, and paranormal systems of belief; we've shown how dangerous it is when people trade their ordinary way of knowing for a blind belief in what they hope to be true. Often this qualification will be added: those methods of knowing are inadequate for the rest of us, because (to paraphrase Thomas Paine) what's revelation to you is just hearsay to me. The scientific method of corroboration, replicative testing, trustworthy instrumentation, and revisable hypotheses has shown itself to be the most reliable way of knowing the world. But here we run into the undeniable fact that we are trying to convince people who are not as concerned with watertight epistemology as we are. While science can so effectively control what's outside of us, unfortunately we cannot so confidently say that it quenches the emotional yearning inside many people.

For some, science is a process to participate in and enjoy; we can measure ourselves by its triumphs. This is roughly the position of E. O. Wilson, Isaac Asimov, and Carl Sagan, for whom the world's material progress maps their own spiritual progress. But it is perhaps too much to expect that all men and women make the world's meaning their own, especially at a time when the specialization of our economy prevents any such transfer.

Still, for those raised in the Western tradition, it is difficult to abandon the scientific method altogether, so many New Age and modern mystical movements claim to accommodate science even as they penetrate spiritual spheres. To be sure, uniting Western mysticism with the Eastern pantheistic traditions can be an ingenious affair. For the sheer volume of systematization of the occult worlds and their astral and etheric beings, the writings of Madame Blavatsky, Alice Bailey, G. I. Gurdjieff, and Rudolf Steiner are bewildering. (Of Steiner especially there has not been nearly enough serious academic examination.) Their philosophies offer the *aroma* of science—its edifices of information, its savory combination of cooperative effort and solitary study—and the hope for unending life that science seems to have crushed.

Claims made by New Age propagandists are sometimes harder to refute than those, say, of dishonest faith-healers or fundamentalists who would repeal the First Amendment; and it is important to remember that flamboyant tricksters like "Ramtha" are merely straw men. That they are making a lot of money from gullible, troubled people makes their claims highly suspect, and we need to call them to account. But to equate the frauds with the movement itself would be a gross error; New Agers generally spurn the oratory of would-be leaders, they have built no powerful churches, and they tend not to seek political power.

Nonetheless, our next great debate may well be with these New Agers. The humanist side must offer positive alternatives as well as rigorous critique. Because 42 percent is a lot.

(Spring, 1987)

V.

Faith-Healing and Televangelism

S atan, come *out!*"
    In early 1987 Satan began to come out in full force—out of the closets
of America's top televangelists and faith-healers, that is. By now there is not
a newspaper or network affiliate in the United States that has not reported on
the transgressions and bizarre antics of God's anointed.

Tammy Bakker's face dripped down every front page as she watched her
multimillion-dollar empire crumble beneath the disclosure of her husband's lurid
sexual and financial dealings. Jimmy Swaggart, too, offered an outpouring of damp
emotion when he publicly admitted to having "sinned" with a prostitute in a New
Orleans hotel room. Pat Robertson attempted to turn this godless nation "back
to its roots" in a failed presidential bid to unite church and state, and Oral Roberts
narrowly escaped meeting his maker when a surprise donation came through at
the last minute and he met, instead, his $8 million fund-raising goal.

Free Inquiry readers were not shocked by any of this. In fact, they were barely
even surprised, for they already knew the depths to which people will stoop in
the name of God and mammon.

James Randi and the Committee for the Scientific Examination of Religion
(CSER) had been investigating faith-healers for more than a year before releasing
their findings in the magazine's Spring 1986 issue. It is this investigation for which
Free Inquiry is perhaps best known. It generated widespread publicity that would
later prove to be the first ripple in a vast and seemingly endless tsunami of media
interest in the topic.

Since the earliest times, religions of many stripes have relied on faith-healing to intensify belief in their gods. But once the con men of the revival tents realized that they could reach out and touch millions of wallets without ever leaving their comfy studios, an industry was born. Access to electronic media raised scamming the flocks to a new height—and breadth—of corruption. Elmer Gantry looks like a choirboy in comparison with modern televangelists.

Not only did television provide an entirely new arena, it enhanced the recognizability factor of these "healers." Many continued to take their shows on the road, where they found, to their endless delight, many thousands of votaries awaiting them at each stop along the way, checkbooks waving.

Needless to say, CSER's investigators were waiting too. And when several of these "men of God" announced engagements in Western New York and Southern Ontario, I was anxious to offer my services as an amateur sleuth.

Like many others, I had seen the latter-day witch doctors on television, and had made sport of their haircuts and their overt chicanery. I had thought that the bulk of their audience was laughing along with me. But I had failed to take into account the power of religious belief and frantic hope. Television had not prepared me for what I encountered in the auditoriums filled with lambs eager to be led to slaughter.

The audiences were made up of blacks and whites, young and old, men and women in equal numbers. Many were poor and uneducated; many sought the mercy of God in cases that were clearly out of the hands of modern medicine. And they were willing to give all they had—and probably much that they did not have—in order to get it. In one evening alone, we estimated a tax-free take of $30,000 for the preacher. That's preacher, 30,000—flock, less than 0.

As the following articles point out, those who needed help the most were almost always ignored by the men and women "of God" they had hoped would save them. This not only disheartened them, it kept them coming back—and donating more "seed money"—in search of the miracle they knew must occur. I knew that these people would believe that it was neither their God nor their preacher who had failed them, but their own lack of faith that had kept them from moving mountains.

We have had to choose just a few of the many fine articles that *Free Inquiry* has published as part of its ongoing investigation—but these provide an accurate overview of the situation, as well as some heartfelt editorial comment.

—*M.B.G.*

'Be Healed in the Name of God!'

James Randi

There is, in the majority of religions, a history of miraculous cures effected by the touch of a prominent individual; contact with a sacred relic, amulet, or place; or anointment with sanctified oil, water, or any other medium presented by chance or intent to the ailing. As in the practice of all magic, participation in these "cures" is an attempt by Man to control nature by means of spells, incantations, or ritual. The effectiveness of these measures has been discussed for centuries, but the power of suggestion is only now beginning to be understood.

Because monarchs ruled by divine right, they were believed to have the ability to heal. Thus originated the "Royal Touch" that was said to be effective against scrofula, a disease known as the "King's Evil." Certainly kings had some effect upon psychosomatic and quite imaginary ailments, and subjects eagerly provided affidavits to support strong faith in this sort of healing.

Healing by contact with or in the presence of holy relics, which enters history in the third century, should be a much bigger business than it is considering the plethora of objects that are said to have been the possessions or actual physical parts of various saints and biblical characters. One avid German collector claimed to have more than 17,000 of these objects, which inspired Pope Leo X to calculate that this devout chap had saved himself exactly 694,779,550.5 days in purgatory by such pious devotion to his hobby. His hoard included bones from the children slain by Herod, a crust of bread from the Last Supper, a jar containing a sample of the Virgin Mary's milk, and a hair from Christ's beard. But he was outdone by the Schlosskirche at Halle, which boasted 21,483 relics in its vaults.

Though all Protestant denominations long ago condemned the veneration of such objects and their use in healing, the Catholic church permits and even encourages the practice. Pieces of the true cross, toenails of St. Peter, the bodies of St. Stephen and the three wise kings, several heads, or parts of one, all claimed to have belonged to John the Baptist, sixteen foreskins of Christ, Mary Magdalene's entire skeleton, and scraps of bread and fish left over from feeding the five-thousand, not to mention a few shrouds—including the one at Turin—are exhibited at various Catholic churches.

Christianity, beginning with the New Testament, has a history of miraculous cures credited to the touch of many of its luminaries. The apostles and their successors were said to have performed the "laying on of hands," taught to them by their master. Reformer Martin Luther, in the sixteenth century, took credit for spontaneous cures, while at the same time savants like Paracelsus were attempting, with highly varying degrees of success, to evolve the superstition of magic into what we know today as the science of medicine. Mormons and Episcopalians have established a history of faith cures as part of their theologies, and Mary Baker Eddy founded her Christian Science church solely on the notions that pain is an illusion and bacteria are the result rather than the cause of disease.

In the 1870s, faith-healing became very popular and widely practiced in London, and it continues to attract followers in England. Elsewhere, the tombs of Francis of Assisi, Catherine of Siena, and others are said to have caused miracle cures for those who visited them. The town of Lourdes, in France, is the site of a shrine that has long been held to bring about healing as a result of a visitation by the Virgin Mary. Though its quite ordinary spring-water has never been officially touted as effective in healing, millions of gallons have been sealed in vials and plastic jugs and sold by mail-order to miracle-seekers around the world. Despite the fact that Lourdes has had a bustling industry of healing for more than 125 years, with tens of millions of afflicted making pilgrimages there, the Catholic church has officially declared only sixty-four miracle cures to have taken place among that multitude.

The Reverend William Branham, a preacher from Jeffersonville, Indiana, is credited with initiating the present evangelical/fundamentalist healing movement in the 1940s. Pastor Branham was so convincing a preacher that, when he died in 1965, his burial was postponed for four months because his flock expected him to rise from the dead at Easter. He didn't.

Radio, and then television, brought the movement into full bloom. Protected by the First Amendment, anyone capable of speaking in public became eligible to dispense interpretations of holy writings. An occasional individual took his or her inspiration from vaudeville, applying psychological techniques and razzmatazz to build an act that the Internal Revenue Service would never trouble, Congress would never question, and the law would find completely insulated by the Constitution against charges of fraud and deception.

Faith-healing is difficult to differentiate from witchcraft, which in its healing aspects is involved with expelling evil spirits from the body. The modern witch-doctor in Africa still calls on primitive "show biz" when he "pulls the thorn" by applying his mouth to a wound or an ailing portion of the body, producing by sleight of hand a thorn, a stone, or a sliver that is said to be either the actual cause of pain or the material representation of a demon or devil. Thousands of doctors and nurses in the United States have joined the International Order of St. Luke the Physician, which stresses a spiritual approach to the practice of medicine, thus identifying with if not actually practicing witchcraft.

A Catholic healer, Father Ralph DiOrio, of Worcester, Massachusetts, specializes in the "slaying of the spirit." During this ritual, the afflicted person falls over when the healer gestures. This is an expected reaction, and it's a case of "monkey see, monkey do." DiOrio claims he has healed every conceivable kind of emotional, physical, and spiritual defect. However, consider the testimony of one healed devotee of Father Ralph, published in *Fate* magazine:

> I suffered a neck injury . . . a long time ago . . . and I have had breathing problems and pain . . . I attended Father DiOrio's charismatic service . . . I was sitting high in the third balcony . . . I heard [him] call my name, saying, "There's a Helen here with a cervical problem, a neck problem—I feel it happening—a healing is taking place." Out of all those thousands of people, I was not certain he meant me, because nowhere was my name or ailment given. But he DID mean me . . . [now] I do not have pain.

True, this woman's name is Helen. But how difficult was it for Father DiOrio to hit on a Helen with a neck pain in the Joe Louis Arena in Detroit, jammed with believers? It is very probable such a coincidence occurred. And, if not, are all the non-Helens ever going to know it? Of course not. A faith-healer can never be wrong with such a maneuver. D'Orio's "call out" allows for more than one interpretation. "Cervical" can refer to problems of the uterus, too, and this could have been a "hit" for "Helen," had she been so afflicted. This fitted-evidence tendency is typical of many reports of miraculous healings.

*   *   *

My investigation of faith-healing has concentrated on one prominent healer about whom a great deal is known and who is more readily accessible than most. He also makes more claims, is more careless about concealing his methods, and is one of the biggest moneymakers in the business. He is a healer of the sick, a minister of God, and a television star named Walter Vinson Grant.

W. V. Grant is the plumply handsome forty-year-old son of another evangelist who rose to moderate fame in Texas. He performs on stage dressed in very expensive well-tailored business suits set off by monogrammed shirts and elegant jewelry, looking like prosperity personified. He runs his mail-order business from a post-office box in Cincinnati, Ohio, and sells a book titled *God's Answers For You* ("made to sell for $30" but available for fifteen dollars with "gold gilted edges"), audiotape cassettes of sermons, Bibles (half-price this month), and record albums and eight-tracks. He also sells booklets written by Grant, Sr., now deceased, as if they were his own. Winning titles among the sixty available (fifty cents each) include *The Great Dictator—The Man Whose Number Is 666, I Was a Cannibal, Men in Flying Saucers Identified, Faith for Finance,* and *Freedom From Evil Spirits.* He also sells a Bible course (sixty-four dollars) that offers the subscriber a purple and gold diploma as a real "Reverend" with an "honorary Doctor's Degree" and a "license to preach" after certain true-and-false questions have been answered. Grant will cut two dollars from the price for each "name of someone who wants this course" supplied to him by a customer.

Every Sunday Grant holds what he describes as "two great miracle services" at his home-base, the Eagle's Nest cathedral in Dallas. He claims his show, "Dawn of a New Day," appears on some three hundred television stations across the continent once or twice a week and that he has to spend more than $8 million annually for air-time alone. In his live revival meetings, as he tours the United States from coast to coast, miracles fall from his fingertips on all present. He fills dental cavities, straightens limbs, adds vertebrae to ailing backs, and cures tumors, deafness, blindness, digestive problems, "broken" and otherwise-damaged hearts, diabetes, paralysis, fractured bones, arthritis, gall-bladder conditions, high blood pressure, colitis, obesity, bone spurs, kidney problems, and almost any other disease our species is heir to—all by mumbling some magical syllables, touching the sufferers, and mightily grinding his teeth. (The magic words transcribe as: "Quah talah mokos! Stee keekeenee bahkus! Dee!")

It appears that Grant can also reverse hysterectomies. "When they opened me up, they found all my ovaries and tubes were back and they just couldn't understand it!" declared one woman. In another case, an afflicted woman had her "leg and foot" problems remedied by the Reverend Grant; "I couldn't wear high-healed [*sic*] shoes for 13–15 years," she wrote in her testimonial. "I praise the Lord that I can now." Is there no end to this man's good works?

At every revival meeting that Grant holds, people are commanded to get up out of their wheelchairs and run, not walk, up the aisle and back. Canes and walkers taken from the lame and crippled are dramatically broken and thrown onto the stage, while those who used them moments before trot about in ecstasy. Folks whose legs are different lengths straddle a pair of chairs onstage while the shorter leg appears to lengthen. The deaf hear, the blind see, tumors vanish, and bacteria are slain at the wave of a hand. Miracles of every sort are plentiful.

Perhaps these wonders needed looking into. Certainly, if *any* of Grant's claims were true, medical literature would have to be entirely rewritten. But I have always heeded an observation made by Benjamin Franklin, to wit: "There are no greater liars than quacks—except for their patients." I suspected that Grant and his peers depend upon the imagination of their clients for success, rather than upon their own hyperbole. Suggestion, too, in cases of psychosomatic illness, could be expected to play a part.

In a slick, full-color glossy (undated) magazine titled *New Day,* which Grant publishes several times a year, I noted the "Crusade Schedule" of Grant's personal appearances from Philadelphia to Honolulu for the upcoming nine months. On November 4, 1985, he was to appear in a huge auditorium in St. Louis, Missouri.

Paul Kurtz, editor of *Free Inquiry,* decided that Grant's claims needed careful scientific investigation. He and the Committee for the Scientific Examination of Religion (CSER) commissioned me to make an investigation and asked Professor Joseph Barnhart, professor of philosophy at North Texas State University, to join me. Barnhart is an expert on religions and proved to be exceedingly valuable to the investigation. Kurtz also contacted Walter Hoops and other members of the Rationalist Association in St. Louis, who readily agreed to assist in the project. We had two questions to answer: Was Grant really healing people? How did he do his impressive "mind-reading" act? By arriving early, we hoped to be in on the entire operation and answer these questions. We also intended to pass out leaflets requesting any allegedly healed persons to contact us through the Rationalist Association's post-office box.

The Reverend Grant would have a rather pedestrian act to offer his audiences if it weren't for one particular attraction. As the traveling medicine shows of yore did, Grant needs a "hook" to grab the crowd. What sells the snake oil is a tactic known in the trade as "calling out" the customers, and it is used by several other evangelists as well. One known as David Paul has a less slick presentation, but uses the same gimmick just as effectively as Grant does. A Fort Lauderdale performer named Epley puts drama into the act by clawing at the air and straining to hear the wings of angels. "Calling out" consists of approaching individuals and addressing them by name, specifying their ailments, and identifying their physicians by name—and perhaps supplying details of their lives known only to themselves. The performer is careful to state that he has never met or spoken to the subject before and says that God has asked him to "call out" this person, giving the evangelist the information through the process of revelation. This ability is said to be one of the "nine gifts of the spirit" granted to certain "anointed" individuals—like W. V. Grant, for example.

If you think this sounds more like a description of the act offered by mentalist Kreskin, take ten points for perception. Kreskin, like Joseph Dunninger, the greatest mentalist who ever lived, offers his act as entertainment rather than religion, however. W. V. Grant, who has denied that what he is doing is "a magic act," not only gains the full attention of his audience by means of these tricks but also convinces them of his closeness to God. How he manages this clever deception, I will discuss shortly.

First, let us look into the question of whether Grant is actually able to heal the afflicted as he says he can. It would seem that checking his healing record would not be at all difficult. It would be a simple matter of following up on as many "healees" as we can find. But that can be a lengthy, harrowing, and often unsuccessful task. For instance, from a videotape of one of Grant's revival meetings in Atlanta, we were able to transcribe—from one healing ritual—the name of a patient, the names of the patient's six doctors, the hospital, the date of a specific planned coronary operation for the patient, and the patient's birthday. (Grant had even correctly divined a comment made by one of those six doctors.) Since the tape had been made less than four weeks before the broadcast, Kurtz and I decided that I should visit Atlanta under the auspices of CSER and find out whether the patient had undergone the operation and what his present condition was.

During his healing process, Grant had told this man that "Dr. Jesus" had put a new heart in his body by means of "closed-heart surgery" and that he no longer needed orthodox "open-heart" surgery. In response to Grant's command, the patient, toothless and very advanced in years, trotted up the aisle and back to demonstrate the new heart. I felt that this case presented an ideal prospect for confirmation, since so much data had been given. In Atlanta, CSER enlisted the help of an associate at a medical school there and he agreed to try to contact the doctors named in the videotape. We were both in for a surprise.

Not one of the six doctors appeared in the current listing of the Medical Association of Georgia (MAG), which lists all of that state's more than eight thousand physicians, whether they are MAG members or not. Nor were those doctors listed as chiropractors. We found that the hospital had no such patient and no such operation planned for the date given. In fact, the hospital officials reported that they had never performed cardiac surgery at that facility. Furthermore, the pastor of the church named could not identify this person as a church member. We had apparently discovered an absolute "ringer"—the man, for one reason or another, had fabricated the whole story. And he made W. V. Grant and Dr. Jesus look pretty good in that videotape.

But another participant in the revival meeting in St. Louis, J. Elmo Clark, was a different story. He'd gone to Grant's service after having sent him a lot of money over a period of years. Mr. Clark was blind in one eye. He had seen Grant heal the sick on television and firmly believed he would be healed, too. We spoke to Clark two days after the meeting, and he was angry and upset. Grant had "called him out" of the audience, and announced his name, his doctor, and his ailment. But J. Elmo Clark is still blind in one eye, despite the fact that he believed he had regained his sight following some mumbo-jumbo by Grant. How this came about, we will learn later. Though Grant led his audience to believe that he'd restored Clark's vision, that claim was just not true.

Looking through *New Day,* we found names of many persons who had testified to their healings. One was a man from Erie, Pennsylvania, who stated, concerning his encounter with Grant eighteen months before, that his healing was still in effect. "For 20 years, I had sugar diabetes," he said, "and thank God I am healed." (Grant refers to diabetes as either "sugar diabetes" or just "sugar"—as in his expression, "You've got the sugar, haven't you?") *Free Inquiry* discovered the man's name and telephone number. When we contacted him by telephone, he was wary. He wanted to be assured that we weren't trying to falsify any of Grant's work. All I could tell him was that we were investigating the whole matter without prejudice. Reassured, he told us that, although he knew his doctor would disagree with him, he no longer had diabetes. He was still taking insulin (the standard treatment for this ailment), but the dose was smaller, he said. The impression I got was that he could not contemplate discrediting faith-healing and that he was clinging to his preferred—and comforting—belief. The fact remains that this man, despite his wishes and his faith and Grant's intercession with supernatural forces, was not and is not healed.

Others who testified in *New Day* could not be found, even though some of their names were quite unusual.

In 1982, Mrs. Pearl Kidd of Racine, Wisconsin, had been angry enough to tell a reporter that a full-color photograph of her husband, Morris, had been run in *New Day* with the caption: "This Milwaukee man was blind all of his life. After Rev. Grant prayed, he saw for the first time." Said Mrs. Kidd, "What miracle?" Her spouse, she said, was still almost totally blind, and she resented this lie appearing in print. First of all, Mr. Kidd had not been "blind all of his life." His sight had been deteriorating only for a few years. The photo and caption were misleading. "It was just a hoax," Mrs. Kidd said, and she suggested that Grant should be "put out of business for lying to people."

Mr. Kidd had been carrying a white cane when he attended the service. Suffering from an incurable, degenerative eye disease, he could see very little. Grant had declared him healed and had thrown his cane up on the stage in a dramatic gesture. At the close of the meeting, Kidd had to ask that his cane be returned to him so that he could make his way out of the auditorium. "[Grant] claimed to have healed him," fumed Mrs. Kidd, "but he lied."

While looking through Grant's various publications and noting the many mailing addresses he uses, I was struck by their variety and geographical spread. The "W. V. Grant, Jr. Evangelical Association" at a Cincinnati post-office box address sounds straightforward enough. Then there are mailing addresses for "W. V. Grant" in Dallas, Texas, one at a post-office box and the other on Grant Street. Grant's Bible course is offered from five different sources: The "21st Century Christ Ministry," "Kingsway Bible College," "TVD Bible College," "International Deliverance Churches," and "Faith Clinic Bible Correspondence Course." The television show is handled by QCI, QC Inc., QCM, and/or QC Advertising. Both "World Headquarters" and the "Eagle's Nest Cathedral" (formerly "Soul's Harbor Church") are located in Dallas on West Davis Street. But there is also the "Cathedral of Compassion" in Cincinnati, to say nothing of "Grant's Faith Clinic" and the "Faith Clinic School" back in Texas. Evidently deciding that consolidation of these several enterprises would be a wise move, the Reverend announced that as of January 1, 1986, he would be receiving mail (and offerings) at a single Dallas address—"The Eagle's Nest Cathedral."

The Reverend Grant pleads for donations to keep his show on television, basing his begging on that $8 million dollars a year for air time. Between October 1985 and October 1986, he will spend $375,700 ($7,225 each week) on one television station alone, KHJ-TV in Los Angeles. But that is his single biggest market. It is also his most expensive by far, since some small UHF stations sell that same time-slot for as little as $500. The Los Angeles bill represents about 10 percent of Grant's annual air-time budget. Actually, his total bill is just half of what he claims, or $4 million.

Grant's program does not even show up in the top ten of the eighty-seven syndicated religious television programs in the United States. (Evangelist Rex Humbard, who appeared on television before some present incumbents were out of puberty, claims there are some 1,100 television preachers operating today, though this estimate may be inflated and surely covers every 10-watt local station.) Robert Schuller with his "Hour of Power" commands the top position in that competition, reaching 1,123,200 households. Second place is occupied by Pat Robertson's "The 700 Club"—a powerful aid to his 1988 presidential ambitions. It is interesting to note that Robertson has of late abandoned his Grant-style healing pretensions, preferring to heal by telephone during his broadcasts. He now says he considers himself more a television journalist than an evangelist, and he compares himself to Walter Lippmann and William Buckley.

Robertson's White House aspirations may not be as fanciful as we may wish. Jerry Falwell and Jimmy Swaggart are both fond of alluding to their phone chats with President Reagan. Certainly, the Falwell organization's gross income of $73 million could easily support any political campaign he might choose to launch. At a prayer breakfast during the 1984 Republican National Convention, Ronald Reagan declared that "religion and politics are necessarily related." Taking advantage of this assurance of access to the presidential ear, five television evangelists promptly presented themselves before the Platform Committee and claimed they represented thirty million television viewers. This was a bold ploy to make themselves important to the media and available for "inside" clues to Reagan's intentions. But, again, reality intrudes. The A. C. Nielsen rating service puts the viewer audience of all top ten television ministries at 9.3 million, a formidable figure but far less than these evangelists claimed. Facts and figures are invented and hyperbolized with little fear that anyone will discover the truth and care to correct them.

It is difficult to imagine how the Reverend Grant would explain the rather large discrepancies between his television coverage claims and the facts as recorded by Arbitron, the New York-based company that since 1949 has been the nation's leading broadcast audience measurement organization. Its latest in-depth survey of religious television programs shows that in yet another respect Grant has perhaps not given us the right figures. He claims to appear on "more than 300" television stations; Arbitron says he shows up on only 93. Grant says he now is seen in more homes than Oral Roberts; Arbitron says that Roberts appears in 1,046,000 households, while Grant is seen in only 198,000. And Roberts actually is shown on 201 television stations, against Grant's 93.

The American way means the freedom to pursue success in the free-enterprise system. There is nothing wrong with making money at a chosen profession. Most of us, but not all, are required to account for our income and pay appropriate taxes for our share of the financial burden of government. Religious organizations are not required to. Though the laws of the United States do not specify that churches are exempt from taxation, the First Amendment has been taken to mean just that. Many churches and religious organizations register with the Internal

Revenue Service as nonprofit organizations, though they are not required to do so. Many evangelists, such as Billy Graham and the Wycliffe Bible Translators, have joined the Evangelical Council for Financial Accountability, a Protestant group that publishes the financial statements of its 350 members for public scrutiny. But W. V. Grant is not a member, nor is his corporation registered as a nonprofit organization. If it were, we would have some way of knowing just how much money goes into the wastebaskets carried about by his ushers at revival meetings and how much is deposited by the mailmen at all the post-office boxes and street addresses he uses for his mail-order business.

Grant's history is uncertain, at best. Consider what Grant, Sr., wrote about his son's early life and what the son recalls of his own youth. The father claimed that during one football game, W. V., Jr., "was knocked unconscious that might. He played for half the game while he was unconscious, scoring three touchdowns." Well, I hardly think that myth needs to be debunked. Suffice it to say that the school that young Grant attended was W. B. Adamson High School in Dallas, and those three touchdowns don't show up in its record books. Grant says that he "led the state of Texas in scoring as a halfback . . . and I had 77 full NCAA football scholarship offers." He scored an average of twenty-two points a game while at Adamson, he says. These stories are denied by Adamson's coach, James Batchelor, who now works with the Dallas Cowboys. He recalls Grant well. "He was not the kind that would get 77 scholarships," says Batchelor. The fact is that W. V. Grant did not receive inquiries from even one school, let alone 77! And no football player in Adamson's history has ever held the record Grant claims for himself. Batchelor says Grant's story is "just not true."

Grant claims to have attended the University of California at Los Angeles (UCLA) in the 1960s, and a certificate hanging on his office wall shows that he received a Doctor of Divinity degree in 1972 from "Midstates Bible College" in Des Moines, Iowa. UCLA has no record that Grant ever attended school. The Iowa Department of Public Instruction never heard of Midstates, nor did it show up in the 1972 phone book. It was never registered as a corporation in the state of Iowa, and neither the American Association of Bible Colleges nor the Association of Theological Schools has any record of its existence. Grant seems to be confused about details of his professional training and qualifications.

Just how much of Grant's disdain for truth creeps into his performance as a healer? We can begin to answer this question by examining the phenomena whereby afflicted persons jump out of wheelchairs and jog up and down the aisles at Grant's command.

*   *   *

Before we entered the auditorium at Grant's meeting in St. Louis, we encountered many invalids in wheelchairs. They included children in advanced states of cerebral palsy. Two chair-bound children, suffering from conditions I would not presume to diagnose, were strapped into their chairs. They made loud noises from time to time and thrashed about uncontrollably while their parents attempted to quiet them. Many older people were hunched over in their wheelchairs and appeared largely unaware of their surroundings. It was a depressing sight, and I wondered what Grant would do when confronted with these cases.

I went inside and sat up front with Joe Barnhart, who had eagerly volunteered to be an usher in Grant's service. This enabled him to obtain much valuable information that would otherwise be unavailable. People in wheelchairs lined the front and the sides of the seating area. Several of these people were subsequently commanded by Grant to get up and walk. But not one of those I'd seen earlier was even approached for healing. They were all placed at the back of the auditorium, and when one of the noisy chair-bound children approached the stage, Grant turned to an aide and told him, out of the range of the microphone, to "get him to the back." Later the child cried out from the side of the auditorium, where he'd again been placed by his parents. Grant, busy with a miracle on the other side, was forced to acknowledge the shriek and said, "I'm gonna git to that in just a minute." But he never did.

Those people who did rise from wheelchairs and run in the aisles did so because they were quite capable of doing so, and always had been. One of them, an elderly black man we later interviewed, told Barnhart that "a pastor told him to sit" in the wheelchair they provided even though he could move about without it. We visited this man at his home and discovered that he lived in a room on the third floor of a walk-up. He managed the trip up and down those stairs several times a day!

The fact is this: Grant supplies the wheelchairs to appropriate subjects. It is no miracle at all that they get up and at his command wheel *him* about in those very chairs. Witnesses assume that the subjects arrived in the wheelchairs and will leave in them—unless treated to a miracle healing. That is just not so. Deliberate, cruel hoaxes are perpetrated to make miracles where there are none.

Following the meeting, I went to the elevator where the real wheelchair cases were preparing to leave in the same condition in which they arrived. I intended to approach the parents of the crippled child who had gotten near the front, in order to learn their reaction to what had occurred. At the last moment, seeing them in tears and comforting one another, their child still in the same pitiable state, I found I could not bring myself to intrude. They wheeled their son out into the night, sadly resigned to their situation, perhaps having enriched W. V. Grant beyond what they could afford in a last desperate hope of a miracle. Their agony was evident.

Supplying canes, walkers, and wheelchairs to those who don't need them is a common practice among healers. And, the believer might ask, is it the fault of the Reverend Grant if he doesn't know that the subject shouldn't be in that wheelchair? Perhaps God misinformed him on this, while correctly whispering the other "called out" information to his anointed minister? Surely, Grant could not correctly guess the subject's name every time unless God supplied him with it. Let's remember Kreskin and the other mentalists who perform just such wonders every night to entertain their audiences.

How does Kreskin do it? There are ways of obtaining information that are not apparent to the layman. We will discuss several of these techniques, and they are not in any way supernatural, merely clever. What's more important is the way that the information is delivered to the subject. The mentalist has various ways of doing this to maximize the dramatic effect. Grant's act rarely rises above mediocrity in this respect.

Grant has adequate means of obtaining the information he needs—without the help of God or any of the "Nine Gifts of the Spirit" he is supposed to have been given as "One of the Anointed." But his revelation of that data is depressingly the same. For example, to give the name of the victim, here are the variations he uses: "I'm hearing, 'Jack,' " "I'm led to say, 'Jack,' " "I want to say, 'Jack,' " or "I'm seeing, 'Jack.' "

Whichever one of these he uses, it is then immediately followed with: "What's your name?"

And the subject answers as below. Or as an alternative, Grant asks: "Who is 'Jack'?" "What's 'Jack' mean to you?" "Why am I saying, 'Jack'?" or "Is there a 'Jack' here?"

To any of these questions, the victim may answer: "I'm 'Jack.' " "That's me," or "That's my name."

To make his dramatic disclosure of the subject's doctor's name, he uses it in a statement; for example: "When you go to see Dr. Meadows at the Grace Hospital, he's gonna tell you that your arth-uh-ritis is gone. Dr. Jesus has took over!" He then quickly follows up with, "What's the name of your doctor?" or, "Who's your doctor?" and obtains the correct reply.

With monotonous but necessary regularity, Grant asks one of these questions while "calling out" information: "Any of these folks [pointing to those within a five-foot circle around the subject] ask you any questions?" "Anyone ask you any questions since you've been here?" or "I ever ask you anything?"

The answer is almost inevitably no. But each of those questions is designed for a very specific situation. The first question is used when Grant himself has already approached the victim and personally asked for the information. Yes, unbelievable as it sounds, Grant's most frequent method of gaining his information is by simply asking the patient beforehand! Two hours before the meeting begins, he is very evident, walking about in his shirtsleeves among the few dozen early arrivals. These are mostly people who want to be healed and arrive early to get seats on the aisle, where they can be touched by Grant. Remember J. Elmo Clark? He's the man who wanted his blind eye restored to sight. Clark had arrived at five o'clock when there were only a few persons in the auditorium. Grant had simply walked up to him, asked him his name, his doctor's name, and his ailment. Later, when Clark was "called out," he knew very well that Grant already had that information, but thought that Grant was *only checking the accuracy of what he remembered Elmo told him!* The rest of the audience were led to believe that God had revealed it all to Grant, since he also asked Clark, "Any of these folks ask you any questions?" and he gestured to those seated around Clark. The subject, of course, honestly answered no, because *none of those persons had asked him a thing!*

Mr. Clark is also angry at Grant because his "healing" was a trick. Grant had covered Clark's *bad* eye and asked if he could see the people around him. Of course he could, and he affirmed that fact. But he never got a chance to explain until we interviewed him.

Mrs. Pearl Kidd said the same trick had been used on her husband, who had been touted by Grant in his publication as having been healed. Grant had approached Morris Kidd hours before the meeting and asked him his name, his doctor's name, and whether he could see a little. Kidd said that when he was "called out" he was asked if Grant or any other staff member had ever spoken to him. (If Grant actually used this question, he obviously erred, and should have phrased his inquiry as he did with Elmo Clark.) "My husband started to answer yes, but he [Grant] sort of cut him off. He would not give him a chance to answer." Remember, the Reverend Grant carries the microphone, which can be kept away from the subject or switched off completely if the answer is not the one desired. Remember, too, that Grant controls the editing of the videotape that is broadcast every week. Awkward moments never reach the air.

Of course the victim can either unintentionally give the information away in conversation with others in the line waiting to enter the auditorium or volunteer the information—with encouragement—while chatting with Grant's people before the meeting.

Some persons we interviewed claimed that they had given no information to Grant. The day after the meeting we attended, we spoke to relatives who had accompanied a man who suffered from several ailments and was barely able to walk. Though he'd been "called out," too, those relatives assured us that Grant had not spoken to him. He'd not written to Grant to say that he'd be there. It had been a last-minute decision. But then they mentioned an important fact. They mentioned that the sick man had gone up to the front and engaged in a conversation with one of Grant's assistants. It turned out to be John Holland, who also ran the public-address system. The next day we planned to interview the subject, who had been declared healed by Grant with much applauding and cries of "Thank yuh Jesus!" but he was so ill that he could not speak or receive visitors.

There is another, much more subtle process that we observed in use at the St. Louis meeting. It involves those persons who could honestly testify that neither they nor any member of their party had told anything to anyone, from the moment they arrived at the meeting. I will discuss that a little further on, since the technique is quite sophisticated in concept and requires detailed description.

First, another question must be answered. Regardless of how Grant gets the information he uses, how does he remember it so well since he "calls out" as many as twenty persons in an evening? Let me leave this discussion for a moment and turn to the art of mnemonics. It is a simply fascinating art, about which today's leading practitioner, Harry Lorayne, has written a number of books. As perfected by Lorayne, mnemonics is a system of memorizing by association. Suppose you must remember the names of several persons to whom you are being introduced. Applying Lorayne's system, you would pick out some prominent feature of each person's appearance (facial details, dress, ornaments, marks, etc.) and associate that detail with either the sound or some characteristic of the name. Now suppose that you have met a man with a bandage on his cheek. His name is Carter. You might imagine the bandage to have a cartoon of Jimmy Carter—with lots of teeth, of course—drawn on it. The connection has been made. When you see that man with the bandage an hour later, the Carter association will come to mind and you will "remember" his name. A woman might be wearing rhinestone glasses and be named Alexander. I would make the association by imagining a former feline pet of mine named Alexander wearing those glasses. Another person named Donahue wearing a loud checkered vest would lead me to associate that vest with television talk-show host Phil Donahue.

Now, without looking at the preceding paragraph, answer these questions:

1. What is the name of the man wearing the loud vest?
2. Who is the man with the bandage?
3. How is the woman with the rhinestone glasses addressed?

If you never had a cat named Alexander, you might have missed the last question. But each person forms his or her own associations, of course. Weeks from now, if anyone asks you those same three questions, you will be able to answer correctly—because of mnemonics. Harry Lorayne, in his public performances, mixes with his audience before the show, meets each of them just once, and then later on correctly calls each and every one of them by name from the stage.

The system as taught by Lorayne also requires that the student learn a list of simple, basic objects that are associated with, say, the numbers from 1 to 25. Thus, a sailboat might stand for the number 5, while a dill pickle represents 15. Equipped with this information, anyone is able to perform apparently prodigious feats of memory.

With mnemonics in mind, let us return to the discussion of Grant's most sophisticated methods. Some of those "called out" could honestly say that they hadn't told anyone their names and hadn't been engaged in conversation with anyone. We suspected that the information had been gained by means of "healing cards," which is a system still being used by some performers. In *The Truth About Faith Healers*, Grant, Sr., wrote about "healing cards" which were filled out by those seeking to be healed, giving permission to the evangelist to try his methods and use the name of the subject in publicity.

It seems evident that the present W. V. Grant has discovered a more sophisticated method that his father would have admired. At six o'clock, a full hour before the service was to begin, Grant mounted the stage and asked for the attention of those who had been sent "special offering envelopes" in the mail. These people were asked to come down a side aisle with their envelopes, in single file (this was emphasized several times), and to give their envelopes to Grant in person, one at a time. They were also carefully admonished not to say anything to the Reverend Grant because he might later "call them out" and wanted to be sure that no one suspected he had obtained any information from them at this encounter. Grant was careful to add that, even if they didn't have these special offering envelopes, they were free to join the line and give him any check or cash they wanted to contribute, and he would personally receive it. Obediently, a long line formed and moved slowly past Grant.

Barnhart and I remarked that Grant seemed strangely distracted as he accepted the envelopes and dropped them into the huge wastebasket at his side. His attitude seemed almost callous at a time when we thought he would have been exuding maximum charm in his personal contacts with these potential sources of income. But, to me, there was something familiar about his unfocused stare and seeming distraction.

There's an important observation to make here. In using mnemonics, you find that as you meet each person, you require a brief moment to establish an association. This almost invariably produces the "dissociated" expression that we observed on Grant's face as he took each envelope. And he glanced at the front of each envelope, then looked directly into the face of each donor.

Now we discovered that there is a section on the front of each envelope where the name of the donor can be written. Persons who have colored envelopes with a dove drawn on the front are those who have previously written to Grant. In return they have received a computer-printed form letter reminding them that Grant will be in their area for a Miracle Crusade, and they are told that if they "have any prayer requests or needs you may have in your life" they are to write them down and send them along with their $20 donation in "the enclosed envelope." They are instructed: "Hand it to me personally when I call for it at the Auditorium. If you have any special requests enclose them as well."

The Reverend Grant reads the name of the donor on the front of the envelope and associates the person's face with the name as the envelope is handed to him. He can then retire backstage, as he did at the St. Louis and Fort Lauderdale meetings we attended, to open the envelopes and establish a connection with the data contained inside. And, of course, since most checks bear the name and address of the account holder, reference to a telephone book would supply further information that could be "called out" during the service to follow, as if it came from on high.

An unorganized crowd of persons pressing around Grant to present their envelopes would interfere with this association and memorization process. For this reason, he specifies that they stay in single file. This, and the insistence both in his letter and in his statement at the meeting that these envelopes must be presented *in person* by those who received them, provide ample evidence that this is one of Grant's methods of obtaining "called out" data. Remember too, that he says such things as, "I want to say, 'Jack' " or "Who is "Jack?" In this way, he avoids blunders resulting from another person having brought the envelope to him, the afflicted having been unable to do so.

At the Fort Lauderdale meeting, we were able to discover two more of Grant's methods for obtaining information. There, he personally collected one batch of "special" envelopes from those who stood in line. He made no move to retreat backstage to memorize the new data. Instead, four-by-five-inch "crib sheets" were prepared backstage by his coworkers and taken to him on stage. During pauses for hymns, Grant studied these sheets, folded and placed them in his jacket pocket, and then proceeded to call out a new batch of subjects.

Much to my surprise, one of my team members noticed one of Grant's associates standing at the back of the auditorium using hand signals and pointing to various parts of his body to indicate where the subject was afflicted. The associate had his own crib sheet and was there to jog Grant's memory if his mnemonics began to fade.

I wanted to get hold of the crib-sheets Grant carried around in his pocket. I stood close up to the edge of the stage as he worked at memorizing one of them. When the meeting broke up, I approached Chuck Saje, one of my colleagues, and suggested that we put a watch on the trash that was thrown out by the Grant crew each night. The first night yielded nothing. Two large dumpsters, each the size of a Grant truck, remained empty except for a few food wrappers. The second and third nights were the same, and even the food wrappers were gone by Saturday, when the Grant caravan departed. I felt that I should probably abandon this surveillance, but made one more forage on Sunday. *Eureka!* Two plastic trash bags had appeared atop some tree cuttings and, to the amusement of several early morning joggers, I made off with them. It was a bonanza.

Chuck and I searched among the coffee grounds, cigarette butts, and french fries, and the first thing we came up with was a note from Shirley Grant to her husband setting up the time and place that they would go to dinner. We knew then that we were behind the scenes of the Grant show, and indeed we were. A total of ninety-seven letters and envelopes, all torn in half, showed up next. One envelope held a letter from a Mary Birchman, a subject who had been "healed" of colon cancer and a swollen leg by Grant at the first meeting. He had "called out" her name. Mary was not healed, and her letter, given in person to Grant, contained every detail he had "revealed" at the meeting. A score more letters were of the same nature, giving intimate details that Grant had been "divinely inspired" to announce.

But the best prize of all was one of the crib-sheets. Recall that Grant had met certain people in selected line-ups as they gave him their beige envelopes containing twenty dollars and a letter. He had associated their faces with their first names (on the envelope). He had then had a dozen or so envelopes at a time taken backstage and, in return, received four-by-six-inch data-sheets from an assistant. He had studied the sheets and added the new data to his memory, then placed the sheets in his pocket. The crib-sheet we saw read, "Anthony—deaf in both ears, and bladder and tumors. Connie—pain in left eye and left jaw, thyroid and arthritis. Digestive problems. Bernadette—psoriasis, arthritis. Michael—deaf in left ear. Syl—high blood pressure."

The Reverend Grant, both in his personal ministry and in his television appearances, had encouraged his subjects to write letters expressing their prayer needs. "I will take each letter and anoint it with this holy oil from Israel, and I will pray over your letters back in my church in Dallas," Grant had promised. But the most callous fact we uncovered was that some letters, some several pages long and filled with heart-rending pleas for the minister's prayers and the intercession of God, had been torn up, crumbled, and tossed into the garbage. They never even reached Grant's hands. Only by piecing together the scraps of the congregation's hopes, bit by bit, were we able to finally see the true attitude of this pastor toward his flock.

Grant says in no uncertain terms that it is as a result of his anointed status that he possesses the Gifts of the Spirit and that he is thus able to call out members of his audience. Accompanied by his down-home bad English and country-boy usage (he refers to the land of "Iz-rull," "paralyzation of the limbs," and the disease "arth-uh-ritis") his magic act is quite effective in convincing many people that they are witnessing miracles. Grant even has the gall to tell them—in several different ways—that he is not doing an "ESP act" or a "magic show." He attributes it all to divine gifts.

"I take dominion over every force of sin! I take dominion over every force of every disease!" he shrieks. Then he quickly adds, "Brothers and sisters, I couldn't heal a fly with a headache—it's Doctor Jesus who heals!" He follows up with an observation based upon a scriptural passage: "There are folks here who will try to tell me that they have 'heart trouble'! Don't they know that's *impossible?* The scriptures tell us that's impossible! Jesus tells us that's impossible! How many know that's impossible? Why? Cause Jesus said, and these are his words, 'Let not your heart be troubled'! There! Jesus' own words! You *can't* have 'heart trouble'!"

As a magician, I recognize the phrasing in Grant's act. Rather than simply reciting or directly declaring the data he has on each person, he couches his information carefully so that if it is wrong or applied incorrectly it will not really miss the mark. Knowing a name listed in a telephone directory will give him a street number. But it may be a former address, or belong to another person. He wisely chooses to create a vignette: "You're coming out of a door. I want to say a number ending in a '9.' [The person begins nodding affirmatively.] Is it '2409'?" And it is. He has made a hit. If there is no recognition, however, he can turn the small scene into the emergence of a former address, of a doctor's office, or any one of dozens of other scenarios. Of course, these comments are all peppered with frequent questions, such as, "Any way I could know all this?" and "Have you told anybody here . . . ?"

W. V. Grant is, to put it bluntly, doing a magic act disguised as religious miracles. Using a mixture of very simple and rather sophisticated techniques learned from observing evangelists like David Paul, David Epley, and others, going back to William Branham, Grant performs his mind-reading tricks in order to prepare his victims to accept the subsequent demonstration of faith-healing. To a large extent, his audience is already "primed" to accept him, by his reputation, his wide exposure on television, and an already established tradition of charismatic healers, with their "slaying of the spirit," "laying on of hands," and other techniques with which many of the believers are familiar. They lose themselves in the inane crying out of phrases like "Praise the Lord!" and endless repetitions of "Amen!" and suspend their thinking processes in hopes that blind faith will win them a place in Heaven.

It is incredible what long-time believers will accept from evangelists. They have been so conditioned to ignore paradoxes and to excuse blatant errors of fact presented to them by the preachers that they actually take pride in their ability to believe in spite of contrary evidence. Anyone who has never attended a revival meeting cannot imagine the assault on reason and common sense to which the audience is subjected. In St. Louis, the Reverend Grant asserted that he only asks for money once a month, knowing that his listeners cannot check on the last stop he's made, nor on the next. He promised just one money appeal during this service but asked eleven times for donations. No one objected or even noticed, it seemed.

Evangelists abuse truth at every opportunity. But surely their victims have doubts? Surely those who know that the Reverend Grant *asked* them their names in person are not going to ignore that fact and continue to believe in his powers? Why don't people say something when they are aware of the farce being played out? These questions are not easily answered.

There are doubts aplenty. But Grant and his colleagues carefully warn their followers that Satan will try to implant doubts in their heads and that they must resist the temptation to listen. Satan will even tempt the believers to withhold that twenty-dollar bill from Grant's offering basket. Most manage to resist that temptation.

Those who are aware of Grant's information-gathering techniques may decide— as did Elmo Clark—that what happened to them was an exception. And, like Mr. Kidd, they get little opportunity to express their doubts and, if they do, they can be cut off and subsequently misquoted.

Where is the forum for those who want to complain? There is none. Any attempt to take questionable evangelistic healers to court has failed because of two major factors: (1) The guilty have simply too much money behind them and too large and powerful organizations to be in danger of prosecution. (2) The First Amendment has legislators so completely cowed that they treat such an action as the very hot potato it is. Taking an evangelist to court could be political suicide.

There is no doubt that performers like Grant are culpable. If he were pretending to heal headaches, backaches, depression, or other psychosomatic ailments, he could to a considerable extent escape condemnation for interfering with the well-being of his victims. But he goes all the way, claiming to treat such problems as cancer, bacterial infections, physical imperfections, bone fractures, organic defects, circulatory disease, and internal disorders simply by praying them away. Grant is literally practicing medicine without any qualifications whatsoever—an infraction that cannot be allowed under law and a process that can lead to the injury and death of his victims.

There are other serious reasons to assign culpability to Grant. For example, during his appeals for money, he promises that donations will be returned to the giver many times over, thus making a financial offering to his audience. Could anyone other than a self-appointed minister of religion make such a presentation without fear of prosecution?

In an interview with one devoted couple, firm believers in the television evangelists, who had even equipped themselves with a satellite dish and a video recorder so that they would not miss even one gospel message or miracle, an interviewer for a television station in Florida discovered their strange reasoning concerning television preachers. Asked what their reaction would be if the preachers were proven to be crooks, the woman smiled and explained that that would be quite all right with her. "You see, it's our job just to send them the money they need to carry on the good work. If any of them is dishonest, God will take care of that in the bye-and-bye!" Again, formula wins out over good thinking.

*   *   *

It is almost beyond belief what W. V. Grant teaches in his Kingsway Bible College correspondence course. Although a considerable portion of Grant's income is derived from black Americans, in *Men in the Flying Saucers Identified*—one of his textbooks—he labels as "communist doctrine" that the "white girls [should] marry the negro boys, or mate with them without marrying." And to point up the import of his observation, he asks us, "You don't take it serious [*sic*]?" Evidently Grant takes all this "serious," because he says in this book that the information came to him "through prophetic utterance and under the anointing of God." He had a revelation in 1953 that demons live "near the moon" and that we will only reach the moon "when Jesus comes."

Grant would also have his students believe that a "mysterious red tide" has appeared in the Pacific Ocean and Niagara Falls and that "the scientists could not tell it from blood." (This may be a far-fetched reference to the "Red Tide" phenomenon seen yearly off the coast of Peru, but *not* at Niagara Falls. It is a well-understood seasonal growth of algae.)

In his textbook *Power to Defeat Demons,* W. V. Grant says that "a demon is assigned to each country to try to control the ruler of that country." He also claims that there is good reason for the backward state of tropical countries:

since demons are "not affected by weather . . . there are more demon possessed people near the equator than in other parts of the world." That's not the least of it, continues Grant. "The devil will make people dress in shorts or bathing suits, or join the nudest [*sic*] camps." Even the demon-casting-out business itself is fraught with peril: "I started to cast a devil out of a lady," he tells his students. "That devil screamed for its companion nearby. Then I discovered there were two spirit mediums in the audience." Later, he asked a demon who it was, and it replied, "I am a Christian Science practitioner . . . I am mean. I'll hurt you."

In another fanciful tirade, Grant teaches his correspondence students that "from two to five thousand Christians are being put to death each day in China alone. The goal is 100,000,000; Christians and others. There are 15,000,000 in America who are on record to go the same way. They are marked." In this way students are brought to understand world politics and the danger of un-Christian philosophies. A booklet titled *Demons at the Doorstep, II* even claims that certain chemists grind up newborn babies to use in the manufacture of cosmetics for painted women to buy. The Reverend Grant has a dire warning for his colleagues— detractors who might doubt his qualifications—in his text *Signs, Wonders, Miracles* that he has "seen several ministers the past few years criticize miracles, signs and wonders. They are now in their graves. They have gone down with heart trouble, cancers, and operations of various sorts."

One of his texts, *A Mark in the Forehead,* gives further details on the tribulations of Christians in communist countries: "There have been 21,000,000 people in Russia and China . . . who have had their heads cut off, or buried alive!" And he delves into astronomy with this statement: "The scientists say that something happens to the stars every two thousand years. Two planets passed each other, for the first time since just before Noah's flood. Six of the eight planets lined up in the west like they were on a parade. This had not happened since just before the birth of Christ." To point out the inanity of these statements would be to insult the intelligence of a twelve-year-old.

But the big surprise of this particular text—only one of the sixty sold by Grant for his correspondence course—is the answer to a burning question concerning those who have "the seal of God in their foreheads." It is a question Grant poses on the cover, and he promises that the answer will be inside. He will give us, he says, the actual "names and addresses of those who have it now!" Who has the blessed mark? "Millions," says the Reverend Grant, "I have it: I was there the night that I received it; I should know. My wife and boy have it." And the addresses? "My address is Box 353 in Dallas, Texas. My wife and boy receive their mail at the same place. . . ." Readers are told that if they are without this mark at the Coming, they are doomed to "battle over 200,000,000 demons!" But, if they do not have this required mark, there is still a small chance for them: "There may be a few saved people who will have their heads cut off and be saved. . . ." (Grant is very fond of head-chopping as a punishment.)

Surely this cannot be legitimate college-degree material? But the advertisements for the Kingsway Bible College aver that it is accredited by the Accrediting Commission for Specialized Colleges and that students will receive a D.D. degree upon having read the texts and answered the true/false questions. I asked Joseph Barnhart to check this out with his sources in Texas, where Grant has his headquarters. He consulted David Kelly at the Coordinating Board of the State of Texas, in Austin, who said he had never heard of these organizations, nor of W. V. Grant. He referred Barnhart to the Accredited Institutions of Post-Secondary Education and the Higher Education Directory (published by the Department of Education), two U.S. reference books that would list legitimate, recognized institutions able to award degrees. No trace of any of Grant's groups showed up there. Kelly reported: "There is no TVD College or Kingsway Bible College authorized to award a degree, including an honorary doctor's degree, or to use the term *college* in its title within the state of Texas."

The correspondence course is mailed out from "International Deliverance Churches," which claims to be "a non-profit corporation in Texas recognized by the Federal Government, to promote education." The blurb accompanying Grant's course says "We are qualified to give ordination." But *any* church, of any kind or scope, can give ordination to anyone it wants, for any reason.

Examination of the Bible course Grant sells shows that it is useless as a source of knowledge. It appears to have been assembled by an illiterate and consists of superstitious nonsense. It is a total misrepresentation, sold to innocent persons who receive several pounds of printed paper accompanied by pleas for donations and little else for their investment.

Can the Reverend W. V. Grant practice medicine, guarantee financial success, promise to perform miracles, pretend to educate and give out college degrees—for a price—without proper qualifications to do so, without any sort of permit, training, or license? Can he do all that and also publish and preach lies that promote fear, hate, superstition, and bigotry to the American people, in the absolute certainty that no one has the power to stop him? The answer is yes. He knows that no matter what emotional, physical, or financial damage he does to any number of people, he will not be prosecuted or even stopped.

Grant's immunity—and the immunity of other evangelists—seems assured. In 1979, the Federal Communications Commission (FCC) was pressured into investigating the "Praise the Lord" (PTL) television evangelism operation run by Jim Bakker. The commission spent three years investigating, then decided in a four-to-three vote to take "no action" on the matter. Its findings were turned over to the U.S. Department of Justice, and that body took three months to decide to drop it as well. Note: Bakker was not vindicated, as he now claims. He was simply not prosecuted. Had either the FCC or the Department of Justice found insufficient evidence that he was not guilty of misdirecting donated funds to the designated charity, as was charged, they would have so declared.

Helen O'Rourke, director of the U.S. Council of Better Business Groups, was asked about the possibility that evangelists might be seriously investigated by that body. "I can't even believe they will ever touch religious organizations," she replied. "It's too political." Paul Tuz, director of the Toronto Better Business Bureau in Canada, says that his desk is crossed daily by letters from victims of television evangelists and healers. He is more optimistic than Mrs. O'Rourke that something can be done, but still concludes that it is a matter of the "let the buyer beware."

A 1984 U.S. Supreme Court ruling threw out all limitations on the amounts a charity—and that includes operations like Grant's—can spend on administrative costs. Since Grant is not required to make any financial disclosure and does not belong to the responsible groups who voluntarily make such statements, he is free to do what he wants with millions of yearly income. The Grant publication *New Day* lists Kenya, Haiti, Mexico, and Nigeria as countries to which Grant donates money from his ministry. Checks of as much as $1,000 are mentioned. And such urgent matters as the distribution of "over 100 King James Version Bibles and good Christian books" are reported to have been distributed in the Nigerian prison system. One can only hope that those books contain better educational material than the Grant Bible course.

(Spring 1986)

Peter Popoff Reaches Heaven via 39.17 Megahertz

James Randi

Sooner or later, it had to come. The flim-flam artists were bound to discover the advantages of high technology and step up into the Computer Age. In my investigation of the faith-healing business, I almost immediately came upon some modern twists that rather startled me.

Evangelist/healer Peter Popoff is headquartered in Upland, California, whence he sends out highly fanciful fund-raising literature that is computer-generated to appear as if it were personally typed and signed. Some of the slickly designed mailings are quite clever, but others are extremely juvenile, appealing only to the least sophisticated of those on Popoff's vast mailing list.

Little is known about Popoff except from what he publishes—in great numbers—in a series of booklets about his life. According to Peter, it all began when he went to Heaven on a visit and received Nine Gifts of the Spirit along with a command to preach to the multitudes. And, apparently, he was told at the same time that a little cheating couldn't hurt.

Being on the mailing lists of more than a dozen evangelists—under several different names on each list—I receive an enormous amount of mail from these highly organized businesses. From Popoff, I've received Russian currency, handker-chiefs, and red felt hearts—to be carried or worn, then each to be sent back with a check attached. Special envelopes and endless appeals for the emergency needs of his ministry arrive every week. Each is personalized at the computer, dropping my first name into the text occasionally and using "Brother Randi" as the salutation. Most of us are familiar with these gimmicks, but the effectiveness of such methods can only be judged by those in the field.

A man preparing to enter the Popoff crusade in San Francisco in February was approached by a television interviewer. "Why are you coming to see Reverend Popoff?" he was asked. "Peter wrote to me," replied the man, "and wanted me to come here today for a special message God has for me." He was blissfully unaware that *thousands* of persons in the Bay Area received identical letters— identical, that is, except for the personalized effect generated by Popoff's computer.

Seeing the elegant laser-printed mailings and the expensive props used by Popoff, I knew that he was using computer technology prosperously. But I was unprepared for witnessing a spectacular show-biz technique when I attended his crusade in Houston, Texas. Members of H-STOP, the Houston Society to Oppose Pseudoscience, were also in attendance.

With me was Steve Shaw, a young man who was half of the team in the Alpha Project. (See *Skeptical Inquirer,* Summer and Fall issues, 1983.) Steve is very active as a "psychic" entertainer, and he proved invaluable in this investigation.

We arrived two hours before the show began in order to observe any "pumping" of the victims—such as that done by the Reverend and Mrs. W. V. Grant (see *Free Inquiry,* Spring 1986). Each H-STOP member was instructed to fill out any "healing cards" that might be given to them and to put down only false information, except for the address. This was so that they could get on the mailing list but might be "called out" by Popoff under the false name and ailment.

Indeed, that is just what happened. Steve Schafersman, chairman of H-STOP, was approached by Mrs. Elizabeth Popoff and interviewed extensively. Curiously enough, as he gave her each detail, she repeated it *out loud,* slowly and clearly. Others reported the same procedure. Steve Shaw had volunteered as an usher and was observing everything from a different and more auspicious vantage point, but he came back with the same report.

At exactly 2:30 P.M., the time set for the beginning of the service, Mrs. Popoff left the floor of the Coliseum and retired behind the curtain.

Finally, following a spirited address and pep-talk by the front man, the Reverend Reeford Sherrell, Popoff himself came screeching onstage amid Hallelujahs aplenty. He stormed about and screamed warnings of Hell and Damnation for thirty minutes. Then he began a remarkable demonstration that made W. V. Grant's show look pretty thin. He "called out" people from the audience fast and accurately. He named them, gave their ailments, named relatives, and even threw in an occasional street address for good measure.

But, after Popoff had dealt with twenty or so people, it became obvious that he was not using W. V. Grant's mnemonic methods, unless he was *very* good at that art. Steve and I looked at each other as the same idea came to both of us.

"He's got something else going for him," said Steve, "and I think I know what I have to do."

"You're going to get up close to Reverend Popoff and get a look—"

"In his ear," Steve finished for me. And off he went to "usher" next to the Man of God.

Moments later, having practically knocked Popoff down to get close to him,

Steve Shaw was back, grinning like a Cheshire cat. "He's wearing a *hearing aid!*" chortled Steve. "You can see the shiny plastic in there, clear as can be!"

*   *   *

Now what, you may ask, might Peter Popoff be doing with a hearing aid? We concluded that he *had* to be getting this wealth of information via some such device. Though we were unprepared to investigate that angle during the Houston meeting, in San Francisco we enlisted Bob Steiner, a magician and former chairman of the Bay Area Skeptics, who supplied us with technician and security consultant Alec Jason. This enthusiastic chap was equipped with highly sophisticated electronic "scanners" that would prove the undoing of Peter Popoff.

As with the Houston group, the Bay Area Skeptics were instructed to attend the San Francisco meeting prepared to give false data to any interviewer and/ or write in the same fictitious data on the healing cards. True to form, supremely confident that her gimmick was impossible to detect, Elizabeth Popoff waltzed around the audience asking questions—and carefully *repeating* all the details given to her by the unsuspecting victims. Hanging from her arm was a huge handbag— *from which every word was being transmitted upstairs to Peter Popoff!* Then, as in Houston, at 2:30 sharp, Mrs. Popoff left the floor to join her husband in the announcer's booth overlooking the arena. There they discussed details about the members of the congregation below—*leaving the transmitter switched on!*

High in the back area of the arena, using an electronic scanner receiver, Bob Steiner and Alec Jason had quickly located the frequency used by the Popoffs— 39.17 megahertz. A tape recorder was attached to the receiver, and every word was heard. When Popoff made his entrance, we heard Mrs. Popoff testing the communications channel: "Hello, Petey. I love you! I'm talking to you. Can you hear me? If you can't, you're in trouble. . . . I'm looking up names, right now."

Transcribing the tape later on, we heard such commentary as: "I have a hot one for you. Robert Kaywood. He's got a chest condition that needs surgery. Robert Kaywood. Kaywood. Kaywood. He needs surgery. His veins aren't formed. He prays that God will heal him today."

Later on, we heard: "Dean. She . . . no, she should be there on your right side. *Right* side. No, that's not her! No, that's *not* her! In the blue. . . . Oh! That—that might be her. Okay. She lives at 4267 Masterson, and she's praying for her daughter Joy, who's allergic to food." This was followed by laughter from Elizabeth and Pam, the wife of Reeford Sherrell.

But the one that really pleased us was: "Tom Hendry. He's praying for restoration of his family, but he's got a drinking problem that's gotten out of control."

"Tom Hendry" was one of the Bay Area Skeptics, Don Henvick, *who was also called out by Peter Popoff two weeks later in Anaheim, under a different name and with a different disease, and later on in Detroit, dressed as a woman named Bernice Manicoff!* Both Steve Schafersman and Don Henvick were used in the next Popoff television broadcast.

How could God, speaking directly to Peter Popoff through one of the Nine Gifts of the Spirit—the Gift of Knowledge— have made such errors?

*   *   *

Popoff, at one point in the Houston meeting, asked his audience to "break free of the Devil" by throwing their medications up onto the stage. What followed surprised even him. Dozens of people came forward and tossed bottles onto the platform. Popoff was ecstatic. But when Steve and I examined the debris after the audience had departed, we were shocked. Prescriptions for digitalis, nitroglycerine tablets, oral diabetes medication, and many unidentified pills had been discarded by people who might well have needed such substances to stay alive! Steve Shaw, who has had experience working in hospitals, was familiar with these emergency medications.

It was even more amazing that Popoff actually included the pill-throwing episode in Houston in his television broadcast! One would think that he would have recognized the seriousness of the implications of this stunt and that he would de-emphasize it, but he broadcast it for all to see.

The old days of the tent-show healers are gone, but their replacements are among us, filling coliseums with many times the people the tents used to hold. They are louder, slicker, and richer by far, assisted as they are by technology that their predecessors would not have imagined. Now, reaching millions via television and radio, they flourish under the protection of the Constitution.

It would be well for you to know about one more aspect of the Popoff ministry. The callous atmosphere that exists backstage at this pathological Mystery Play is amply demonstrated by the following transmission to Peter Popoff as he ministered to his adoring flock. It was recorded in Anaheim, following an obvious interruption of the radio broadcast from the trailer:

(Elizabeth Popoff speaks.) "Reeford's got a *hot* one!" (Laughter.) "Reeford's so excited! He came running in back here and scared us half to death! You ready for a *hot* one? Okay! Want a hot one? *Hot* one! Hot off the press! Ruby Lee Harris. Ruby Lee. She is standing in the far back where there's no chairs." (Long pause.) "Reeford got a hot one. Hot one! Reeford's got a hot one, Ruby Lee Harris. She's against the back wall. Ruby Lee Harris. She's against the back wall. She's got lumps in her breast. You might want to whisper it—Have her walk down—Have her *run* up there. *Run.* Oh! *Look* at her *run!*" (Loud laughter.) "She's got knots in her breast." (Laughter and giggles.) "A home run! A home run!"

(Then, later on, giggles are heard, and Pam speaks.) "At any rate, she should kick him in the face!" (Laughter.)

(Elizabeth speaks.) "Pam says to make her—Pam thinks that you should have *her* kick *him* in the face!" (Giggles.)

I suggest that the heartless exploitation of the elderly, the ailing, and the emotionally unstable citizens of this country will continue until someone in government decides that these "faith-healers" have abused, deceived, and milked enough people. Perhaps a St. George, rather than a Don Quixote, is waiting in the wings. Let us hope so.

(Summer 1986)

God Helps Those Who Help Themselves

Thomas Flynn

"Do you want some money?" writes the evangelist. "I want to send it to you. God wants to see your faith! God wants to know if you would feel better if you received an extra $700.00 (SEVEN HUNDRED DOLLAR) Money Blessing. Show God you have faith enough—send a [*sic*] $18.00 Donation for the Ministry."

No, the above is not taken from a segment of "Hill Street Blues" dealing with religious bunco. Nor, unfortunately, is it a fabrication. It is a direct quote from a sophisticated circular thousands of Americans found in their mailboxes in 1984. In its consummate, if cynical, craftsmanship, it exemplifies the way some conservative national televangelists use direct-marketing techniques to fund their ministries.

Direct Marketing (DM)—a term that has largely replaced "direct mail" in the business lexicon and embraces such varied techniques as catalog sales, direct mail, and telemarketing (semi-automated telephone solicitation)—is undergoing an unprecedented renaissance in America today. "Junk mail" has been a familiar annoyance for decades, of course. But technological developments of the past decade, which have made the building and maintenance of huge lists of prospects easier and more efficient, have tremendously increased the attractiveness and power of DM techniques. Legitimate businesses use DM to sell books, records, and other consumer products, to promote industrial products and supplies, and to advertise business management seminars, to use only a few examples. Nonprofit and political organizations use its methods effectively to promote their viewpoints and solicit contributions. A growing variety of media are available to the DM user, from television to special newspapers and magazines designed specifically to serve as DM marketplaces. But the mails have continued to hold their own as a popular and powerful DM medium.

America's national fundamentalist ministries are active DM users. Many televangelists who depend on buying air-time from local stations are reluctant to actively solicit funds on their programs lest station managers take offense. The televangelists may sell reasonably priced merchandise or even offer gifts to induce viewers to write in. When the viewers write and identify what offer prompted them to do so, their names go on a DM list and the fund-raising begins in earnest. This article will explore a representative sample of the fund-raisers' output, discuss some of the techniques that go into the design of a successful DM mailing, and evaluate the evangelistic mailings according to the standards that apply to other, nonreligious direct-marketers.

To begin, let us return to the mailer quoted at the beginning of this article—the one that speaks so elliptically of a "$700.00 Money Blessing." Its design reflects sophisticated DM design philosophies. Its source: the Reverend Ike of the United Christian Evangelical Association, whose address is a post office box in New York City.

Ike's mailing contains several separate pieces; each piece repeats the core message with a slightly different slant. DM researchers say this technique improves the effectiveness of almost any mailing—if the cover letter fails to "hook" the reader, perhaps another one of the enclosures will. Many of the pieces also bear the mark of contemporary word-processing technology, which allows the recipient's name to be injected into the copy at almost any point, "personalizing" the letter. This technique has been found to increase readership, even though most readers know the mailing is not truly personal.

Other proven design techniques inject a disingenuous degree of phony informality. Ike's mailing is printed to look as though it were typewritten on a page torn from a child's school notebook. And the page is emblazoned with underlines, circles, and margin notes in various colors, as though the writer emphasized key points by using a small arsenal of felt-tip markers. The resulting cacophony of multichromatic marginalia could be used as evidence to support a claim that the Reverend Ike tapes his pieces to the outside of New York subway cars before they are mailed.

Another powerful technique is to force the reader to become physically involved in the act of responding to an offer. Many magazines, including *Free Inquiry,* use subscription solicitations in which the respondent must punch out or peel off a medallion-like "acceptance token" and attach it to the order form. Research suggests that respondents who have gone to this much trouble are thereby insulated to some degree against changes of heart until after the acceptance is in the mail. Still another proven force-multiplier: give the recipient exact and detailed instructions as to how to respond. Reverend Ike exploits various current marketing methodologies. He specifies the peculiar donation amount of eighteen dollars, and then requires the recipient to check off some boxes and return the enclosed tiny swatch of carpet—allegedly trimmed from the Reverend's prayer rug—with the donation. In return, Ike promises to send each respondent a "Three Day Good Luck Package." (Even after prolonged inspection, no language was found describing a specific procedure for obtaining the above-mentioned $700.00 Money Blessing.)

Another Reverend Ike mailing includes a scrap of cloth that is almost— but not quite—claimed to have come from a garment of Christ. The copy eventually admits that the swatch came from Ike's prayer robe. "I have touched this garment with both hands, and I prayed over it for you and your needs," Ike writes with passion. "Now I ask you in the name of Jesus to take this little piece of blessed heavenly garment out and touch it to your forehead three (3) times." Ike specifies further rituals to be performed with the cloth, then gets to the point: "Now the first thing tomorrow morning, I want you to return this piece of 'Heavenly Hem' [a colored underline in the original]. Please send it back to me along with the $33.00 faith donation!!! As soon as I receive it back from you in faith and belief I will start a prayer cycle for you, then I shall close my eyes and pray a special 'TREATMENT' prayer for you—Then I will send you 'GOD'S GOODIE' package."

The Reverend never explains what this package is, except to say that if you are a lucky recipient and "work with it . . . you will find happiness, good luck, good fortune and money as your faith increases." To climb aboard this gravy train, one turns to the order form—which bears the headline: *"Touch this garment . . . you will be well!"*—checks off some boxes, returns the fabric swatch, and encloses the thirty-three dollars.

Lincoln is reputed to have said, "God must love the poor—He made so many of them." Using the same standard of evidence, we can confidently conclude that the Reverend Ike must love his DM mailers. Another Ike mailing follows the same pattern. No costly carpet samples or scraps of cloth here; this one contains only a cocktail napkin. But no ordinary cocktail napkin, as Ike assures us in fervid prose:

> Inside the envelope . . . You'll find one of my favorite and personal napkins— it has my name and address on it—I'm letting you keep this napkin as a gift of love in exchange for a napkin from you with your name on it. . . .

Now Reverend Ike, however strongly he may believe that "God will provide," is not a man to take chances:

> If you don't have a napkin within your home, I have enclosed one for you to print your name on and mail back to me.

This napkin mailer represents one of Ike's most generous bargains for his faithful. By returning the napkin and a mere twelve dollar donation (that sum is pre-circled on a list of suggested donations) one can receive the "GOD'S GREAT-

EST GIFT" package. Whatever it is, Ike promises that he will send a follow-up letter that will give the lucky recipient "instructions as to how to work with" it.

*　　*　　*

Lest the reader begin to feel that the Reverend Ike has been unfairly singled out, let us proceed to examine the DM productions of other televangelists. It will be apparent that Ike's colorful packages are typical. In fact, the sharp-eyed observer may begin to wonder whether all of these DM slicksters retain the same communications consultant.

The Reverend Al (not to be confused with the Reverend Ike—Al's the one from Fresno with the "Prayer Family") sends a mailer in a tinted window envelope emblazoned with a photograph of the Reverend and the headline "Living On A Shoestring!" It should by now come as no great surprise that inside the envelope can be found a real shoestring. Next to it, a specially punched sheet shows an illustration of (What else?) the "Shoe of Faith." The recipient is to thread the laces through the little holes and check off the problems in his or her life. One reads, "Dear Lord, I don't have the money to pay my bills . . . this shoestring existence has got to go!" One then encloses "a beautiful gift from your heart." Beauty is, of course, in the eye of the beholder, so Reverend Al lets you know he finds $10, $20, $25, or a "special tithe" especially beautiful.

Another mailing—perhaps the most astounding of them all—comes not from the Reverend Al but from his "Prayer Family," or headquarters staff. It asks for thirty-three dollars—one dollar for each year the Reverend Al and his wife, Sister Wilma, have shared wedded bliss—to send the loving and holy couple on a vacation! "There are so many deserving things we could do for them," the letter explains in a naïvely charming approximation of English grammar and syntax, "but don't you think it would be wonderful if we could send them to some place for a few days of good rest? They have been pushing themselves so hard for others. . . ."

Jimmy Swaggart, based in Baton Rouge, Louisiana, takes a simpler approach. In a telegramlike piece headlined "High Priority," he announces his declaration of "war." After the computer-personalized greeting, Swaggart writes, "Jimmy Swaggart Ministries has declared war on Satan. . . . Due to a shortage of funds, this warfare against the enemy will be hindered. Without 'ammunition' from home, the big guns of the Gospel will soon fall silent." Swaggart lets recipients choose their own level of giving, and responds to any gift by sending "a free cross and dove lapel pin." Using the dove symbol in a declaration of war must be judged, if nothing else, a creative touch.

Ernest Angley in Akron, Ohio, is an old-fashioned faith-healer. He makes grandiose claims regarding his power to heal the sick in the name of the Lord.

So healing-oriented are his services that on a 1984 European tour Angley was arrested by officials in Munich, Germany, for practicing medicine without a license! Angley may come the closest to the Reverend Ike's combination of down-home sincerity, deliberate naivete, and avarice. One Angley mailer features a picture of Noah's ark, inside which one is supposed to write the names of those among one's family and friends who are not yet saved. "PLEASE DO TAKE THE TIME TO DO THIS!" Angley thunders. "IT COULD MEAN HEAVEN FOR SOME OF YOUR LOST!"

The recipient is now physically involved. Here comes the pitch:

STEP NUMBER TWO: Make a blessing covenant pact with the Lord. Send you [sic] financial support seed faith and tell God you are going to send something every month to this Jesus ministry. Don't try to send more than you can afford, but as God blesses you, you can increase your amount as He leads you.

Don't think, "Lord, I have such a little to give that I am ashamed to send it." My attitude about giving to God has always been: "If I give my best to God, then I can expect His best for me." DOING YOUR BEST IS ALL GOD EXPECTS!

Angley devotes a great deal of prose—six paragraphs—to the need for the reader to sow the most generous possible "seed faith." It is no surprise, then, that when we turn to the reply card, the recipient is permitted to choose the "seed faith" amount, from five dollars to five hundred dollars. Presumably, Angley could wax less eloquent about gift size if he simply took a page from Reverend Ike's book and specified the gift amount—thereby sparing his flock the agony of choice.

Another Angley classic asks the recipient to write down all his or her problems on a paper cross and mail it back. It hardly seems necessary to explain what *else* one is expected to enclose in addition to the paper cross! On his very next trip to Jerusalem, Angley pledges, he will have the paper cross stuffed into his pocket when he kneels to pray in the very tomb of Jesus, hallelujah. "I want to make certain you receive The Tomb Anointing!" he coaxes.

Oral Roberts also issued a mailer—indeed, a rather austere one—to promote his pending trip to the Holy Land. He asks recipients to list their unsaved loved ones so that he can pray for them when *he* prays on the very soil Christ trod. Perhaps so as not to stumble over the Reverend Angley, Roberts tells us he plans to fly to Bethlehem and "to kneel on that sacred spot where Mary gave miraculous birth to our Savior, the Holy Child Jesus." Another Oral Roberts mailer is somewhat more complex—it includes plenty of color underlining and an autographed picture of Roberts himself. "I want you to have your miracle breakthrough so much that I'm going up in the Prayer Tower . . . to travail in prayer for you." But Roberts will not travail alone.

He asks each believer to send a snapshot of himself or herself that he can use as "a point of contact" during his prayers. Most readers have already guessed what is supposed to accompany the snapshot.

A very sophisticated Oral Roberts piece dated March 1985 solicits support for an ambitious, ultramodern "Healing Center." He encloses a tiny bag of cement. "Partner," he writes, "return this cement bag to me with your Seed-Faith gift today. As we pour the piers [for the new building], we will combine your cement with the cement from my other Partners to symbolize our faith joining together for the great things God is going to bring to you through this Healing Center."

Roberts is not alone in the construction business. Pat Robertson in Virginia Beach is hard at work on Phase IV of his ambitious Christian Broadcasting Network (CBN) Center project. Robertson will send a brand new teaching tape and the *CBN Ministry Handbook,* which is "filled with tested biblical solutions to life's deepest problems," to anyone who donates $100 or more.

This mailing, with its textured-paper cover letter and paired four-color fliers (one describing the construction project and another describing the premiums) makes an impressive package. The real DM *putsch* came about a month later, when Robertson's flock received an *exact copy* of the letter. The word COPY was stamped in red at its top; and attached to its face with two strong staples was a yellow "message slip" with a pseudo-handwritten message from Robertson, begging those readers who didn't send one hundred dollars the first time to buckle down and respond to this second mailing.

But perhaps the prize for unmitigated gall must go to Jim Whittington, a Greenville, North Carolina, evangelist. The very envelope, boldly emblazoned with the "handwritten" headline "You Were Chosen!!!" should tell the believer that this is no ordinary piece of junk mail. Indeed, it is very special junk mail—so special that Whittington begins by disparaging other DM-using evangelists who use word-processing to personalize their letters:

> You see, I can write to you and call you by your name as I sometimes do; but anyone can write to you and use your name. But only a friend can write to you from their [*sic*] heart. . . .

Whittington is only warming up:

> I can not choose the ones to answer the call in this letter. . . . Friend, those who are not chosen might not understand this letter at all. Some might read it and get mad. Some might read it and make fun. . . . It might fall into the hands of an unbeliever or a relative of someone who has passed away and they may turn it over to a TV reporter or newspaper or some agency to get some publicity or get me attacked again and talked about.

What is Whittington worried about? Read on.

Are you one of the 99 to send a special one time gift of $1,000.00 to help defeat the financial attack the devil has made against me and this ministry. [*sic*]

Your eyes have not deceived you. Jim Whittington wants one thousand dollars. "Has God chosen you?" he writes. "Do you fill [*sic*] a tug at your heart strings telling you that you must do whatever it takes?" Whittington wants exactly ninety-nine people to send in one thousand dollars: "I can only take 99. Anything less will not please God. Anything more must be turned away. You must send that $1000.00 now."

One thousand dollars is a lot to give, but not the way Whittington sees it:

You may feel like you can't but you can. The Americans on that cruise ship [an apparent reference to the *Achille Lauro*] paid more than $1000.00. Many people have paid $500.00 for a ticket to see a world series game. . . . Take it out of savings. (Banks are failing every day anyway.) Borrow it. (We borrow for everything else in this world.) . . . The chain must not be broken. As soon as I receive your prove-God offering of $1000.00, I will send you your number and you will know what position in the chain you hold. Don't let the chain have a missing link. . . . Remember there's just so many that can get in. Don't wait too late and live to regret it.

*   *   *

What do these mailings have in common? What makes them work? (We must conclude from the fact that so many televangelists structure their mailings so similarly that this DM technique is quite effective.)

First, most—if not all—of the pieces use one or more "personalizing" techniques, from simulated felt-tip underlining to injecting the recipient's name into the copy. Some users employ "felt-tipping" to preselect options, such as the amount of a gift—effectively creating the feeling of a decision opportunity where none really exists.

Second, most of the mailings include a novelty item, such as the Reverend Al's shoestring or Oral Roberts's bag of cement. In the trade, such add-ons are known as "unordered merchandise." Much of the unordered merchandise used in fundamentalist DM mailers is intended to serve as the focus of physical activity to involve the recipient, who is asked to do something with the novelty and return it with the offering. In the case of the Oral Roberts snapshot, the novelty was intended as a symbol of the action the recipient was asked to undertake.

Third, the mailings generally contain thinly veiled promises of awesome rewards awaiting those who respond in time. Ministers who rely heavily on faith-healing, such as Angley and Oral Roberts, speak fuzzily of diseases cured and a return to well-being. Others hint—in the case of the Reverend Al's shoestring mailer, rather directly—at miraculous rewards of prosperity. At other times, writers rely on promises of undefined miracles. This quote is from Oral Roberts's "trip to Bethlehem" mailer:

> There on my knees I'm going to raise your name and needs to the Lord and believe him to give you the miracle breakthrough you've got to have—on or before Christmas.

> Here's what I want you to do QUICKLY:

> FIRST. Make up your mind this won't be just another Christmas. Start dreaming right now you're going to get your biggest miracle.

Careful reading of these paragraphs will show what Roberts has really promised his readers: nothing. But the structure—with sinewy, forceful, and memorable phrases strung like beads between the obfuscations—is clearly designed to impress a less critical reader as a promise: *Do what I ask and send in your dollars, and I WILL get you a miracle from the Lord.*

Fourth and most important, all the mailings conclude with a plea for money. In very few cases is the appeal phrased in terms like "We need your help. Give what you can." Specific or substantial amounts are the goal, and the mailers go to great lengths to create the feeling in the recipients that they will get their money's worth. From the complexity of the mailings themselves, to the layers of activity that are to accompany the donation (checking off boxes, writing down names, performing prescribed rituals upon the unordered merchandise, and so on), to the tangible or intangible items one receives in return (from "your greatest miracle" to a set of teaching tapes), every effort is made to make the recipient feel his or her donation is but a single element of a vast and complex web. It is very much like the negotiation and performance of a contract.

Obviously, the faithful who receive these mailers do not perceive the appeal for money they all contain as detracting from their supposedly religious purpose. Anyone who chooses to support a cause-oriented organization understands the need for periodic contributions to support the organization's operations. But believers in these televangelists are willing to be told how much to give, and in many other ways tolerate a level of pushiness (for lack of a better word) that no secular organization would dare use in its appeals. To some degree, televangelists rely on sheer bluster to force reader acceptance. When you're offering your readers not only eternal salvation but also future prosperity and cures for disease, you can afford to be more direct in your appeals than, say, the Cousteau Society.

But even the men and women behind these mailers feel the need for circumlocution. The donations are called "prove-God offerings," "blessing covenant pacts," or "seed-faiths." The term *seed-faith* is most prevalent; several of the DM packages I sampled used it. Oral Roberts provides a fascinating glimpse into the pastoral theology that underlies the term and apparently makes it a successful cover for direct and pointed fund-raising:

> I know this: God cannot order your miracle harvest until your seed is in His hand.

> Have you ever given a sacrificial seed to Jesus at Christmas? Well, I'm led to offer you the opportunity to plant a seed out of your need—a seed against your problem—a seed to empower your life with your own personal Christmas miracle breakthrough. You can't buy it—but the Bible teaches you can Seed-Faith for it.

> Remember this, every person who got their miracle at that first Christmas gave God their best, including gifts of money.

Obviously, the "seed-faith" concept effectively masks or sanctifies the essentially pecuniary nature of many of these mailings. Secure in their faith, the recipients fail to recognize when their spiritual shepherds have shifted their allegiances to another, older God—one we know today as Mammon.

To the sophisticated reader, these mailings are transparently—and offensively—acquisitive in their outlook. They are every bit as disturbing and absurd as the impassioned pleas for support most of us have heard or seen on episodes of these preachers' broadcast ministries—but with the added element of hard copy, which allows us to hold their ravings in our hands and contemplate them at leisure. Studying these cynical circulars, one can feel only pathos for the hapless individuals—trapped by loneliness, limited intellectual horizons, or the strictures of a misdirected faith—who are their intended targets. Those who write and design these mailers betray a numbing confidence that they can tell their flocks virtually anything, however manifestly self-aggrandizing, and tell them it came from God—and get results.

This point cannot be overemphasized: these mailings work insidiously well. Since professional religious in the United States need not release their financial statements to anyone, there is no way to quantify the returns these mailings bring in. But practical wisdom assures us that such complex and relatively expensive mailings would not be used time and time again, and would not be designed so similarly by so many media ministries, unless they represented a proven and mature technology for making money. Nor can we be too far wrong in concluding that the people for whom these gross appeals are best tailored to extract funds—the desperate, the uncritical, the lonely, and the undereducated—are the very persons who can least spare those funds.

Obviously, no ordinary cause organization or profit-making venture could long employ such openly manipulative strategies in its mailings without running afoul of the United States Postal Service, consumer agencies, or the Direct Marketing Association (a Washington-based trade association whose attempts to police the DM industry have been relatively successful of late). But televangelists enjoy the same advantages in their use of the mails as they exploit in other phases of their operations: the enormity and inherent ambiguity of their promises, and the condition, seemingly analogous to diplomatic immunity, that attends upon their status as men of the cloth.

Compare televangelists with other direct marketers. K-Tel promised only that their Veg-O-Matic would slice, dice, and otherwise relieve kitchen drudgery. The Sharper Image promises only that its high-tech gadgets will work as their manufacturers claim. Almost all televangelists offer salvation, whatever that is; some go on to include healings, a restoration of well-being, and future prosperity. Promises of this nature powerfully resist verification in your garden-variety product-testing laboratory.

*   *   *

Before we conclude our examination of fundamentalist DM practices, it may be enlightening to examine three of the forty articles in the Direct Mail Association's Guidelines for Ethical Business Practices. It is doubtful that any of the telepreachers whose work we have examined could survive judgment by these principles:

Article #1

All offers should be clear, honest and complete so that the consumer may know the exact nature of what is being offered. . . . Before publication of an offer, direct marketers should be prepared to substantiate any claims or offers made.

Advertisements or specific claims which are untrue, misleading, deceptive, fraudulent or unjustly disparaging of competitors should not be used.

One Reverend Al order-form says, "After checking or writing your most urgent need to God, read it again as a prayer to Him. Begin Praising and Thanking God with all sincerity for the answers you're about to receive." Is that "clear, honest, and complete" in any but the most pedantic sense?

An Oral Roberts piece shrills, "You need a miracle breakthrough this very month, and I can help you get it." Is the Reverend Roberts prepared to substantiate that claim?

Or reflect on the Reverend Ike's colossal pronouncement.

When I answer your letter and send you this "GOD'S GOODIE" package, you are going to receive the answer as to how to get rid of bad luck, evil, setbacks, hardships, and all the other things that cause you to be unhappy. . . .

It would be interesting to see this claim judged on the basis of DMA's "untrue, misleading, deceptive . . ." language.

Article #25

Direct marketers should only offer merchandise when it is on hand or when there is a reasonable expectation of its receipt.

It would be challenging indeed for the Reverend Al to prove what solutions to "shoestring problems" he really has on hand, or for Ernest Angley to substantiate to the satisfaction of a court that he has truly stocked enough Tomb Anointings to go around. After hundreds of years, philosophy has finally and all but unanimously ruled as to whether there is a "reasonable expectation" of receiving the kind of "merchandise" televangelists offer. And the answer is no.

Article #26

Merchandise should not be shipped without having first received a customer's permission. The exceptions are samples or gifts clearly marked as such, and merchandise mailed by a charitable organization soliciting contributions, as long as all items are sent with a clear and conspicuous statement informing the recipient of an unqualified right to treat the product as a gift and to do with it as the recipient sees fit, at not cost or obligation to the recipient.

Some DM-using evangelists could be plunged into very real legal hot water on this point if prosecutors in any state having similar laws on the books were so inclined. Though the "unordered merchandise" is typically of negligible value (e.g., Oral Roberts's bag of cement, the Reverend Ike's carpet scraps, fabric swatches, and napkins), the copy usually allows recipients very little freedom as to what to do with the merchandise and seldom, if ever, refers to the enclosures as gifts. No, the Reverend Al wants his shoelace back, laced through the Shoe of Faith but not tied. Oral Roberts needs that pinch of cement back so he will have enough to complete his multimillion-dollar building project. And one quails at the thought of the retributions the Reverend Ike might call down upon the miscreants who send in the required eighteen-dollar donation without returning his prayer rug.

To the educated reader who is fortunate enough to be situated outside these preachers' arena of belief, most of the mailings appear little more than humorous. But the laughter is muted when we realize that these mailings must be working—and when we contemplate the type of believer who must therefore constitute the rank and file of those forces.

(Spring 1986)

Does Faith-Healing Work?

Paul Kurtz

The Reverend Ernest Angley is a popular television preacher. His "Ernest Angley Hour" and the "Ninety and Nine Club" are beamed to a growing number of television stations. Ernest W. Angley Ministries claims the two programs air in over more than one hundred markets in the United States, Canada, the Philippines, and Africa. A native of North Carolina, Angley came to Akron, Ohio, in 1954 and built his Grace Cathedral there in 1957. He recently purchased his own television station in Akron, TV-55, and in 1985 took over the extensive television production facilities of Rex Humbard, who had been located in Akron but moved away after suffering financial difficulties. Although all Akron's tire factories have virtually closed, it still holds forth as a kind of gospel center.

The image Ernest Angley portrays is actually rather comical. He is short and chunky, and his thick brown hair looks very much like a toupee. His speech is unpolished, has a deep Southern (somewhat feminine) accent, and closely resembles an old-time populist preacher. He stretches the word "Jesus" ("Jee-ee-su-us") into four syllables and often implores his viewers to put their hands on the television screen as he shouts "Hee-ea-ul."

Angley has gained surprising notoriety as a faith-healer. On his television shows he goes through his curious antics of "healing" all kinds of afflictions: from cancer, diabetes, multiple sclerosis, and alcoholism to deafness and blindness. The magazine he edits, *The Power of the Holy Ghost,* contains enthusiastic testaments of healing: One woman reports that Angley cured her of back trouble; another testifies that he cured her anorexia bulimia; still another claims that an aneurism at the base of her skull disappeared after she made a phone call to Angley's hotline.

A Safari to Ernest Angley Country

With this in mind *Free Inquiry* and the Committee for the Scientific Examination of Religion (CSER) decided to investigate Angley's healing firsthand. On January 10, I assembled a seven-member team and we set off for Akron to attend one of Angley's services. We drove to Grace Cathedral, a handsome building on the outskirts of the city. On the adjacent grounds stands a gleaming white marble statue of an angel, which I am told represents Angley's deceased wife.

The Friday-night service was to begin at 7:00 P.M.; however, the doors were open at 6:00 P.M., and invalids were admitted still earlier by a side entrance. The plan was that James Randi would pose as a decrepit cripple and that I would lead him in by the hand. Randi, with his white beard and flowing brown cape, played the part well. He had a cold and kept coughing pathetically as he limped along. He looked terrible! We went up to the side door and were beckoned to come right in by two sympathetic attendants. We were helped into a wing of the church where several ill and crippled people were already waiting, some in wheelchairs. I kept assuring Adam Jersin (Randi's pseudonym), in a voice loud enough for everyone to hear, that he would feel much better after the service and that, in any case, "when you get back to the hotel you can put on a hot-pack to relieve the pain." Shortly thereafter an attendant helped us to two of the seats up front that had been cordoned off and reserved for invalids. Seated behind us was a partially paralyzed elderly woman who had been helped out of her wheelchair. We discovered that most of those present, in the front rows, at least, knew one another and seemed to attend the services regularly. Soon another elderly cripple arrived on crutches and was greeted by the ushers and by several other people nearby.

The church gradually began to fill up. Our colleagues entered through the front door and positioned themselves in various parts of the auditorium. Two of them were equipped with tape-recorders, and Randi and I were carrying hidden recorders to tape the proceedings. The stage set the tone of what was to follow: it was decorated with two huge bouquets of flowers and various shrubs and trees— all of which appeared to be fake.

The service began promptly at seven o'clock with lively musical entertainment. There was a fifty-piece choir and musical ensemble, including three trumpets, four guitars, a drum, a piano, and an organ. The music was very well done, aping a Broadway show, with a sprinkling of jazz and gospel music.

Thirty minutes later the Reverend Angley appeared, nattily dressed in a gray suit and a tan striped tie. Early in the program Angley began his appeal for funds, first asking for a "tithe offering" and then a "love offering." As the ushers came up the aisles, Randi flashed a twenty-dollar bill, but he managed to palm it and put an empty envelope into the collection plate. I enclosed a five-dollar bill and filled in my name and address because I wanted to get on Angley's mailing list. We calculated that there was a hefty take that evening since an estimated eight hundred people were present, and most of them gave twice.

Angley droned on, delivering an incomprehensible sermon. He complained that he had many enemies but considered their criticism free advertising. (Angley's TV-55 had been attacked in the *Cleveland Plain Dealer* the previous week for its daily programming of grade-B Hollywood movies with lots of sex and violence, which Angley had previously deplored.) Basically, Angley's message was that we must be absolutely obedient to God and on guard against Lucifer. If we were to trust everything to God, he promised, our troubles would disappear. He also promised his expectant audience that the presence of God would soon manifest itself in the cathedral and miracles would occur.

*   *   *

Angley had his own troubles in 1984, which he recounts in the little booklet *Cell 15,* on sale at the book table in the church. On July 11, 1984, while on a tour of Western Europe, he was imprisoned in Munich. He had been charged with practicing medicine without a license and with promising "sure cures." He was held on suspicion of fraud.

Angley's trip to West Germany was accompanied by considerable fanfare. He had taken out full-page ads in German newspapers announcing himself as "Wunderheiler." There were 187 public-relations men, guards, attendants, and other camp-followers in his entourage, and his arrest caused a great deal of confusion among them. When he was released on bond, he threatened to sue, but left Germany hastily.

What Angley does not mention in *Cell 15* is that on July 8, 1984, a Swiss woman, Anna Berner, had died of a heart attack at one of his healing sessions. Moreover, German law requires a license to practice medicine at public gatherings. Angley claimed that it was not *he* who healed but *God* and that he was only an instrument of God's power. According to Angley, his arrest provoked an international incident. He also took credit for a storm that hit Munich the day after his departure, hurling hailstones "as big as tennis balls and grapefruit" on the city, injuring three hundred and inflicting severe damage. He insists that Jehovah had vent his wrath on the citizens of Munich because of his arrest.

Is Angley a healer? Does he cure people? In *Cell 15* he recounts the death of his wife, Angel, which he says was a terrible blow to him. As nearly as we can determine, his wife's name was Esther Lee and she died in 1970 of colitis. According to Angley, one day "Angel" suddenly became ill. He called the family physician in Cleveland and was told to bring her to the hospital in an ambulance immediately. An hour later she died. Angley collapsed upon hearing this grim news. Why couldn't he save her? His rationalization runs as follows: About five or six weeks before her death "an anointing" came upon her to go to heaven. Angel told Ernest that the only reason she didn't want to go to heaven was that she didn't want to leave him. Angley replied: "I will tell you one thing . . . if the Lord ever starts to take you, I promise you I won't stand in your way." He then goes on to say that when "I made such a bold promise, I didn't think I would ever have to face it; but in just a few weeks, suddenly, I was confronted with the horror of keeping that promise. Angel was dying" (p. 27). This is the pretext Angley gives for being unable to save his own wife.

*   *   *

Let us return to the cathedral. Angley's sermon began to build up to a crescendo as he announced to the hushed audience that supernatural events would ensue and that miracles would occur. He then left the stage and moved out front. He went up to one woman, who one of his ushers had apparently seated in the front row near us, touched her on the forehead, shouting, "Hee-ea-ul, Jee-ee-su-us!" She immediately fell back into the arms of the three attendants standing behind her and was then laid out flat on the floor and covered with a blue silk cloth.

Angley quickly proceeded down to the front of the church, touching three more persons, each of whom fell back in a swoon into the arms of the attendants. He next went to Randi, who came hobbling forth. "I command the evil spirit to leave you. In the name of Jesus I pronounce you whole." He touched Randi on the forehead, and Randi immediately fell back and was caught and laid out on the floor. Later he said that he had wanted to play along with the act to find out what was going on.

Angley next approached me and beckoned that I come forth. "Oh my gosh," I thought to myself, "Randi was the alleged cripple, not me." Angley must have thought I didn't look too well either. I quickly covered my tape recorder with my hat and stood up. He touched me on the forehead and cried out, "In the name of Jesus, he-ea-ul." I was not going to take part in this charade, so I stood my ground and did not fall back. Angley again hit me on the forehead, somewhat harder, and the attendant held my shoulder, but I didn't give in. I looked Angley straight in the eye. He said, "Do you wish to be saved? Are you born again? Is there anyone in your family that you wish to be saved? In Jesus' name I command these to happen." He put his arm behind me and forcibly tried to push me down, but I steadfastly refused to fall. We were eyeball to eyeball, and I thought to myself, "Look, you son-of-a-gun, don't try anything on me." But I didn't want to let on who I was because we were there to investigate what went on. Angley tarried a bit, and then left me, moving on to the next victim as I reclaimed my seat on the bench. Randi was still stretched out on the floor. All around me people were crying. On my left a woman was talking gibberish, "speaking in tongues."

Angley continued this for well over an hour, moving up and down in the front of the auditorium. As the people came up to him, he asked what their problems were. One young man, Steve Bruch, age twenty-one, came back three times, was touched by Angley and fell back each time. After the third time Angley questioned him and declared that a miracle had occurred. Steve attested to the fact that he could now straighten his knee and the pain had disappeared.

Angley called out, asking that any alcoholics or drug addicts who wished to be healed come forth. Several people moved to the front. One elderly gentleman in a dark pin-striped suit who said he was an alcoholic fell back in tears when Angley touched him. Later, Angley returned to question him, examined his hand, and declared that another miracle had occurred.

In another case, a man presented his twelve-year-old son to Angley. The boy wore a hearing aid in each ear. The father said the boy had a 90-percent hearing loss and had difficulty with his speech. Angley ordered the boy to take off his hearing aids and then walked around him, shouting "Hallelujah! Hallelujah!" He said to to the boy, "Say Jee-ee-su-us," which he did, though it was barely audible. Yet Angley declared that this was another miracle and that this young lad's hearing and speech would improve when he returned home.

Angley repeated several times that miracles had occurred. The loudspeaker system was adroitly turned off and on and raised and lowered to highlight only some conversations. Generally it only picked up Angley's voice and not what was said by those he talked to—unless he wanted it that way. So one could not always verify what Angley's subjects said before and after the "healings." One woman, accompanied by her son, reported that she had brought the boy there five years earlier when he had a large tumor. Angley prayed for him, she said. The boy had surgery immediately thereafter, the tumor was removed, and he recovered rapidly. She attributed his recovery to the Reverend Angley, and he again declared, "Hallelujah!" Another miracle had occurred!

Next Angley walked back and forth pointing to one section of the auditorium at a time. He said that there was a person in one section with a bad kidney. "You've got your miracle," he proclaimed. Pointing to the next section he said there were eight people with back trouble and that they would be healed. In the next, he said that someone had chest pains and heart trouble and would be healed. I was doubtful about all of these claims, since very few people verified his pronouncements or his prophecies.

Nonetheless, the audience remained transfixed. Approximately half of those present—some four hundred people—came to the front to be healed. Most of those assembled were dramatically involved, intensely emotional, and simply overwhelmed.

As the healing session concluded, several hundred moved toward the front of the church lustily singing hymns; many were tearful, others joyful, still others babbled in tongues. Angley was in complete control of the audience. One got the impression that he could have commanded them to do almost anything and that they would have obeyed. I was reminded of Jim Jones's hypnotic power over his flock in Guyana.

As the meeting began to break up, Randi, the rest of our team, and I attempted to contact those for whom Angley had proclaimed a miracle. Given the hustle and bustle, it was virtually impossible to do so. Nonetheless, I managed to question two people. The first was Steve Bruch. I learned that he was unemployed and lived with relatives in Wellington, a town about an hour from Akron. Steve had come to the front and fallen down three times. "What was your ailment?"

I asked. He replied that he had cartilage in his knee that caused it to go out of joint and made it painful to use his leg, and that Angley had repaired it.

"Had that ever happened before?" I asked.

"Yes" said Steve, "The knee often goes out."

"But if you stretch it does it go back in?" I asked.

"Yes," he said.

"Was that a genuine miracle?" I asked. He just smiled.

Next I encountered the man who said he was an alcoholic. He was being led from the auditorium by a large, buxom woman, no doubt his wife. "Excuse me, sir," I said. "I was intrigued by the fact that the Reverend Angley pronounced a miracle over you. Are you an alcoholic?"

"Yes," he said.

"How long have you been drinking?" I asked.

"Oh," he said, "I stopped drinking many years ago. Indeed, twice."

"But why are you an alcoholic?" I asked.

He replied, "Well once an alcoholic, always an alcoholic."

"What was the miracle?" I asked him.

He said that he had shown Angley a finger he had broken a few months before and that it had been bent. He showed me his crooked finger. "It's still bent," I said.

"Yes" he replied "But it is a bit straighter than before." This was Angley's miracle.

Evaluating the Claims of Faith-Healers

According to Angley, a great number of people in the auditorium that night had been cured, but this is highly questionable. On television, Angley proclaims healings week after week. What are we to make of these alleged miracles? Are they genuine? It is clear that we have to be extremely skeptical about any claims that a miracle has occurred. Likewise, we have to be extremely careful about the accuracy of subjective reports of such healings by the recipients. Several steps should be taken before accepting the claims of a faith-healer:

1. One would need to diagnose the case beforehand. Often what we get are garbled accounts by patients of what their preexisting conditions were. We need careful documentation of their conditions, including X-rays, blood tests, and other medical records. Often we hear the claim that "the doctors had given up" or that "the doctors could do no more for me," or that the person was "incurable." But are these statements accurate? There are no doubt some cases of mistaken diagnoses. Facile public proclamations of illnesses need medical corroboration.

2. One needs to follow up such cases after the fact to see whether the subjects' conditions have actually improved and whether orthodox medical treatment is being given currently. Simple testimonials by preachers or their parishioners are not sufficient in themselves. Yet that is what most of the claims of cures are

based upon. Television evangelists like Pat Robertson, who report telephone conversations with people they claim were cured, provide no independent corroboration that such claims are accurate.

Clearly we must recognize the psychosomatic nature of many illnesses. When an illness has a psychological component, a patient may very well be helped by a dramatic healing session, especially if he believes in the healer. Suggestion can be a powerful tool. But it is not Jesus or God who helps the patient but the *belief-state* itself, which acts as a placebo. This may be the case in some hysterically induced illnesses (such as paralysis), as Charcot and Freud observed. Hence, in some situations the healer, in spite of his evoking God, may function as a psychotherapist. Faith-healing *may* provide some help in alleviating symptoms of stress-induced illnesses like ulcers and asthma. The "bedside manner" of the physician or the psychiatrist plays a role in many healing situations. The state of mind of the patient, especially the confidence that he or she will get better, may be therapeutically self-fulfilling. Given the emotionally charged atmosphere of a mass healing session, many people may be carried away by the infectious enthusiasm and may feel better, at least momentarily, and even may be persuaded that a "miracle" has taken place. A "miracle" is a product of ignorance. The word is used in connection with "healing" when a patient's actual physical condition and the possible natural causes of a cure are unknown.

The question, of course, is whether the cure will be lasting, if indeed there was an affliction in the first place. A follow-up study of so-called cures is necessary. Some patients may be psychologically harmed by faith-healers, particularly when their infirmities are not helped by the healing session and they attribute the failure to their own lack of faith.

The real issue is whether faith-healers can affect *organic* illnesses like diabetes, arteriosclerosis, cancer, infectious diseases, and broken bones. Interestingly, television healers blithely maintain that they are able to do so. It is here that the serious questions of malpractice and fraud emerge; there may be considerable danger to patients who believe they will get better and neglect or delay seeking competent medical treatment in the hope of a miracle. If a subject's condition has not been previously diagnosed and he puts his faith in the healer, he may ignore medical therapy. It can be a life-or-death situation.

A story reported in the Charlotte, North Carolina, *Observer and News* on January 1, 1978, told of a woman who died of a heart attack moments after Angley prayed for her; after she fell back in the customary swoon, she was allowed to lie on the floor unattended for twenty minutes. Angley denied that she was "slain in the spirit" and maintains that she remained in the back of the hall and died later in the hospital. But protestations notwithstanding, healers are tampering with the health and lives of countless people. They should be called into account for practicing medicine without proper credentials. They insist that they are dealing with religion and not medicine, but a quack is a quack no matter what he calls himself. CSER is now embarked on a follow-up study of patients whom Angley allegedly healed, and we hope to publish results of this inquiry when it is completed.

*   *   *

There have been at least two important scientific studies of faith-healing in recent years. One is *Faith Healing* (1968), by Louis Rose, a British clinical psychologist. In this book, Rose examines the history of faith-healing. He also investigates some modern faith-healing in Britain, such as that by Harry Edwards, Christopher Woodward, and Christian Science practitioners. According to Rose it is extremely difficult to do follow-up studies. What we would need to accept it as genuine, he says, is at least one incontrovertible case of paranormal healing that stands up under meticulous scrutiny. The basic problem, however, is that there is an abysmal lack of evidence in support of the faith-healing hypothesis. After examining literally hundreds of cases of purported cures over the years, Rose narrowed his quest to a search for just a handful of cases, perhaps only a single case, "in which the intervention of a faith-healer had led to an irrefutable case" (p. 175). It would have to be a cure not in the vague sense that the patient felt better or in the sense that a progressive disease had been limited but "in the sense that as a result of the healer's work alone, a demonstrated pathological state had been entirely eliminated." But Rose concludes that he has not found "one miracle cure."

It is important to point out that some illnesses are misdiagnosed, some (such as cancer) go into remission, and some simply run their course and cure themselves in time. What is needed is a definitive illustration of a healer's cure.

Rose examined ninety-five instances of purported cures in detail. In fifty-eight cases, it was impossible to see medical or other records to confirm the cure. In twenty-two cases the records were at such variance with the claims that it was considered useless to proceed with an investigation. In other cases, temporary improvement was followed by a relapse, or improvement occurred concurrent with orthodox medical treatment. There was no clear-cut, unambiguous cure by a faith-healer. Here is Rose's evaluation of some typical cases:

> M.R., a boy aged 9, was suffering from pseudohypertrophic muscular dystrophy. When I examined him in December 1951 he was free of spinal deformity. He later visited Mr. Edwards (the faith healer) who told him he "would get better and that he had straightened his back. "The family general practitioner wrote in February 1953: "I am sorry to report that in my opinion the condition is very definitely worse." [p. 164]

> Mrs. M.H. was the subject of an article in a well-known pictorial magazine: the patient sent in her own history. After several X-ray and anesthetic examinations the hospital could do nothing more for her: she had been obliged to continue wearing her surgical belt for thirteen more years and could not get out of bed without it, but in 1949 she went to a healer at whose hands she was "cured."
>
> When I examined the hospital records, they revealed that Mrs. M.H. had had an appendectomy in 1934 and a curetage for cervical erosion. In 1936 there was a barium investigation revealing nothing more than visceroptosis and in 1943 there was a further examination, all with negative findings. Her doctor subsequently wrote

in terms which did not substantiate her claims or those of the publication and gave his opinion that there was a large factor of functional exaggeration. [pp. 156–157]

The boy J.R. was according to the headlines "permanently cured": "Psychic healing succeeded when doctors failed," one of these read. "He was given up by professors and doctors who examined him as a hopelessly incurable case. He was born paralyzed in legs and arms, he was dumb and he had a distended stomach. After four years he received one treatment and the paralysis left him" the account continued, "the next morning he spoke and could run. . . . J. has now grown into a fine young man, leading a normal, happy life."

In answer to my request, the hospital concerned reported that J.R. was an in-patient for two months in 1934, suffering from rickets, and was discharged "improved." From September 1934 to February 1935 he was treated for coeliac disease, chicken-pox and whooping cough and again discharged "improved." December 1948 to February 1949 he was suffering from Brodie's abscess of the ankle and was discharged with satisfactory results. There was no record of any other disability, temporary or permanent. [p. 157]

Mr. R.B. A biopsy was carried out on this patient in June 1953, and a week later Mr. B. was informed that he was suffering from cancer of the larynx calling for a major operation. Mr. B. applied to Harry Edwards for direct healing, and during the interview his hoarse voice began to improve in quality and gain in volume. Then, on 21 July 1953, Mr. B. was re-examined under an anaesthetic in hospital and informed that the pathologist's report was at variance with the previous one. Independent examination was arranged and a later report ran: "In all Mr. B. has been examined by five throat specialists, one of whom is considered the greatest authority on cancer in this country. The two specialists who examined him after he had had the direct healing from Mr. Edwards both reported "no cancer now." One of the surgeons wrote to me in December 1953: "I doubt if anyone will give a definite reply. . . . My own belief is that it was pure fortunate coincidence that this man had a piece removed for biopsy and it had happened to contain all of the carcinomatous tissues." [p. 158]

Another important study is by William Nolen, a surgeon from Minnesota. In his book *Healing: A Doctor in Search of a Miracle* (1974), Nolen recounts the growth of his interest in various forms of faith-healing and his investigation of its effectiveness. Probably the most popular faith-healer a generation ago was Kathryn Kuhlman. Nolen visited her healing sessions, where hundreds, even thousands, of afflicted people would come forth and be declared healed. He describes what occurred: "At one point a young man with liver cancer staggered down the aisle in a vain attempt to claim a 'cure.' He was turned away, gently. . . . When he collapsed into a chair I could see his bulging abdomen—as tumor-laden as it had been earlier" (p. 59). Nolen concludes that "all the desperately ill patients who had been in wheelchairs were still in wheelchairs. In fact, [the] man with . . . kidney cancer in his spine and hip . . . was now back in his wheelchair. His 'cure,' even if only a hysterical one, had been extremely short-lived" (p. 60).

Dr. Nolen was able to record the names and addresses of twenty-three people who were allegedly miraculously healed by Kuhlman. He followed up on these cases. One woman had been announced by Kuhlman to have been cured of lung cancer, but the disease persisted. Another woman with cancer of the spine had discarded her brace and followed Kathryn's command to run across the stage. The next day her backbone collapsed. Four months later she was dead. Nolen's follow-up studies showed that none of the patients he examined who had been claimed as "cures" at the service "had in fact been miraculously cured of anything by either Kathryn Kuhlman or the Holy Ghost" (p. 81).

The more Nolen studied the results of Kuhlman's miracle services, the more doubtful he became that "any good she was doing could possibly outweigh the misery she was causing" (p. 89).

In the course of his investigation, Nolen also tracked down many other healers and patients who were supposedly cured, but still to no avail. There were no miracles to be found. Nolen thus raises the question: Does faith-healing help people? And he concludes that in cases of functional disorder or psychosomatic illnesses it may be of some help—particularly where suggestion plays a role and the autonomous voluntary nervous system is involved. Even here, though, patients may be only temporarily relieved of symptoms. Whether there are any long-lasting cures is another matter. However, any pretense of a cure does not apply to organic diseases. One cannot grow a limb, or cure a diseased gall bladder or a hernia by willing it. Nolen recognizes that many cases of cancer in remission do occur. There are far fewer cases where the cancer disappears entirely. It is estimated, he says, that perhaps only one in ten thousand or perhaps as few as one in one hundred thousand cases of cancer actually are spontaneously regressed. We don't always know the causes for this, he observed, but we have no evidence at all that they are due to miracles or to the intervention of a faith-healer.

Conclusion

Thus we are faced with a serious problem: although some forms of faith-healing may relieve psychosomatic symptoms, there is no clear evidence that faith-healing can cure organic illness; and yet faith-healing has become fashionable. Countless numbers of people are now being deceived in healing sessions and by television reports of these services. Faith-healers are practicing medicine without licenses. Their religious beliefs are appealed to in order to provide immunity from criticism. It is time that they be called to public account.

(Spring 1986)

VI.

Biblical Criticism

E very week, millions of worshipers jam churches and temples to inherit the party line from Father Conner, Pastor Goodman, and Rabbi Stern. Most, if they bother to read the Bible at all, never think to question its blatant contradictions, glaring inaccuracies, and muddled linguistics. If they did, they would likely receive only the answers their religious hierarchy wants them to hear. The answers the hierarchy wants them to hear, of course, consist of considerably less than what the hierarchy itself knows about the Bible—and even that is considerably less than most people would like to believe.

The powerful rational analysis of religion that developed from the eighteenth century through the first two decades of the twentieth has been dissipated by various forms of neo-orthodoxy that have reintroduced outdated religious and metaphysical principles by means of the ambiguous use of language and the assertion that men and women can live adequate lives only if they immerse their uncertainties in ancient myths, symbols, and rituals. This new obscurantism is perpetuated by mainline theological scholars who seldom have their views scrutinized or challenged. The public is thus led to believe that the claims of religion are more genuine than is the case.

So said the editors in *Free Inquiry*'s Spring 1982 issue, and the Biblical Criticism and Research Project was born. Its purpose was to submit the Bible to careful scientific and scholarly analysis, drawing on disciplines ranging from archaeology to folklore to literature, and to disseminate to the public the results of biblical research. Though the project itself is now a subcommittee of the Committee for the Scientific Examination of Religion (CSER), its purpose remains the same.

And it is as necessary today as it was at its inception—if not more so—for most people are not even aware of the existence of a body of knowledge collectively known as "biblical criticism," though there is scarcely a traditionally held belief about the life of Jesus that has not been called into question by linguists, archaeologists, historians, comparative religionists, or philosophers. Moreover, a large percentage of religious believers consider the Bible to be "literally true, divinely inspired, and the ultimate source of human salvation," though scholars agree that it is clearly the product of human imagination drawing on received mythology.

This, of course, is due in part to the widespread conviction that the Bible should be approached from a standpoint of faith. According to this view, it is sacrilegious to examine it critically, as a product of worldly time and place. There is a great deal of hostility in the religious community toward the objective scholarly analysis of the Good Book, and this hostility is easily transferred to the millions who do not wish to have their beliefs challenged. This, in turn, creates an enormous gap in Western thought.

Gerald Larue, the founding chair of the Biblical Criticism and Research Project, summed up the problems in this way:

> In synagogue and church, more than a generation of biblical illiterates have become easy prey for media evangelists, simply because they are unfamiliar with the methodologies and information with which to reject the claims of fundamentalists.
>
> What is equally disturbing is the vigorous campaign being launched by right-wing evangelicals against modern scientific inquiry and free thought. Their persistent pressure, based on their interpretation of what the Bible teaches and their insistence that biblical ethics become the law of the land, threatens free choice of reading materials in public libraries, the teaching of evolutionary theories in public schools, the freedom citizens enjoy in their private lives, sexual behavior not endorsed by the Bible, the efforts of women to achieve equal rights under the law, etc.

Over the years, *Free Inquiry* has provided a forum for some of the best writings in biblical criticism. Herewith, a short sampling of those essays.

—*M.B.G.*

Was Jesus a Magician?

Morton Smith

Scholars are generally agreed that the four Gospels now in the Bible were written in the last thirty or forty years of the first century C.E. In the following century they enjoyed great success and, by the year 185, Clement of Alexandria already equated them with "the Law" (i.e., Genesis-Deuteronomy), "the Prophets," and "the Apostles" as revelations of "the one God." From then on most Christians read the Gospels as timeless expressions of their God's eternal truth. Historical study of their texts—the attempt to explain their origins, pinpoint their differences, and determine the particular events behind them—was usually sporadic and undertaken only to prove one or another dogmatic point. Only with the rise of rationalism in the eighteenth century and the consequent development of historical understanding did Christian scholars generally come to conceive of Jesus not as an incarnate god sacrificed for the salvation of humanity but as a first-century Jew crucified on the charge of fomenting a revolution.

The first thorough attempt to give a historical account of Jesus' career, explaining it by the hopes and expectations of his day, is generally said to have been made by the German rationalist Hermann Reimarus (1694–1768) in his work *The Goal of Jesus and His Disciples*. Reimarus began by taking the Gospels at face value. He pointed out that the main concern of the authors was to make their readers believe that Jesus had been "the Messiah"—in Greek, "the Christ." The authors themselves unquestionably believed this, and all reported that Jesus himself had made the claim. Since "the Messiah" was thought to be a king who would deliver the people from their oppressors, the claim could be understood as revolutionary; this understanding is implicit in the reports of the trial of Jesus (especially in Luke 23:2) and in the official statement posted on the cross to give the reason for the execution, "This is the King of the Jews." Accordingly Reimarus thought Jesus was a failed revolutionist and that after his failure his disciples misrepresented his teaching.

This initial position shaped a century-long dispute of which Albert Schweitzer has given a classic description in his great book *The Quest of the Historical Jesus*. Although many complications were introduced, the central issue remained the question of Jesus' messianic claims. The Gospel evidence for them gradually brought critical opinion around to acceptance of—essentially—Reimarus's position, albeit in disguise. Schweitzer's persuasive presentation of it (with a little cosmetic surgery and a lot of homiletic makeup) became the most common scholarly interpretation of the Gospels in liberal Protestant circles through the first quarter of this century.

Conservative embarrassment at the Gospel evidence was therefore an important factor in the success of Rudolf Bultmann's *History of the Synoptic Tradition,* which brilliantly discredited most of the reports in the Synoptics (the first three Gospels). Bultmann analyzed the material section by section and found everywhere traces of composition—introductions and conclusions added to earlier stories, sections of connective material put in by editors, evidences of excision and alteration, and so on. These findings were almost completely speculative. Almost none of the supposed pre-Gospel forms of the stories have been preserved, and the hypothecated Christian communities in which they were supposed to have been made up do not resemble those found in Acts, Paul, the other Epistles, and the Apocalypse, which do not seem to have had such concerns. Thus the evidence for Bultmann's analyses was almost wholly the inconcinnities in the present Gospel texts, the details that "look like" traces of addition, conflation, and so on. Nevertheless, these appearances are so persuasive and so numerous that by now almost all competent scholars are persuaded of the truth of Bultmann's essential claim: behind the present texts of the Gospels lay a long period of tradition, partly written, but mostly oral, during which many stories and sayings of Jesus were invented, and even the genuine ones were remodeled, often to such an extent that their original meanings were concealed.

If so, which are genuine? To this question Bultmann's literary analysis could give no answer. After distinguishing the original elements, he fell back on his prejudices—those of a Protestant existentialist. "Jesus," he decreed, "was not an apocalyptic preacher"—so the apocalyptic elements were spurious. Of course he did not claim to be the Messiah. Also, he was not a visionary; so the visionary elements were thrown out. He was, however, a Palestinian Jew, and Palestinian Jewry was almost untouched by Hellenistic elements, and by this (demonstrably false) principle anything that could be identified as "Hellenistic" were also spurious. But neither did Jesus teach Jewish "legalistic" morality, so unwelcome Jewish parallels could be disposed of. And so on and on. In the end the original elements were reduced to the crucifixion and a handful of sayings into which Bultmann could read, by homiletic exegesis, just what he wanted. The resultant Jesus was a disembodied Bultmann—a great preacher of "repentance" and "absolute obedience" to God. (The Greek words meaning "obedient" and "obedience" do not occur in the Gospels, but the theme was popular in Germany during World War

I, when Bultmann's book was written, and became catastrophically so with the rise of the Nazis, when the book was reissued.)

Bultmann's position was ultimately indefensible—to suppose that four accounts of a historical figure, written by his followers within sixty or seventy years of his death and based on yet earlier sources, should contain so little reliable material is implausible; but to suppose that a first-century Jew should have rejected all the major elements of the Palestinian thought of his time and have made himself the preacher of a twentieth-century German moral philosophy is absurd. Nevertheless, Bultmann's work touched off a long dispute in which various scholars advanced various criteria that they thought might be used to determine which of the stories and sayings of Jesus were primitive. The resultant cats' concert of contradictions proved only what should have been clear in the first place—that we cannot get at Jesus from the Gospels, or even the New Testament, alone. Imitation of Bultmann's textual analyses by critics of every persuasion showed that the analytical technique was not foolproof—it could be made to seem to yield whatever results the critic wanted—and attempts to determine the authentic by questions of internal consistency led to endless arguments about indemonstrable suppositions. Objective controls turned out to be necessary. Jesus had to be located in his time and his society (about which Bultmann's notions were sometimes grotesque: of his *Primitive Christianity in Its Contemporary Setting,* A. D. Nock once said to me. "It is less a work of history than a Wagnerian Opera; I should say, *The Flying Dutchman").*

First of all we must begin with the objective facts of Jesus' life, which are not matters of serious dispute. Practically everybody will agree that he was a Jew, born about the beginning of the present era, who grew up in Galilee, came to John the Baptist for baptism, returned to Galilee and there became famous as a miracle worker, went to Jerusalem and there fell foul of the authorities, who, fearing he might start a messianic revolt, turned him over to the Romans for crucifixion.

This outline poses a practical problem. How did he attract enough followers to make the Jerusalem authorities think him dangerous? Certainly not by preaching existentialist sermons! Bultmann's notion that he was a preacher of repentance can appeal to a few Gospel sayings, but not to the reported facts. We find no stories of extensive repentance consequent on his preaching—in fact, it is denied—and there are very few stories of individual penitents. He himself came "eating and drinking" (Matt. 11:19; Luke 7:34); his followers did not fast, but were compared to a bridal party (Mark 2:18f., and parallels); and most of those who came to him wanted, not forgiveness, but cures.

Similarly the notion that Jesus was plotting a violent revolution or even cooperating with revolutionists fails utterly for lack of evidence. The fears of the Jerusalem authorities can be justified only by the supposition that the evangelists expunged from the Gospels everything that would have justified them, i.e., by the admission that there is no substantial supporting evidence. S. G. Brandon's defense of this interpretation has sufficiently refuted it.

The report that Jesus was called "rabbi" may be true, but the word must have been used in its nontechnical sense, to mean simply "master" or "sir." No official "rabbinate" was organized until half a century after his death, and his relations with its forerunners seem to have been hostile. Beside, no official rabbi is known to have produced similar beliefs and visions in his pupils. If Jesus was a rabbi he must have been one of a peculiar sort, and we are back to the original question. What was the peculiarity? (That he came from any such closed, puritanical ghetto as that of Qumran is completely incredible.)

No doubt he occasionally prophesied—most of us do. But he is never said to have said, "Thus saith the Lord." His reported prophecies, though they have certainly grown with reporting, are still a minor part of his reported teaching and play no demonstrably important role in his career. Some people occasionally thought so and called him a prophet, but the full breadth of his activity cannot be forced into the narrow prophetic shoe.

That he claimed to be the Messiah is practically certain, as Reimarus recognized and Schweitzer established. But this claim is more likely to have been the consequence of his following than the cause of it. Messianic claimants were probably then, as they are now, a dime a dozen. (We have one currently at Columbia— a unfortunate middle-aged Messiah who goes about distributing fly sheets to warn faculty and students of his second coming. So far as I know, he has attracted no followers.) Even if we should suppose that the messianic claim was primitive, we should still have to explain why Jesus attracted as many followers as the Gospels report, and why the Gospels do not commonly connect the followers with the messianic claims but represent the claims as believed by almost no one or, at best, as matters of speculation about which the crowds were uncertain. Even at the height—and almost at the end—of his career, at his "messianic entry" of Jerusalem, when his followers and the people around them were shouting "Hosannah to the Son of David," "the whole city" asked, "Who is this?" and "the crowds said, 'This is *the prophet* Jesus, the one from Nazareth of Galilee'" (Matt. 21:9–11).

We have had to review all these conjectures because critics have been unwilling—some because of piety, some because of rationalisms—to accept the Synoptics' adequate, unanimous, and repeated explanation that great crowds came to him "because of his cures" (Mark 1:28, 32ff.; 3:7–11; Luke 5:15; 6:17–19; 7:18–23; Matt. 8:16f.; 15:30 f.). Such citations could easily be multiplied. These, however, suffice to settle the matter. If we want to describe Jesus' role as first conceived by those who thronged to him, we must call him a healer, *not* "a doctor." He never prescribed medicine; when he told a patient to do something, it was not as treatment for the disease but a demonstration of trust and obedience. He healed simply, most often immediately, and always miraculously.

The question, How could Jesus perform miracles?—especially, how could he quiet hysterical persons (i.e. "cast out demons") and cure psychosomatic complaints (blindness, deafness, paralysis, aphasia, and so on)?—would take us into questions of psychotherapy, which the preserved material is inadequate to answer and which perhaps, in the present state of our knowledge, cannot be answered. However, it is a familiar anthropological fact that occasional persons, especially in primitive cutures, do have such curative powers. The evidence indicates that Jesus was such a person; the supposition that he was explains his following; and the following explains his execution, not only because it frightened the Jerusalem authorities, but also because it, together with the miracles, may have led Jesus to believe that he was in fact the Messiah. But what would he have called himself before he decided he was the Messiah?

Prophets and rabbis, too, were believed to perform miracles. We have seen that some people thought Jesus a prophet and others respectfully addressed him as "Rabbi." But neither prophet nor rabbi was characteristically a miracle worker, and neither classification would account for Jesus' other actions and sayings. The figures whom he most closely resembles are the "divine men" (as their followers called them; or, as their enemies called them, "magicians") of the Graeco-Roman world of which Palestine was part. Another miracle man of the same sort was active in Jesus' time in Samaria, just to the north of Jerusalem: "Simon the magician," as the Christians called him, "had been for a long time astonishing the Samaritans by his magic arts" and had persuaded many of them to believe that he was an incarnate "power of God" (Acts 8:9-11). Later on, as the political situation in Palestine disintegrated, such men began to collect sizable bands of followers to whom they promised miraculous deliverance from the Romans. Josephus says they were numerous and distinguishes them as "magicians" from the ordinary revolutionists, whom he calls "bandits." He says they promised to perform miracles and claimed to be prophets. Perhaps some, too, were led to think themselves messiahs. The Romans had to take military action to disillusion them (Josephus, *War* 2:258-263; *Antiquities* 20:97, 167-271, 188). Of such magicians Josephus's reports are hostile, but when magic involved no political dangers he was proud of it as an art derived from Solomon for exorcising demons and curing illnesses by the use of seals and drugs and incantations prescribed by the great king (*Antiquities* 8:45-48).

These are the social types by which the career of Jesus can be understood, but the relation has not hitherto been generally recognized—partly because of piety which put Jesus in a class by himself, partly because of rationalistic prejudice which left magic out of consideration, partly because little was known of ancient magic and its similarities to Gospel material could not be seen. Now that about a hundred magical papyri, some of book length, have come to light and we have thousands of shorter texts, the situation is different. The Gospel stories can often be paralleled point by point from magical material. Many of these parallels are collected in my book *Jesus the Magician* (currently a Harper and Row paperback). Here I must refer to it for details and citations, since the available space barely suffices for an outline of the main categories, which are as follows:

1. The Gospels report that Jesus' career began just after his baptism, when a spirit descended on him and he was declared a son of God. Getting a spirit was the first step for many magicians; hence we have many rites for doing it

and some of them show striking similarities to the Gospel story (heavens open, spirit comes down as bird). There is also a rite for ascension into the heavens, which leads to the magician's being declared "the Son." I should guess that "getting a spirit" or "becoming the Son" referred, in modern terms, to some sort of major psychological change. At all events, the large number of such rites and the importance evidently attached to them seem to indicate that they had some sort of powerful effect.

2. The story of Jesus' being "driven by the spirit into the wilderness," fasting there, and eventually meeting and overcoming a demon is a variant of the common accounts of shamanistic initiation. (See M. Eliade, *Shamanism.*)

3. After the initiatory ordeal, Jesus went to Galilee and began calling disciples and performing miracles. There are many spells represented as enabling magicians to call anybody they want and make those called follow them. In these stories then, as in the following, Jesus is credited with doing the things magicians were expected to do, and evidently tried to do. Personal attraction is still very little understood, and so speculation about the effect of magical practices in developing it is useless. I have already remarked that the miracles with which Jesus is most often credited—"exorcisms" and cures of psychosomatic conditions—are those most often effected by psychotherapy. Ancient magical texts provide spells for all of them. A number of other magicians are also said to have raised the dead; whether such stories resulted from false diagnoses or from mere exaggeration is indeterminable.

4. The structure of the Gospels and the picture of Jesus' life that they give—a series of episodes connected by a main character who goes from place to place and adventure to adventure—are paralleled by the structures and pictures of other lives of magicians, because all reflect the actual lives of such itinerants.

5. Jesus was reportedly able to order spirits about and permit them to enter other bodies (Mark 5:13; 7:29; John 4:50; Luke 7:6ff.). John 13:27 indicates that he sent Satan into Judas by giving Judas a specially prepared piece of bread. The ability to control and use spirits in such ways was often claimed by magicians. Magical texts promise it and provide rites to achieve it.

6. He was said to have given his disciples "the mystery of the kingdom of God" (Mark 4:11) and to have empowered them to perform miracles like his own. Many magicians are said to have instituted "mysteries" (initiatory rituals) and to have trained disciples to carry on their practices.

7. Like many magicians, Jesus was credited with supernatural knowledge of other people's thoughts and private actions, and also with extensive prophecies about the coming end of the world—such were then in fashion—and other matters. Rites for knowledge of private thoughts and affairs are plentiful in the papyri, and a number of other magicians were credited with prophecies, expecially eschatological ones.

8. Of the obviously false miracle stories—multiplying food, calming a storm, withering a fig tree, turning water into wine—the first four have parallels in stories of other magicians, the last is due to imitation, by John 2:1–11, of the myth

of a Dionysiac festival popular in nearby Sidon.

9. Another distinguishable group of miracles are those involving Jesus' body —walking on the sea, transfiguration, institution of the Eucharist. (Resurrection and ascension, miracles of "the risen Christ," will be dealt with later.) Walking on water was claimed by, and reported about, many magicians. The transfiguration story may reflect visions that Jesus induced in his disciples (cf. M. Watkins, *Waking Dreams)* but, as we have it, it is a variant of a well-known type of magical tale, "the interrupted ritual," in which an untoward remark or act by some participant in a rite breaks the spell and leaves the whole party back where they were at the start. The Eucharist is a variant of a form of love magic for which directions are given in several papyri: The magician identifies himself with a god and, by divine power changes various edibles, most often wine, into his blood and/or body and gives them as food to persons whom he wishes to bind to himself in love. The reports that Jesus actually used this ritual differ in details, but are substantially unanimous in all the Synoptic Gospels and also in Paul (1 Cor. 11:23ff.). Moreover, its place in the narrative—just before the betrayal, when Jesus had most reason' to try to bind his disciples to himself—is historically plausible.

10. Many of Jesus' sayings, especially those in John, have close parallels with and sometimes appear verbatim in magical rites. e.g. "I am the son of the living God." "I am the one who came forth from heaven," "I am the truth," "I am light." "You are in me and I in you." The list of substantial, but not verbally close, parallels would be a long one.

11. Besides these specifically magical parallels, many af the stories told about Jesus—his attitude toward money, his everyday practices, his attempt to reform the Temple, his practice of secrecy and praying in secret, his hostility to "those outside," his thanksgiving to his god for revealing the mysteries to him alone, and his claim to be the image of and to reveal his god—all these and many more are paralleled in stories told of magicians or in prayers used and claims made in magical rituals.

12. Finally, from a historical point of view, the most important thing Jesus did was "to rise from the dead," i.e., to condition his disciples so that shortly after his death a number of them saw him and became convinced he had risen. The immediate causes of these hallucinations were no doubt abnormal psychological conditions of the individual disciples, but the fact that similar hallucinations reportedly appeared about the same time to a number of disciples suggests that for these there was some uniform preparation. So does that fact that they seem to have been unique in the Judaism of this period—no rabbi's disciples saw their deceased masters in this way. The transfiguration story (Mark 9:2–8 and parallels) may reflect the sort of visions Jesus trained his disciples to see, and may thus account for those they saw after his death. Its resemblance to the resurrection stories has often been noticed. It also resembles the Ascension story, apparently a group hallucination. Many magicians are said to have gone up to heaven, and rites for doing so are preserved.

The preceding list has picked out only the most important and conspicuous classes of parallels between the Gospels and magical material, but I think these sufficient to show that the Jesus stories and the magical stories and spells are cut from the same piece of goods—the popular religion and superstititon of the ancient Graeco-Roman world. The Jesus material has a lot of Jewish elements sewn in, but they do not suffice to conceal the common pattern.

Recognition of this pattern brings us face to face with the basic problem posed by magic—it is false, but it often works. That problem must be left to psychologists, but a secondary one confronts the historian: given the fact the magic often works, where can one draw the line in evaluating reports about magicians and their miracles? Frankly, I don't know. The area of uncertainty can be narrowed. One can confidently rule out stories involving changes in physical objects (as distinct from the ways they are perceived). Notice that Jesus is never said to have practiced major surgery or restored missing limbs; such restraint speaks in favor of the cures reported. Conversely, one can confidently admit as possible those "miracles" involving changes only in psychological conditions (e.g., "exorcisms"). But between these there is still an immense gap. Also one must realize that, in the ancient world, where practically everybody believed in the efficacy of magic, the magicians believed, too. Of course there were many frauds, but in this field fraud and belief are not incompatible. If the spell does not work, that is because of some neglect or accident; the failure this time must be glossed over, but next time. . . . The magician's pattern and goals were established in the society. Individuals could and did deliberately set out to follow the pattern and achieve the goals. Consequently, stories reporting expected practices, and even sometimes achievements, have a certain claim to be considered probable, at least as records of self-deception.

In sum, we find in ancient magical texts, and in stories about ancient magicians, a large body of ancient material, closely related by vocabulary and content to the Gospels, and presenting a type of historical figure that fits Jesus' career and sayings better than does any other known.

(Winter 1982/83)

Jesus in Time and Space
Gerald A. Larue

Within fifty years of the death of Jesus, Christian writers began efforts to anchor his life in time and space. Paul was dead, and his expectation that Jesus would soon return and set up his kingdom had not materialized. Roman soldiers had destroyed the Jewish Temple and had wiped out the Essene community at Qumran. Masada had fallen after a brilliant assault by the Romans. It was clear that the leaders of Judaism and its offspring, Christianity, had to redirect their thinking and their missions.

Paul had paid scant heed to Jesus' life-story in his letters. Whether or not he made more of Jesus' biography in his preaching cannot be known; nor can we know what stories circulated about Jesus' life among his followers. Sometime after 70 C.E., the Gospel of Mark was written, and Mark began his account with Jesus' baptism by John the Baptizer at the river Jordan. At this time Jesus was already an adult.

Greater interest in Jesus's biography is apparent in the Gospels of Matthew and Luke and, because Mark's Gospel, which was used as a guide, contained no account of Jesus' beginnings, Matthew and Luke filled in those missing years with separate and conflicting accounts. Matthew claimed that Jesus was born in Bethlehem during the reign of King Herod the Great and that the family fled Egypt and returned only after Herod was dead. According to the Jewish historian Josephus, Herod died following an eclipse of the moon (*Antiquities,* XVII, vi). Modern astronomers inform us that eclipses visible in Palestine occurred on March 14 in 4 B.C.E. and January 10 in 1 B.C.E. so that, depending upon which eclipse is meant, Jesus was born either before 4 B.C.E. or before 1 B.C.E.—dates that are not very helpful in fixing Jesus in history.[1]

Luke, also, said that Jesus was born during Herod's reign and linked the birth to a worldwide census instigated by Caesar Augustus (Gaius Octavius) who reigned between 30 B.C.E. and 14 C.E. and at a time when Cyrenius (P. Sulpicius Quirinius) was governor of Syria, which was in the years 6 and 7 C.E.. The fact that Luke mentions that this was the first census has prompted some scholars to suggest that there may have been a second census by this same governor. Perhaps the 6–7 C.E. census that we know about is the second census, and perhaps Cyrenius was governor at an earlier time. There is a gap in the list of governors, and that gap falls between 3 and 2 B.C.E., so perhaps Cyrenius is the person whose name is missing.[2] This would make the Lukan account and the Matthean account agree and, using the 1 B.C.E. date for the lunar eclipse, it could be estimated that Jesus was born between 3 and 2 B.C.E. This is a neat theory, but whenever one runs into a series of "perhapses" and "maybes" rising out of lack of evidence, it is time to become uneasy. These separate and different accounts do not provide much help in estimating a date for Jesus' birth.

Nor does the wondrous star that guided the wise men provide any help. Attempts to interpret what that star might have been are as old as Johannes Kepler's efforts (1603) and include everything from triple conjunctions, meteors, fireballs, comets, and, in more recent times, alien spaceships.[3] It must be admitted that the idea of a hovering star shining above the birthplace is best suited to the spaceship interpretation; but for most of us the star is simply an item of religious fiction and provides no help in establishing a date for Jesus' birth.

Both Matthew and Luke tell us that Jesus was born in Bethlehem, and Matthew relates the birthplace to a statement found in the Book of Micah 5:2: "But you, O Bethlehem Ephrathah, who are little to be among the clans of Judah, from you shall come forth one who is to be ruler in Israel, whose origin is from old, from ancient days."

Now this particular passage is one of those added to the Book of Micah by some unknown writer who lived not in the eighth century, at the time of the prophet, but in the sixth century, during the Jewish exile in Babylon. He looked to the restoration of Judah under a Davidic-type king—perhaps one of the descendants of the Hebrew king who had been captive in Babylon. The prophecy has nothing to do with Jesus, but, in the words of one of my conservative Christian colleagues, "Isn't it wonderful that the Holy Spirit could give the passage one meaning in the sixth century and a whole new meaning in the first century!" I call this the "double-bounce" theory of biblical interpretation. My colleague admits that the same passage might be given another meaning still at a later time by this same Holy Spirit.

But there is a Church of the Nativity in Bethlehem, built, so we are informed, over the very grotto where Jesus was born. In fact there is a star set in the floor where the baby rested. Over the centuries hundreds of thousands of pilgrims have worshiped at this spot, believing that this was the birthplace. Can they all have been in error?

Matthew and Luke disagree on the nature of the birthplace. Matthew has the wise men visit Jesus in a house, presumably the place where he was born (2:11). There are those who suggest that this visit occurred after Joseph and Mary found suitable lodging and that the story in Luke that has the birth occur in a stable is to be preferred (2:7). By the middle of the second century the birthplace was identified as a cave—a not unreasonable assumption, because caves were and still are used to house animals. Justin Martyr wrote, sometime between 150 and 160 C.E., that "when the child was born in Bethlehem, since Joseph could not find lodging in that village he took up his quarters in a certain cave near the village" (*Dialogue with Trypho,* 78). Later, between 246 and 248 C.E., Origen wrote: "Corresponding to the narrative in the Gospel regarding his birth, there is shown at Bethlehem the cave where he was born, and the manger in the cave where he was wrapped in swaddling clothes" (*Against Celsus,* I, 51). Jerome, who lived in Bethlehem from 386 to 420 C.E. wrote that from the time of Hadrian (117–138 C.E.) the cave was overshadowed by a Tammuz grove and that lamentations from Tammuz were made in the cave (*Letter 58, to Paulinus 3*). It is quite possible that in Hadrian's time efforts were made to desecrate the birthplace, just as in that same time, according to Jerome, Jesus' burial place was desecrated by statues of Jupiter and Venus.

It was, apparently, above this same cave that Helena, mother of King Constantine the Great, dedicated a church that was to be the foundation of the present-day Church of the Nativity. But there is one problem: most modern scholars believe Jesus was not born in Bethlehem but in Nazareth. The birth stories are pious legends designed to portray Jesus as the fulfillment of Jewish prophecy concerning the Messiah. References to governmental figures serve to locate Jesus in time, and the identification of the birth cave and the subsequent erection of a church on that spot are efforts to locate Jesus in space. Worshipers' needs are met because through this sacred place they are enabled to come into intimate contact with the founder of the religion.

As one might imagine, the birth legends did not stop with the erection of the church. There is a "milk" grotto where it is said a drop of milk from Mary's breast fell to the ground and magically turned the limestone white. There is another grotto where the very coffins of children killed by King Herod in his efforts to annihilate the Messiah are shown. In each locale a priest waits for true believers with a collection basket at hand.

*   *   *

As the Jesus story progresses, once again Matthew and Luke are in conflict. According to Matthew, Joseph, Mary, and Jesus fled to Egypt to avoid Herod's soldiers (2:13–15). Luke states that Jesus was circumcised and then taken to the temple in Jerusalem for purification rites before the family returned to Nazareth (2:21–39). There was a time when the church was able to show the artifact of circumcision, but I have been unable to discover what has happened to it in more recent times.

There seems to be no doubt that Jesus grew up in Nazareth in Galilee as the son of the carpenter, Joseph. Research into the history of Nazareth indicates that, although it was inhabited as early as Neanderthal times (c. 70,000–35,000 B.C.E.), in Roman times there was only a small, insignificant Jewish colony there— a village so small that it was ignored in the geographical references recorded in the first century of the Common Era. Therefore the Church of the Annunciation that commemorates the place where the angel Gabriel informed the Virgin Mary that she was to be divinely impregnated when the Holy Spirit would "come upon" her and "overshadow" her (Luke 1:35) is a late structure built in the Byzantine period, probably in the fifth century. All the other structures associated with the life of Jesus in Nazareth are also late. Perhaps the only authentic relic of the past that might possibly be associated with Jesus is 'Ain Myriam, the one spring from which water has been flowing for centuries.

In the Gospels, Jesus is referred to as *rabbi,* a word that means "master" or "teacher" and which has usually been assumed to refer to one trained in the Law. The question immediately arises: Where did Jesus get his training? As the son of a carpenter he would be apprenticed to that work. The Galilee was not considered to be a center of learning in Jesus' time; indeed, there is some evidence to suggest that a Galilean accent was not well respected in the sophisticated circles of Jerusalem. Some modern biographers have suggested that he had, perhaps, traveled to India and sat at the feet of some master there. Or perhaps he went to a lamasery to be trained by a Tibetan monk. More recently it has been suggested that Jesus got his master's degree from the Essene university on the shores of the Dead Sea at Qumran.

The idea that Jesus may have been affected by Essenic thought is not new. Indeed, back in 1893, Professor H. Graetz, in his monumental *History of the Jews* (II, 146), wrote that John the Baptizer

. . . led the same life as the Essenes, fed upon locusts and wild honey, and wore the garb of the prophets of old, a cloak of camel-hair fastened with a leather girdle . . . John dwelt with the other Essenes in the desert, in the vicinity of the Dead Sea, presumably in order to be ever at hand to teach repentant sinners the deep moral significance of baptism.

Jesus, of course, came to John to be baptized, and after John's imprisonment, he carried on John's work. Graetz comments:

Jesus must, from the idiosyncrasies of his nature, have been powerfully attracted by the Essenes, who led a contemplative life apart from the world and its vanities. When John the Baptist—or more correctly the Essene—invited all to come and receive baptism in the Jordan, to repent and prepare for the Kingdom of Heaven, Jesus hastened to obey the call, and was baptized by him. Although it cannot be proved that Jesus was formally admitted into the order of the Essenes, much in his life and work can only be explained by the supposition that he had adopted their fundamental principles. [p. 150]

Professor Graetz suggested that the fundamental principles included disdain for wealth, the aversion to marriage, the community of goods, the eschewing of oath-taking, and the performance of miraculous cures, including exorcism of demons, which, he writes, "were often made by the Essenes, so to say, in a professional capacity" (p. 151).

The discovery in 1945 by a Ta'amireh tribesman of what we now call the Dead Sea Scrolls and the subsequent translation of these scrolls and the excavation of the Essene headquarters at Qumran have provided scholars with fresh, new material about the Essenes. Much of what Professor Graetz wrote in 1893 has been substantiated and new alliances in thought between the Essenes and the New Testament writers have been put forth together with clear evidence of differences. What is still lacking is a roster of members, so that there is no clear-cut proof that Jesus or John the Baptizer had anything to do with the group. On the other hand, the circumstantial evidence cannot be dismissed. At this time, the nature of the relationship must remain *sub judice* and open to further scholarly study.

So far it can be said that excavations at any of the sites associated with Jesus in the Christian Scriptures have produced nothing that sheds light upon his life. This is also true when we look at the environs of Jerusalem. Of course the Mount of Olives is still there, virtually peppered with sacred spots. There are the ruins of the Eleona Church, where Jesus is supposed to have instructed his disciples about the end of the world; there is the Church of the Lord's Prayer, where Jesus is supposed to have taught his disciples to pray; there is the Mosque of Ascension, formerly the Church of the Ascension, marking the spot from which Jesus made his ascension into heaven; there is the Franciscan chapel *Dominus flevit,* where Jesus is said to have wept over Jerusalem; there is the Church of Mary Magdalene; the Garden of Gesthemene Church; the Grotto of the Betrayal, where Judas betrayed Jesus; the Tomb of the Virgin Mary, where her body rested before ascending to heaven; and, finally, the entrance to Jerusalem and the Via Dolorosa—the way of sorrows, or the way of the cross.

Within the city of Jerusalem, the site of the ancient Jewish Temple is obscured by the presence of magnificent Muslim shrines—the Harem es-Sharif— the sacred enclave. We can learn nothing of the Temple in Jesus' time from this locale, except, perhaps, that the Western wall, where pious Jews still weep over the destruction of the Temple in 70 C.E., is a testimonial to the kind of protective walls that once surrounded it.

The streets that Jesus walked are not the same as those where the faithful Christians today carry wooden crosses, observe the stations of the cross, and try to ignore the souvenir merchants with their olive-wood artifacts. The streets of Jesus' day are ten to fifteen feet below the present walkways, and there is no way of determining whether the way of the pilgrims corresponds to Jesus' journey. Perhaps that is unimportant to the faith. What does matter is to be in Jersualem, the Holy City, and through some sort of spiritual empathy to come into an affect relationship with the past and with the tradition. I have watched the pilgrims as they come singing down the rough path from the Mount of Olives to enter the Via Dolorosa. The Jesuit with me commented on the pilgrims' stupidity in believing they were really walking where Jesus walked. I watched their faces as they passed, waving their palm branches on Palm Sunday, singing their hymns. Some were the bored faces of Jerusalemite guides, who made this processional for recompense. But there were others who seemed to be transported by the experience—solemn, joyous, meditative, involved—and I had no desire to deny them that experience. But they need to know the truth—the experience is one thing, but the reality is another. Human progress is threatened when the fiction becomes more important than the fact.

There is a bit of exposed pavement known as the *Lithostratos* in an excavation in the church built by the Sisters of Sion. The stones appear to have been part of the Praetorium or courtyard of the Antonia—the fortress tower named by King Herod to please Mark Antony. Portions of this same courtyard have been found in excavations under the Convent of the Flagellation and the Greek Orthodox Convent that suggests that the *Lithostratos* covered an area of some 1,500 square meters. It is quite possible that Jesus stood somewhere on this pavement, when he was judged by Pilate.

The Via Dolorosa leads to the Church of the Holy Sepulchre, which incorporates both the place of the Crucifixion and Jesus' burial site. The place of the Crucifixion was called Golgotha, the place of the skull (Matt. 27:33; Mark 15:22; Luke 23:33; John 19:17), which was located "near the city" (John 19:20), or outside the city (Heb. 13:12). Certainly the burial ground would be outside of the city walls and probably the place of execution would be too.

It is recorded that, when Hadrian visited Jerusalem in the second century, he erected a sanctuary to the Roman god Jupiter on the site of the Jewish Temple, which had remained a desolate wreckage since the destruction in 70 C.E. Many see this as a deliberate attempt at desecration—which it may have been—but it is well known to archaeological researchers that holy places retain their magic and, because a site has been sacred to one god, there is no reason why it cannot be transformed into a holy place for another god. Therefore, whether Hadrian was actually attempting to desecrate a Jewish holy place, or whether he was honoring a Roman god on a place already declared sacred, can be a matter of interpretation. However, Hadrian did bar the Jews from Jerusalem, no doubt in part as a reaction against the revolt of the Jews that had shaken Rome's eastern empire just before he assumed the throne in 117 C.E. and the Bar-Cochba revolt after he became emperor. He did erect a shrine to Jupiter on the holy mountain Gerazim, which was sacred to the Samaritans, and he did erect a temple to Venus on Golgotha. There is reason to suspect that at least part of his motivation was humiliation of the Jews and desecration of their holy places.

Perhaps the early Christians did remember the place of the Crucifixion. Perhaps Hadrian deliberately built the Venus temple on a place sacred to the Christians, but it was not until Jerusalem became a Christian city, when it was conquered in 325 C.E., that Golgotha became a Christian shrine. By this time Venus had been adored at the site for nearly two hundred years. Now Constantine ordered the Venus shrine destroyed, and during the demolition the tomb of Jesus was discovered. By 335 C.E. the Christian church that forms the foundation for the present-day Church of the Holy Sepulchre was erected on the site of the temple, but only fragments of the Constantine structure remain.

But wondrous discoveries associated with the Christian shrine were made. Queen Helena had a dream in which the hiding place of the cross was disclosed. And sure enough, while workers probed a pit as the queen sat nearby, the three crosses were found. At this point, I prefer to let the great American writer Mark Twain tell the story as he learned it when he traveled to Palestine in 1867 and which he published in *The Innocents Abroad* in 1869.

Here, also, a marble slab marks the place where St. Helena, the mother of the emperor Constantine, found the crosses about three hundred years after the Crucifixion. According to the legend, this great discovery elicited extravagant demonstrations of joy. But they were of short duration. The question intruded itself: "Which bore the blessed Savior, and which the thieves?" To be in doubt, in so mighty a matter as this—to be uncertain which one to adore—was a grievous misfortune. It turned the public joy to sorrow. But when lived there a holy priest who could not set so simple a trouble as this to rest? One of these soon hit upon a plan that would be a certain test. A noble lady lay very ill in Jerusalem. The wise priests ordered that the three crosses be taken to her bedside one at a time. It was done. When her eyes fell upon the first one, she uttered a scream that was heard beyond the Damascus Gate, and even upon the Mount of Olives, it was said, and then fell back into a deadly swoon. They recovered her and brought in the second cross. Instantly she went into fearful convulsions, and it was with the greatest difficulty that six strong men could hold her. They were afraid, now, to bring in the third cross. They began to fear they had fallen upon the wrong crosses, and that the true cross was not with this number at all. However, as the woman seemed likely to die with the convulsions that were tearing her, they concluded that the third could do no more than put her out of her misery with a happy dispatch. So they brought it, and behold, a miracle! The woman sprang from her bed smiling and joyful, and perfectly restored to health. When we listen to evidence like this, we can not but believe. We would be ashamed to doubt, and properly, too. Even the very part of Jerusalem where this all occurred is there yet. So there is really no room for doubt.

Today, fragments of the "true cross" are to be found in Roman Catholic churches throughout the world. Just who hacked the cross to pieces is not known. Some scholars have conjectured that wood fragments in the area around the Church of the Holy Sepulchre were gathered and accepted as fragments of the cross. There has been some estimate that there are enough fragments to represent several crosses. Although many Roman Catholics continue to accept these bits of wood as authentic relics of the cross, modern scholars tend to place them in the same category as the bones of saints and other relics adored by naive believers—the category of pious superstition.

*   *   *

There are other relics in the Church of the Holy Sepulchre that have been associated with Jesus. For example, just inside the entrance is a huge slab of marble known as "the stone of unction," which is now worn smooth from worshipers' tears, kisses and caresses. It is supposed to be the slab on which Jesus' body was prepared for burial. There is the "pillar of flagellation"—or at least part of it—which is supposed to be the post at which Jesus was scourged. There is a chapel associated with the Roman soldier whose spear pierced Jesus' side when he hung on the cross. There are holes to represent the exact places where the crosses stood for the Crucifixion. And of course there is the tomb itself. These creations of pious imagination encourage pilgrims to believe blindly and to give willingly to support the shrines.

There have been challenges to the Church of the Holy Sepulchre. There is the so-called Garden Tomb, which is located outside the present Turkish walls of Jerusalem. Apparently those who accept this place as the actual site of the burial disdain the ancient church because it is within the present walls of the city. We think we now know the course of the ancient walls, and if that tracing is correct then the Church of the Holy Sepulchre is definitely outside the walls of ancient Jerusalem and in a not improbable place for the burial. The Garden Tomb is a late discovery and is accepted as authentic only by the millions who follow the fundamentalist television preachers. Indeed, I saw two programs during the past Passover-Easter celebrations in which television pastors were shown standing in the true tomb—the Garden Tomb. No present-day scholar attributes any validity to these claims.

There have been other discoveries associated with Jesus' lifetime. A stele bearing the name of Pontius Pilate was found at Caesarea, and this provides tangible evidence of the presence of the procurator in Palestine. A skeleton of a man named Yehohanan, who was crucified about two thousand years ago, was found at Givat Hamivtar in northeastern Jerusalem in 1968. It provided interesting details about crucifixion.

Perhaps the most dramatic claims of an artifact associated with Jesus is the so-called Shroud of Turin. Few readers of the popular press know that this was only one of several shrouds purported to be the burial cloth of Jesus that existed during the fourteenth century. Few have read the critical reviews; most have read the accounts of those who believe in the authenticity of the Turin Shroud and who account for the image with such imaginative explanations as "bursts of radiant energy" and coin such terms as *radiation scorch*.[4] Our best investigations have demonstrated that the shroud is a fourteenth-century invention and, like the multitude of other relics shown from that same period, was designed to bring pilgrims to specific shrines to enhance the status and financial health of those holy places.

*   *   *

I have no quarrel with those who utilize sacred space to renew and deepen their faith. I can appreciate that, since the establishment of the Church of the Nativity and the Church of the Holy Sepulchre in the fourth century, millions of Christians have made pilgrimages to these places and have paid homage to their beliefs. And those who go to these churches today are, by their very presence, linked to the thousands of others who over the centuries before have also gone to Bethlehem and Jerusalem. But to make a pilgrimage that links one to a Christian fellowship that extends back through time and deepens one's commitment to the highest values of the Christian faith is quite different from going in the belief that these are sacred spots physically associated with Jesus.

To listen, as I did during the Passover-Easter week, to fundamentalist preachers advertising their trips to Jerusalem as they stood before what they claimed was the authentic tomb of Jesus—the Garden Tomb—insults my intelligence, encourages naiveté, promotes ignorance, and discards the best results of conscientious modern scholarship.

To the degree that the church, with its clergy, its teachers of clergy, and its membership composed of thinking human beings, abandons its rich tradition of higher education, and tends to move away from the use of logic, and seems to be prepared to ignore the best findings of historical and archaeological research, it denies the validity of the best thinking that the human race has produced through the centuries. It denies philosophy and philosophical logic, it denies history and the search for that which really happened, it denies the best research into our past and into the understanding of our past, and it encourages blind, unthinking, uncritical belief. I am uneasy and disgusted with colleagues who become insecure with their own research and take the leap of blind faith.

As an educator in the humanities, committed to producing a culturally literate society and to educating students and the public in the best understanding of the past, I am frustrated by the number of students who come from liberal churches and from good high-schools where modern scientific thought has been watered down, where the best Bible scholarship is ignored, and where faith replaces reason.

Jesus is an important figure in Western thought, but the Jesus who seems to matter most is the Jesus of religious fiction, the so-called Christ of faith. As a symbol, Jesus can inspire the finest ethical traditions humans have developed, but what must be kept clear is that we are dealing with a symbol and that the historical figure is lost in the mists of time. The Christ of faith is the creation of religious believers, of clergy and teachers who took a historical figure and clothed it in mythological swaddling bands—just as ancient Egyptians took Osiris, who may indeed have been an historical figure, and mythologized him, clothing him in the garments of divinity and sanctifying sacred spots associated with his fictionalized life. And there are others—Gilgamesh, Moses, Buddha—who have become divine humans who model and wrestle with the meaning of human existence. There is no problem here. We can enjoy symbolic figures. We can learn from them. We can draw psychological models from them, as Freud did from Oedipus and as Camus has done from Sisyphus. We do not have to insist that they are solidly anchored in history or that the sacred spots associated with them have any basis in fact.

Our problem is twofold. The first part lies in the greed of towns, cities, and churches who seek to bring tourists and pilgrims to their shrines, men and women who will spend their time gawking at places that may have little relation to what their guides are telling them, and who will spend money for food, housing, travel, artifacts, and souvenirs to enrich the guardians of the sacred places.

The second part embraces the educated clergy and teachers in this part of the world, who for whatever reasons—perhaps fear of parishioners, fear of being challenged, fear of controversy—fail to acquaint their parishioners or their students with the best evidence we have of the past. There are, of course, pressure groups that constantly threaten those who do not conform to their interpretation of the past, of the Bible, of Jesus, or of life itself. When we fail to challenge their assumptions, when we fail to set forth the best evidence, when we bow to these special groups, we fail our highest calling as teachers, leaders, and guides in education.

We can locate Jesus in a general sort of way in time. Our dates are not as firm as we would like them to be. We can locate Jesus vaguely in space, but the locales that are now associated with him are questionable.

Notes

1. Gerald A. Larue, "Astronomy and the Star of Bethlehem," *Free Inquiry,* Winter 1982/83, pp. 25ff.

2. Jack Finegan, *Light from the Ancient Past* (Princeton: 1959), pp. 256ff.

3. For a discussion see Larue, op. cit.; David Hughes, *The Star of Bethlehem* (New York: 1979).

4. Joe Nickell, *Inquest on the Shroud of Turin* (Prometheus Books: 1983); "Update on the Shroud of Turin," *Free Inquiry,* Spring 1985, pp. 10–11.

(Summer 1985)

The Origins of Christianity

R. Joseph Hoffmann

The answers to the following ten commonly asked questions about Christianity are as brief and factual as anyone has the right to expect from a historian, and they are briefer and more factual than anyone would get from a theologian, many of whom are as uncurious about the origins and historical context of the charter documents of Christianity as Supreme Court justices are about the intellectual life of the eighteenth century. It seemed best to me to be blunt, even flatfooted, with respect to the difficult historical problems involved in the study of Christian origins and the New Testament. I say this not out of disrespect for the text, but because I am convinced that bluntness has its place, both as a response to the Enthusiasmos of the fundamentalist fringe now claiming exclusive ownership of the Bible and to the learned quasi-theological histories of the biblical text that bury significant information beneath the freighted prose of the religious establishment.

1. In what language or languages was the New Testament originally composed?

Greek. From time to time one hears of "lost" Aramaic gospels, purported to stand nearer to the historical Jesus than the present text of the synoptics (Matthew, Mark, Luke). There is absolutely *no* solid evidence, either of a linguistic or of a textual variety, that warrants assuming the existence of an "Ur-gospel"—an original gospel, older than the text of our earliest canonical Gospel, Mark. It is true that the Gospels were written on papyrus and that papyrus has a habit of rotting in the course of a century or two; thus some have used the absence of papyrus evidence to argue that the Greek Gospels are really translations from original Hebrew or Aramaic sources. The perpetrator of this fable is a second-century writer named Papias—a dilettante if ever there was one—who claimed that Matthew had recorded the words of Jesus in Hebrew. In fact, Papias was reporting from hearsay a tradition that linked the First Gospel with the tax-collector disciple named in Matthew's Gospel.

Today scholars agree that Greek is the primary language of the Gospel of Matthew and that Papias, whatever other virtues he may have possessed, was a pretty bad historian. The Gospels, the letters of Paul (those written by him and forged in his name), and the rest of the canonical material were written in the *lingua franca* of the Hellenistic world, Greek. Put differently, the "records" of Jesus' life and teaching are both linguistically and culturally removed by at least one stratum from the language he is assumed to have spoken and the ideas he is thought to have espoused.

2. How many original manuscripts (signatures) of the New Testament have survived?

None at all. When one hears of the New Testament—or the Bible generally—being the word of God, one assumes that we possess ancient papyrus scrolls signed by the authors of the various books and witnessed by the first-century equivalent of a notary public. Such thinking is dangerous and unhistorical. In fact, our earliest papyrus fragment of the New Testament dates from no earlier than the middle of the second century (known as the John Rylands papyrus) and is no bigger than the average thumbnail. It is assumed to be a fragment of the Gospel of John but may be a piece of a gnostic text, since the fragment was discovered in Egypt where gnostic Christians were in the majority. Needless to say, this tiny scrap bears no authorial ascription, nor in fact does any surviving papyrus fragment bear the name of its writer, the pieces being for the most part hypothetically assigned to the fuller Gospels preserved in later—chiefly fourth-century—collections known as "codices." Hence none of the original manuscripts of the New Testament has survived, nor have any direct copies of the original manuscripts.

What we possess are copies of copies, so far removed from anything that might be called a "primary" account that it is useless to speculate about what an original version of the Gospel would have included. Into these copies crept the errors of theologically motivated scribes, together with the additions and omissions that they or their superiors found it necessary to make. This should not surprise us. The sacred scripture of earliest Christianity was the Old Testament; there was no imperative—real or supernatural—to copy the Gospels and Epistles word for word; and as no text can be better than the one from which it was copied, we must assume that our modern texts of the Gospels—translations of imperfect copies—are very far removed from the events they describe.

3. Was there no protection against manuscript error? After all, the early Christians must have known that they were charged with a task of monumental importance and would have taken care to guard against contamination.

There were no safeguards against such error. We know, for example, that early manuscripts of the New Testament can be classified into "families," the classification being based on certain regional or theological characteristics that set one manuscript group apart from another. Errors, corrections, and additions made in Rome were perpetuated in manuscripts copied at Rome and not at Antioch or Alexandria. Each religious center would preserve and add to its own peculiar readings, and gradually texts in and around these regional centers took on their own characteristics. When copied, the characteristics, including the errors, were transmitted.

4. Isn't it the case that in about 90 percent of the New Testament the manuscripts agree and that the differences occur in a small percentage of passages and do not affect fundamental Christian doctrine?

The percentage is higher than 10 and approaches nearer to 20 if we take into account the full range of manuscript disagreements. Not only is that a substantial figure, but disagreement affects even the most fundamental of Christian doctrines: the doctrine of the trinity. In certain poor manuscripts dating from the fourteenth century, the text of 1 John 5:7f. carries the following reference: "There are three who bear witness in heaven, the father, the Word and the Holy Spirit." This verse is missing in all Greek manuscripts of early vintage and in the original (Eastern) translations of the Latin Vulgate Bible. It was first introduced into the mainstream of Bible transmission in 1519 by Erasmus in the third edition of his Greek New Testament. From these Greek editions, the passage made its way into the received text of the Bible. Without exception, this verse is regarded today by scholars as a later addition without historical pedigree; consequently, reliable modern translations omit it, although it is still to be found in all printings of the "authorized" (King James) Bible of 1611 and is still the most frequently cited "prooftext" for the Christian doctrine of a triune God.

5. Is it because the King James translation of the Bible was based on the best manuscript evidence available that warrants its being called "authorized"?

The King James Bible, so named after its royal sponsor, James I of England, is based on an undistinguished text known as the Byzantine version, which originated in the late third or early fourth century around Antioch. For this reason, it is also (and more appropriately) known as the Antiochene or Syrian text. Adopted officially in Constantinople during that city's ascent to imperial hegemony, it soon predominated in the Byzantine world. So dominant was this version after the eighth century that it became the text found in almost all late manuscripts and the basis for the first printed editions of the Greek New Testament in the sixteenth century. Technically, it is characterized by conflations (that is, combinations of readings from other manuscripts) and revisions of a stylistic and theological character. The term *authorized* as applied to the English translation of this text has absolutely nothing to do with a divine mandate. It means only that the British monarch approved and supported the work of a group of Oxbridge translators and subsequently authorized their translation (and no other) for use in the Church of England. It is worth noting in passing that the Bible upon which the Christian commonwealth of the New World was founded was not the King James (the

Puritans having removed themselves from England to Leiden before the 1611 Bible gained currency) but a pirated translation compiled in Geneva in 1560 by English-speaking refugees to Switzerland. It was this Bible that came over on the Mayflower.

6. Were the Gospels written before or after the letters of Paul?

After—by about a generation. The earliest of Paul's letters, 1 Thessalonians, was written around the year 50; the earliest Gospel, the one assigned to Mark, was not written until after the destruction of the Temple in Jerusalem in the year 70. What looks like a "prophecy" in Mark 13:1–4—a prediction of the fate of the Temple—is rather obviously put onto Jesus' lips by an author, or authors, familiar with the Jewish Wars of the years 66–70, culminating in the burning of the Temple by the Roman legions under Titus. The fiction is even plainer in Luke's telling of the story: "When you see Jerusalem surrounded by armies, then know that its desolation has come near" (Luke 21:20f.).

Such allusions, once recognized as belonging to the time of the author of the story rather than to Jesus' lifetime, help us to date the Gospels. The order Mark, Matthew, Luke, John approaches chronological correctness, though the traditional order (Matthew, Mark, Luke, and John) is sometimes defended. It may even be the case that the Gospel of John, the most theologically advanced of the four, is in part older than the Synoptic accounts, though this view is still considered radical on the silly assumption that the more "biographically orientated" narratives—Mark, for instance—with their use of sayings, traditions, and strings of miracle stories are indisputably older than the Fourth Gospel with its high-blown doctrine of Jesus as the eternal logos (word) of God. We shall never know exactly which Gospel is the oldest, but there is reason to suppose that either an early version of Mark or a proto-version of Luke was around by the end of the first century, and that in another quarter of Christianity (Ephesus?) a rather different looking Gospel, that assigned finally to the apostle John, was in circulation and in process of revision to bring it (more or less) into line with other Gospels.

The dating of Paul's letters, a hotly debated issue, is not usually taken to be a matter of such urgent historical and religious significance as the dating of the Gospels. This is so because the Gospels purport to tell the story of Jesus— to reproduce his message and the proclamation about him (i.e., that he was, and claimed to be, the Son of God, the Messiah, the savior of the world, and so on), as well as those characteristic actions (miracles, healings, and the like) and events (crucifixion, resurrection) that were passed along in the "traditions" of the early Christian communities. History or not, the Gospels have been perceived as historical in character—accurate records of an individual's life, teaching, and significance. The earlier a Gospel can be shown to be, the reasoning goes, the closer we approximate "what really happened." While the majority of New Testament scholars and church historians find such reasoning naive, it persists in determining the course of twentieth-century theology. The fact of the matter is that even the earliest Gospel, contrary to popular belief and church piety, is a *theological treatise and not a historical annal*. And the earliest surviving works of the Christian movement, the letters of Paul, show just how thoroughly popular belief succeeded in displacing the historical details of Jesus' life and teaching by the year 50 at latest. Paul shows almost no interest in—and perhaps had very little knowledge of—the biography of Jesus of Nazareth. Whatever reliable information the Gospels contain must be weighed against the certainty that the historical Jesus was of practically no moment to the earliest missionaries, and that the Gospels are to one degree or another pious historicizations of popular belief, worked out in terms of Old Testament prophecies.

By and large it was controversy that called forth the historical figure—the need to prove his messianic status, to explain away his execution, to show the felicity of his teaching, and to encourage believers in their faith that the end of time was about to dawn (though its arrival was long overdue). The notion that the historical figure was significant enough—as teacher, miracle-worker, and political rebel—to produce the encompassing myth that became his life story still holds sway in scholarly circles. Largely this is so because the pattern of history— from Alexander the Great to John Fitzgerald Kennedy—has been to mythicize heroes, conquerors, and great religious leaders. Such a pattern is discernible, however, precisely because we have other empirical traces of the man to go by, whereas in the case of Jesus of Nazareth the myth is the whole of the record. What "looks" historical about the Gospels can as easily be explained by examining the needs of a growing cult of apocalyptic enthusiasts as by postulating the existence of a historical individual whose unique personality gave rise to the movement that bears the name "Messiah-people" (= Christians). In short, one must at least entertain the possibility that the Gospels tell the story of a god becoming man on the order of other ancient theophanies—Herakles, Horus, and Mithras, to name only a few. Pagan writers like Celsus made just this point about the Gospels in their day, indicting them as inferior versions of ancient myths. That the Gospels tell the story of how a man was legendized into godhood remains the standard assessment, but it is an assessment based on a faulty reading of the evidence as skewered attempts to write historical narrative or else to exaggerate events that really took place. The superhuman proportions of Jesus Christ can only be understood in terms of the controversies that called forth his words, deeds, and prophecies, and these belong not to a human person but to the Christ cult of the late first century. The message *about* Jesus determined the message assigned to him from the beginning.

7. Is it not the case that the Gospels were written by men who had followed Jesus and thus would have had intimate knowledge of his teachings and actions?

This seems not to have been the case. It is certainly true that the early church, in developing its patriarchal idea of authority and government, also developed certain criteria for determining what books and letters possessed the prescribed authority. From an early date, but not before the first decades of the second century, it became a matter of piety and finally of tradition to ascribe the most widely used Gospels and letters to Jesus' followers and to members of the inner circle of disciples. Thus we have inherited two letters ascribed to the apostle Peter, neither of which can plausibly be assigned to him (nor in fact to the same author!). One dates from as late as the year 150. The same holds true for the letters ascribed to James, Jude, and John, and to nearly half of the letters assigned to Paul. *The New Testament is by and large a collection of pseudonymous writings*— works written under the name of an author whose reputation or prestige, based on his proximity to Jesus, would serve to legitimate the material. Neither Paul nor any of the writers to whom such material has been assigned seem to have been eyewitnesses of the ministry of Jesus. What the Gospels offer for the most part are traditions handed down in local communities and traditions about these traditions: ethical manuals (such as the beatitudes), theological traditions (the story of Peter confessing Jesus as the Christ and Son of God), and pseudobiographical traditions, such as the story of the Crucifixion, based mainly on Psalm 22 and assorted other Old Testament passages rather than on the testimony of witnesses. Another and perhaps blunter way of putting this would be to say that the Gospels are the handiwork of early churches and that there are, accordingly, manifold contradictions in the traditions they preserve. These contradictions point to the fact that different churches "remembered" and believed different things.

8. But the church teaches that the Gospels are without contradictions and that the object of faith is to learn to overcome the apparent inconsistencies in the New Testament.

Even the church fathers were aware that the Gospels were far from consistent in their telling of the story of Jesus Christ. Origen of Alexandria, one of the greatest thinkers of the early church, acknowledged that the accounts of the life of Jesus lacked the sophistication of pagan biography and the literary beauty of popular literature. He also realized that the contradictions in the accounts were a great advantage to the opponents of the Christian movement. Origen thought that to solve the problem, whenever the Gospels contained apparent contradictions, one should look beyond the literal meaning of the text to the higher spiritual reality that the text embodied. But such thinking was defensive. What is significant is that writers like Origen were unwilling to use "faith" in defense of the Gospels; rather, they argued their case from the laws of Greek rhetoric and Stoic logic and in so doing never denied that there were real problems with the text.

9. Are there contradictions in the New Testament that have direct bearing on Christians' beliefs?

Clearly there is no room to cite every instance of contradiction in the Gospels. A few will suffice to illustrate the general problem encountered by New Testament scholars and biblical theologians.

1. The earliest Gospel, Mark, dates the beginning of Jesus' divine status from

his adoption to the sonship of God at the time of his baptism by John (Mark 1:9f.). Matthew and Luke offer (contradictory) accounts stressing that Jesus was not "adopted" as the son of God but was God's son by the miraculous union of the holy spirit and a virgin—a tale obviously gleaned from Graeco-Roman legends about the birth of Plato, Alexander the Great, Pythagoras, and other heroes. Both Matthew and Luke offer genealogies to support their contention that Jesus was a lineal descendant of David and thus entitled to be called the "Messiah of Israel"; their accounts, however, contain a discrepancy of some four hundred years, and both cf. 23:38ff.) present the reader with the dilemma of choosing between virgin birth and the paternity of Joseph. If the intention for presenting the genealogies is to be maintained—to argue lineal descent through the male parent—then the virgin birth must go. If the story of the virgin birth is the one to be credited, then the lineal descent of Jesus from David through Joseph must be discredited. Further complications ensue when we turn to the Gospel of John, where still another explanation of Jesus' divinity is put forward: namely, that Jesus was God's son neither by adoption at baptism nor by birth to a virgin, but rather was a full-fledged idea (logos) preexisting in the mind or will of God throughout all eternity, and ultimately made visible in the flesh in the person of Jesus Christ (the incarnation).

2. The synoptic Gospels (Matthew, Mark, Luke) claim that Jesus was not baptized by John; the Gospel of John maintains that John did not baptize Jesus and carries contradictory reports concerning whether Jesus himself baptized any-one (John 3:32 v. 4:2f.). In any event, it looks as though the gospel writers were at a loss to cover up the fact that Jesus (historical person or idea) was a derivative figure—either someone preached by John who never materialized (and whose death became the explanation for his disappearance) or, if historical, a man who had followed John as a disciple and later rose to prominence by furthering the Baptist's message of repentance and apocalyptic doom.

3. The synoptic Gospels offer no clear idea of Jesus' learning. It is certainly commonplace that the appeal of the Christian movement, at least in the first two centuries of the common era, was greatest among the uneducated—those memorialized in the Gospels as the "poor in spirit." Even the language of the Gospel of Mark, unliterary and stylistically spare as it is, offers proof of the sort of person to whom the message of Christianity seemed credible. Pagan philosophers like Celsus did not hesitate to say that Christianity was a "religion for old women, yokels, and little children," a conclusion not altogether unwarranted by the Gospel evidence (Mark 1: 13–16). At the same time, Jesus himself is represented as being the cleverest of teachers, always ready with the right answer, always winning out over his rather obtuse pharisaic opponents with their questions about the law, tax collecting, resurrection from the dead, and adultery. That a follower of John the Baptist (Mark 1:14f.), a wandering preacher who sought to emulate the style of the Old Testament prophets by remaining on the outskirts of "official" Judaism, should be presented as a rival of the great teachers of Torah, is remarkable enough. But in fact it is only the Gospels of Matthew

and Luke, with their great "teaching sections," that Jesus comes off as a rabbinical prodigy (Matt. 5–7; Luke 6:20–49), and here both evangelists rely on a source (or sources) that perhaps had originally nothing to do with Jesus.

More instructive is the way in which the tradition has been altered for the purpose of making a teacher of the unlettered preacher. Mark, for example, has Jesus (followed by unspecified disciples) return to "his own country" (Nazareth?) in order to teach in the synagogue. The writer is careful to point out that everyone who heard Jesus was astonished, less at his teaching (assumed in any case to be earth-shattering) than at its source: "Where did this man get his wisdom," they ask: "Is he not a carpenter's son . . . and aren't his sisters still with us? And they took offense at him" (Mark 4:2f.). Luke, disliking the notion that the son of God was considered ignorant by his audience, alters the Markan text to read as follows: "And he went to Nazareth where he had been brought up, and he came to the synagogue, as was his custom on the sabbath day; and he stood up to read, and a book was given to him, the book of the prophet Isaiah, and he opened the book and found the passage where it stands written, 'The spirit of the Lord is upon me, because he has anointed me to preach good news to the poor. . . . And he closed the book and gave it back to the attendant, and sat down, and all the eyes of the synagogue were upon him. . . . And all spoke well of him, and marvelled at the gracious words that came from his mouth" (Luke 4:16ff.). Luke has tried, albeit inconsistently (cf. Luke 4:29), to remove the offense taken at Jesus' want of credentials by positing his literacy: he reads from a book; he customarily sits with the rabbis, even as a child, Luke reports; he has fingertip control of the scroll of the Book of Isaiah. Postulating a difference of perhaps twenty or twenty-five years between the writing of Mark's gospel and that of Luke, we might conclude that the need to present Jesus as having magisterial authority—a rhetorical swordsman always ready with the right assault and defense—has been responsible for the graying over of an early tradition that Jesus was a traveling evangelist—one perhaps of remarkable power, but one who constantly came up against the brick wall of pharisaic logic. If there was a historical Jesus, it could have been no other way.

At the same time, the existence of these "controversy" stories in the Gospels does not prove the existence of a historical person. Instead, we may chart in the shift from Mark to Luke the transition from a movement self-consciously defensive about its membership (so, too, Paul in 1 Corinthians!) to a cult-church on the verge of attracting its share of literate men and women—a theme Luke is very keen to emphasize. One may thus see Jesus as the personification of this transition.

4. Nor is there any consistency in the record of Jesus' words: Mark (10:11) reports that Jesus recognized the right of a woman to divorce her husband as well as the right of a man to divorce his wife. Yet it is well known that Jewish women of the first century had no such right (though Roman freewomen could initiate divorce proceedings in some circumstances). Further, Mark makes all cases of divorce adulterous, whereas Matthew, who omits Mark's reference to the right

of a woman to divorce her husband (Matt. 5:13f.) records Jesus as saying unchastity constitutes grounds for divorce. Confusion—enough at least to lead to the English reformation under Henry VIII and the confounding of civil law ever since—comes still later in Mark's Gospel: "What God has joined together man cannot divide" (Mark 10:9), and the declaration (also recorded by Matthew) that divorce was an expedient granted to the Jews by Moses "for their hardness of heart," and never intended to be a permanent dispensation (Mark 10:2). Confusion on this point is hardly mitigated when we consider that the "sayings" of Jesus about divorce probably have nothing to do with his teaching but reflect the varying practices of Christian communities in their shift from Jewish divorce practice to gentile provisions concerning marriage, divorce, almsgiving, the care of widows, and the duties of parents.

5. Even in the most trivial matters the Gospels show no consistency; or to be plainer, they do not show the sort of consistency one would expect if the words attributed to Jesus were firmly fixed in the historical memory of the early communities. Thus Mark reports Jesus charging his disciples, "Take nothing for your journey except a staff . . . but wear sandals, and do not put on two tunics" (Mark 6:8f.), while Matthew writes "Take no gold nor silver . . . no bag for your journey, nor two tunics, nor sandals, nor a staff" (Matt. 10.9f.). Matthew suggests (10:5) that Jesus instructed his disciples to "go nowhere among the gentiles, but only to the lost sheep of the house of Israel." As the kingdom was coming soon, there would be little time for them to engage in a worldwide mission. Yet a later editor of the same Gospel, confronted with the disconfirmation of early Christian belief in the immediate return of the son of man, shows Jesus saying after his resurrection, "Go—make disciples of all nations" (Matt. 28:16–20), a missionary vision emphasized still later by Luke (Acts 1:6) in response to a question put to the risen Jesus by an idealized apostolic college: "Lord, will you now restore the kingdom to Israel?" "It is none of your business to know what time or date has been established by the Father," Jesus is made to reply; "after you receive the holy spirit, you will be my witnesses in Judaea, Samaria [territory forbidden them in Matt. 10:5] and even to the very ends of the earth." Here again, the "contradiction" does not point up the existence of a historical person who was wont to change his mind but to sayings contrived to meet the changing geographical and cultural circumstances of an expanding movement—one that had rationalized its apocalyptic hopes and come to terms with the empirical, largely political reality of growth as power.

6. Even with respect to the matters one would suppose free of contradiction— the account of the crucifixion and resurrection of Jesus, for example—the Gospels provide no coherent picture. The trial scenes seem to derive from two orginally discrete traditions: one that blamed the death of the Messiah on the Jews, another that named the Romans. Echoes of the former can still be detected in Paul's letter to the church at Thessalonike (1 Thess. 2:15f.) and in certain passages preserved in the Talmud. The two tales have been woven together on the premise that the Sanhedrin lacked the power to execute Jesus for the crimes he was al-

leged to have committed; but it is well known that in the time the scene is set—
the procuratorship of Pontius Pilate—the Sanhedrin lacked no such power, and
Mark 14:55 and the very abrupt transition between Mark 14:64, where the guards
set upon Jesus, and Mark 14:66f., the story of Peter's denial of Jesus, point to
the possibility of a rather different ending to the trial before the Jewish council.
Nor is there any clear statement of the charges against him: Luke offers political
rebellion and the preaching of tax evasion as the offenses (23:2–5) but the point
of the trial before the priests seems to be that he was charged with preaching
himself as the Messiah (Mark 14:62 f.), although this in itself was not a capital
offense. Sharing Pilate's perplexity about the specifics of the crime, we may conclude,
as church piety requires, that Jesus suffered because he was innocent. Whether
he suffered crucifixion at the hands of the Romans or was stoned as a blas-
phemer by the Jews is in the long run a matter of little consequence; the Romans
as the actual executioners (a point on which there is marginal agreement) is surely
offset by the rhetorical efforts to make the Jews the true villains of the piece
and to exculpate Pilate (Luke 23:15; Mark 15:15; John 19:12; etc.). There is no
easy way to explain this fundamental contradiction except to say that the early
Christians were as reluctant in their preaching to the Jews to claim that their
Lord had suffered rejection and death at the edict of the priests who opposed
his Messiahship as they were also abashed to blame the death on the imperial
powers to whom they looked increasingly for favors and for their continued existence as a cult. The confusion reflects not conflicting *historical* details, therefore,
but the central dilemma of early missionary Christianity. (One may also wish
to compare Jesus' stoic silence as the Isaianic suffering servant in the synoptic
Gospels to his speechmaking defenses in John 18:19 ff. As to the ensuing events:
three Gospels suggest that Jesus did not carry his cross, but that a passerby,
Simon of Cyrene (the paradigm of suffering apostleship), was impressed for the
duty; one Gospel stresses that Jesus bore the cross for himself (John 19:17).

There is no agreement about the day, hour, or location of the crucifixion,
nor about what witnesses were present: the Synoptics, following Mark, stick to
the story that only women watched the events on Golgotha; the Fourth Gospel
places the "beloved" disciple (a pseudonym for the author?) at the foot of the
cross. Reports about the resurrection, the central datum of Christian faith, are
even more confused, doubtless because the ancient churches guard their versions
of the events of Easter morning rather jealously, and there was proportionately
less chance to bring the tales into alignment. Thus Mark 16 possessed no story
of the appearances of Jesus, ending (in its earliest form) at 16:8, or just after,
with the tale of the discovery of the empty tomb by some women (two Marys
and Salome); the women see a young man, get the news that Jesus is on his
way to Galilee ahead of them, are told to spread the news to Peter and the
others (who had fled home in chapter 14), but end up saying nothing to anyone
(Mark 16:8). Matthew tells us that *two* women went to the tomb, where an
earthquake (one of Matthew's favorite devices, cf. Matt. 27:51) announces the
descent of an angel from the heavens. In front of their eyes he rolls the stone

away from the tomb. The guards are said to have "become like dead men at the sight," but are bribed by the Jews (28:11 ff.) to spread the story that the disciples of Jesus stole his body away, thus making the Jews believers in the Resurrection and the soldiers doltish accomplices willing to accuse themselves of sleeping through the events they were posted outside the tomb to prevent! Luke (24:1ff) agrees with Mark on the trivial detail that the stone was found already rolled away, but does not specify who the visitants are (though it is implied that an array of women were present [cf. 23:49]). Luke, dissatisfied with one angel/young man, decides on two, "in dazzling apparel," who tell the women not to go to Galilee (where the apostles have relocated in Mark and Matthew) but to Jerusalem, where they have already formed something like an apostolic college in preparation for Pentecost and the coming of the Holy Spirit (Acts 1:12ff.). John, to compromise, offers in successive chapters (20, 21) appearances of Jesus both in Galilee and in Jerusalem, although he cuts the number of women visitors to one and introduces the race to the tomb by Peter and the "beloved" disciple. And Paul, reflecting yet another stratum of tradition in 1 Corinthians 15 mentions appearances of Jesus to Peter (= Cephas), five hundred others, to James, the other apostles, and then to Paul himself. Later apocryphal Gospels also stress the great numbers of those who had "seen" the Lord, and by Paul's day at least it had become an indispensable entry on a missionary's *curriculum vitae* to be able to boast at least one vision of the risen Christ (Gal. 1:13; 2 Cor. 12:1ff.).

10. In the case of the Old Testament, centuries are reckoned to have passed between the lifetime of a prophet or patriarch and the recording of words, yet it is assumed that only about two generations elapsed between the Crucifixion and the time of the earliest Gospel. Is this not an argument in favor of the historical accuracy of the Gospels? Eyewitnesses must have been around at the time of their composition.

Christian evangelists are fond of this argument; beginning with the postulate of a historical individual, educed from the very texts under examination, they go on to reason that the individual's actions and deeds have been accurately recorded because the accounts are chronologically near to the time when the protagonist of the text is supposed to have lived. What Shaw said of capital punishment—("Hanging the wrong man will deter crime as easily as hanging the right one")—has a peculiar application here, since texts may as easily reflect an ideal figure—a hero or god—who exists solely in the collective mind of the believing community as a real one. It may be of course that there was a historical Jesus who, in some way we shall never recover, called such a community into existence by the strength of his personality or the marvels he performed (in the perception of his followers, anyway) or the success with which his memory survived the circumstances of his death. Such a figure, as Schweitzer recognized at the turn of this century, is lost to us forever, having been replaced by the Jesus of Gospel and church doctrine—a Jesus who never had any existence. As to comparing the Old Testament accounts of prophets and patriarchs and the account of Jesus in the Gospels, we have but one Book of Genesis (with its three accounts of creation!) and one Book of Jeremiah. Had we four books of creation and an accordingly larger number of creation stories, we would be better disposed to see the spinning of such myths as belonging to the history of culture and unfit matter to be regarded as scientific "theory"; so, too, had we four books of Jeremiah, offering us different stories of his birth, his mission, his sayings and prophecies, we would perhaps still believe in prophets but we would have a difficult time arriving at a picture of the historical "Jeremiah"—or the historical Moses, or any biblical figure. Confronted with a multitude of sources, we might want to do what is so often done in the case of the Gospels: namely, to declare it all true; to conflate the birth stories, sayings, deeds, and other details to form one grand picture. Tatian did precisely this when he produced his great *Diatessaron*—the first attempt to make one consecutive gospel of the four he credited. But in this case we will have enshrined contradictions and ignored the fact that the "great fourfold gospel" never had any existence except in the minds of Christian apologists and theologians.

The problem for Christianity, in its claim to be a religion of supernatural authority based on a historical individual, is the diversity it has enshrined in its canon of four Gospels. Only the heretic Marcion, in cutting the number from four to one, anticipated the difficulty the new religion would confront in basing its revelation on a panoply of theological narratives. Doubtless Luke (1:1ff.) and perhaps also the author of John tried to end the process of tale-spinning and gospel writing by making their narratives (different as each is from the other) normative for Christian faith; but it was the fate of their writings to be assimilated and finally canonized alongside, not instead of, the others. Not only did they fail to provide the church with an official story—such a feat was never really possible given the political dimensions of the second-century church in its struggle with "heretical" as well as with "orthodox" communities. But they failed to forestall the process of gospel writing, a process that continued apace for the next two centuries. Only in the fourth century, with the virtual triumph of the usage doctrine (canonical gospels being those in use in the "canonical" churches—Rome, Antioch, Ephesus, Constantinople, etc.) and the rise to power of bishops Athanasius, Cyril of Jerusalem, and Ambrose of Milan) with the political clout to suppress what they considered unappealing, does the process slow and the paint on the picture of Jesus harden.

(Spring 1985)

Keeping the Secrets of the Dead Sea Scrolls
John M. Allegro

"Perhaps it would have been better," said the professor ruefully over his port, "if the Scrolls had been left at the bottom of the Dead Sea." It would have saved a good deal of contention, certainly. The learned professor, holding one of the senior chairs of the Old Testament in an English university, was bemoaning the fact that at the time, in the fifties, controversy was raging over almost every aspect of these famous documents—on their finding, dating, origin, interpretation, and the manner of their editing—to the exclusion, it seemed to him, of every other subject in the field of biblical studies. He could not believe that they were worth the trouble.

In the past thirty years, the amount of attention devoted to these important documents has declined, not least for want of fresh evidence, since a great deal that was recovered from the caves has yet to appear in edited form. But the professor was wrong: the Dead Sea Scrolls were, and are, worth the trouble. However, the essential consideration in any piece of original research is that the inquirer wants to know the answer, and, unhappily, many of those first charged with the study and interpretation of the Dead Sea Scrolls were interested in only part of the answer, or were fired less with enthusiasm for seeking completely new perspectives on their subject than with countering claims that what had come from the dust of the caves necessitated a radical reassessment of traditional views on the nature and origins of Christianity.

Nevertheless, there have been and are real problems in the editing and interpretation of the scrolls. First, as with so many of the great archaeological discoveries of the past, the initial find was quite accidental. In 1947, a young Arab shepherd had followed a straying animal from his flocks up a steep cliff on the western side of the Dead Sea. He came upon a cave containing several tall earthenware jars, in which were seven parchment scrolls in varying states of preservation. The largest turned out to be a copy of the biblical book of Isaiah, dating probably to the first or second century before the turn of the era, a thousand years or so older than any Hebrew manuscript of the Old Testament then known. Exciting though this discovery was, the Isaiah scroll was not the most important of the documents from that cache. Included also was a treatise that its American editors called the "Manual of Discipline"—the rules for the internal government, doctrines, hymns, and prayers of a Jewish sect known from history as the Essenes. Most of what had been hitherto understood about this fringe group of Judaism had come from the writings of early historians like the first-century Josephus, Philo of Alexandria, and the natural historian Pliny the Elder, but this was the first original evidence for their doctrines and discipline that had been seen. The discovery was the more welcome because archaeologists had always maintained that no really old manuscripts would ever be found in Palestine, since they could not have survived the damp climate prevailing in that country. The experts, of course, had overlooked the extremely dry western fringes of the Dead Sea, deep in the great Rift Valley. With an average rainfall of some two inches a year in that area, the interiors of the deep limestone caves are as dry as any Egyptian desert. When systematic searches began to be made along the coast after the shepherd's sensational discovery, it became apparent that this part of the Judaean Wilderness was a veritable treasure-house of antiquities, and not only of early manuscripts, but of wooden artifacts dating from Chalcolithic times, 3000 to 4000 B.C.E.

But the accidental nature of that first find meant that, for many valuable months, nothing was known of the discovery in the outside world, and the manuscripts and accompanying archaeological evidence were dispersed, making certain dating more difficult and allowing the widest range of speculation about the provenance of the scrolls. When the cave itself was rediscovered and searched and the manuscripts brought together and edited, the evidence had to be separately assessed in an unhappy country sorely divided politically and, in the most crucial period, militarily. For this was the time of the establishment of the State of Israel and the tragic division of Palestine into warring factions. Three of the seven scrolls from the shepherd's cave had been taken into custody by a professor from the Hebrew University of Jerusalem; the other four were smuggled from Jordan by an ecclesiastic and sold in New York for a quarter of a million dollars, and only then taken back to rejoin their fellows in the Israeli side of the divided city. Meanwhile, the Bedouin tribesmen of the Dead Sea area had been alerted to the potentialities of their old grazing lands as a rich source of antiquities, and they went scroll-hunting in earnest. Soon other caves were found near the original one, yielding scraps of parchment and papyrus that the Jordanian authorities with their very limited funds had to buy into safety, ever mindful that they could be too easily smuggled from the country and perhaps lost forever. The biggest cache of all was recovered by the Bedouins in 1952, and, to the chagrin of the archaeologists, it was found only a stone's throw from the excavations they had been supervising.

*   *   *

When the shepherd's cave was located by the Jordanian authorities—itself an arduous and time-consuming process, the principals initially involved in the recovery and dissemination of the first scrolls having, by oversight or design, omitted to inform the antiquities department—the archaeologists set about looking for other material remains of the owners of what appeared to be an important library. A mile or so away from the first cave were the tumbled and dust-strewn remains of an ancient settlement, long-noticed but never before investigated. This site was excavated over the next five seasons and turned out to be the Essene monastery whose existence by the shores of the Dead Sea had been noted by Pliny in the first century. The workmen employed for the excavation included local Bedouin shepherds. Showing more resourcefulness and imagination than their employers, they searched the immediate vicinity in their spare time and in 1952 found a chamber artificially hollowed out of the marly plateau on which the settlement was sited. In the absence of the archaeologists, the Bedouins scrabbled in the dust chamber floor and soon came upon tens of thousands of manuscript fragments of parchment and papyrus—the remains, as it subsequently transpired, of some four hundred different documents of the Essene library. In this case, presumably because danger from attack threatened the monastery, the inhabitants had torn up their precious scrolls and thrown them into the chamber they had previously prepared, perhaps for just this kind of emergency, and left them to rot. So while the first scrolls were comparatively well preserved, having been stored in jars and wrapped about in linen cloths for the intervening two thousand years, these small fragments, many no larger than a fingernail, have had to be individually cleaned, photographed, painstakingly pieced together as far as possible, identified, although usually out of literary context, and then edited for publication.

Clearly the work was more than could be accomplished by one or two scholars, and it was decided by the Jordanian authorities that an international team of editors (of which I was a part) should be called together to work in Arab Jerusalem for as long as it took to prepare this new, exciting cache for publication. They knew it would take several years, but no one then guessed that the work would drag out for three decades and that by 1984 only a small part of the material would have been published. Many different factors have caused this delay, not the least being that not all the team members have shown as much enthusiasm for distributing the texts in their charge as quickly as the rest of the scholarly world might reasonably expect. Also, although the eight of us ranged in our religious affiliations from Jesuit to Lutheran Protestant to myself, an unbeliever, no Jews were present of course since they would not have been politically acceptable in a Muslim country at that time. So the team was from the first philosophically, religiously, and denominationally unbalanced, where perhaps a wider spread of faiths or allegiances might have introduced some measure of competition and urgency into what has become an altogether too leisurely process.

The excuses now being advanced to explain the unacceptable delay in the publication of some 80 percent of the fragmentary material include the political state of the country since 1967, when the Israelis took over East Jerusalem and could determine the fate of antiquities remaining in Jordanian territory west of the Jordan and the Dead Sea. In fact, the Israeli authorities permitted the work of editing to continue in Jerusalem. (Only I was barred from returning, but not, as far as I am aware by the Israelis but by the then editor-in-chief, the late Father Roland De Vaux. I had, in any case, already completed the major part of my work, and had published the most important documents in my section in preliminary form over the years since 1953 in the learned journals. A year later, in 1968, my whole group appeared in its definitive edition in the Clarendon series.)

It now appears, from a recent broadcast interview by Professor Yiggael Yadin, former deputy prime minister of Israel, that, following the Six-Day War, he had been under considerable pressure by his academic colleagues to defy international conventions and seize the scroll fragments from the Rockefeller archives in order to hand them out to Jewish scholars to edit and publish. He resisted these attempts and made an agreement with De Vaux to allow time for the original team to complete their work. He now wonders whether this was an overgenerous act on the government's part and feels that the impatience of his friends cannot be restrained much longer. In fact, from my own observation, the fragments have periodically been brought over into East Jerusalem for much-needed conservation treatment, even exhibited in the so-called Shrine of the Book museum devoted to the display of the scrolls in Israeli hands.

Much has been said about the inevitable delays caused by the physical difficulties of our work. It is true that working with such small pieces of parchment, and even more with tiny squares and rectangles of disintegrated papyrus documents, is very time-consuming and often extremely tedious and eye-straining. Many of the parchments had over the centuries become blackened with age, often eaten at the edges by worms, or still showed the rough handling they received when they were wrenched asunder by the Essenes themselves, who were fearful of their secrets being revealed to unauthorized eyes. The result was that we could often be sure that the piece was inscribed at all only by studying infrared photographs to penetrate the blackness of the skin. Even when, through matching scribal hands and general context, we could be sure that we had adjoining parts of this massive jigsaw puzzle, the depredations of worms or skin warping made edge-to-edge joins impossible.

So sustained work on the fragments was necessary, and most of us were only able to come to Jerusalem to work in the room that we called the "Scrollery" at the Rockefeller Museum as and when other duties and finances permitted. In this last respect there was a fund available, instituted by the Rockefeller trustees, but as time went on this ran short, or so we were told, and in any case it was intended to subsidize the cost of publication of the definitive edition of the texts as well as to pay traveling expenses. I myself had only one such grant from this fund and was otherwise subsidized on one occasion by a subvention from a British educational foundation and at other times from my own meager resources, which were fortunately enhanced at the time by royalties from a successful book on the scrolls published by Penguin Books in 1956. My American colleagues found their universities more generous in financing overseas travel and study, and of course the Catholic fathers experienced no difficulties in undertaking protracted periods of attendance at their work and were boarded in nearby religious institutions for as long as they wanted. In any case, when we were away from Jerusalem we took with us the infrared plates of our documents so that editing could continue at home away from the originals. It cannot therefore be maintained that shortage of funds really accounts for the long delay in publication.

Of course, there are great difficulties in working with texts of works never before seen, or versions of previously known writings differing in language or textual tradition from the norm. For instance, works of the Pseudepigrapha—apocalypselike parts of the Testaments of the Twelve Patriarchs, Enoch, and Jubilees, well known in later translations, such as Greek, Latin, Syriac, Ethiopic, and so on—have now appeared in the Essene library for the first time in their original Hebrew or Aramaic. These fragments have first to be recognized for what they are by careful comparison with known translations, a major undertaking in view of the hundreds of documents represented in the cache and the fragmentary nature of the new exemplars. Even biblical texts that, in comparison, might be thought more easily identified pose their own problems. Our concordances are, of course, based upon the received, or standard (Massoretic) text of the Bible, the medieval exemplars of which have hitherto been our earliest recensions. But it is now clear that before the end of the first century of our era, when this standard form of the text was designated the "official" version and other variant forms allowed to go out of use, there existed other recensions that had free circulation. One good reason for believing this prior to the discovery of the scrolls was the existence of significant variants in the Greek edition of the Old Testament, the so-called Septuagint, the Bible of the early church, and of Jews in the Greek-speaking communities around the Mediterranean for whom the translation had been made. It has always been recognized that this Greek version probably presupposed an original Hebrew text differing from the received edition that is the basis of our Hebrew Bibles. That this is certainly so has now been dramatically demonstrated by the recovery from the Essene library of biblical fragments that show differences never before seen or supported by later translations. Clearly, in such cases our concordances are of limited use, and a great deal of patient work and ingenuity have to be employed in identifying chapter and verse, or even in deciding whether the fragment under scrutiny is biblical at all.

Another group of writings from the caves, those for which I had responsibility, present an intriguing mixture of biblical text and commentary: a few words from the prophets, for instance, are followed by a passage of exposition in Essene terms, often fancifully interpreting (or, we might say academically, misinterpreting) the scriptural words to give some valuable insight into their expectations for the future, or explanation of the past, in the history of the sect, or of its encounters with spiritual and political enemies.

Now this kind of study is exciting to the specialist scholar, but also very time-consuming. There has to come a point in our work where we have to admit that, for the purposes of disseminating the texts of the documents as quickly and efficiently as possible, such detailed treatment by the first editors is unnecessary. What our colleagues around the world really want at this stage are the infrared photographs, a transliteration of the script into printed form (always with the proviso that we may be reading the script wrongly, for the quality of handwriting varies considerably and the surface of the skin is often too rubbed or broken to make identification of the letters quite certain), and our suggested translations where they may be necessary or helpful. There is some evidence that not all of us see our work quite this simply; one suspects that some members of the team are reluctant to let the world see the precious texts in their charge before they have extracted every scrap of information they can from them to swell the initial presentation of their material. This can only mean that their definitive editions will be overburdened with their doubtless valuable, but not entirely indispensable, comments, and publication must be almost perpetually delayed. This may be human nature in conflict with scholarly objectivity, but it is extremely frustrating to other specialists who have been waiting thirty years to further their own research and have been unable to complete it for want of new information they know to be lying unpublished in some desk drawer until the appointed editor can spare enough time from his teaching or other official duties to make the final, definitive statement on the new text.

Such monopolistic tendencies in the academic world are not, of course, new. Something of the same regrettable possessiveness occurred in the story of the treatment accorded the comparably important Gnostic documents from Nag Hammadi in Egypt, which were discovered in 1945 in not dissimilar circumstances from that attending the finding of the Dead Sea Scrolls. Again, in the past century, a cache of important medieval Hebrew documents was found in the *genizah* or storeroom of an old Cairo synagogue. Their editor is said to have made a condition of his depositing them in the library of a British university that no one but he should have access to them, not only while he was actively working on their editing but for fifty years after his death! To the eternal shame of that institution's trustees, they apparently accepted this outrageous condition, with the result that the hoard, far more than could ever be handled by one scholar, however prolific, is still not fully published or is ever likely to be.

In the case of the Dead Sea Scrolls, there is a further consideration that cannot fail to be far from the minds of disinterested observers. It is well known that these documents are of most importance for the light they can throw upon the origins and nature of early Christianity. The Essenes had long been suggested as the possible "missing link" between normative Judaism and the church, and examination of their firsthand records indicated from the first that this would be their main interest, and also their most controversial. The late Edmund Wilson, in his series of articles for the *New Yorker* magazine in 1955, suggested that the church might be reluctant to accept conclusions from the new studies that detracted from the originality and thus the uniqueness of the faith and that this would affect the Christian attitude toward the discoveries and their editing. I well recall the heated reaction of my ecclesiastic colleagues in the Scrollery when these articles appeared. It seemed to them an insult to their scholarly integrity that they should wish to withhold information from the documents on which we were working or that they could be anything but enthusiastic for new information or ideas about the origins of their religion. Besides, they were at one in rejecting the very idea that anything in the scrolls could possibly conflict with the revealed truth as dispensed by the church. That was, indeed, the official line taken by the Vatican, in order to quiet the fears of the faithful about the new finds from the Dead Sea.

Wilson's suggestion that the church was none too happy to see fresh, uncontrolled evidence appearing on the admittedly shadowy background of Christianity proved in the event a remarkable stimulus to general interest in the scrolls. Many speculations were advanced to account for the significant parallels that were being adduced between the documents and the New Testament: that Jesus had been himself an Essene; that John the Baptist had been a member of the Dead Sea community and passed on Essene ideas to the Nazarene master and his friends; that the story of Jesus owed much to the history of the Essenes' own leader, the so-called Teacher of Righteousness, and so on. The church's reaction to all such suggestions was in general predictable: the parallels adduced, even when substantiated by their own scholars, were interesting but of limited consequence, for the differences were far greater. As far as the Teacher of Righteousness was concerned, he was not regarded with the awe accorded Jesus by the church, was not claimed to be the Messiah by his followers, let alone the Son of God, and had not risen from the dead. Nothing in the Gospels could be said to reflect the person, character, or fate of the Essenes' Teacher.

*   *   *

About that time, a fresh consignment of scroll fragments was received in the Scrollery from the Bedouins, part of the cache from the underground chamber by the monastery. Among them were several large pieces, obviously part of a biblical commentary on the Book of Nahum, and thus falling into my section for editing. They contained the first of the very few references we have seen to actual historical events. The Essenes were not, as a rule, interested in the history of their time or of their immediate past: their eyes were set on the future, and the coming of their Messiah, or Christ, and the Millennium. The particular event noted in the scroll was the revolt against the hated priest-king Alexander Jannaeus and his terrible revenge against his own Jewish subjects, when, in 88 B.C.E., he had several hundred of them crucified before him under the horrified gaze of the victims' wives and children. Clearly these happenings had affected the Essenes greatly, to the extent that they could regard them as one of the "signs of the times" of cosmic significance. I felt that this was too important a document to be left to the final publication of my section, and I gave it preliminary exposure in a specialist journal as soon as possible. I was also able to include the gist of it in my Penguin volume previously mentioned, then in preparation, and to speak of it in a broadcast I gave on a British radio station, coupling the crucifixion reference to the suggestion that the reason for the Essenes' interest in the awful event could most probably be explained by assuming their own participation in the revolt against Jannaeus and the possibility that their Teacher had, like Jesus, been crucified. We knew from references elsewhere in the scrolls that the Teacher had been persecuted by his enemies and that on one occasion, a Day of Atonement, he had been dramatically confronted by his arch-enemy, the so-called Wicked Priest. This suggestion added so much fuel to the fire of speculation about parallels with the Jesus story that while I was in England my colleagues in the Scrollery banded together to write a letter to the *London Times* dissociating themselves from my thesis, and denying that anything in the document I had edited gave any reason for linking Jesus with the Teacher, or even that it provided evidence for his death by crucifixion. The division of interests between myself and my religious colleagues could not have been more forcefully illustrated; and it did little to quell the suspicions aroused by Edmund Wilson that the church was at the least touchy, if not paranoid, over the newly recovered evidence from the Dead Sea caves.

I continue to publish the most important pieces of my section of documents in advance of the final, definitive volumes. My colleagues published very few, though urged to do so from all sides. In 1952, an extraordinary new discovery was made, this time by the archaeologists themselves. It comprised several parchment scraps from the Essene library found in a cave to the north of the monastery, and with them, in two pieces, a scroll that had been inscribed, quite uniquely, on copper sheets and riveted at the edges in imitation of the sewn skins in a normal parchment scroll. The copper had completely oxidized over the two millennia it had lain in the cave, and for three years the brittle scroll lay in a showcase in the Rockefeller Museum, defying all attempts to open it by normal means and remaining the subject of much speculation about its contents. At length, I suggested to the director of Jordanian Antiquities that in my own university the necessary enterprise and technical skills might be found to cut the scroll open, since it was clear that there remained no other way of ascertaining its message. The Jordanian government agreed to the attempt, and in 1955 and 1956 the pieces were brought to England and operated on in the then College of Science and Technology (now the University of Manchester Institute of Science and Technology). I supervised the work on the behalf of the Jordanian government, and, as the strips of cut scroll came from the operator, I read the message concealed for two thousand years. It was, in fact, an inventory of buried treasure—the last thing we expected to find in a community dedicated to voluntary poverty. Almost certainly the treasure referred to was the wealth of the Jewish Temple in Jerusalem, hidden away by the Zealots who had control of the sanctuary before the Romans arrived in 70 C.E. and destroyed it by fire. The hiding places were in various locations in and around Jerusalem and included, in my opinion, the site of the Essenes' own settlement by the Dead Sea. Indeed, the archaeologists had earlier found, buried under the floor of one of the monastery rooms, a cache of three jars filled with silver coins in mint condition.

I reported my readings immediately to the antiquities department in Jordan and to my colleagues in the Scrollery. There came no response. Eventually, I was told formally that a decision had been made to release news of the successful cutting operation, but that I was on no account to reveal to the press anything about the contents of the strange document. Apparently the archaeological authorities were fearful lest the news should stimulate local treasure-seekers to dig up every site in Palestine looking for the Jews' buried treasure. It seemed to me to set a very unwise precedent to deliberately withhold information about the contents of one of the Dead Sea Scrolls, however religiously uncontroversial. However, six months after the scroll's opening, news of its contents was released, coupled with what seemed to me an arbitrary and insufficiently supported opinion that the inventory was the work of imagination, inscribed (presumably at considerable cost in materials and effort) by a "fanatic"; it was said to have no historical or actual relevance and of comparatively little importance. The responsibility for the press release was given to the technician concerned with the opening, and once again I was told to stand well back and contribute nothing to the official statement.

*　　*　　*

One cannot help wondering, then, with that precedent set on a matter involving only apprehensions about the safety of archaeological sites, whether such restraint might not be far more readily shown by ecclesiastics in the publication of documents relating to religiously sensitive issues. This is not to say that such concerns necessarily lie behind the thirty-year delay in the publication of the scroll fragments. Nor should we accord any significance to the interesting fact that the Catholic scholar responsible for most of the unpublished, nonbiblical, and thus theologically most interesting material obtained a dispensation from his church to leave the priesthood and marry. The inexplicable delay is, nevertheless, bound to raise the same questions posed by Wilson at the start of the scrolls' story. And with the unhappy record of the church for destroying documents and whole libraries of which it disapproved, as well as its predeliction for controlling the reading habits and opportunities of the faithful, one can only continue to be apprehensive about the church's attitude when religiously sensitive information come into its hands, as could very well happen under the kind of circumstances attending the discovery of the Nag Hammadi documents and the Dead Sea Scrolls.

It is customary now for scholars to brush aside suggestions that there is anything in the still unpublished material that could prove embarrassing to the church. That view was recently put in a broadcast by the Jewish custodian of the Israeli scrolls in Jerusalem, who has seen the fragments in the Rockefeller

Museum, even if he has not studied them all in detail. He assured his listeners that there was nothing there that was not already generally known. Yet I have recently published in an appendix to my recent book *The Dead Sea Scrolls and the Christian Myth* a document that has never figured in any review of the contents of the cache and which I for one consider of first importance for an understanding of the Essenes, the meaning of their name, their therapeutic practices, and for the significance of the title Cephas accorded Peter in the New Testament. It so happened that although this piece was not in my original section of material and was therefore not for me to include in my definitive volume, I had arranged some thirty years ago with the Catholic scholar referred to previously to publish it provisionally if the occasion offered in return for transferring into his section a very much longer text that fell between our respective genres of literature. I had long been aware of the importance of this small piece, but fully expected my colleague to publish it earlier, either in provisional form or in his long overdue definitive edition. Since I needed its evidence to supplement the thesis of the book, I decided to present it in this publication, along with a short philological commentary and infrared photograph. So one may well inquire that if this small but significant document has remained unnoticed for so long, how can any person who has not studied in the fullest details every one of the several hundred works lying unrevealed in that large group talk so dismissively about what importance may or may not be attached to them? The fact is that no one but the appointed editor has had the opportunity to submit the scroll fragments to such intensive examination as would warrant any assumption about their significance, and even then a fresh eye can often detect a meaning or vital relevance unsuspected by one to whom the text has become perhaps overfamiliar.

Perhaps there is no way of ensuring that purposeful suppression of information from new discoveries does not ever happen in the future. At least, the public should be aware of the dangers that exist, even in this supposedly enlightened age, and by demanding the prompt publication of all newly acquired documents as soon as reasonably possible, and the free and unrestricted discussion of all matters affecting the issues involved, we might do something to ensure that truth is not made subject to the strictures of any one interested party.

(Fall 1984)

VII.

Battles in Science

S ince 1987 *Free Inquiry* has published "The Affirmations of Humanism" on its back cover. The first and third affirmations read: "We are committed to the application of reason and science to the understanding of the universe and to the solving of human problems"; "We believe that scientific discovery and technology can contribute to the betterment of human life." By the end of the nineteenth century these principles were accepted by practically everybody—certainly the educated. Even occult mysticisms and Christian fundamentalists couldn't resist science's appeal—or at least its veneer—so we got things like Rudolf Steiner's "spiritual science" and Mary Baker Eddy's Christian Science church.

There's been some retrenchment since then. Science is now seen by many—religious and otherwise—as the cause of humanity's greatest woes: the possibility of nuclear holocaust, and the chemical despoliation of the earth and its atmosphere. Moreover, with the strength of technology most often in the hands of the moneyed classes, science is no longer seen as a neutral (let alone benevolent) application of human thought. It seems to threaten and enslave us.

Its reputation thus tarnished, the methods of science have to be defended now as never before. The most public battle has been over the teaching of Darwinian evolution in the public schools. L. Sprague de Camp's "The Continuing Monkey War" is a vivid recounting of the history of that battle, which reached its pitch with the Scopes Monkey Trial in the 1920s and again—to the dismay of the scientific establishment—in various cases brought to court by fundamentalist "creation scientists" in the 1980s.

Martin Gardner's sparring match with Paul Feyerabend shows that the debate stretches beyond Darwin and the fundamentalists. Feyerabend, an "epistemological anarchist" and professor at the University of California at Berkeley, writes that science "must admit that standards, like theories and measuring instruments, constantly change and that the only *general* statement that can be made about science is: Anything Goes." Gardner writes that "to most philosophers Feyerabend is a brilliant but tiresome, self-centered, repetitious buffoon whose reputation rests mainly on the noise and confusion he generates." Feyerabend's retort: "I do sympathize with Gardner and his fellow ideologues. They grew up in a well-equipped and confident church; they were and still are nourished by it, both intellectually and financially; they spent long hours trying to understand and master its gospel; they enjoyed the authority their knowledge gave them in society; and now it seems that their knowledge is but one opinion among many, and without inherent advantages."

For Sir Karl Popper, the "inherent advantages" of the scientific spirit are monumental. Popper is perhaps best known for his doctrine of "falsifiability"—that in order for a scientific hypothesis to be worthwhile, it must be presented in such a way that, if false, it can be *proved* false—has become an invaluable tool in scientific theorizing. Indeed, for Popper the hypothesis is the key: "New hypotheses . . . whether true or false, are most valuable, because they are so very rare, and we are always in need of more." The impact on science is obvious—but here, in an essay honoring Andrei Sakharov, the "impersonal" critical thinking that generates the testable hypothesis can perhaps be most useful in the political realm. Reason: "From the point of view of biology and natural selection, the main function of the human mind and especially of critical thinking is, indeed, that they make possible the application of the method of trial and the elimination of error without the elimination of ourselves. . . . With the emergence of mind and human understanding, selection needs no longer be violent: we can eliminate false theories with nonviolent criticism."

—R.B.

The Continuing Monkey War

L. Sprague de Camp

The young assistant attorney general for Arkansas, Don Langston, sounded embarrassed. The case, he told the Supreme Court, began under a previous administration, and it was his task to see it through.

Chief Justice Earl Warren asked: "What was the significance of that?"

"I was just giving you background, Your Honor," replied Langston.

"I thought you were telling us your administration doesn't like the statute."

"I am not prepared to say that, Your Honor."

"It might not be too late, you know," smiled Chief Justice Warren.

Langston went on to argue the State's side of *Epperson* v. *Arkansas.* The case began in 1965, when Susan Epperson, a pretty young red-haired biology teacher in Little Rock Central High School, filed suit in the Pulaski County Chancery Court. She sought to have the Rotenberry Act, Arkansas's "monkey law," declared unconstitutional. Patterned on the more famous Butler Act of Tennessee, the Rotenberry Act forbade teaching, in public schools and colleges, "the theory or doctrine that mankind ascended or descended from a lower order of animals and it shall be unlawful for any teacher, textbook commission, or other authority . . . to select textbooks . . . or use in any such institutions a textbook that teaches the doctrine" in question.

Mrs. Epperson was backed by the Arkansas Educational Association and represented by attorney Eugene R. Warren. The chancellor, Murray O. Reed, found the law unconstitutional on the ground that it infringed on the teachers' freedom of speech. The state appealed. In a two-sentence opinion, the Arkansas Supreme Court reversed Judge Reed, holding the law a legitimate exercise of the legislature's power to control the curriculum. Lawyer Warren in turn appealed. Now, on October 16, 1968, the Supreme Court of the United States was hearing the arguments.

Eugene Warren had already asserted that the law was unconstitutionally vague because it did not define the scope of the verb "teach." This might mean "to teach as true, to indoctrinate or proselytize." Or it might mean merely "to mention or describe in class," without saying whether the teacher agreed with the doctrine.

Moreover, continued Eugene Warren, Arkansas used a standard biology text, Otto and Towle's *Modern Biology,* which had evolutionary sections on the development of life and the origin of man. This placed teachers in a strange position. Some told their pupils: "It is illegal to read this next chapter," knowing that this was a sure way to get pupils to study the material. If the law were broadly construed, it would even be illegal to refer pupils to a standard dictionary or encyclopedia, all of which have articles on evolution.

Now it was Langston's turn to address the Court, and the austere justices saw fit to have a little fun with him. Chief Justice Warren asked if a state might outlaw the mention of geometry.

Justice Marshall asked: "Since your Supreme Court has disposed of the lower court's opinion in two sentences, would you object to us disposing of that one in one sentence?"

Justice Stewart added: "What if Arkansas would forbid the theory that the world is round?"

With a fiendish grin, Justice Douglas put in: "How about sex? Does Arkansas have any prohibitions on teaching in the field of sex?"

Smiles and discreet laughter spread around the courtroom, where Mrs. Epperson sat with her husband, an Air Force mathematician. The hearing was over in half an hour.

The Epperson case was a late battle in a dwindling war of ideas, which has raged and sputtered in the United States for more than a century. In the 1870s, American Protestant leaders became aware of two disturbing developments. One was the fact that European scholars were scrutinizing the Bible more closely than ever before. They had concluded that it was not, as Christians had long believed, a book dictated by God and therefore infallibly true. It was, instead, a disorderly anthology of ancient myths, legends, history, law, philosophy, sermons, poems, fiction, and some outright forgeries. They pointed out, among other things, that Genesis contains not one creation story but two different and mutually inconsistent ones, clumsily spliced together, and that there are likewise two divergent stories of Noah's flood.

The other development was the spread of Charles Darwin's theory of evolution by natural selection, which included the idea that man had descended from some apelike or monkeylike primate. The general concept of evolution had been the subject of occasional speculation at least from the time of Anaximandros in the sixth century B.C.E.

In his *Origin of Species* of 1859, Darwin not only presented a mass of evidence indicating the evolution of all living things but also advanced a convincing explanation of why evolution took place. His concept of natural selection—the "survival of the fittest"—is Darwinism in the strictest sense.

Since *Origin* appeared on the eve of the American Civil War, it had little popular impact for a decade in the United States, although it gained quick acceptance from most scientists. Then an uneasy awareness of these novelties aroused the churches. Some divines accepted them; others rejected them with repugnance.

At yearly Bible conferences, conservative leaders inveighed against the menace of liberalism at home and destructive biblical criticism abroad. They fiercely pursued those whom they accused of corrupting the minds of the people by the new teachings. Some preachers lost their pulpits and some professors their chairs in consequence. The most celebrated victim was the geologist Alexander Winchell, who was dismissed from Vanderbilt University for telling his students they were descended from pre-Adamite organisms.

Late in the century, an annual gathering of orthodox Protestants, the Niagara Bible Conference, listened to speeches and issued publications. In 1895, this conference put forth a statement reducing Christian doctrine to five essential points:

1. The inerrancy or infallibility of the Bible.

2. The divinity of Jesus Christ.

3. The virgin birth of Jesus Christ.

4. The substitutionary atonement of Christ—the doctrine that Jesus' self-sacrifice freed men from the sin inherited from Adam.

5. The physical resurrection of Christ and his eventual Second Coming.

Although the last point combines two doctrines, making six in all, the "Five Points" became famous and were set forth, with variations, on later occasions. Since the first point, the inerrancy of the Bible, demanded literal belief in the Creation myth of Genesis, it brought the Bible into collision with Darwinism.

In 1907 millionaire brothers, Lyman and Milton Stewart, founded the Los Angeles Bible Institute. Then they chose a committee to codify the tenets of the faithful. The result was a dozen pamphlets, issued in 1910 as *The Fundamentals*. Circulated by the Stewarts' generosity, these pamphlets set forth the committee's version of the Five Points and furnished the basis for the fundamentalist movement, which grew during the next few years.

The First World War distracted American minds from fundamentalism; but as soon as it ended, the fundamentalists sprang back into action. When the Eighteenth Amendment was adopted, the fundamentalists, flushed with triumph, sighted upon their next target: the ape in man's family tree. Leaders included William Bell Riley of the First Baptist Church of Minneapolis; John Roach Straton of the Calvary Baptist Church of New York; Aimee Semple McPherson of the Angelus Temple of Los Angeles; and William Jennings Bryan (1860–1925), lawyer, politician, orator, reformer, Sunday-school teacher, lecturer, journalist, editor, anti-liquor crusader, real-estate promoter, lobbyist, thrice-defeated candidate for president, one-time U.S. secretary of state, and prominent Presbyterian layman.

Bryan was an upright, virtuous, kindly, likable, eloquent, magnetic, and majestically wrong-headed man. Not unintelligent, he was wholly superficial, with unshakable faith in slogans as solutions to problems, and unable to grasp any idea that conflicted with his preconceived convictions. In 1921 he moved from Nebraska to Florida. For several years he lobbied for Latin American governments seeking loans, sold real estate he had bought near Miami, lectured on the Chautauqua circuit, and supported the fundamentalist cause.

Like other Adamist leaders, Bryan wrote, lectured, and appeared before legislatures to urge bills to ban the teaching of evolution. Probably the greatest American orator of all time, he was much more moderate and reasonable than some of his followers, who wanted to forbid evolutionary beliefs on pain of death by crucifixion or burning. Bryan was satisfied to have legislatures pass simple anti-evolutionary resolutions, without penalties. In private, he showed himself less than dogmatically sure of his Adamism, remarking to younger associates in the Scopes case: "Now, you boys will probably live to see whether or not evolution is true. I won't."

In public he hid these doubts for the sake of presenting a united front with other Fundamentalists. In the early 1920s, under fundamentalist urging, several monkey bills were narrowly beaten in state legislatures. In 1923 Oklahoma passed an act against evolutionary textbooks, but it was repealed three years later.

In 1925, the farmer-legislator John Washington Butler introduced into Tennessee's House of Representatives an anti-evolutionary bill that passed without debate—75 to 5. Many non-fundamentalists voted for it to curry fundamentalist votes or do Butler a favor, expecting the Senate to kill the bill. Pursuing the same logic, the Senate passed the bill expecting the governor to veto it. At first dismayed, Governor Peay, under pressure from his fellow Baptists, signed it on March 21, 1925. He issued a rambling, contradictory statement asserting that "nobody believes that it is going to be an active statute." He was mistaken.

On May 4, the *Chattanooga Daily Times* reported that the American Civil Liberties Union would finance the defense of a case to test the constitutionality of the Butler Act. The afternoon of the fifth, an argument arose in Robinson's Drug Store in the small town of Dayton, in southeastern Tennessee. The disputants were Walter White, superintendent of the Rhea County Schools; Sue K. Hicks, a young lawyer (male, despite the name); and George W. Rappleyea, a young New Yorker and manager of a bankrupt local coal company. Rappleyea, one of the few evolutionists in town, opposed the law. White and Hicks, though not convinced fundamentalists, favored it.

Why not, suggested Rappleyea, have the proposed test case right here? It would put Dayton on the map! He appealed to White: "Well, we will make it a sporting proposition. As it is, the law is not enforced. If you win, it will be enforced. If I win the law will be repealed. We're game, aren't we?"

He soon won over Hicks and White. For a sacrificial victim they chose their friend John Thomas Scopes, a twenty-four-year-old science teacher in the Dayton High School. Scopes—unmarried, modest, and popular—was the obvious candidate. He had been teaching evolution not only because he believed in it but also because the official biology textbook affirmed it.

Summoned to the drugstore, Scopes was talked into accepting his role in the drama. Rappleyea wired the ACLU about his plan. Receiving a favorable reply the next day, he swore out a warrant against Scopes.

For attorneys, Scopes retained an ex-judge, John L. Godsey, and a gifted but eccentric professor of law, John Randolph Neal. Hicks wrote Bryan, offering him a place on the prosecution. When Bryan accepted, Clarence Darrow, America's best-known defense attorney and a noted agnostic, offered his services and those of his friend Dudley Field Malone, a New York divorce lawyer. They were joined on the defense by Arthur Garfield Hays, attorney for the ACLU. Several more attorneys joined one side or the other, while Godsey, fearing for his reputation, dropped out. The prosecution finally included Bryan's son, W. J. Bryan, Jr., and A. T. Stewart, attorney general for the Eighteenth Circuit. The volunteers on both sides served without pay.

The trial did indeed put Dayton on the map. It received enormous publicity. More than a hundred journalists arrived, including two Britons and the celebrated gadfly H. L. Mencken. A swarm of evangelists, cultists, eccentrics, fanatics, and demented persons converged on Dayton, converting that neat, quiet, conventional, orderly, humdrum little town into a madder tea party than Lewis Carroll ever imagined. A white-whiskered prophet announced himself as John the Baptist the Third. Showmen appeared with chimpanzees that they tried to rent to the litigants to lend zip to their arguments.

In blistering heat, the trial began on July 10, 1925. Judge John T. Raulston, a fundamentalist, tried to run a fair trial. This proved difficult, because of the circus atmosphere and because the judge himself was more than a little bewildered. Normally fair-minded, Raulston, while competent in his usual bootlegging and homicide cases, was unqualified to conduct a trial involving such profound philosophical issues. He soon succumbed to a lust for publicity.

The first three days were devoted to the choice of the jury and to pre-trial maneuvers. There were endless arguments over the motion to quash the indictment and over the propriety of Raulston's opening each session with prayer. On Wednesday, July 15, the trial proper got underway. A series of schoolboy witnesses for the state (carefully coached by Darrow) testified that Scopes had taught them evolution.

The defense had persuaded a dozen scholars and scientists to come to Dayton as expert witnesses for the defense. Most were comparatively young and obscure. The older and more eminent savants invited, by and large, begged off, alleging pressure of work or plans for foreign travel. Some of their reasons were probably genuine; in other cases, they may have been pretexts to cloak fear of loss of dignity.

However, when the defense proposed to call these witnesses to prove that evolution was a well-established fact and that it did not necessarily conflict with a liberal, allegorical reading of the Bible, the prosecution objected. A day was spent on the question, with the jury absent. There were eloquent speeches by Bryan and Stewart and a super-eloquent one by Malone, which brought an ovation even from those who disagreed with him.

The defense lawyers, especially Darrow, made good impressions. At first the Daytonians looked warily at these lawyers from afar as dangerous infidels but ended by esteeming them as men of charm, character, and wisdom. Not so for H. L. Mencken. His dispatches to the *Baltimore Sun* describing the locals as "gaping primates" and "anthropoid rabble" so enraged the townsfolk that Mencken narrowly escaped a coat of tar and feathers.

Raulston ruled out the scientific witnesses as irrelevant. Darrow lost his temper and insulted the judge, who cited him for contempt. Next day, Darrow apologized and was forgiven. For the record, Hays, again without the jury, read a summary of what the defense experts would have said had they been allowed to speak.

On the afternoon of the twentieth, fearing for the safety of the picturesquely ugly old courthouse building, Raulston moved the trial out on the courthouse lawn. There the defense played its trump card.

Hays said: "The defense desires to call Mr. Bryan as a witness . . ."

The judge goggled, and Bryan's palm-leaf fan froze in his hand. The other prosecution lawyers jumped up shouting. It was unheard of, they protested, to call an attorney in a case as a witness in that same case. But the defense persisted. Raulston put it up to Bryan, who agreed to testify if he might in turn examine the defense attorneys.

For an hour and a half, Darrow mercilessly grilled Bryan about the Bible, the history of civilization, and the origin of man. Did the whale swallow Jonah? Had Joshua stopped the earth from spinning? Was the earth created in 4004 B.C.E.? What about civilizations known to be older than that? Did the fishes survive the Flood? What did Bryan know about Buddhism and Confucianism? Did linguistics support the story of the Confusion of Tongues? Did God really fear that the builders of the Tower of Babel would use it to invade Heaven? Bryan sweated, hedged, and evaded but time and again was forced to admit his ignorance of subjects on which he had pontificated.

Darrow ground on. Where did Cain get his wife? How old was the earth? How could there have been "days" of creation before there was any sun? To the dismay of the fundamentalists, Darrow trapped Bryan into admitting that the earth might be millions of years old.

Finally, how did the Serpent walk before God commanded it to go on its belly? Did it hop along on its tail? The crowd guffawed.

Bryan rose, shaking his fists and screaming: "The only purpose of Mr. Darrow is to slur at the Bible . . ."

Darrow roared back; the spectators were excited almost to the verge of a riot. With a terrific smash of his gavel, Raulston adjourned the court. That night, District Attorney Stewart told a resentful Bryan that he might not examine Darrow; the trial had been enough of a circus already.

On the morning of the twenty-first, Raulston expunged the Darrow-Bryan debate from the record and called in the jury. In his closing address, Darrow hinted that he wanted a verdict of guilty, to make possible an appeal. The jury obliged, and Raulston ordered Scopes to pay a fine of $100.

The gathering broke up. The lawyers, the journalists, the spectators, the evangelists, the showmen, the concessionaires, and the eccentrics streamed away, leaving the Daytonians to wonder whether the publicity they had obtained was the kind they wanted. Scopes became a graduate student at the University of Chicago and went on to a quiet but honorable career as a petroleum geologist. After the trial, he privately confessed that he had never actually taught the evolutionary lesson for which he was convicted. He had been too busy that day coaching the football team.

William Jennings Bryan temporarily remained in Dayton. Although he seemed in good health and spirits, five days after the trial he quietly died during an afternoon nap. The exact cause was never learned. He was an elderly diabetic who cheated on his diet and ate voraciously. Darrow's inquisition, together with the infernal heat, had doubtless worn him down.

The defense filed its appeal. The ACLU was riven by a conflict between those who disapproved of Darrow's tactics and wanted to oust him and those who wished him to stay with the case.

The months after the Monkey Trial saw a surge of anti-evolutionary activity. Many bills were introduced into state legislatures. A host of anti-evolutionary societies blossomed: the Bible Crusaders, the Bryan Bible League, the World Christian Fundamentals Association, the Supreme Kingdom, the Defenders of the Christian Faith, and two weirdly misnamed groups—the Reseach Science Bureau and the American Science Foundation. They talked of an anti-evolutionary amendment to the U.S. Constitution—an idea with which Bryan had also toyed.

In Meridan, Mississippi, the high-school superintendent held a public bonfire of evolutionary pages torn from textbooks. William Bell Riley joyfully cried: "Within twelve months, every state in the Union will be thoroughly organized." Many evolutionists feared he might be right and that a new Dark Age was on its way. In Mississippi, a bill like the Butler Act became law in February 1926.

The following May, Darrow and his colleagues appeared in Nashville, Tennessee, to argue their appeal. The verdict was announced on January 15, 1927. Of the five justices, one disqualified himself, one held the Butler Act unconstitutional for vagueness, one held it valid but not violated, and the remaining two, while making no secret of their dislike for the law, found it constitutional and violated.

Normally the opinion of these last two would have prevailed. But alas for George Rappleyea's grand design! The court also held that Raulston had blundered in levying the fine, because the Tennessee constitution ordained that fines over $50 must be assessed by a jury. The court seized upon this technicality to remand the case to the lower court and advise District Attorney Stewart to nol-pros it. "We see nothing to be gained," quoth the court, "by prolonging the life of this bizarre case." Stewart complied, leaving the law intact and Scopes unpunished.

Through 1926 and 1927, Adamists continued to bustle and shout, to resolve and exhort. Yet it transpired that something ailed the anti-evolutionary movement. The steam had gone out of it. Of the monkey bills presented to state legislatures during this time, only Mississippi's passed. The rest failed, some by maneuvers that forestalled a vote. Delaware's monkey bill of 1927 was referred to the Committee on Fish, Game, and Oysters, where it died a quiet death. Many legislators disliked monkey bills but did not wish to vote openly against them for fear of losing support at the next election.

The crusaders won a few local victories. Here and there they persuaded local school officials to ban the teaching of evolution or to sack some unlucky pedagogue. They also intimidated many textbook publishers into omitting evolution from biology texts or skimming over the subject with vague platitudes.

In 1927, a monkey bill was introduced into the Arkansas House of Representatives by A. L. Rotenberry and backed by the Reverend Ben M. Bogard's American Anti-Evolution Association, an organization open to all save "Negroes and persons of African descent, Atheists, Infidels, Agnostics, such persons as hold to the theory of Evolution, habitual drunkards, profane swearers, despoilers of the domestic life of others, desecrators of the Lord's Day and those who would depreciate feminine virtue by vulgarly discussing sex relationship." When the bill failed to pass, Bogard got enough signatures to put the question on the ballot for a referendum the following year.

Charles Smith, president of the American Association for the Advancement of Atheism, campaigned against the proposal by handing out inflammatory anti-religious literature on the streets of Little Rock. For this, Smith was jailed under a mildewed blasphemy statute. His antics probably made more votes for the Rotenberry bill than against it, for it passed the referendum by 108,991 to 63,406.

Still, the assault on evolution continued to weaken. One by one, the Adamist leagues vanished. Gerald B. Winrod kept his Defenders of the Christian Faith alive longer than the rest by reviling the Jews in the way that was bringing success to Hitler.

Several factors hastened the wane of the Adamist crusade. One was the rise of opposition. Writers, teachers, scientists, and other intellectuals had been frightened into giving their time to writing, lecturing, and appearing before legislatures to oppose monkey laws, or paying the costs of those who did.

Another factor was boredom. Since many crusaders were only semi-literate, the endless repetition of their limited stock of ideas, crudely phrased and easily contradicted, wearied many of those to whom they were addressed.

The death of Bryan, although it gave the movement a martyr, robbed it of a widely known and respected leader. Most of the surviving leaders were too individualistic, egotistical, quarrelsome, and personally ambitious to cooperate. The movement also suffered from the personal shortcomings of some of these leaders, such as E. Y. Clark, a crook and racketeer eventually convicted of mail fraud. In 1926 the fundamentalist congressman John W. Langley was jailed for stealing liquor from government warehouses.

In the same year, Aimee Semple McPherson vanished from a California beach and was given up for drowned. On June 24, she reappeared in Mexico with a tale of being kidnapped by the hirelings of her enemies: gamblers, dope peddlers, and evolutionists. It transpired that she had merely been enjoying a holiday from Christian austerity with her former radio operator, Kenneth G. Ormiston, in a love nest at Carmel-by-the-Sea.

J. Frank Norris, the gunman-preacher of Fort Worth, departed even further from Christian ideals. In 1926 he began a violent campaign against the Roman Catholic church. When a Catholic named Cripps went unarmed to his office to complain, Norris shot and killed him. The following January, with the support of the Grand Dragon of the local Klan, Norris was acquitted on grounds of self-defense.

Although legally indecisive, the Scopes trial had some effect. Darrow's manhandling of poor Bryan made many politicians wary of supporting anti-evolutionism, not for love of science but for fear of ridicule.

By 1929 the anti-evolutionary crusade seemed to have withered. America still had millions of fundamentalists and a host of preachers to stir them up; but the zest had gone. No more monkey bills passed, although Adamist forces were strong enough to defeat attempts to repeal those already enacted. Public interest drifted to more pressing matters: the stock market crash, the Depression, repeal of Prohibition, the rise of fascism and Japanese imperialism, and the preliminaries to the Second World War.

During the subsequent half-century, anti-evolutionary sentiment slowly dwindled as millions of Americans learned about geological ages and prehistoric life. Books, articles, and movies helped to spread this knowledge. Several attempts were made to repeal Tennessee's Butler Act, each try coming closer to success than the last. In May 1967 the law was repealed. Mississippi's was repealed in April 1972.

Dayton may be called the Gettysburg of the Monkey War, remembering that the Civil War lasted for nearly two years after Gettysburg. So the Monkey War has sputtered on, with the Adamists rallying and occasionally winning local victories, but on the whole losing ground.

Evolution is still not presented over much of the nation. Some states have local-option provisions by which a fundamentalist school district may use non-evolutionary textbooks. Even where fundamentalist pressure is minor, evolution is still often not taught. Curricula are crowded. Many high-school students hate to learn anything at all and resist the learning process. Textbook publishers often skip evolution in biology texts rather than risk loss of sales in Adamist areas. And timid teachers prefer to dodge the subject rather than risk stirring up the smallest minority of noisy Adamists.

These conditions tend to perpetuate themselves, because pupils grow up without hearing, save vaguely and disparagingly, about evolution. They reach maturity believing in Adam, Eve, and the Serpent. Then, when the subject of evolution comes up, in fear of having their fixed opinions disturbed, they close their minds like so many startled clams snapping shut their shells.

One university coed was reported as saying of a professor: "When he began to lecture on evolution, I just sat back and laughed. I wasn't going to believe any of that stuff."

Many such know-nothings in their turn became teachers, parents, and school-board members. Thus ignorance, like a precious heirloom, is passed down to the third and fourth generation.

On November 12, 1968, Justice Fortas delivered the opinion of the Supreme Court in the Case of *Epperson* v. *Arkansas*. The majority held that, since the purpose of the Rotenberry Act was plainly to forbid any teaching that gainsaid the fundamentalist view of Genesis, the act did, in effect, establish a religious doctrine. This is forbidden under the First and Fourteenth amendments to the U.S. Constitution. "It is clear that fundamentalist sectarian conviction was and is the law's reason for existence." Therefore the law was unconstitutional, and "the judgment of the Supreme Court of Arkansas is *reversed.*"

Three justices filed concurring opinions. Justice Harlan agreed with the majority but objected to some of their peripheral discussion. Justice Black thought the law should have been struck down solely for vagueness. Justice Stewart thought the essential point was that the state not only forbade the teaching of a subject but also levied criminal penalties against the violator. That, he said, violated freedom of speech.

More recently, encouraged by the nation's swing toward political conservatism, Adamist forces have tried a new tactic. They promote laws not forbidding the teaching of evolution but requiring the teaching of the creation myth of Genesis, transparently disguised as "creation science," alongside it. Laws to this end were unsuccessfully pushed in California in 1973 and in Iowa in 1979. In California a civil suit by a fundamentalist resulted in a waffling decision by the judge, who demanded that evolution be presented only as a "theory" and not as a "fact." (This distinction, of which much has been made—by Ronald Reagan among others—is unreal. Everybody considers his own convictions "facts"; to a flat-earthian, the world's flatness is a "fact" and its roundness a mere "theory."

A bill requiring the teaching of creationism was declared unconstitutional by a federal judge in Tennessee in 1975. Undaunted, creationists pushed through a similar law in Arkansas in March 1981; this law was declared unconstitutional by District Court Judge William Overton on January 5.

The closing skirmishes of the Monkey War will doubtless go on for many decades. Adamist influence will continue to shrink, because of long-term influences against it: the urbanization of the American people; the Supreme Court's reapportionment reform, ending the over-representation of rural areas in legislatures; and the never-ending advance of science. But Adam, Eve, and the Serpent will, I suspect, still have their believers in the twenty-first century. After all, we still have flat-earthians who insist that flights into outer space are a hoax.

However advanced thinkers deplore the fact, reactions like those of the Adamists to evolution are normal. Any new doctrine that conflicts with well-established beliefs evokes violent opposition, no matter how weighty the evidence or cogent the arguments in its favor. At the same time, such conservatism serves a useful purpose. It helps to weed out the host of beguiling new ideas that constantly spring up but turn out to be wrong.

Considering the record of mankind in such doctrinal struggles, the American Monkey War seems comparatively humane. After all, nobody has been burned at the stake. Yet!

(Winter 1981/82)

Anti-Science: The Strange Case
of Paul Feyerabend

Martin Gardner

How to formalize the rules by which science operates, and why those rules work, are deep questions in the philosophy of science. There is little agreement among experts, but almost without exception they regard scientific method as a rational procedure. Science, they are persuaded, makes authentic progress. Not only does it discover new "facts" about nature; it also formulates laws and theories that provide increasingly better predictions about what will be observed in the future.

The most notorious dissenter from these commonplace views is Paul Karl Feyerabend (pronounced fire-AH-bend, with the accent on a long *a*). He was born in Vienna in 1924, and received the Iron Cross for his service in the German army during World War II. After studying science in Vienna and London (it was in London that he and Imre Lakatos, an influential Hungarian philosopher who died in 1974, became good friends), he settled in California, where he has been teaching philosophy at the University of California, Berkeley, since 1958.

In recent years Feyerabend has become the guru for a vague, scattered group of admirers. Some are counterculture physicists who are involved in Eastern religions and parapsychology. Others are sociologists who are down on scientific "orthodoxy" and so reluctant to take strong stands on scientific controversies that they constantly berate the scientific community for not taking time to engage in serious debate with promoters of astrology, the cosmology of Velikovsky, and similar nonsense. In what follows I will use AM to identify page references in Feyerabend's first book, *Against Method* (1975), and SFS for its sequel, *Science in a Free Society* (1978). For several years Feyerabend has been working on *The Rise of Western Rationalism,* but a publication date for this eagerly awaited treatise has not yet been set.

Feyerabend likes to call himself an "epistemological anarchist," or, better, a "flippant Dadaist" (AM, p. 21). His rallying cry, put forth partly as a joke, is "Anything goes!" By this he means that any scientific procedure, no matter how foolish it seems, can lead to progress, and any procedure, no matter how sound and rational it seems, can impede progress (SFS, pp. 165–166, 179, 188–189). There are no methodological rules, including rules of logic, that have not been violated, and rightly so, in the actual practice of science (SFS, pp. 13–15, 98–100, 212–213).

Nowhere in either book does Feyerabend mention any of the leaders of pragmatism: Peirce, James, Schiller, or Dewey. Nevertheless, he calls his basic approach a "pragmatic philosophy" (SFS, p. 19), and it is difficult to distinguish it from John Dewey's "instrumentalism." Science cannot, of course, operate without temporary rules, but the rules are constantly being transformed by the research process. Feyerabend leaves open the possibility that if the universe has a finite structure, and the human race lasts long enough, scientific method may eventually congeal into precise, permanent rules, but this seems unlikely. In any case, there are no signs of it happening. The history of science will continue to be careless, sloppy, and fundamentally irrational (AM, p. 179) in the sense that both its claims and its procedures are corrigible, perpetually being altered by experience (SFS, p. 99).

If Feyerabend were content to leave it at that, seeing science as a tool that is constantly improving as it enlarges our understanding of nature, few philosophers of science would object. But Feyerabend doesn't leave it at that. He pushes his tolerance for pseudoscience, and for eccentric ways of getting useful information about nature, into such an extreme relativism that science ceases to be a rational enterprise superior to the visions of the mystics. The search for better and better knowledge becomes such a foggy process that it is almost impossible to distinguish good science from bad.

Feyerabend does not deny that science keeps improving its instruments of observation and its engineering technology. We obviously build faster spaceships and smaller and more powerful computers, learn more about the moons of Saturn, and so on. But when it comes to theories, such as relativity, quantum mechanics, quark theory, and evolution, we enter a subjective realm where choices depend less on reason than on metaphysical and religious beliefs, cultural pressures, and personal aesthetic tastes (AM, pp. 175, 285; SFS, pp. 8, 28). Feyerabend sees theories the way he sees moral systems. Competing theories and rival ethical systems are "incommensurable" in the sense that we can apply to them no objective yardstick (AM, pp. 171ff.; SFS, p. 65ff.). In AM (pp. 226ff.) he reproduces several optical illusions of the shifting gestalt type to model our constantly shifting visions of both nature and morality (AM, pp. 226ff.). " 'Objectively' there is not much to choose between anti-semitism and humanitarianism. But racism will appear vicious to a humanitarian while humanitarianism will appear vapid to a racist" (SFS, pp. 9, 27).

For Feyerabend, science is more like a church than a rational undertaking, and its theories no closer to final truth than myths and fairy tales (AM, pp. 295–309; SFS, pp. 73–76). Science is only one tradition among many for seeking truth, perhaps not even the best (SFS, pp. 106–107). For this reason, Feyerabend recommends a free society (the "immortal Mill" is one of his heroes) in which there are open debates, and all traditions, including old and discarded ones, are allowed to proliferate (SFS, pp. 9, 29, 134). We do not have such a society now because science has hardened into a dogma as rigid as Roman Catholicism. It not only dominates the world's democracies, it is even supported by their governments.

To allow freedom for all traditions, Feyerabend wants as sharp a separation between science and state as we now have in the United States between church and state (SFS, pp. 31, 106–107). If the government funds science, it should also fund churches. If taxpayers believe in such things as astrology, Chinese herbal medicine, Hopi cosmology, parapsychology, faith-healing, acupuncture, creationism, voodoo, or ceremonial rain-dances, then those theories must be taught in state-supported schools (AM, pp. 299–301; SFS, pp. 87, 134). "Three cheers to the fundamentalists in California who succeeded in having a dogmatic formulation of the theory of evolution removed from the textbooks and an account of Genesis included" ("How to Defend Society Against Science," a 1974 talk by Feyerabend that is reprinted in *Introductory Readings in the Philosophy of Science,* 1980, ed. by E. D. Klemke, Robert Hollinger, and A. David Kline).

Feyerabend repeatedly expresses admiration for Chairman Mao's decree that revived the teaching of ancient Chinese medicine (AM, pp. 50–51, 220, 305–306; SFS, pp. 88, 102–105). He favors similar action in the United States (though by democratic legislation rather than government fiat) to force state-supported schools to teach all traditions, not just orthodox science (AM, pp. 52, 216; SFS, pp. 107, 178). Science must be cut down to size, given a more modest role (AM, p. 204). A committee of laymen should be set up to determine if evolution is really as well established as biologists claim, and to decide whether rival theories of life should be taught in government-funded schools (AM, pp. 307–309; SFS, p. 96).

Feyerabend's extreme distrust of orthodox medicine pervades all his writings. In SFS (pp. 136–137) he goes into embarrassing details about a twenty-year illness that caused him to lose twenty-five pounds and to endure double vision, stomach cramps, and other symptoms so severe that he once fainted on a London street. Orthodox doctors in England made him more miserable with their standard tests, but could find nothing wrong. Finally he located a "quack" who massaged the acupuncture points for his liver and stomach. The treatment stopped his long-lasting dysentery and cleared up his urine. Now in Berkeley, where he says he regularly sees an acupuncturist and a faith-healer, he is slowly recovering.

This agonizing experience convinced Feyerabend that there is valuable medical knowledge around that establishment doctors treat with contempt. He is firmly persuaded that traditional Chinese medicine is superior to Western, both in diagnosis and in therapy (SFS, pp. 103, 175–176).[1] Thousands of women, he declares, have lost their breasts when they could have been cured by massage, diet, acupuncture, and herbs (SFS, pp. 175, 206). Children have been cured of leukemia by similar treatments (SFS, p. 206). Since his personal experience with Western medicine, he has avoided all scientific doctors "like the plague" (SFS, p. 194). Asked whether, if he had a child with leukemia, he would take it to a witch doctor or to Sloan Kettering, Feyerabend opted for the witch doctor. So, too, he adds, would many people he knows in California (SFS, pp. 205–206). Even voodoo has a firm material basis, and a study of it would enrich science.

So would the study of astrology. Feyerabend does not think much of astrology as now practiced, but he believes it has made genuine progress, just like other sciences. It contains profound ideas, and should be taken seriously by philosophers (AM, p. 100; SFS, pp. 91–96, 194). Under Feyerabend's photograph on the jacket flap of SFS is not a biographical sketch but a reproduction of his astrological chart. Even the efficiency of rain dances should not be dismissed out of hand. "Who," he asks, "has examined that matter?" (SFS, pp. 78, 138).

Anything goes! "The epistemological anarchist has no compunction to defend the most trite, or the most outrageous statement. . . . he has no everlasting loyalty to, and no everlasting aversion against, any institution or any ideology" (AM, p. 189). He is against all programs, including his own. The rhapsody continues:

His aims remain stable, or change as a result of argument, or of boredom, or of a conversion experience, or to impress a mistress, and so on. Given some aim, he may try to approach it with the help of organized groups, or alone; he may use reason, emotion, ridicule, an "attitude of serious concern" and whatever other means have been invented by humans to get the better of their fellow men. His favourite pastime is to confuse rationalists by inventing compelling reasons for unreasonable doctrines. There is no view, however "absurd" or "immoral," he refuses to consider or to act upon, and no method is regarded as indispensable. The one thing he opposes positively and absolutely are universal standards, universal laws, universal ideas such as "Truth," "Reason," "Justice," "Love" and the behaviour they bring along, though he does not deny that it is often good policy to act as if such laws (such standards, such ideas) existed, and as if he believed in them. He may approach the religious anarchist in his opposition to science and the material world, he may outdo any Nobel Prize winner in his vigorous defence of scientific purity. He has no objection to regarding the fabric of the world as described by science and and revealed by his senses as a chimera that either conceals a deeper and, perhaps, spiritual reality, or as a mere web of dreams that reveals, and conceals, nothing. He takes great interest in procedures, phenomena and experiences such as those reported by Carlos Castaneda, which indicate that perceptions can be arranged in highly unusual ways and that the choice of a particular arrangement as "corresponding to reality," while not arbitrary (it almost always depends on traditions), is certainly not more "rational" or more "objective" than the choice of another arrangement: Rabbi Akiba, who in ecstatic trance rises from one celestial sphere to the next and still higher and who finally comes face to face wtih God in all his Splendour, makes genuine observations once we decide to accept his way of life as a measure of reality, and his mind is as independent of his body as the chosen observations tell him.

Asked why he takes airplanes instead of brooms, Feyerabend's reply is: "I know how to use planes but don't know how to use brooms, and can't be bothered to learn" (SFS, p. 190). Lakatos wanted to know why Feyerabend, if he doesn't believe in objective standards of truth, never jumps out of fifty-story building windows. Because, he answered, he has an innate fear of death, not because he can give rational reasons for such a fear (AM, pp. 221–222).

"People who genuinely have fears which they also sincerely consider irrational," writes Ernest Gellner (in an essay I will cite later in this article), "have no objection to being cured of those fears, if a painless cure is available. In fact, certain drugs are said to induce fearlessness in people in such circumstances. I am, however, convinced (not irrationally, I believe) that the reluctant anarchist, when offered the appropriate drug on the fiftieth floor, will also firmly refuse it."

As I have said, if Feyerabend's views are taken as no more than idiosyncratic distortions of Deweyan instrumentalism, they make a certain amount of sense. And who doubts that science often makes revolutionary leaps by shifting paradigms, to use Thomas Kuhn's language, in a way that sometimes resembles the changing of religious systems? But Feyerabend's relativism and his attacks on all rules are so extreme that not even Kuhn can buy them. "Vaguely obscene" was what he called them in a contribution to *Criticism and the Growth of Knowledge* (1970), edited by Lakatos and Alan Musgrave. To most philosophers Feyerabend is a brilliant but tiresome, self-centered, repetitious buffoon whose reputation rests mainly on the noise and confusion he generates, and the savagery with which he pummels everybody who disagrees with him.

Karl Popper, for instance, is a "mere propagandist" (SFS, p. 114), who likes to express "simple matters in pompous language" (SFS, p. 166). "Popperism is not a court but at most a tiny outhouse" (SFS, p. 208). And these epithets are mild compared to what Feyerabend has to say about lesser philosophers: "intellectual fascists" (SFS, p. 207), "intellectual midgets" (SFS, p. 217), blindmen, liars, illiterates, incompetents, and so on. Feyerabend's attitude toward modern philosophers of science can be summed up crisply: They are all crazy except himself and Lakatos, and he thinks Lakatos was slightly crazy. A great admirer of comic plays (he once attended an actor's school), Feyerabend writes that he has seriously considered a career as an entertainer preferable to teaching philosophy. George S. Kaufman, he adds, rates higher on his scale of values than "Kant, Einstein and their anaemic imitators" (SFS, p. 122).

For a restrained attack on Feyerabend's views see Ernest Nagel's latest collection of papers, *Teleology Revisited* (1979). A less inhibited attack is Ernest Gellner's essay, "Beyond Truth and Falsehood, or No Method in My Madness," in his *Spectacles & Predicaments* (1979). Gellner has no objection to good-natured clowning when it is combined with humanity and humility, but he finds Feyerabend's buffoonery

> persistenly rasping, boastful, derisive and arrogant; its attitude to what is rejected is aggressive and holier-than-thou, and opponents are not allowed to benefit from the all-permissive anarchism; the frivolity contains a markedly sadistic streak, visible in the evident pleasure taken in trying (without success) to confuse and browbeat the "rationalists," i.e. people who ask questions about knowledge in good faith. This is why what might otherwise seem a harmless piece of Californian-Viennese Schmalz leaves such a disagreeable taste in the mouth.

Note

1. David Jarovsky, reviewing Feyerabend's two books (*New York Review of Books,* June 28, 1979), makes a telling point about Feyerabend's obsessive praise of Mao's attempt to place traditional Chinese medicine on an equal footing with Western medical science. Nowhere does Feyerabend consider the hilarious effort by the Chinese government to persuade women that an effective means of birth control is to swallow a live tadpole. The result of this campaign was the discovery that the method doesn't work. If anything goes, and if the tadpole theory persists (as it does) in Chinese folklore, why should the government now persuade its women to use other methods? There must be some reason why so many folk medicine practices (blood-letting, for instance) have been abandoned by modern medical science. "I'm not sure I know," writes Jarovsky, "when he [Feyerabend] is clowning or crying or philosophizing. I'm not sure it matters."

Feyerabend's angry reply ("One might as well," he says, "talk to a Barbie doll") appeared in the October 11 issue, with a rejoinder by Jarovsky. For an excellent report on Mao's vast effort to revive Chinese folk remedies, see "Medicine in China," by Peggy Durdin, *New York Times Magazine,* February 28, 1960. Mao's effort was the greatest attempt by a government to promote pseudoscience since Hitler's support of Aryan anthropology and Stalin's support of Lysenkoism.

(Winter 1982/83)

SCIENCE: CHURCH OR
INSTRUMENT OF RESEARCH?
PAUL FEYERABEND

Martin Gardner quotes some of my assertions but says little about the reasons behind them: he tells only part of the story. I shall start my reply with a sketch of the missing ingredients.

During the nineteenth century philosophers and some scientists made the following two assumptions: (1) there are limits to scientific theorizing, and (2) these limits are determined by philosophical analysis, not by scientific research.

They protect science; they guarantee that it remains science; they cannot be displaced by science. Examples of the limits discussed were: a stable boundary between subject and object; causal explanations; the laws of classical logic.

Modern science (relativity, quantum theory, cosmology, gestalt psychology, etc.) started from a denial of assumption (2) and led to the overthrow of assumption (1). Scientists like Mach, Boltzmann, Einstein, and Bohr asserted that what plays a role in science must be subjected to scientific scrutiny and discovered that the limits just mentioned collapsed under this scrutiny. Historians then found that older scientists had shown a similar disrespect for principles in their research, though they had continued to refer to them in their more philosophical moods.

It is clear that a methodology adapted to this situation can at most describe what works in a certain area at a certain time—it cannot put lasting restrictions on research. It must admit that standards, like theories and measuring instruments, constantly change and the only *general* statement that can be made about science is: Anything goes. Who would have thought that the boundary between subject and object would be questioned as part of a scientific argument and that science would be advanced thereby? Yet this was precisely what happened in the quantum theory. Who would have thought that the theological notion of a beginning of the universe would again play an important role? Yet Friedmann's calculations and the discoveries of Hubble and others had this result. Who would have thought that scientific theories could be upheld in the face of unambiguous negative evidence and that science would profit from such a procedure? But Einstein, who more than once ridiculed the concern for "verification of little effects," made progress in just this manner. Nobody can foresee such developments; no philosopher can forbid them once they have occurred. All a philosopher can do now is either participate in scientific research or catalogue the discoveries that have been made: he must become a scientist or a historian.

General accounts of science are as dead as a doornail. Even the very vague characterization used in arguments against creationism (*McLean* v. *Arkansas Board of Education,* reprinted in *Science,* vol. 125 [1982], p. 983), viz., that science is falsifiable and testable against the empirical world applies only to some scientific episodes, not to others. Of course, every scientist and every group of scientists when doing research carefully selects special theories, procedures, presuppositions from a great variety of alternatives, but the *temporary* and *local* boundaries created by such a selection are constantly being redrawn and may change from one research project to the next. The judgment against creationism takes this into account: Science is "what scientists do." This concludes the first step of my argument.

The second step begins with the observation that a science without stable rules and limits obtains authority only by decisions that stop research at a particular point. For, if all principles and all rules are subjected to the ongoing process of research and if, as is frequently the case, this process may produce discoveries when supplied with ideas that clash with it, then rejecting ideas *because* of the clash means detaching a certain part of science from the ongoing research process and freezing it. One cannot rationalize such a decision by saying that the chosen parts are highly confirmed and therefore strong enough to overrule all alternatives. The reason is that a comparison of an unsupported, absurd, and "unscientific" assumption with a scientific opponent often leads to an exchange of evidence so that the unscientific assumption becomes scientific while its scientific opponent lands on the dungheap of history. This occurred during the so-called Copernican revolution: the idea of a moving earth was in conflict with observations, basic physics, and common sense. But Galileo, following hints given by Copernicus himself, took it seriously and by careful analysis transferred to it the very same evidence that had prevented its acceptance. And this also explains why ideas that today form part of the scientific world-view (atomism, the motion of the earth, the idea that nature produces a great variety of individuals and creates the known species by selection, the idea that the universe has a beginning in time), though often defeated in the course of scientific progress, could return and defeat their defeaters. A science as described in step one can therefore eliminate alternatives only on the basis of decisions that interfere with the ongoing process of research.

Now such decisions have often far-reaching consequences. They affect not only experts, but the rest of society as well; and they affect not only material conditions, but the very soul of people (John Donne saw this clearly in the case of Copernicus): they are political decisions. In a democracy, political decisions are made by democratic councils, not by experts. (We have here an extension of a method already used in trials by jury.) Note how this restriction of the authority of the sciences in society depends on the extension of their authority to matters that before were in the hands of philosophers (and theologians). Conversely, the attempt of some philosophers to keep at least some principles out of the reach of scientific research can now be seen to have anti-democratic tendencies. (The same is true of the attempt to "civilize" the sciences by a combination with the humanities; in both cases scientific matters are to be kept within the walls of academia.)

It must be emphasized that the existence of political ingredients right in the center of science does not reveal any faults but is a basic feature of all our knowledge. We all have to make decisions that take only a tiny fraction of possible paths into account, and our actions, epistemic actions included, are excursions into the unknown. In a democracy collective excursions into the unknown—such as wars, social programs, basic changes in medicine or in education—are subjected to the judgment of the voters. This does not reduce the ignorance but brings it to the fore: everybody's judgment is now as good as everybody else's. Judgments involving the authority of the sciences belong in the same category. The value of the sciences is not denied thereby. I am not anti-science. But I do object to its ideological distortion, which turns ignorance into "'well founded knowledge," removes the "knowledge" from supervision by the public, and regards people as equal only to the extent that they are capable or willing to accept it.

What I have said so far is an (extremely condensed) abstract argument. Abstract arguments can always be countered by equally abstract objections. The *case studies* block such escape routes by making it evident that abstract reason is much too crude an instrument for comprehending the historical phenomenon science (as opposed to its ideological distortion). The two books discussed by Gardner contain four case studies: Einsten and Brownian motion; Galileo's dynamics and his telescopic observations; the transition from Homeric common-sense to the "science" of the pre-Socratics; Maestlin's reception of Copernicus. Gardner doesn't mention any of them. Yet they are absolutely essential. Without them the argument is as reasonable as the attempt to judge the arts of a certain period from catalogues and aesthetic treatises and not from a direct inspection of the art works themselves.

What does Gardner have to say about this situation and the reasons proposed? The answer can be given in a single word: nothing. There are only two comments in his vignette that have some evanescent substance. The first is that my views are "extreme." Considering the general backwardness of modern thinking about the sciences, this may well be the case. But the question is not if my views are mild, or groovy, or boring, or extreme; the question is if they are correct—and here Gardner keeps a chaste silence. His second comment is that "it is almost impossible to distinguish good science from bad." Now, this is the point at issue. I try to show that it is indeed impossible to draw a distinction independently of concrete scientific research and that scientists engaged in such research may draw it in surprising places. I also provide case studies to explain the situation in detail. What does Gardner offer in return? A sullen replay of my conclusion, i.e., again—nothing. The tadpoles, Gardner's only concrete criticism, even support my case. They show that Chinese medicine can be as silly as its Western counterpart and thereby argue for a plurality of institutions and ideas and close collaboration between them. But this is precisely the arrangement I propose.

For the rest we have insinuations, rumors, and plain scandalmongering—though of a rather unreflected sort. For example, Gardner reveals what "most philosophers" think about me. Now there are about ten thousand philosophers in the United States and Canada alone, and many more writing in languages not accessible to the average reviewer. Does Gardner really expect the reader to believe that he interviewed a fair sample of them? The sample Gardner did manage to assemble is even more intriguing. It contains the enormous number of two (two!) individuals. And a fine pair they are! The essay from which Gardner lifted his final blast contains the following passage: "One way to treat this book [i.e., *Against Method*] would be to concentrate on the extensive parts that argue this [i.e., my] viewpoint in connection with the history of modern physics . . . Such a procedure would be reasonable and perhaps the most sensible one to adopt." Gellner does not choose this way. "I am not going to adopt it," he says. His reason (explicitly stated in his essay): lack of competence. Instead, Gellner decides to deal with the "rest," about 10 percent of the book, containing summaries and asides comprehensible only to a reader who has followed the argument. But this argument, Gellner says, he did not understand and, therefore, did not consider. A fine witness! Joravsky's reading habits can be gauged from the fuss he makes about the tadpoles (which, as I showed above, support my case) and his comment on my "obsessive" concern with Chinese medicine: the Chinese fill no more than three pages (out of 550). Besides, the reader does not need to take my word for it. Joravsky's talents as a critic were put in perspective by a well-known conservative historian of science, Kevles, writing in the same issue of the *New York Review of Books* Gardner quotes toward the end of his note. Was it that difficult to get intelligent support?

I do sympathize with Gardner and his fellow ideologues. They grew up in a well-equipped and confident church; they were and still are nourished by it, both intellectually and financially; they spent long hours trying to understand and to master its gospel; they enjoyed the authority their knowledge gave them in society; and now it seems that this knowledge is but one opinion among many, and without inherent advantages. Small wonder they are disappointed and want to restore the status quo. But I would also point out that the developments they deplore (and which started long before I or even Dewey started writing) come from the very same process of inquiry whose results they so often admired in the past and are in harmony with a humanism that values all products the human race has to offer and not only the concoctions of a small and spoiled elite. And I would add that their procedure is excellent proof for a statement made earlier in this note, viz., that any enterprise claiming authority ceases to be an instrument of research and becomes a political pressure group.

MARTIN GARDNER REPLIES:

Professor Feyerabend complains that I focused on his minor assertions, ignoring his main arguments. Let me reply first with a fable.

Suppose an English professor of a distinguished American university writes a big book about poetry, most of it devoted to the sensible thesis that cultural forces strongly condition literary tastes. A poet with a high reputation in one age is forgotten in the next, while poets considered minor are elevated to top rank. We should, therefore, be humble in our enthusiasms and recognize the absence of ironclad rules for distinguishing between good poetry and doggerel. Dante and Shakespeare are incommensurable. In poetry, anything goes.

Mixed into these commonplace observations are remarks in which the professor berates his colleagues for their contemptuous neglect of Edgar Guest and Ella Wheeler Wilcox. Why, he asks, are there no college courses and Ph.D. theses devoted to the work of these two popular bards? Footnotes disclose that he has been reading Guest with gusto. On the book's flyleaf, under the author's photograph, are these immortal lines by Eddie:

If it's worth while and you're sure of the right of it,
Stick to it, boy and make a real fight of it!

Can you blame the reviewer for ignoring the book's broad conventional arguments to concentrate on the author's eccentric tastes? Similarly with Feyerabend. Of course anything goes in science if this means that standards, theories, and observing instruments constantly change and that there is no way to foresee how they will change. It is hard to predict, Bohr once said, especially the future. And who today wants to deny that social and political forces play roles in shaping science? Everything human beings do is something human beings do, and therefore is part of culture. These are views John Dewey took for granted. And Russell and Carnap and Popper. But it does not follow from these views that competing theories are incommensurable and that "everybody's judgment is as good as everybody else's."

It is here, where Feyerabend pushes his relativism to extremes, that he starts to peddle nonsense. We all know that a wild theory, such as Alan Guth's new inflationary model of the Big Bang, may or may not be fruitful (compelling evidence is too thin). But astrology? Or the efficacy of rain dances?

Feyerabend repeatedly likens the science community to the Roman Catholic church in the inflexibility of its dogmas. I can think of no comparison less apt. The speed with which modern science can overturn old dogmas and the zeal with which it tries to falsify present dogmas are awesome developments in human history. It was not until 1980 that the pope initiated an inquiry to determine if the Inquisition acted properly in condemning Galileo. Einstein abandoned Newtonian physics, and quantum theory discarded classical causality, in just a few decades. How soon does Feyerabend expect the Roman church to discard the virgin birth and the immaculate conception?

Last week I was favored with a copy of a paper by a Muslim scientist, Mostafa A. Abdelkader, of Alexandria, scheduled to appear in a journal called *Speculations in Science and Technology*.[1] It is titled: "A Geocosmos: Mapping Outer Space into a Hollow Earth." No, it is not a joke. Mr. Abdelkader revives an old hypothesis that the earth is hollow and we live on the inside of the shell, but he defends it with remarkable sophistication. First he performs a geometrical inversion of conventional spacetime that exchanges every point believed by establishment cosmologists to lie outside the earth with a point inside. Then he adjusts all physical laws accordingly. Straight rays of light become circular arcs, and the speed of light decreases as it gets closer to the center of the hollow earth. All galaxies hitherto considered enormous become microscopic objects inside, much smaller than the moon. Everything appears to us exactly as we in fact see it. The great merit of this inside-out cosmology, the Egyptian scientist maintains, is that it relieves us of the anxiety of believing in a universe of such fantastic size that our earth becomes infinitesimal.

It is not easy to see how the geocosmos can be falsified. Indeed, its logical consistency raises deep questions about the role of convention in cosmology. "Since both universes are equally possible," Abdelkader writes, "there is no valid reason for astronomers . . . to confine their attention exclusively to the study" of Copernican cosmology. He is convinced that "the only way to ascertain conclusively which of the two vastly different universes is our actual one is by piercing the earth vertically to a depth of 12,742 kilometers, a project which does not seem to be possible in the foreseeable future."

I am not sure that drilling through the earth would decide conclusively between the two theories—there are clever ways to get around an unfavorable result by modeling the cosmos in various kinds of closed hyperspace—but that is beside the point. The point is, does Feyerabend think Abdelkader is crazy?

If so, why? If the geocosmos is unworthy of empirical testing, on what basis is such a value judgment made? Should the geocosmos be taught in Muslim universities as a serious and incommensurable rival to Copernican cosmology? If not, why does Feyerabend think fundamentalist creationism, with its flood theory of fossils, should be taught here in state-supported schools? If the geocosmos doesn't go, why doesn't it go? And if it doesn't, what is wrong with saying that competing theories are commensurable, and that, although scientific "truth" is pragmatic and hence fallible, there are excellent grounds for ruling out astrology as worthy of research. What is wrong with maintaining that there is no such thing as "well founded knowledge," or that the history of scientific theories displays rational progress of a sort qualitatively unlike progress in metaphysics and the arts?

Feyerabend accuses me of statistical fudging when I say that "most philosophers" do not buy his extreme relativism. It is true that I cited only four thinkers (Feyerabend forgot about Thomas Kuhn and Ernest Nagel), but I know many other philosophers personally who, although they have not published anything about Feyerabend, have a much lower opinion of him than I have. If Feyerabend doubts my "most," let him hire an impartial pollster to sample the opinions of one hundred leading philosophers. In view of his repeated insistence that all living philosophers of science except himself are incompetent, it seems odd that he would expect the outcome of such a poll to contradict my estimate.

Although there is nothing in Feyerabend's response that he has not said over and over again, I am surprised by the uncharacteristic mildness of his ad hominem remarks tossed my way. It makes it a pleasure to exchange banter with him.

Note

1. *Speculations in Science and Technology* is an Australian journal, now in its sixth year, "devoted to speculative papers in the physical, mathematical, biological, medical and engineering sciences." Feyerabend is on its editorial board.

(Summer 1983)

The Importance of Critical Discussion
Karl Popper

Sixty years ago, a great physicist was born. For the good of us all, he became a great thinker, a great humanitarian, a great hero, and, above all, truthful and truth-seeking.

Andrei Sakharov's great achievements as a physicist were acknowledged in 1953, when at the age of thirty-two he became a full member of the Academy of Sciences. I suppose that this honor and the other great honors he received were connected with his basic work on the hydrogen bomb. However this may be, like those atomic scientists in the West who founded the famous *Bulletin of the Atomic Scientists,* he became greatly concerned about nuclear weapons. Since 1957, he has dedicated his life to doing everything possible to reduce the most terrible danger to mankind: the danger that is a consequence of the wonderful discoveries in atomic theory, which, due to Hitler, led to nuclear armaments and to the armament race that may so easily bring about the destruction of life on Earth.

Now the supreme importance of criticism and of critical discussion—of *free* critical discussion—seems to me to be central to Sakharov's thinking. For this reason, I have made the problem of critical discussion the center of this paper. Many of the points I shall make are due to Sakharov; and my other points are such as, I hope, he would approve of. But since I know nothing of him and his work except what has been published in English translation, I cannot, of course, be certain of his approval; and the responsibility for what I am saying is obviously mine alone.

Now I hold, with Sakharov, I think, that there is the most urgent need for criticism: for free critical discussion. This discussion *must* be free in the sense that theories ought to be freely proposed and their consequences freely examined. The discussion need not be and, in my opinion, *should* not be free in the sense that aspersions can be freely cast on those persons who happen to hold a theory that is under critical attack. There is an almost universal tendency, perhaps an inborn tendency, to suspect the good faith of a man who holds opinions that differ from our own opinions, whether those opinions are religious, scientific, or political. This tendency is, admittedly, as widespread in the West as in the East; and the only people whose professional education somewhat counteracts this tendency are scientists doing research in the natural sciences. This tendency has been for many centuries the source of religious intolerance and religious persecution; and for these and other reasons, we all should combat it strongly and suppress it in ourselves. It obviously endangers the freedom and the objectivity of our discussion if we attack a person instead of attacking an opinion or, more precisely, a theory. We have all to learn to be purists in this matter. It is highly desirable that in a critical discussion the theory to be criticized be clearly and simply formulated and the reasons that speak for its rejection be clearly stated, independent of the motives of those who hold it. Of course it may be admissible to name a person and to say that he or she actually holds the theory criticized. This is sometimes necessary in order to make clear that one is not fighting windmills.

But we should never impute motives to those who hold a mistaken theory. After all, each of us makes mistakes, serious mistakes, all the time. We should remember what Voltaire said: "What is toleration?" asks Voltaire. And he answers: "It is a necessary consequence of our being human [and therefore fallible]. We are all products of frailty: fallible and prone to error. So let us mutually pardon each other's stupidities. This is the first principle of the law of nature [the first principle of human rights]."

Voltaire's principle of tolerance is, indeed, the basis of all rational discussion. Without it, rational discussion is impossible. And it is the basis of all self-education. Without consciously admitting our fallibility to ourselves, we cannot learn from our mistakes; we become infallible dogmatists.

It is a credit to the schools in which Sakharov was educated and to the scientific training he received—but, above all, to his devotion to truth—that he could change his mind on many points and in a truly critical and revolutionary way. I am not now speaking about the question of what the result of this change of mind was: this is another question. I am speaking about the change as such: the ability to change one's mind radically; the difference between a dogmatic mind and a critical mind. Some people are totally inflexible. Some have the ability to change their theories just once. But the ability for critical thinking, for revising one's theory again and again is, unfortunately, very rare. It seems to be the result of training, of participation in many free critical discussions, and of self-education. However this may be, Sakharov has shown that he has this ability. Even more important, he has been able to change his social and political theories critically, in spite of the fact that he was not helped, but hindered, by most of the criticism directed at him. And he has been hindered not only by the actual criticism but also by his generally precarious situation. Clearly, he was prepared for great sacrifices; and he took great risks.

I have read somewhere that Sakharov had been accused of acting in order to be praised in the West. I can only say that, so far as I know, he received far more praise in the West for his older theories than for his later ones. And this cannot have surprised him; for in his later publications he criticized these earlier theories, which had become perhaps the most fashionable among Western intellectuals. He described them as "faddist". Thus he certainly did not think of praise or recognition, or fame, either in the East or in the West. He pursued other aims—the only aims worth pursuing: he tried to get a little nearer the truth, even though he had to contradict some things he had said before. And he tried to think of what could be done to save his country, and mankind as a whole, from destruction. They are indeed aims worth pursuing and they are worthy of a scientist—a great scientist.

The distinction between dogmatic ways of thinking and critical ways of thinking is of great importance. From the point of view of biology, dogmatism corresponds to *lack of adaptability;* and since life demands constant adaptation to a constantly changing environment, dogmatism—and especially the inflexibility of a society— leads almost of necessity to extermination. Critical thinking corresponds to adaptability. It is, like adaptability, decisive for survival. Darwin might have spoken of the survival of the adaptable rather than the survival of the fittest; or he might have said that the fittest organisms are those that are the most adaptable. They are certainly not the biggest or the most powerful ones. On the intellectual level, this means that the most self-critical thinkers, the most imaginative thinkers, the most flexible thinkers, are needed by every society if mankind is to survive. Or, to use another term, the most revolutionary thinkers are those who can carry out revolutions in their own imaginative minds; those who can try out different revolutions in their minds, compare the results, and choose the best. This is precisely how *science* progresses. Such intellectual revolutions, carried out in one's mind or on paper, are obviously far superior, far cheaper, and far more successful than revolutions carried out by killing people. Use words instead of swords! Use tentative theories instead of warheads! This is the method of the intellect. It is not only the humane method but also infinitely more effective and successful. It is clearly the method that Sakharov adopted when he gave up forging swords. As a great scientist, he had always used this method when he *was* forging swords.

Indeed, one can see the history of mankind in may ways, as a war of classes or as a war of religion or ideologies, or perhaps even a war of races. But perhaps the most convincing way, as implied by Marx, is to see it as a war between means of production, between more improved and less improved tools and instruments. This, however, would be a war between dogmatic and critical ways of thinking, or between less and more mental flexibility.

In history, the less flexible were usually in the majority. And, like Louis XIV, or Napolean, or Kaiser Wilhelm, or Hitler, they usually had a monolithic and highly centralized organization. Often they even had the first shot. The more flexible ones were often less well prepared; and they were at best an alliance of states, states in which there were two or more parties competing for power.

Nevertheless, it was flexibility, critical thinking, that counted in the end.

What I am trying to describe as critical or flexible thinking, in contradistinction to dogmatic inflexibility, is simply *the method of learning from our mistakes.* We are all fallible, we are all prone to error; in fact we are making mistakes all the time. On the biological level, many mistakes occur, mainly in the form of unfavorable mutations. And natural selection consists in eliminating these mistakes by eliminating the organism that is the carrier of the mistake. On the human level, dogmatism often means that a man does not learn from his mistakes but perishes with them. Critical thinking consists in formulating in a human language, and thus outside our skins, our conjectural theories, which are often mistaken—in fact, far more often than not. This became possible with the invention of human language, of writing, and especially of printing. It allows us to submit these theories and hypotheses to critical discussion and thus to expose them to the full force of natural selection, without danger to us. In fact, we do more: we submit them to the severest test we can design: we add to the pressure of *natural* selection the *artificial* selection pressure contrived by our cunning. We do so with the help of scientific discussion, in which we appeal to the results of our cunningly designed experimental tests.

In this way, *we let our hypotheses, our ideas, die in our stead.* This is precisely what scientists do. The so-called scientific method is nothing else: it is an attempt to eliminate our many errors of thought; the more, the better. It is a form of the method of trial and the elimination of error. It is the way in which we learn from our mistakes and in which we can make fertile our almost always erroneous hypotheses.

For this reason, a real scientist would not dream nowadays of personally attacking another scientist for having proposed a mistaken conjecture. For he knows only too well that almost all our conjectures are erroneous and that they are extremely valuable nevertheless. They are just as invaluable as red traffic lights. To criticize the scientist rather than those specific consequences of his hypothesis that are mistaken shows a typically uncritical attitude. It is the typical attitude of religious dogmatism, of precritical intolerance, of religious persecution. In the field of politics it is a symptom of failing to learn from science the main thing a politician can and ought to learn from it: its ways of thinking critically—self-critically.

What is particularly important in this connection is that new hypotheses, new ideas, whether true or false, are most valuable, because they are so very rare, and we are always in need of more. We have to wait until they emerge under the pressure of difficult problems, or under the stimulus of an exciting discussion. This makes free discussion almost indispensible: we need many new theories, and we need peaceful coexistence between the new theories so that they can compete in order that we can select the fittest—the most flexible, the best adaptable, and the best-adapted ones. We need a pluralism of ideas and of theories; and therefore we need a pluralistic society. This is exactly what Sakharov tries to propagate. I have no doubt that he is right in saying that this is what his country needs most urgently. But pluralism needs toleration; and this too Sakharov has seen very clearly. We need a tolerant society in order to find among this plurality of competing ideas, of competing theories, the true ones—or those that get nearest to the truth. A pluralist and tolerant society, one in which we can discuss theories freely, is what I described more than forty years ago as an open society. Obviously, a society can be more open or less open, more free or less free. but a good measure of freedom or openness is needed, especially if the society in question competes with another, with one that is freer and more open. The idea of freedom became part of our Western history in the fifth century B.C.E., when an alliance of a few tiny democratic Greek city states succeeded in resisting the colossal might of the Persian Empire.

This brings me to the problem of democracy. Since I do not like to speak about the meaning of words, I shall say nothing about the meaning of the term *democracy*. I shall confine myself to speaking about its merits and demerits, starting with a remark by Winston Churchill.

Churchill once said something like this: Democracy is the worst form of government except for all other known forms of government. I think this is excellently put. Yet I still prefer to say that there are two kinds of governments, those you *cannot* get rid of without bloodshed and those you *can* get rid of without bloodshed. I am an adherent of this second kind, whatever beautiful names you might give to the first and whatever ugly names you may give to the second.

The second kind of government—for brevity's sake, let us call it "democracy"—is certainly not a method to ensure the rule of the wisest or the best; and it has often been criticized for this reason. But only a very unwise person can believe that any method exists that ensures the rule of the wisest or of the best. At any rate, Socrates was certainly right that wisdom consists in realizing our own lack of wisdom.

Democracies have serious drawbacks. They certainly are not better than they ought to be. But corruption can occur under any kind of government. And I think that every serious student of history will agree, upon consideration, that our Western democracies are not only the most prosperous societies in history—that is important, but not so very important—but the freest, the most tolerant, and the least repressive large societies of which we have historical knowledge.

I have said this before, of course. It would be almost criminal not to say it if one believes it. One must fight those who make so many young people unhappy by telling them that we live in a terrible world, a kind of capitalist hell. The truth is that we live in a wonderful world, in a beautiful world, and in an astonishingly free and open society. Of course it is fashionable, it is expected, and it is almost demanded from a Western intellectual to say the opposite, to lament loudly about the world we live in, about our social ills, about the inherent injustice of our society, and especially about the alleged terrible inequalities, and the impending days of reckoning.

I do not think that any of this is true. It is true that there are a few people who are very rich. But what does it matter to me or to you? It is most certainly not true that anyone suffers *because* a few are very rich, not to mention that quite a few of the few who are rich spend much of their money on such things as founding universities and lectureships and on scholarships and cancer research.

The truth is that Western democracies are the only societies in which there is much freedom, much welfare, and much equality before the law. Of course our society is very far from perfect. There is much misuse of drugs, of tobacco, and of alcohol. But from our experiment with Prohibition we know that these things are difficult to combat; especially if we cherish freedom. It will be answered: "But these things are just symptoms of the people's unhappiness. They are unhappy about such things as social inequality and unemployment." If by social inequality is meant that some people have more money than others, then I should say that, so long as those others can live reasonably well, I don't care. Unemployment is of course a very different matter.

I am very much aware of the fact that unemployment is a terrible thing, a real social ill, the most terrible of all our social problems. I certainly do not know how to cure it, but of one thing I am sure: it is an ill that every democratic government would not only wish to cure but would make great sacrifices to cure if it only knew how.

Our Western democratic societies are far from being perfect. But discussion of their faults is welcome in all of them; and practical steps to remedy matters are constantly being searched for, and being taken—certainly more than ever before and certainly more than anywhere else.

Our Western democracies are the most flexible, the most anxious for reforms: the reforms I have witnessed in my lifetime amount to several social revolutions. Of course we have made great mistakes, and some of them have not yet been corrected. Obviously, democratic public opinion is not always very wise. But there is an infinite amount of good will about. Peace on earth and good will toward men: this is the hope of millions. I know nothing and I can prove nothing, but I believe that millions on both sides of the Iron Curtain would willingly give their lives if they knew that by doing so they could establish peace.

Meanwhile we have built up those institutions that have made freedom reasonably secure, and with it all those wonderful rights that we enjoy: habeas corpus; a parliament or a house of representatives to look after our rights and to help us defend ourselves if our freedom is invaded or merely threatened; and especially the freedom to hold unconventional theories and to discuss them freely— in other words, toleration. It is plain that without toleration and freedom, pluralism would be impossible and we would become a monolithic society without, or at best with diminished, flexibility. But toleration is also a necessary precondition for the East and West to live together without destroying the world.

Sakharov and others speak of "peaceful coexistence." But during the past years, this combination of words has become debased. No one in the West can any longer hear these words without feeling that they have become a symbol of sheer hypocrisy.

There is a nice story somewhere by Emerson about a guest in his house. He writes: "The more he talked of honesty, the faster we counted our silver spoons." I am afraid we all feel today that "the more he talks of peaceful coexistence, the faster we ought to count our ballistic missiles." This is a most serious situation: we do not any longer believe in what the U.S.S.R. promises. It is a situation that is very difficult to reverse and which adds—in fact, adds immeasurably— to the danger of the nuclear arms race.

The hope of establishing a state of peaceful coexistence was high in the West for a long time because it was so obvious to us all that peaceful coexistence was the only alternative to total mutual destruction. Thus it was in the interest, in the self-interest, of both sides to be honest about peaceful coexistence. But our hopes were systematically destroyed. The U.S.S.R. exploited every opportunity to improve its military position at the cost of the West. But, what is infinitely more important, the U.S.S.R. continued to do so even after signing, in Moscow in 1972, a solemn declaration stating the "Basic Principles of the Relations Between the U.S. and the U.S.S.R." and promising that neither of the two powers would "try to obtain unilateral advantages at the expense of the other." The Soviet leaders must have known that to continue after this declaration with their earlier policy was a dangerous game. But it seems they did not see the greatest danger: the destruction of our faith in their trustworthiness, in their capacity to be taken seriously as possible partners in a peace treaty.

Immanuel Kant, a philosopher venerated by many, and also by Karl Marx, foresaw the possibility of such a development. He discussed it in his marvelous essay *On Eternal Peace*. "No state," Kant writes, "ought to allow itself to commit those kinds of hostile acts that are likely to undermine mutual confidence in a future peace." This, Kant shows, is a sheer commonsense principle of self-interest: since the future is never fully predictable, the violation of this principle can easily become suicidal for the transgressor. So wrote Kant in 1795, before wars had become national wars (with Napoleon); or total wars (with Hitler); or nuclear wars (with our own destruction of Hiroshima and Nagasaki).

The disappearance in the West of trust in The Soviet's word was a lengthy process. The process was lengthy not only because of the typical inclination of a democracy to believe in words of peace and to disbelieve or discount acts that belie these words, but also for more rational reasons. It takes some time to convince oneself that rational people are acting against their own obvious self-interest. Now the self-interest of all parties to avoid common suicide by universal extermination is obvious; and so is the self-interest of acting in accordance with Kant's principle.

There is a school of utilitarians that says that morality is nothing but enlightened self-interest. I do not believe this; in fact, I think it is blatantly untrue. But in the present world situation, it is blatantly true that morality and the rational self-interest of the great powers do coincide with the establishment of mutual trust in each other's signatures.

Two events led to the collapse of our trust in both the sincerity and the rationality of the rulers of the U.S.S.R.: the complete disregard of the Helsinki agreement on human rights and the invasion of Afghanistan.

After the invasion of Afghanistan it was felt by everyone in the West that the U.S.S.R.'s talk of peaceful coexistence and her solemnly signed agreements were parallel to Hitler's announcement that the Rhineland—then Austria, then Czechoslovakia, then Poland—was definitely his last demand.

I do not know any one in the West who is any longer interested in what happens at the Madrid Conference. Treaties are no longer taken seriously. If Russia wishes a reversal of this terrible situation (which did not arise in Lenin's or even in Stalin's days), only her acts—drastically different acts—will be able to achieve it.

I think that the U.S.S.R. ought to have learned from Hitler's errors, and the West ought to have learned from our own errors. The West gave in to Hitler many, many times: we wanted to convince him that we were ready, without hypocrisy, for what is now called peaceful coexistence. He took it for weakness— a fatal error, as it turned out: fatal for millions, fatal for him. So Hitler proceeded, like Louis XIV, like the two Napoleons, and like the Kaiser, from victory to victory and from treachery to treachery. He had failed to learn from their mistakes.

The Soviets, like Hitler's Germany, refused to be convinced of our sincerity concerning peaceful coexistence. They took it for weakness. This was a great mistake, and they are now on a dangerous path. A first turn away from this path—a turn that they should take in any case, not only in the interest of humanity but in their own self-interest—would be to fulfill what they had promised and signed in Moscow and in Helsinki and reverse their policy toward the valuable and constructive criticism of the so-called dissenters, and stop the violation of human rights.

The constant emphasis of the U.S.S.R. on our alleged hostility and on our alleged hypocrisy seems to be a relic of the most dangerous of superstitions: the belief in the predictability of history; more especially, the belief in the historical inevitability of the triumph of communism, whether through war or through the piecemeal surrender of the West. At least some of the Soviet leaders seem to be caught in this ideological trap, or to be dazzled by this fantasy.

This would explain why they have forgotten or, rather, repressed the memory of our Great Alliance in the war against National Socialism and our fulfillment of our obligations throughout the war and at the end of the war.

It would also explain why they have forgotten, or, rather, repressed such events as the help rendered to Russia by the unforgettable Fridtjof Nansen, the High Commissioner of Refugees at the League of Nations. I remember as if it were yesterday how Lenin thanked Nansen for saving the lives of millions of Russians in the three years from 1921 to 1923. The help from the West was rendered at a time when revolutionary Russia was in a precarious situation and when the class structure of Western society was very different from what it is now: far less equalitarian. Nevertheless, it is clear that we in the West have made at least as many mistakes as those in the East. One of these mistakes is that in England and America we have forgotten Nansen. And we did not learn from our own fateful mistakes in our attempts to convince Hitler of our nonaggressiveness. Yet I feel certain that *we can learn.* An obvious first step, already much discussed, would be the refusal to cooperate with the Soviet Union in cultural and scientific matters, including, of course, technology. This would not be a countermove to blackmail; but, to use that florid language that they often use and which they therefore may understand, it would be "a spontaneous demonstration of our solidarity with our suffering brethren in the East."

I wish to end with an optimistic consideration. At least I have been somewhat cheered by it. Natural selection and selection pressure are usually thought of as linked to *violence,* to a more or less *violent* struggle for life. But all this changes with the emergence of the human mind, of the higher function of human language that permits us to formulate theories, hypotheses, and especially impersonal critical discussion. We may let our *theories* fight it out—we may, as I said before, let our theories die in our stead. From the point of biology and natural selection, the main function of the human mind and especially of critical thinking is, indeed, that they make possible the application of the method of trial and the elimination of error without the elimination of ourselves. In this lies the great survival value of the human mind and the human language. Thus in bringing about the emergence of mind, of language, and of critical thinking, natural selection transcends itself and its original violent character. With the emergence of mind and human understanding, selection needs no longer to be violent: we can eliminate false theories by nonviolent criticism. Nonviolent cultural evolution is, from the biological point of view, not merely a utopian dream; it is, rather, a *possible* result of the emergence of mind through natural selection. It is possible for us to make the leap from the world of necessity and violence into the world of freedom and peace. Peaceful coexistence is *possible,* and to bring it about remains our task. Our task is not merely to interpret the world but to change it.

Peaceful coexistence is what Sakharov wishes to bring about. We must support him in this task.

(Winter 1981/82)

VIII.

Courting the Constitution

The late former Senator Sam Ervin, Jr., described himself as a religious man: "a Presbyterian whose Scotch-Irish, English, and French Huguenot ancestors came to America before the Revolution. All of them were Protestants. Most of them dissented from the established churches in the lands of their origin." You can imagine, then, how Senator Ervin inherited a reverence for tolerance and freedom as well as for the Christian God. In his essay "The Constitution and Religion" Senator Ervin provides a dismaying catalogue of religious intolerance:

the casting of Christians to the lions in the Colosseum at Rome; the bloody Crusades of the Christians against the Saracens for the possession of the shrines hallowed by the footsteps of the Prince of Peace; the use by the papacy of the dungeon and the rack to coerce conformity and of the fiery faggot to exterminate heresy; the unspeakable cruelties of the Spanish Inquisition; the slaughter of the Waldenses in Alpine Italy; the jailing and hanging by Protestant kings of English Catholics for abiding with the faith of their fathers; the jailing and hanging by a Catholic queen of English Protestants for reading English Scriptures and praying Protestant prayers; the hunting down and slaying of the Covenanters upon the crags and moors of Scotland for worshiping God according to the dictates of their own consciences; the decimating of the people of the German states in the Thirty Years War between Catholics and Protestants; the massacre of the Huguenots in France; the pogroms and persecutions of the Jews in many lands; the banishing of Baptists and other dissenters by Puritan Massachusetts; the persecution and imprisonment of Quakers by England for refusing to pay tithes to the established church and to take the oaths of supremacy and allegiance; the banishing, branding, imprisoning, and whipping of Quakers, and the hanging of the alleged witches at Salem by Puritan Massachusetts; and the hundreds of other atrocities perpetrated in the name of religion.

He quotes his mentor on the North Carolina State Court, Chief Justice Walter P. Stacey: "It would be unbelievable, if history did not record the tragic fact, that men have gone to war and cut each other's throats because they could not agree as to what was to become of them after their throats were cut." So it is with the deepest respect that Senator Ervin writes of Thomas Jefferson and James Madison, the architects of this nation's "wall between church and state," a wall built into the Bill of Rights.

Former Senator Lowell Weicker, in an essay originally delivered with Ervin's at *Free Inquiry's* "Religion in American Politics" symposium in March 1983 at the Washington Press Club, shares this respect. Criticizing then-President Ronald Reagan for declaring 1983 the "Year of the Bible," Weicker writes, "I don't believe it is up to a congressman or a senator or even the president to espouse or encourage any one religion, or even religion in general. It is not our job to do the convincing, to take up on Monday where the minister left off on Sunday or the rabbi on Saturday. . . . So I say to my fellow citizens: Face 1983 with the Constitution. And I say the same to my colleagues in the Congress. For we serve our constituents best when we do our best by that document." Adds Daniel Boorstin, Librarian of Congress emeritus and author of *The Discoverers:* "After the American Revolution, Washington, Jefferson, and others could see what the New England Puritans could not see, that their government was not described and foremodeled in the Bible but was the prudential product of human struggle, compromise, and the pursuit of decency."

—R.B.

The Constitution and Religion
Sam J. Ervin, Jr.

Religion is man's belief in and reverence for a superhuman power recognized as the creator and governor of the universe. Believers call this power God.

I am a Presbyterian whose Scotch-Irish, English, and French Huguenot ancestors came to America before the Revolution. All of them were Protestants. Most of them dissented from the established churches in the lands of their origin.

Religious faith, which is tolerant of other beliefs, is, in my opinion, the most wholesome and uplifting power on earth. Religious faith is not a shelter to which men and women can flee to escape the storms of life. It is, instead, an inner spiritual strength that enables them to face those storms with courage and serenity.

The Constitution makes two references to religion. One appears in Article 6, Section 3, of the original Constitution, and the other is found in the first words of the First Amendment and the Bill of Rights.

Article 6, Section 3, provides that all legislative, executive, and judicial officers "of the United States and the several States shall be bound by oath or affirmation to support this Constitution, but no religious test shall ever be required as a qualification to any office or public trust under the United States."

The First Amendment provides in pertinent part that "Congress shall make no law respecting an establishment of religion, or prohibiting the free exercise thereof."

If we are to understand the meanings of these provisions, we must understand the historic events that prompted the Founding Fathers to embody them in the Constitution.

Religious Intolerance

The ugliest chapters in history are those that recount the religious intolerance of the civil and ecclesiastical rulers of the Old World and their puppets during the generations preceding the framing and ratifying of the First Amendment.

These chapters of history reveal the casting of Christians to the lions in the Colosseum at Rome; the bloody Crusades of the Christians against the Saracens for the possession of the shrines hallowed by the footsteps of the Prince of Peace; the use by the papacy of the dungeon and the rack to coerce conformity and of the fiery faggot to exterminate heresy; the unspeakable cruelties of the Spanish Inquisition; the slaughter of the Waldenses in Alpine Italy; the jailing and hanging by Protestant kings of English Catholics for abiding with the faith of their fathers; the jailing and hanging by a Catholic queen of English Protestants for reading English Scriptures and praying Protestant prayers; the hunting down and slaying of the Covenanters upon the crags and moors of Scotland for worshiping God according to the dictates of their own consciences; the decimating of the people of the German states in the Thirty Years' War between Catholics and Protestants; the massacre of the Huguenots in France; the pogroms and persecutions of the Jews in many lands; the banishing of Baptists and other dissenters by Puritan Massachusetts; the persecution and imprisonment of Quakers by England for refusing to pay tithes to the established church and to take the oaths of supremacy and allegiance; the banishing, branding, imprisoning, and whipping of Quakers, and the hanging of the alleged witches at Salem by Puritan Massachusetts; and the hundreds of other atrocities perpetrated in the name of religion.

It is not surprising that Blaise Pascal, the French mathematician and philosopher, was moved more than three hundred years ago to proclaim this tragic truth: "Men never do evil so completely and cheerfully as when they do it from religious conviction."

One of my life's most rewarding experiences was that of serving for a time on the North Carolina Supreme Court with the late Chief Justice Walter P. Stacy, one of America's wisest jurists of all time. He possessed an uncanny capacity to phrase truth in unforgettable words.

When he wrote his opinion in *State* v. *Beal,* 199 N.C. 278, 302 (1930), Chief Justice Stacy made these comments on the nature and history of religious intolerance:

> There are those who feel more deeply over religious matters than they do about secular things. It would be almost unbelievable, if history did not record the tragic fact, that men have gone to war and cut each other's throats because they could not agree as to what was to become of them after their throats were cut. Many sins have been committed in the name of religion. Alas! the spirit of proscription is never kind. It is the unhappy quality of religious disputes that they are always bitter. For some reason, too deep to fathom, men contend more furiously over the road to heaven, which they cannot see, than over their visible walks on earth.

Religious intolerance was fostered in Great Britain and virtually all the nations of Europe by unholy alliances between governments and particular churches recognized and established by law as the sole custodians of religious truth.

The objective of the unholy alliance in each nation was to persuade or coerce the people to accept and practice the political and religious orthodoxy sanctioned by the state and the established church. As pragmatists, state and church sought to accomplish this objective by imprisoning the minds and spirits of the people within intellectual and spiritual jails.

The British Parliament made the Church of England the established church in Great Britain. It created the crime of seditious libel to punish those who spoke ill of the government or its officers, and the crime of blasphemous libel to punish those who spoke ill of the established church. Besides, the British Parliament enacted laws compelling the people to pay tithes or taxes for the support of the established church, and to attend its worship services, denying those who dissented from its doctrines the capacity to hold civil office in government, and forbidding ministers of dissenting congregations to administer the sacraments to their members.

As a consequence of these attempts to regulate relations between men and religion, dissenters from the established church were compelled to make contributions of money for the propagation of religious opinions they disbelieved, required to listen to the exposition of religious doctrines they rejected, and denied the right to hold civil offices in government. Besides, they sometimes had their marriages annulled and their children adjudged illegitimate for daring to speak their marital vows before ministers of their own faith rather than clergymen of the established church.

Established Churches in the Colonies

While they were joined by many Germans and French Huguenots and smaller numbers of Dutch, Swedes, and Swiss, natives of the British Isles constituted by far the greater part of those who migrated from the Old World to the thirteen British colonies in America.

A substantial proportion of the colonists were dissenters from the churches established by law in the lands of their origins.

Like the colonists who conformed to the established churches, these dissenters came to America to better their economic lots. But they were also motivated by the hope that they would find in the New World the political and religious freedom denied them by the civil and ecclesiastical rulers of the Old.

When they reached America, however, they discovered to their disappointment that in many of the colonies predominant groups had set up established churches here and that they were compelled in such colonies to pay taxes for the support of established churches whose doctrines they disbelieved. Moreover, most of the colonies had established religious qualifications in their oaths for public office holders. As a rule, these tests were designed to exclude dissenters, Catholics, Jews, deists, or unbelievers.

There is more than a modicum of historical truth in this statement of Artemas Ward, a humorist of a bygone generation:

> The Puritans nobly fled from a land of despotism to a land of freedom, where they could not only enjoy their own religion, but could prevent everybody else from enjoying his.

The colonies of Virginia, North Carolina, South Carolina, Georgia, and Maryland had established churches, and the Anglican church was the favorite under their laws.

In the colonies of Massachusetts, Connecticut, and New Hampshire, the Congregational church was the established church.

In the colony of New York, the Dutch Reformed and Anglican churches were, in turn, established by law.

The people in these nine colonies were compelled by law to pay taxes for the support of these established churches, and in some cases to attend their services.

The dissenters were outraged by these requirements. They believed it tyrannical for government to attempt to regulate by law the relationship between an individual and his God. Moreover, as they pondered verses 15 to 22 of Chapter 22 of Matthew, "Render, therefore, unto Caesar the things that are Caesar's, and unto God the things that are God's," they concluded that in addition to being tyrannical, the attempt to regulate religion by law was also sinful.

Separation of Church and State in the States

The dissenters accepted as absolute truth this declaration, which had its origin in the North Carolina Constitution of 1776:

> All persons have a natural and inalienable right to worship Almighty God according to the dictates of their own consciences, and no human authority shall, in any case whatever, control or interfere with the rights of conscience.[1]

As a consequence, they demanded the separation of church and state in America.

During the Revolution and the years immediately following it, the dissenters found staunch allies in their fight for separation of church and state among non-churchmembers and those adherents of established churches who believed that it was abhorrent to reason as well as for earthly government to regulate the relationship between human beings and religion.

The separation of church and state presented no problems in Rhode Island, where Baptists led by Roger Williams had settled under a royal charter granting complete religious freedom to all, or in Delaware, New Jersey, and Pennsylvania, where establishment never acquired a foothold.

When their revolt against Great Britain converted the thirteen colonies into self-governing states, Rhode Island retained separation under its original charter, and Delaware, New Jersey, and Pennsylvania did so under constitutions adopted in 1776. North Carolina, New York, Georgia, and Virginia granted the right of freedom of worship to all and disestablished religion within their borders before the drafting of the First Amendment, and South Carolina did likewise before the amendment was ratified.

Hence, the only states maintaining any financial and legal relationship to religion at the time the First Amendment became a part of the Constitution were Connecticut, Maryland, Massachusetts, and New Hampshire. These four states were able to do this after the adoption of the First Amendment because the amendment applied originally to the federal government and not to the states.

But in those four states there was no single established church at that time. As a concession to those demanding complete separation of church and state they had substituted for single established churches multiple establishments and were providing for an impartial use of taxes for the support of all churches they deemed respectable.

The last of these four states to terminate such relationships to religion was Massachusetts, which did so in 1883.

The Statute of Virginia for Religious Liberty

It is not surprising that James Madison hated religious intolerance and loved religious liberty. As a student at what is now Princeton University, he sat at the feet of the great educator and patriot John Witherspoon, the Scottish divine, who taught that mere tolerance of differing religious views was not enough, that every man was entitled to worship God as he chose or not at all, and that every church should be supported by the contributions of its own members and not by taxation.

On entering politics in his native Virginia, Madison adopted as his wise and trusted counselor Thomas Jefferson, the great apostle of liberty, who had sworn on the altar of God eternal hostility to all forms of tyranny over the mind of man.

Jefferson, the theorist, and Madison, the pragmatist, were an ideal combination. They led the fight for the disestablishment of religion in Virginia. Madison subsequently authored the religious clauses of the First Amendment. For these reasons, the fight for religious freedom in Virginia illuminates the meaning of these clauses, and merits detailing.

In 1776, Virginia, as an independent commonwealth, adopted a new constitution. James Madison was a member of the constitutional convention that drafted it, and he succeeded in writing into it the proposition that all men are equally entitled to the free exercise of religion according to the dictates of conscience.

Shortly after the adoption of the new constitution, the Virginia legislature met, and a conflict ensued between the members who demanded total separation of church and state in Virginia and those who favored supplanting the single established Anglican church by an establishment of all the churches deemed to be respectable.

As a member of this legislature, James Madison was able to persuade his colleagues to provide that no dissenters should be compelled to pay taxes to the Anglican church, which had been established in Virginia in 1629. He also secured the enactment of law that suspended for the time being the requirement that members of the Anglican church should pay taxes for its support.

But the legislature of 1776 expressly reserved for the future the crucial decision of whether general taxes should be levied for the support of all the denominations that the controlling element in the Virginia Legislature deemed to be respectable.

The conflict was renewed in the Virginia legislature of 1779, when James Henry introduced a bill for multiple establishment, and John Harvie, a member of the general assembly, introduced a bill that was drafted by Thomas Jefferson, which is known to history as the Bill for Establishing Religious Freedom.

James Henry's bill undertook to establish by law virtually all of the Christian churches of Virginia as the established churches of Virginia and to levy taxes for the support of all of them on an impartial basis. It is significant that in this bill reference to an establishment appears at a number of points, in contexts that clearly show that James Henry and the others of his day understood the term "an establishment of religion" to mean an official connection between the state and one or more churches whereby the state recognized such church or churches and provided for taxation for its or their support.

The bill for religious freedom is one of the great documents that preceded the writing of the Constitution. It was designed to effect complete separation of church and state in Virginia.

To this end, the bill laid down these propositions in its preamble: First, "Almighty God hath created the mind free"; second, "to compel a man to furnish contributions of money for the propagation of opinions he disbelieves is sinful and tyrannical"; third, "the proscribing of any citizen as unworthy of the public confidence by laying upon him an incapacity of being called to offices of trust and emolument, unless he profess or renounce this or that religious opinion, is depriving him injuriously of those privileges and advantages in which in common with his fellow citizens he has a natural right"; fourth, such action "tends only to corrupt the principles of that religion it is meant to encourage by bribing with a monopoly of worldly honors and emoluments those who will externally profess and conform to it"; fifth, "to suffer the civil magistrate to intrude his powers into the field of opinion, and to restrain the profession or propagation of principles on supposition of their ill tendency is a dangerous fallacy, which at once destroys all religious liberty, because he being of course judge of that tendency will make his opinions the rule of judgment, and approve or condemn the sentiments of others only as they will square with or differ from his own";

sixth, "it is time enough for the rightful purpose of civil governments for its officers to interfere when principles break into overt acts against peace and good order"; and, seventh "truth is great . . . and has nothing to fear from the conflict" with error, and "will prevail" over error, and error will cease "to be dangerous" unless by human interposition "truth is disarmed by her natural weapons, free argument and debate."

On the basis of these propositions, the bill proposed that the Virginia legislature make these enactments: First, "that no man shall be compelled to frequent or support any religious worship, place or ministry whatsoever"; second, that no man "shall be enforced, restrained, molested, or burthened in his body or goods" or "otherwise suffer on account of his religious opinions or beliefs"; third, "that all men shall be free to profess, and by argument to maintain, their opinion in all matters of religion, and that the same shall in no wise diminish, enlarge, or affect their civil capacities"; and, fourth, that "the rights hereby asserted are of the natural rights of mankind, and . . . if any act shall be hereafter passed to repeal the present or to narrow its application, such act shall be an infringement of natural right."

The opposing forces in the Virginia legislature of 1779 were so nearly equal in power that it was impossible to secure the enactment of either the James Henry bill for a multiple establishment of religion or the Jefferson bill for complete religious freedom.

The contest was renewed in the Virginia legislature of 1784. This time James Madison presented Jefferson's bill for religious freedom and Patrick Henry sponsored a new bill for a multiple establishment.

Patrick Henry's bill, which was entitled "A Bill Establishing a Provision for Teachers of the Christian Religion," undertook to recognize the legal interest of Virginia in virtually all the Christian churches functioning within its borders, and to impose taxes on all Virginians for their support.

When the legislature was apparently on the verge of passing Patrick Henry's bill, Madison persuaded it to postpone a final vote until its next session, which was scheduled for November 1785.

Between that time and the next meeting of the legislature, Madison composed a most convincing and eloquent appeal for religious freedom, which he called "The Memorial and Remonstrance Against Religious Assessments." In it Madison said:

> It is proper to take alarm at the first experiment on our liberties . . . The same authority which can establish Christianity, in exclusion of all other religions, may establish with the same ease any particular sect of Christians, in exclusion of all other sects . . . The same authority which can force a citizen to contribute three pence only of his property for the support of any one establishment, may force him to conform to any other establishment in all cases whatsoever.

This document is crucial in determining what the Founding Fathers meant when they yielded to the insistence of James Madison and wrote into the First

Amendment the provision that Congress shall make no law respecting an establishment of religion.

In this document, which was a protest against the bill sponsored by Patrick Henry to levy taxes for the support of virtually all Christian churches in Virginia, Madison used the word *establishment* at least five times in contexts that showed that in his mind "an establishment of religion" meant an official relationship between the state and one church or many churches or all churches, and the imposition of taxation for the support of one church or many churches or all churches.

Madison caused "The Memorial and Remonstrance Against Religious Assessments" to be widely distributed throughout Virginia. By so doing, he ensured his victory. When the members of the legislature that was scheduled to convene in November 1785 were elected, those who supported Jefferson and Madison in their fight for religious freedom were in an overwhelming majority. Upon convening, they enacted into law Jefferson's bill for religious freedom.

Jefferson's Appraisal of the Statute

We cannot overmagnify the importance that Jefferson and Madison attributed to the Virginia Statute for Religious Liberty.

Jefferson gave cogent testimony on this score when he chose the epitaph to be carved upon his gravestone. As one ascends the hill that leads to Jefferson's home at Monticello, he passes the spot where the mortal remains of Thomas Jefferson rest in the tongueless silence of the dreamless dust. On the gravestone of Thomas Jefferson is the epitaph, which speaks with as much eloquence as Jefferson used in writing the Declaration of Independence or the Statute of Virginia for Religious Freedom. The statement is as follows:

> Here was buried Thomas Jefferson, author of the Declaration of American Independence; of the Statute of Virginia for Religious Liberty; and the father of the University of Virginia.

At the time that Jefferson decided that those were the words he wished to have engraved on the stone that marks his last resting place, he had been a member of the legislature of Virginia; he had been governor of Virginia; he had represented Virginia in the Continental Congress; he had served as American Minister to France; he had officiated as secretary of state in George Washington's cabinet; he had been vice president of the United States under John Adams; and he had been twice elected to the highest office within the gift of the American people— the presidency itself.

Yet Thomas Jefferson was not concerned that he should be remembered for the high offices he had filled; he was concerned that he should be remembered as the author of the Virginia Statute for Religious Freedom, one of the greatest documents ever conceived by man.

The First Amendment

After the Constitution of the United States was drafted and submitted to the states for ratification or rejection, many Americans were dissatisfied with it because it did not contain any bill of rights, or any provision relating to religious freedom other than Article 6 prescribing that no religious test should be required as a qualification for any office or public trust in the United States.

When New York, New Hampshire, and Virginia ratified the Constitution, they adopted resolutions that insisted that the Constitution should be amended by incorporating in it guaranties of religious freedom and freedom from taxation for the support of religion.

North Carolina and Rhode Island both postponed ratifying the Constitution and their conventions resolved they would not ratify it unless it was amended to provide for the disestablishment of religion.

As a result of the actions of these five states and the demands of multitudes of Americans in the other original states, the Constitution was amended in these respects by the First Amendment, which, as part of the Bill of Rights, was adopted by the requisite number of states by December 15, 1791.

The Constitution was so amended as a result of efforts of James Madison, who was elected a representative from Virginia to the First Congress, which met after its ratification.

As soon as this Congress convened, Madison began his great fight to have the First Amendment added to the Constitution. Some of his colleagues did not want the amendment to deny to government the power to support religion, and others insisted that the religious clauses of the amendment should merely prohibit a *single* established church.

But Madison contended at all times that the First Amendment should embody in it provisions that Congress should pass no law respecting an establishment of religion or prohibiting its free exercise.

He triumphed after much effort. On September 23, 1789, Madison made a report to the House of Representatives concerning the action of the conference committee of the Senate and House, which had been appointed to reconcile varying views as to the language of the First Amendment. This committee agreed with Madison and recommended the words that are now incorporated in the First Amendment. Hence James Madison, whom historians call the Father of the Constitution, really phrased the establishment and free-exercise clauses of the First Amendment.

As has been observed, the First Amendment was originally an inhibition on the federal government and not on the states.

In July 1868, the Fourteenth Amendment was added to the Constitution. Section 1 of this Amendment provides that no state shall deprive any person of liberty without due process of law.

The Supreme Court clearly adjudged for the first time in *Cantwell* v. *Connecticut,* 310 U.S. 296, which was decided in 1940, that the fundamental concept of liberty embodied in the Fourteenth Amendment embraced the liberties guaranteed by the First Amendment relating to religion, and that in consequence the First and Fourteenth amendments in combination forbid the states as well as the federal government to make any law or take any action respecting the establishment of religion or prohibiting its free exercise, and thus secure to all people in the United States religious freedom. This ruling has been subsequently reaffirmed by the Supreme Court in many cases.

The First and Fourteenth amendments do this by erecting a wall of separation between government and religion at all levels and in all areas of the United States. By prohibiting any official relationship between government and religion, they forbid government to undertake to control or support religion and deny any religious group or groups the power to control public policy or the public purse.

The constitutional separation of government and religion is best for government and best for religion. It enables each of them to seek to achieve its rightful aims without interference from the other. Besides, it is wise. History reveals that political freedom cannot exist in any nation where religion controls government and that religious freedom cannot survive in any nation where government controls religion.

Moreover, constitutional separation of government and religion is indispensable to the domestic tranquility of the United States, "whose people came from the four corners of the earth and brought with them a diversity of religious opinion." As the Supreme Court revealed in *Abington School District* v. *Schempp* and *Murray* v. *Curlitt,* 374 U.S. 203, 214 (1963): "Today authorities list 83 separate religious bodies, each with a membership exceeding 50,000, existing among our people, as well as innumerable smaller groups." These organizations compete for the religious allegiance of the people.

By securing the absolute equality before the law of all religious sects and requiring government to be neutral in respect to them, the constitutional separation of government and religion makes the love of religious freedom and the other things that unite our people stronger than their diversities and enables Americans of varying religious faiths to live with each other in peace.

As made applicable to the states by the Fourteenth Amendment, the religious clauses of the First Amendment accomplish their wholesome objectives in their entirety in these ways:

1. They prohibit the federal government and the states from establishing any religious test as a qualification for any public office at any level of government.[2]

2. "The establishment of religion clause of the First Amendment means at least this: neither a state nor the federal government can set up a church. Neither can pass laws that aid one religion, aid all religions, or prefer one religion over another. Neither can force nor influence a person to go to or remain away from church against his will or force him to profess a belief or disbelief in any religion. No person can be punished for entertaining or professing religious beliefs or disbeliefs, for church attendance or non-attendance. No tax in any amount, large or small, can be levied to support any religious activities or institutions, whatever they may be called, or whatever form they may adopt to teach or practice reli-

gion. Neither a state nor the federal government can, openly or secretly, participate in the affairs of any religious organizations or groups or vice versa. In the words of Jefferson, the clause against establishment of religion by law was intended to erect a wall of separation between church and state."[3]

3. The free-exercise clause of the First Amendment secures to every person the absolute right to accept as true the religious beliefs that appeal to his conscience and to reject all others, to practice the religious beliefs he accepts in any mode of worship not injurious to himself or others, to seek by peaceful persuasion to convert others to his religious beliefs and practices, and to be exempt from taxation for the support of religious activities or teachings. A person is denied religious freedom if he is taxed to support any religious faith, including his own.[4]

Opposition to the First Amendment

Numerous Americans of the utmost sincerity are not in intellectual and spiritual rapport with the First Amendment's separation of government and religion. Whether they are hostile to the principle of separation itself or do not understand what it entails, I do not know and will not surmise.

One group demands that the public schools of the states teach religion to the children attending them; and the other group demands that government provide public funds to aid and support private schools maintained by various churches to teach their religious doctrines to the children attending them. In so doing, the second group demands that the taxes of Caesar be used to finance the things of God.

While one is concerned with the public schools and the other with private religious schools, both groups base their demands on the assumption that governmental fidelity to the First Amendment frustrates the religious education of children.

This assumption is without foundation. While it forbids government to teach religion, the First Amendment leaves individuals, homes, and nongovernmental institutions ,such as Sunday schools, churches, and private schools, free to do so. Indeed it encourages them to do so by securing religious freedom to all.

Churches should look to their members and their friends only for the financing of their undertakings, and no church should engage in any undertaking, no matter how laudable it may be, that its members and friends are unable or unwilling to finance.

The Public Schools

For generations before the school-prayer cases, the public schools of various states conducted religious exercises each school day conforming to the religious beliefs that prevailed in the communities where the schools were located. The school-prayer cases are *Engel* v. *Vitale, School District of Abington Township* v. *Schempp,* and *Murray* v. *Curlitt.*

The *Engel* case, 370 U.S. 421 (1962), involved the constitutionality of a New York regulation requiring the following prayer to be said aloud by each class in a public school in the presence of a teacher at the beginning of each school day: "Almighty God, we acknowledge our dependence upon Thee, and we beg Thy blessings upon us, our parents, our teachers, and our country."

The *Abington School District* and *Murray* cases, which were consolidated for decision, involved the constitutionality of a Pennsylvania statute that required that "at least ten verses from the Holy Bible shall be read, without comment, at the opening of each public school on each school day," and a rule of the School Commissioners of Baltimore, Maryland, that required the holding of opening exercises in the schools of the city consisting primarily of "reading, without comment, of a chapter in the Holy Bible and/or the use of the Lord's Prayer."

It was provided in each instance that any child would be excused from participating in the prescribed religious exercises on the request of his parent or guardian.

By a vote of 6 to 1 in the *Engel* case and 8 to 1 in the *Abington School District* and *Murray* cases, the Supreme Court ruled that by using their public school systems to require these religious exercises, New York, Pennsylvania, and Maryland violated the establishment clause of the First Amendment, and that the regulation, statute, and rule requiring them were therefore unconstitutional.

The Court dismissed as immaterial the circumstance that any child was excused on request from participating in the exercises on the ground that governmental coercion is not an essential ingredient of government establishment of religion.

The rationale of the rulings was thus summarized in the opinion in the *Abington School District* and *Murray* cases: "They are religious exercises required by the state in violation of the command of the First Amendment that the government maintain strict neutrality, neither aiding nor opposing religion."

These rulings shocked sincere people throughout the nation. It is not surprising that this was so. The custom of holding religious exercises in public schools had been followed in many states for generations, and the school authorities in these states had acted on the assumption that it was proper for these schools to teach the religious beliefs that prevailed in the communities in which they operated.

Many sincere persons charge that the school-prayer cases show the Supreme Court to be hostile to religion. This charge is untrue and unjust. In these cases the Supreme Court was faithful to its judicial duty. It enforced the First Amendment, which commands government to maintain strict neutrality respecting religion, neither aiding nor opposing it.

In these and other cases, the Surpeme Court recognizes the supreme value of religious faith in the lives of individuals and through them in the life of the nation.

The First Amendment forbids the states to teach religion to the children attending their public schools. Without impairing this principle to any degree, the Supreme Court makes this observation in its opinion in the *Abington School District* and *Murray* cases:

It might well be said that one's education is not complete without a study of comparative religion or the history of religion and its relationship to the advancement of civilization. It certainly may be said that the Bible is worthy of study for its literary and historic qualities. Nothing we have said here indicates that such study of the Bible or of religion, when presented objectively as part of a secular program of education, may not be effected consistently with the First Amendment. [374 U.S. 203, 225]

It is to be noted, moreover, that the school-prayer cases do not question the soundness of the prior ruling in *Zorach* v. *Clauson,* 343 U.S. 306 (1962), where the Supreme Court held that the New York system of released time for religious instruction did not violate the First Amendment. Under this system, the state authorities in charge of public schools released from their customary studies an hour a week children who, acting without any pressure from them, desired to receive religious instruction in churches or church schools outside public school property.

Those who demand that public schools be made instruments to teach religion to the children attending them suggest varying ways to achieve their objective.

Since these school-prayer cases adjudged the religious exercises involved in them to be repugnant to the First Amendment because they were required by state authorities, they propose initially that state authorities sanction voluntary religious exercise in public schools. Despite their good faith, this proposal is fatally defective. In the nature of things, religious exercises sanctioned by public authorities are not, in reality, voluntary.

They proposed secondarily that Congress deprive federal courts of jurisdiction to hear and determine cases in which states are alleged to have taught religion to the children attending their public schools in violation of the First Amendment. If it should take such action, Congress would nullify the First Amendment in substantial part by abolishing judicial enforcement of one of the amendment's commands.

They propose finally that Congress and the states amend the Constitution to authorize the states to teach religion to children attending their public schools. If consummated, this forthright proposal would repeal the First Amendment in substantial part insofar as it applies to the public schools.

As a general rule, those who demand that the public schools of the states be made instruments to teach religion are motivated by their desire to have the children attending them taught the religious beliefs of their particular sect of Christianity.

The word *religion* as used in the Constitution is not restricted in its meaning to any particular sect of Christianity, or to the Christian religion in general. It embodies Buddhism, Judaism, Islam, Shintoism, and all other religions; and the Constitution confers on all persons of all religious persuasions an equality of constitutional right. If those who demand that the public schools be made instruments to teach religion would pause and ponder these things, the ardor of their demand might abate.

Private Schools That Teach Religion

The Supreme Court held in *Pierce* v. *Society of Sisters,* 268 U.S. 510 (1925), that a state statute requiring all children to attend the public schools was unconstitutional because the guaranty of liberty of the due process clause of the Fourteenth Amendment gave Catholic parents a constitutional right to send their children to a Catholic school to receive both secular and religious instruction from it.

Although many Catholics revere and understand the First Amendment in its entirety and oppose taxation of any Americans to support the teaching of any religion, Catholics comprise the majority of those who insist that government give financial aid to private schools that teach religion.

The Catholic church establishes and operates its parochial schools to teach the children of Catholic parents its religious doctrines and observances. Since the First Amendment forbids the public schools to teach any religion, Catholic parents who desire their children to be taught the Catholic faith send their children to parochial rather than public schools. As taxpayers, these Catholic parents pay taxes to help the state to maintain the public schools; and as parents, they bear the added expense of the instruction of their children in parochial schools.

Many of these parents and others demand that government should provide public funds either directly or indirectly to aid and support the parochial schools. They base their demand on the propositions that it is unjust to compel Catholic parents to pay taxes for the support of public schools and bear the additional expense occasioned by sending their children to the parochial schools, and that the Catholic church saves the government enormous outlays of money because Catholic children go to parochial rather than public schools.

Without questioning the validity of the unadorned facts underlying these assertions, these observations are of crucial import:

1. The Catholic parents voluntarily impose the additional financial burden on themselves by sending their children to the parochial schools to obtain instruction in the Catholic faith, instruction that the First Amendment forbids the public schools to give them.

2. The Catholic church operates the parochial schools to ensure that it rather than government will control the education of Catholic children.

Justices Jackson and Rutledge present irrefutable reasons in their dissenting opinions in the *Everson* case why government must refuse to give financial aid and support, either directly or indirectly, to parochial and other private schools that teach religion if the religious freedom the First Amendment establishes is to endure in the United States. Justice Jackson added the warning that government may regulate the private schools it subsidizes.[5]

Conclusion

As Justice Jackson stated in his dissent in the *Everson* case, 330 U.S. 1, 22–28, the First Amendment occupies first place in the Bill of Rights because its objective occupied first place in the minds of the Founding Fathers. He made the objective of the Bill of Rights clear in the opinion he wrote for the Court in *West Virginia Board of Education* v. *Barnette,* 319 U.S. 624, 638 (1943):

> The very purpose of a Bill of Rights was to withdraw certain subjects from the vicissitudes of political controversy, to place them beyond the reach of the majorities and officials and to establish them as legal principles to be applied by the courts . . . One's right to freedom of worship . . . and other fundamental rights may not be submitted to vote; they depend on the outcome of no elections.

The Oklahoma court proclaimed truth when it said in *Cline* v. *State,* 9 Okla. Crim. 40, 130 P. 510:

> The crowning glory of American freedom is absolute religious liberty, every American has the unquestioned and untrammeled right to worship God according to the dictates of his own conscience, without let or hindrance from any person or any source.

It is just as sinful and tyrannical now as it was in the day of Jefferson and Madison for government to tell people what they must think about religion, or to compel them to pay taxes for the propagation of religious opinions they disbelieve.

May America cherish the First Amendment and thus keep religious freedom inviolate for its people as long as time shall last.

Notes

1. North Carolina embodied this declaration in its constitution of 1776, "that all men have a natural and unalienable right to worship Almighty God according to the dictates of their own conscience," and added to it as an amendment in 1835 the words "and no human authority should, in any case whatever, control or interfere with the rights of conscience."

2. *Torcaso* v. *Maryland,* 367 U.S. 488 (1961).

3. The statement revealing the meaning of the establishment clause appears in the majority opinion in *Everson* v. *Board of Education,* 330 U.S. 1, 15–16 (1947), which was written by Justice Black. In this case the Supreme Court upheld the constitutionality under the establishment clause of a statute that required New Jersey to use state funds to reimburse the cost of transportation of children to the state's public schools and Catholic parochial schools. The state was not permitted, however, to reimburse the cost of transportation of children attending private schools operated for profit.

The majority and dissenting opinions illuminate the establishment clause. The justices did not disagree as to its meaning. They disagreed only as to its application to the New

Jersey statute.

The majority concluded that the expenditures required by the New Jersey statute was comparable to governmental expenditures for fire and police protection and were for the public purpose of promoting the safety of the children traveling between their homes and the public and parochial schools. The dissenters maintained that the expenditure did nothing to increase the safety of the children over that of other patrons of the transportation system and was for the private purpose of aiding parochial schools to teach the Catholic faith to the children attending them.

Some years after the *Everson* decision, the Supreme Court explained in the first school-prayer case, *Engel* v. *Vitale,* 370 U.S. 421 (1962), that the establishment clause is unlike the free-exercise clause in that governmental coercion is not an essential ingredient of it, and enunciated the several reasons why the Founding Fathers embodied the establishment clause in the Constitution.

4. *Cantwell* v. *Connecticut,* 310 U.S. 296 (1940); *Jones* v. *Opelika,* 316 U.S. 584 (1942); *West Virginia Board of Education* v. *Barnette,* 319 U.S. 624 (1943); *Follett* v. *City of McCormick,* 321 U.S. 573 (1944); *Kovacs* v. *Cooper,* 336 U.S. 77 (1949); *Sherbet* v. *Verner,* 374 U.S. 398 (1963); *Flast* v. *Cohen,* 392 U.S. 83 (1968).

Justice Rutledge made the meanings of both the establishment and free-exercise clauses plain in his dissent in *Everson* v. *Board of Education,* 330 U.S. 31–63 (1947). He said:

Not simply an established church, but any law respecting an establishment of religion is forbidden. The Amendment was broadly but not loosely phrased. It is the compact and exact summation of its author's views formed during his long struggle for religious freedom. In Madison's own words, characterizing Jefferson's Bill for Establishing Religious Freedom, the guaranty he put in our national charter like the bill he piloted through the Virginia Assembly, was a "model of technical precision, and perspicuous brevity." Madison could not have confused "church" and "religion" or "an established church" and "an establishment of religion."

The Amendment's purpose was not to strike merely at the official establishment of a single sect, creed or outlawing only a formal relation such as had prevailed in England and some of the colonies. Necessarily it was to uproot all such relationships. But the object was broader than separating church and state in this narrow sense. It was to create a complete and permanent separation of the spheres of religious activity and civil authority by comprehensively forbidding every form of public aid or support for religion. In proof the Amendment's wording and history unite with this Court's consistent utterances whenever attention has been fixed directly upon the question.

"Religion" appears only once in the Amendmnent. But the word governs two prohibitions and governs them alike. It does not have two meanings, one narrow to forbid "an establishment" and another, much broader, for securing "the free exercise therof." "Thereof" brings down "religion" with its entire and exact content, no more and no less, from the first into the second guaranty, so that Congress and now the states are as broadly restricted concerning the one as they are regarding the other.

No one would claim today that the Amendment is constricted in "prohibiting the free exercise" of religion to securing the free exercise of some formal or creedal observance, of one sect or many. It secures all forms of religious expression, creedal, sectarian or nonsectarian, wherever and however taking place, except conduct which trenches upon the like freedoms of others or clearly and presently endangers the community's good order and security. For the protective purposes of this phase of the basic freedom, street preaching, oral or by distribution of literature, has been given "the same high estate under the First Amendment as . . . worship in the churches and preaching from the pulpits." And on this basis parents have been held entitled to send their children to private, religious schools, *Pierce* v. *Society of Sisters,* 268 U.S. 510 (1925). Accordingly, daily religious education commingled with secular is "religion" within the guaranty's comprehensive scope. So are religious training and teaching in whatever form. The word connotes the broadest content, determined not by the form or formality of the teaching or where it occurs, but by its essential nature regardless of those details.

"Religion" has the same broad significance in the twin prohibition concerning "an establishment." The Amendment was not duplicitous. "Religion" and "establishment" were not used in any formal or technical sense. The prohibition broadly forbids state support, financial or other, of religion in any guise, form or degree. It outlaws all use of public funds for religious purposes.

Two great drives are constantly in motion to abridge, in the name of education, the complete division of religion and civil authority that our forefathers made. One is to introduce religious education and observances into the public schools. The other, to obtain public funds for the aid and support of various private religious schools. . . . In my opinion both avenues are closed by the Constitution. Neither should be opened by this Court. The matter is not one of quantity, to be measured by the amount of money expended. Now, as in Madison's day, it is one of principle, to keep separate the separate spheres as the First Amendment drew them: to prevent the first experiment upon our liberties; and to keep them from becoming entangled in corrosive precedents. We should not be less strict to keep strong and untarnished the one side of the shield of religious freedom than we have been of the other."

5. After pointing out that parochial schools are established and maintained by the Catholic church to teach "Catholic faith and morals," and that its Canon Law prescribes that they shall be "schools where religious and moral training occupy the first place," Justice Jackson declared in his dissenting opinion in the *Everson* case, 330 U.S. 22–28:

It is no exaggeration to say that the whole historic conflict in temporal policy between the Catholic Church and non-Catholics comes to a focus in their respective school policies. The Roman Catholic Church, counseled by experience in many ages and many lands and with all sorts and conditions of men, takes what, from the viewpoint of its own progress and the success of its mission, is a wise estimate of the importance of education to religion. It does not leave the individual to pick up religion by chance. It relies on early and indelible indoctrination in the faith and order of the Church by the word and example of persons consecrated to the task.

Our public school, if not a product of Protestantism, at least is more consistent with it than the Catholic culture and scheme of value. It is a relatively recent development dating from about 1840. It is organized on the premises that secular education can be isolated from all religious teaching so that the school can teach all needed temporal knowledge and also maintain a strict and lofty neutrality as to religion. The assumption is that after the individual has been instructed in worldly wisdom he will be better fitted to choose his religion. Whether such disjunction is possible, and if possible is wise, are questions I need not try to answer.

I should be surprised if any Catholic would deny that the parochial school is a vital, if not the most vital part of the Roman Catholic Church. If put to the choice, that venerable institution, I should expect, would forego its whole service for mature persons before it would give up education for the young, and it would be a wise choice. Its growth and cohesion, discipline and loyalty, spring from its schools. Catholic education is the rock on which the whole structure rests, and to render tax aid to its Church school is indistinguishable to me from rendering the same aid to the Church itself.

It is of no importance in this situation whether the beneficiary of tax-raised funds is primarily the parochial school and incidentally the pupil, or whether the aid is directly bestowed on the pupil with indirect benefits to the school. The state cannot maintain a church and it can no more tax its citizens to furnish free carriage to those who attend a Church. The prohibition against establishment of religion cannot be circumvented by a subsidy, bonus, or reimbursement of expense to individuals for receiving religious instruction and indoctrination . . .

I agree that this Court has left, and always should leave to each state, great latitude in deciding for itself, in the light of its own conditions, what shall be public purposes in its scheme of things. It may make public business of individual welfare, health, education, entertainment, or security. But it cannot make public business of religious worship or instruction, or of attendance at religious institutions of any character. There is no answer to the proposition . . . that the effect of the religious freedom to our Constitution was to take every form of propagation of religion out of the realm of things which could directly or indirectly be made public business and thereby be supported in whole or in part at taxpayers' expense. That is a difference which the Constitution sets up between religion and almost every other subject matter of legislation, a difference which goes to the very root of religious freedom. . . . This freedom was first in the Bill of Rights because it was first in the forefathers' minds; it was set forth in absolute terms, and its strength is its rigidity. It was intended not only to keep the state's hands out of religion, but to keep religion's hands off the state, and, above all, to keep bitter religious controversy out of public life by denying to every denomination any advantage from getting control of public policy and the public purse. . . .

This policy of our Federal Constitution has never been wholly pleasing to most religious groups. They are all quick to invoke its protections; they are all irked when they feel its restraints . . .

But we cannot have it both ways. Religious teaching cannot be a private affair when the state seeks to impose regulations which infringe on it indirectly, and a public affair when it comes to taxing citizens of one faith to aid another, or those of no faith to aid all. If these principles seem harsh in prohibiting aid to Catholic education, it must not be forgotten that it is the same Constitution that alone assures Catholics the right to maintain these schools at all when predominant local sentiment would forbid them, *Pierce* v. *Society of Sisters,* 268 U.S. 510 (1925). Nor should I think that those who have done so well without this aid would want to see this separation between church and state broken down. If the state may aid these religious schools, it may therefore regulate them. Many groups have sought aid from tax funds only to find that it carried political controls with it. Indeed this Court has declared that "It is hardly lack of due process for the government to regulate that which it subsidizes."

But in any event, the great purposes of the Constitution do not depend on the approval or convenience of those they restrain.

(Summer 1983)

The Bible or the Constitution?

Lowell P. Weicker, Jr.

My perspective on religion in America is not that of a historian or a theologian, and I have been accused by at least one New Right politician of flunking constitutional law. That is not true by the way, but neither do I pretend to know it as well as Sam Ervin or Leo Pfeffer. No, my perspective is that of a Member of Congress sworn in all I say and do to uphold the Constitution of the United States, as written by the Founders, amended by Congress and the states, and interpreted by the Supreme Court. And if upholding the Constitution means opposing the president and the tide of public opinion on any of a number of church-state issues before the Congress, then so be it. The choice is not mine to do differently.

During the Ninety-seventh Congress, a coalition was built around the issues of religious liberty and the separation of powers. By standing together, we were able to stop Senator Jesse Helms from seeing his school-prayer bill enacted into law. Unfortunately, Senator Helms is from the "try, try again" school of politics, and in March he presented his calling card to the Ninety-eighth Congress in the form of another bill to promote school prayer. The president is again pushing his alternative: a constitutional amendment to do the same. Tuition tax credits and vouchers for private and parochial schools are again on the agenda, with the administration optimistically factoring them into future deficits.

Abortion, another issue with serious church-state ramifications, is likely to come up again in an appropriations rider, if not a full-fledged bill or constitutional amendment.

So while we can celebrate the fact that the First Amendment emerged from the Ninety-seventh Congress relatively unscathed, we must be prepared to link arms again in the Ninety-eighth.

In my home state, our license plates proudly proclaim Connecticut to be

"The Constitution State," a motto dating back to 1650, when we were the first state to adopt a bill of rights. And it was Mark Twain's "Connecticut Yankee in King Arthur's Court" who decried established religion because it invariably "means death to human liberty and paralysis to human thought."

Unfortunately, Connecticut's record in this regard is not without blemish. Until its disestablishment in 1818, nearly two hundred years after the Pilgrims came to America in search of religious liberty, Congregationalism was Connecticut's official creed. This no doubt made life difficult for the Baptists in Danbury, to whom in 1802 Thomas Jefferson wrote a now famous letter: "Believing with you that religion is a matter which lies solely between man and his God," wrote Jefferson, "I contemplate with solemn reverence the act of the whole American people which declared that their legislature should 'make no law respecting an establishment of religion or prohibiting the free exercise thereof' *thus building a wall of separation between Church and State."* (Emphasis added.)

That wall, embodied in the First Amendment, is perhaps America's most important contribution to political progress on this planet. For as Theodore White put it, "Never in civilization, since the earliest ziggurarts and temples went up in the mud-walled villages of prehistoric Mesopotamia, had there been any state that left each individual to find his way to God without the guidance of the state."

By building this wall between church and state, we stop either from putting barriers between people and their own beliefs. From the first, this was a wall under constant barrage from both sides. It has been battered by courts and Congresses, local governments and boards of education, preachers and presidents. James Madison noted this tendency when as a small boy he happened by a window of the local jail and heard one of the prisoners, who turned out to be a persecuted Baptist minister, preaching the Gospel to a crowd outside.

As a young man just out of Princeton, Madison used livid language in a letter to a friend to express his horror that such practices continued in Virginia. "That diabolical, hell-conceived principle of persecution rages among some," wrote Madison, " and to their eternal infamy, the clergy can furnish their quota of imps for such business."

Just a few years later, he would muster his great skills of persuasion and his reading of John Locke and other writers of the Enlightenment to author "A Memorial and Remonstrance Against Religious Assessments." When I rediscovered that document during the Senate floor debate on school prayer last year, I couldn't resist reading it in its entirety to my colleagues. What genius it contains.

When Madison was engaged in debate in the Virginia legislature with the equally eloquent Patrick Henry, Henry is reported to have named city after ancient city that had fallen after religion decayed. He further asserted that the lack of a tax for support of the church in Virginia was the reason for what he called an alarming decline of morals in that state. Henry appeared to have won the day, but Madison one-upped him in the history department. In every one of those ancient civilizations, said Madison, the church had in fact become an established church, and that was the cause of its decay.

History books are full of such examples, but so are the daily papers of 1983. In India, we read about Hindus killing Muslims. We read about Shiite Muslims battling Sunnite Muslims in Iran and elsewhere in the Middle East. We read about Protestants and Catholics terrorizing each other in Belfast, Northern Ireland. Where does it all end? The answer is that it doesn't until that wall between church and state is solidly in place and held together with the mortar of cooperation and good will.

And it does no good for the folks on one side of the wall to keep their side in good repair if the others let it fall into ruin. That is why every generation of clergy, lay people, and politicians alike must prop up the wall. Today, we do that by fighting radical rewrites of the First Amendment that are masquerading as good, old-fashioned morality.

The most religious among us should actually take the lead against such proposals, because they are the ones with the most to lose if religious liberty becomes a freedom of the past. Indeed, on the national level, many church leaders have come out against school prayer because at best it would be "a least common denominator prayer addressed to whom it may concern." But the message hasn't yet filtered down to the congregations and parishes. It hasn't reached the people who make up the school-prayer majorities in the Harris polls. People need to be reminded that not so many years ago, right here in America, Baptists were being thrown in jail for preaching the Bible as they knew it. They need to be reminded that Catholics, until the election of John F. Kennedy in 1960, were considered by many to be unfit to hold high public office. They need to be reminded that Mormons and Jews were mocked and shunned and excluded from clubs and communities. People need to be reminded, because it could happen again.

I should think my Catholic friends would be especially wary of mixing government with religion. American history is rife with examples of discrimination against them. In the mid-nineteenth century, a struggle ensued in the New York City school system over the daily reading of the King James Version of the Bible and the use of other texts disparaging of the Catholic church. This Protestant bias in the public schools was a primary reason that the archdiocese decided to set up a system of parochial schools.

School-prayer supporters vow that the prayer they have in mind would be both non-denominational and voluntary. But to a child who is six, or even twelve, no prayer recited in school will be truly voluntary. Peer pressure is often at its strongest then—when everyone else bows their head, you bow your head; and when everyone else mutters a prayer, so do you, whether or not you believe it, whether or not it goes against everything you have been taught at home and at church.

I myself attended a private school where not only prayer but worship was mandatory, and believe me it was Protestant in form. As a WASP with an Archbishop of Canterbury among my ancestors, I had all the right credentials to feel at ease; but even I felt uneasy, because the form of worship was Presbyterian. My Jewish and Catholic friends were forced to participate or go stand in the park. And we looked on them as something different, just as they must have looked on themselves. Now this school, mind you, was private. No one was there because they had to be. They chose to be, or their parents chose it for them. Public school students have no such choice. Their attendance is compulsory.

Many clergy are sincerely concerned about the fall in church attendance and the dwindling numbers of applicants to seminaries, and well they might be. But making prayer and other forms of religious expression a government program won't help matters. Government itself is suffering many of the same symptoms. Fewer and fewer people are bothering to vote. Many young people look down on politics as a profession. Political parties, like many churches, have become complacent, too comfortable with their monopolies to get out there and compete. People look at our two-party system and find the ideas and the candidates they have to offer stale and uninspiring. There's the problem with politics and with the church.

Yet, rather than go about fixing up their respective failings, church and state are proposing to join forces. As chairman of the Small Business Committee, I must say that I have never seen a merger between two weak companies succeed, and that is what is being attempted here. In this country, government and religion must stand on their own. If they cannot, then the fault lies not in the Constitution but in those institutions themselves.

We should take to heart Madison's prescription for a free yet moral secular society. According to biographer Irving Brant, Madison's remedy lay in fair laws, proper administration of them, the education of youth, and better adult example. We hear a lot of talk about law and order, but almost always it is in terms of crime on the streets. We underestimate the demoralizing example set by some of the most privileged and best educated in the country who break the law on a daily basis. Whether we are talking about Abscam or Watergate or whatever, we see a privileged group acting as though they were above the law, acting as though because their crime is more sophisticated it bears no similarity to sticking a knife in someone's back. Yet these same individuals may at the same time be some of the most vocal proponents of school prayer. Better adult example, that is what is needed today, not school prayer, or a ban on abortion based on some people's religious beliefs, or even a law proclaiming 1983 the "Year of the Bible."

In a recent radio address, the president urged Americans to "face 1983 with the Bible." I don't believe it is up to a congressman or a senator or even the president to espouse or encourage any one religion, or even religion in general. It is not our job to do the convincing, to take up on Monday where the minister left off on Sunday or the rabbi on Saturday. What I *can* and do encourage, espouse, promote, and plead for is greater understanding of the principles on which our nation was built. So I say to my fellow citizens: Face 1983 with the Constitution. And I say the same to my colleagues in the Congress. For we serve our constituents best when we do our best by that document.

I was recently reelected to my third term. Two years ago, when I began the first of the filibusters against bills seeking to strip the federal courts of jurisdiction over busing, abortion, and school prayer, the common wisdom was that messing with any one of these issues was tantamount to writing your political obituary. But I am living proof that that just isn't so. In fact, these issues may well have provided my margin of victory. Not that the majority of Connecticut voters necessarily agreed with me on school prayer, or abortion, or busing. Many disagreed, and vehemently so. But what they did endorse was the notion that the Constitution represents the best of what American is about. They may not refer to it as a matter of course in their daily lives. But they know it is a tough document that sets some high standards for us all, and they want their senator to stand up and fight for those standards.

People are like this in Connecticut and all over this country. They may say they favor the president's constitutional amendment for school prayer, but when the issues are laid out for them in plain language that is simple and straightforward, they think twice. They begin to consider the consequences. They begin to understand what Madison meant when he urged the American people "to take alarm at the first experiment on our liberties." They begin to realize that by allowing a simple prayer in school today, we invite an inquisition tomorrow. "One is the first step," said Madison, "the other the last one in the career of intolerance."

But before this deeper kind of understanding can take place, somebody has to take the time and the trouble to put the issues in perspective. Somebody has to be the first to stand up and say: "Wait a minute. This may sound like a good idea but it's not." It is hard. It won't win you friends, at least not right away. Sometimes even your loved ones won't understand. But it has to be done.

I'd like to ask you to imagine with me the scene in *A Man for all Seasons,* after the hero, Sir Thomas More, a devout Catholic and leading citizen, has refused to bless the annulment of the king's first marriage. King Henry, hoping to get even, has sent a spy to More's household. Recognizing him for what he is, More's daughter cries: "He's a spy. Arrest him. Father, that man is bad."

More answers: "There's no law against that." But his son-in-law interjects: "There is. God's law." More replies: "Then God can arrest him."

Meanwhile, More's daughter is becoming more and more exasperated as it becomes clear that the spy will be allowed to escape. "While you talk, he's gone," she complains.

"And go he should if he was the Devil himself," says More, "until he broke the law."

Sarcastically, his son-in-law inquires: "So now you'd give the Devil the benefit of the law?"

"What would you do?" More asks him. "Cut down a great road through the law to get after the Devil?"

And his son-in-law replies, "Yes, I'd cut down every law in England to do that."

That was when More had him. "Oh?" he said, "and when the last law was down, and the Devil turned around on you, where would you hide, the laws all being flat? This country's planted thick with laws—man's laws, not God's— and if you cut them down do you really think you could stand upright in the winds that would blow then?"

The wall of separation between church and state is just this sort of law. With it, we are sheltered from the winds of intolerance. Without it our nation could hardly stand as it does today, a haven where people of all religions can live together in peace.

In conclusion, what we are all fighting for is the freedom to interpret life and the world around us as we choose. Our purpose is not to promote Catholicism or Judaism or Buddhism or the faith of Islam. For, indeed, it may be that none of these is the true faith. Perhaps there is one but it has yet to be proclaimed. And when the day comes to pass when it is proclaimed, then in America, if nowhere else on this planet, it will be taught and it will be heard. We hold that door open to the future by fighting for religious freedom today.

(Summer 1983)

The Founding Fathers and the Courage to Doubt

Daniel J. Boorstin

In late winter of February 1790, when Benjamin Franklin at the age of eighty-four was gravely and painfully ill and suspected that he did not have much longer to live, he received a letter from his old friend Reverend Ezra Stiles, then president of Yale, asking him for the specifics of his religion. It was a serious matter for Stiles. He had spent some years experimenting with electricity at Franklin's suggestion, and then spent many years reflecting on whether he really believed in the Christian doctrine when he accepted ordination.

Franklin's reply was laced with Franklin wit. He said, "I believe in one God, Creator of the universe. That He governs it by His providence. That He ought to be worshiped. That the most acceptable service we render Him is doing good to His other children." But Stiles had also asked him what he thought of the divinity of Jesus. To which Franklin replied, "I think the system of morals and his religion as he left them to us, the best the world ever saw or is likely to see; but I have, with most of the present Dissenters in England, some doubts as to his divinity; though it is a question that I do not dogmatize upon, having never studied it, and think it needless to busy myself with it now, when I expect soon an opportunity of knowing the truth with less trouble."

With his usual political concern, Franklin added the request that Stiles should not make his letter public because, Franklin said, "I've never let others enjoy their religious sentiments, without reflecting on them for those that appeared to me unsupportable and even absurd. All sects here, and we have a great variety, have experienced my good will in assisting them with subscriptions for building their new places of worship; and, as I never opposed any of their doctrines, I hope to go out of the world in peace with them all."

I think this parable represents the beliefs of at least many of the Founding Fathers and the spirit that formed their making of much of the Constitution. I would like, from the vantage point of Franklin's skepticism, to try to offer a larger historical perspective, to take the discussion of religion in politics out of the halls of legislatures and try to put it in the macrocosm of world history.

The United States was the first modern nation founded on purpose in the bright light of history. The mere existence of the nation itself was a kind of Declaration of Independence from the folk gods and religious and semireligious myths that had always and everywhere surrounded governments and their rulers. Kings and queens were customarily crowned and hallowed by priests, bishops, cardinals, and popes. And they had good reason to want the odor of sanctity. Queen Elizabeth I, for example, made trouble for an author who wrote too freely describing the dethroning of her predecessor Richard II. Prudent divine-right sovereigns saw their protection lay in controlling the prying research of inquiring historians. They preferred simply to legitimize themselves by descent from the Trojans or from the gods.

Some would say that religious liberty is probably the most distinctive and certainly one of the greatest contributions of the American experience to all human progress. Religious liberty in the United States is the product of not only the courageous personal humility of the Founding Fathers, as well as a by-product of some happy facts of American history. These are no less important because they appear obvious, but we're inclined to ignore them.

First, since the founding of a nation—by an act of revolution and by the framing of a Constitution—was accomplished in a relatively brief time, living men and women could see that it was a product of their struggles, discussion, and handiwork, not the fiat of some sanctified, myth-enshrouded past.

Second, the nation was created from areas with diverse sects. Oddly enough, the fact that the colonies already had their several and various established churches contributed to this necessity. A federal nation was plainly not founded on an orthodox religious base. In Europe, the Protestant Reformation came as a disruptive force into the relatively monolithic world of the medieval church. In England, for example, Protestant orthodoxy was indelibly identified with national identity. In the American colonies, religious variety preceded political unity and had to be accommodated within it.

Third, the diffusion of American colonial settlements with no one capital, the great distance of colonial urban centers from one another, and the oceanic separation from London or Rome, all made religious independence a fact of geography as well as of theology. So much of the population was at the edges and out beyond the range of the churches. One of the consequences of this was a different line of historical development of the relation between church and state, one which is so grand and so unique that we are perhaps inclined to ignore it. Over there, the development was generally from religious orthodoxy enforced by the state, to toleration—and only later to religious liberty. Historically speaking, of course, religious toleration is to be sharply contrasted to religious liberty.

Toleration implies the existence of an established church, and toleration is always a revocable concession rather than a defensible right. In the United States, for the first time in modern Western history, the nation leaped from the provincial religious preference of its regions into religious liberty for the whole nation. The Founding Fathers despised the condescension that was implied in the very concept of toleration. That was a stage necessary for Old World nations, but not for our New World nation.

Religious persecution, that is to say, the punishment, torture, execution, or civil disability of individuals for their refusal to embrace a particular religious doctrine, is a modern Western and especially a Christian invention. It was virtually unknown in Greek and Roman antiquity. Socrates was condemned to death for essentially a political crime. In Rome, where religion seems to have been more in the nature of a patriotic ritual than an affirmation of doctrinal orthodoxy, the execution of Christians in the first three centuries was less because of governmental opposition to their theology than for their refusal to participate in the imperial rites. It is well known, of course, that as the Roman empire expanded the Romans simply incorporated the local deities into the Roman pantheon.

Judaism, monotheistic and theocratic, did offer more basis for intolerance. While the Jews detested and opposed idolatry, their religion remained in many respects national or perhaps even tribal. Of the Eastern religions, Buddhism was notoriously free from intolerance. The only example of Buddhism appearing to become the basis for persecution—in seventeenth-century Japan—turns out to have been for political and not for theological purposes and was stirred by the fear of Christian missionaries. Hinduism, with its wealth of pantheistic lore, was not a persecuting religion and did not encounter problems of religious warfare and genocide until it encountered Islam, which was of course a successor to Christianity.

Christianity then, along with its benefits, sought also the spirit of intolerance and persecution. The Protestant Reformation did not help much against these particular evils. It brought a new version of religious (now Protestant) persecution, and it was a long time before the Reformation brought political liberalism and religious liberty. Some of the most bitter religious wars in Western history—the Thirty Years' War, for example, between 1616 and 1648, which we are told killed one-tenth of the population of Germany, mainly for religious doctrinal reasons—were taking place at the very time that the New England Puritans were settling in the New World in quest of their own religious liberty, and incidentally, their freedom to persecute in their own way.

But after the American Revolution, Washington, Jefferson, and others could see what the New England Puritans could not see, that their government was not described and foremodeled in the Bible but was the prudential product of human struggle, compromise, and the pursuit of decency.

From the force of circumstances, as well as from long and deep reflection, our Founding Fathers brought forth this nation in the wholesome atmosphere of the courage to doubt. Federalism in politics meant pluralism in religion, which incidentally meant a faith in the wisdom of mankind but a doubt of the wisdom of orthodox man. Their spirituality, their God, was a God of common human quest and not the God of anybody's dogma.

There is no more eloquent apostle of the courage to doubt than Jefferson. Belief in the happy diversity of mankind and human thought was for him probably his first religious axiom after belief in God. "Rebellion to tyrants is obedience to God," was the motto that Jefferson chose for his seal in 1776. Jefferson's God was a God not of orthodoxy, but of diversity. "As the creator has made no two faces alike," Jefferson said, "so no two minds, and probably no two creeds," and he substantiated this view with the latest psychology and medicine of his day. He believed that the study of the variety of creation itself was an act of worship. In 1811, when Jefferson was about to resume friendly relations with his old friend John Adams, from whom he had been separated by bitter differences of opinion, he asked, "Why should we be dissocialized by mere differences of opinion in politics, in religion, in philosophy, or anything else? His opinions are as honestly formed as my own. Our different views of the same subject are the result of a difference in our organization and experience." So it's not surprising that Jefferson refused to accept the dogma of any religious sect. He made his own humanist anthology of the teachings of Jesus and we reap a rich harvest of his differences with John Adams from his treasure trove of correspondence in his last years.

An eloquent and reverent expression of the implications of this courage to doubt—a belief in religious liberty and the creator's delight in the multiformity of men's minds—was offered by Thomas Paine, who was a prophet and publicist of the American Revolution and never a favorite of dogmatic theologians.

This is what Paine wrote in the *Rights of Man* in 1792: "If we suppose a large family of children who . . . made it their custom to present to their parents some token of their affection and gratitude, each of them would make a different offering, and most probably in a different manner. Some would pay their congratulations in themes of verse and prose, by some little devices as their genius dictated, or according to what they thought would please, and, perhaps the least of all, not being able to do any of those things, would ramble into the garden or the field and gather what it thought the prettiest flower it could find, though, perhaps it might be but a simple weed. The parent would be more gratified by such a variety. . . . But of all unwelcome things, nothing could more afflict the parent than to know that the whole of them had afterward gotten together by the ears, boys and girls, fighting, scratching, reviling, and abusing each other about which was the best or the worst present."

In this way, Paine, as Jefferson did on so many occasions, affirmed his belief in some divine ordination of diversity and man's duty to preserve the opportunity to express that diversity.

The courage to doubt, on which American pluralism, federalism, and religious liberty are founded, is a special brand of courage, a more selfless brand of courage, than the courage of orthodoxy. A brand that has been far rarer and more precious in the history of the West than the courage of the crusaders or the true believer who has so little respect for his fellow man and for his thoughts and feelings that he makes himself the court of last resort on the most difficult matters on which wise men have disagreed for millennia.

(Summer 1983)

IX.

The *Free Inquiry* Interview

The interview is not always the most edifying of literary genres. The temptation to chitchat, or to pontificate, is not easily resisted. On the other hand, interviews with important thinkers and creators can offer something even their best work can't: a stimulating, surprising back-and-forth. Moreover, such occasions provide these thinkers and creators the opportunity to answer their critics, to review their own career, to revise or clarify their positions, and to publicly declare their future course.

Free Inquiry has sat down with prominent humanists from time to time and explored the sources of their work. There is no chitchat here—the themes most often returned to are the role of science in our culture and throughout history, the religious mind, and the survival and future of humankind. Importantly, there is also very little "summing up"; the interviewee remains as interrogative as the interviewer. In other words, everything's open to question. Says Isaac Asimov: "Nothing is sacred, at least in a country that considers itself intellectually free."

That goes for Asimov's own opinions, which are always open to change. That does not mean Asimov believes everything is relative. "I have an article of faith," he notes: "the universe makes sense." It makes sense when penetrated by rational principles—not religious ones. He is therefore understandably perplexed by Bible believers—especially those who regard the Bible as a kind of science textbook. "If we insist on the Bible being literally true, then we must abandon the scientific method totally and completely." The quest of science has made him an astonishingly prolific author—there's 450 books and counting—as well as "an atheist, out and out." The Bible was written by human beings, "not some superhuman one."

But this does not mean that the question of religion is not amenable to the scientist's approach. E. O. Wilson, for example, has written that the "religious impulse" might be programmed into our very genetics. What does humankind do now that our old faiths, the great revelatory religions, no longer convince in the age of scientific materialism? Says Wilson in this interview with Jeffrey Saver: "I abandoned the doctrines of my religious background rather early, in the traditional manner of an emancipated young college student and intellectual. Yet I remained very sensitive to the deep religious needs of people that I had perceived so vividly when I was growing up. . . . I saw the power of the charismatic religion all around me, in my family and the people I lived with, and therefore could appreciate the strength of the need that people have for some kind of satisfaction of the religious impulse. Probably a major motivation in my later research . . . has been to recapture that religious feeling but in a more sustainable form." This is no merely academic pursuit. "The emotional power of religion is too easily captured by nationalism and madmen's fantasies." Our future depends on finding something to capture it back in the very near future.

B. F. Skinner agrees. "My first and ultimate concern [is] for the present and *future* well-being of the human species. I would almost be willing to say simply *future*." When pressed on the subject by *Free Inquiry* editor Paul Kurtz, Skinner does not shy away from the less popular aspects of his behaviorist theory, especially his thoughts on self-determination—traditionally a humanistic virtue. In *Beyond Freedom and Dignity* Skinner has argued that our valued sense of individualism may mean the death of the species. Here, Skinner claims that "Western civilization is suffering from *libertas nervosa*."

Any future society will be educated largely by television. No one appreciates this fact—with more hope and dread—than Steve Allen, inventor of the television talk show and emcee of one of television's finest series, "Meeting of Minds." Allen doesn't dispute the common wisdom that television has become a wasteland, but he knows that it is also our best chance for intellectual and moral amelioration. Legislation written to make us behave better won't work. "You can never order people to be virtuous," says Allen. But "virtue can be encouraged by example."

—R.B.

Isaac Asimov on Science and the Bible

Paul Kurtz: In your view is the Bible widely known and intelligently read today?

Isaac Asimov: It is undoubtedly widely known. It is probably owned by more people than any other book. As to how widely it is read one cannot be certain. I suppose it is read very widely in the sense that people just look at the words and read it mechanically. How many people actually think about the words they read, I'm not at all certain. They can go to a house of worship and hear verses read without thinking about what the words mean. Undoubtedly millions of people do.

Kurtz: There used to be something called the Higher Biblical Criticism. What has happened to that?

Asimov: I am constantly hearing, from people who accept the Bible more or less literally, that the Higher Criticism has been outmoded and discredited, but I don't believe that at all. This is just something that people say who insist on clinging to the literal truth of the Bible. The Higher Criticism, which in the nineteenth century, for example, tried to show that the first few books of the Bible contained several strains that could be identified and separated. I think is as valid today as it ever was. Fundamentally, there is a J-document and a P-document in the early chapters of Genesis and an E-document later on. I have no doubt that as one continues to investigate these things one constantly learns and raises new questions.

Kurtz: But by and large the public does not know much about this skeptical, critical interpretation of the Bible. Would you say that is so?

Asimov: Yes. Just as by and large the public doesn't know about any of the disputes there have been about quantum theory. The public knows only what it reads in the newspapers and sees on television, and this is all extremely superficial.

Kurtz: One thing I am struck by is that today in America we don't have a free market of ideas in regard to religion and the Bible. You are an outstanding exception. You have taken the Bible seriously and have submitted it to critical analysis. Would you agree that, although free inquiry concerning the Bible goes on in scholarly journals, and perhaps in university classes and in some books, the public hears mostly pro-religious propaganda—such as from the pulpits of the electronic church, from various religious publications, and from the daily press— and very rarely any kind of questioning or probing of biblical claims?

Asimov: I imagine that the large majority of the population, in the United States at least, either accepts every word of the Bible as it is written or gives it very little thought and would be shocked to hear anyone doubt that the Bible is correct in every way. So when someone says something that sounds as though he assumes that the Bible was written by human beings—fallible human beings who were wrong in this respect or that—he can rely on being vilified by large numbers of people who are essentially ignorant of the facts, and not many people care to subject themselves to this.

Kurtz: Do you take the Bible primarily as a human document or do you think it was divinely inspired?

Asimov: The Bible *is* a human document. Much of it is great poetry, and much of it consists of the earliest reasonable history that survives. Samuel 1 and 2 antedate Herodotus by several centuries. A great deal of the Bible may contain successful ethical teachings, but the rest is at best allegory and at worst myth and legend. Frankly, I don't think that anything is divinely inspired. I think everything that human beings possess of intelligent origin is humanly inspired, with no exceptions.

Kurtz: Earlier you said that the Bible contained fallible writings. What would some of these be?

Asimov: In my opinion, the biblical account of the creation of the universe and of the earth and humanity is wrong in almost every respect. I believe that those cases where it can be argued that the Bible is not wrong are, if not trivial, then coincidental. And I think that the account of a worldwide flood, as opposed, say, to a flood limited to the Tigris-Euphrates region, is certainly wrong.

Kurtz: The creationists think there is evidence for the Noachian flood.

Asimov: The creationists think there is evidence for every word in the Bible. I think all of the accounts of human beings living before the flood, such as Adam and Eve and Cain and Abel, are at best very dim memories of ancient Sumerian rulers; and even the stories about Abraham, Isaac, and Jacob I rather think are vague legends.

Kurtz: Based on oral tradition?

Asimov: Yes, and with all the distortions that oral traditions sometimes undergo.

Kurtz: In your book *In the Beginning,* you say that creation is a myth. Why do you think it is scientifically false? What are some of the main points?

Asimov: Well, all of the scientific evidence we have seems to indicate that the universe is billions of years old. But there is no indication whatsoever of that in the Bible if it is interpreted literally rather than allegorically. Creationists insist on interpreting it literally. According to the information we have, the earth is billions of years younger than the universe.

Kurtz: It is four and a half billion years old.

Asimov: The earth is, and the universe is possibly fifteen billion years old. The universe may have existed ten billion years before the earth, but according to the biblical description of creation the earth, the sun, the moon, and the stars were all created at the same time. As a matter of fact, according to the Bible, the earth itself existed from the beginning, whereas the stars, sun, and moon were created on the fourth day.

Kurtz: Yes, so they have it backward.

Asimov: They have that backward, and they have plant life being created before the sun. All the evidence we have indicates that this is not so. The Bible says that every plant, and every animal, was created after its own kind, which would indicate that species have been as they are now from the very beginning and have never changed. Despite what the creationists say, the fossil record, as well as very subtle biochemical evidence, geological evidence, and all sorts of other evidence, indicates that species have changed, that there has been a long evolutionary process that has lasted over three billion years.

Kurtz: It's not simply biology that they are questioning, but geology, astronomy, and the whole basis of the physical sciences.

Asimov: If we insist on the Bible's being literally true, then we must abandon the scientific method totally and completely. There's no way that we can at the same time try to discover the truth by means of observation and reason and also accept the Bible as true.

Kurtz: So what is at stake in this debate between evolution and creationism is not simply the principle of evolution in regard to living things but the whole status of the sciences themselves?

Asimov: That is what I believe. But I have letters from creationists who say that they don't deny the scientific method, that they are just trying to examine the inconsistencies in the evidence presented by the evolutionists. However, that is not what should be the chief job of the creationists. What they should do is present positive evidence in favor of creationism, which is something they never do. They confine themselves to pointing out inconsistencies in the evolutionary view, not hesitating to create those inconsistencies by distortion and, in my opinion, in some cases by outright fraud. Then they say that they have "proved" that evolutionary theory is false, and therefore creationism is correct.

Kurtz: Of course you don't deny that *how* evolution occurs is not fully or finally formulated.

Asimov: Certainly there are many arguments over the mechanism of evolution, but our knowledge about the evolutionary process is much greater than it was in Darwin's day. The present view of evolution is far more subtle and wide-ranging than Darwin's was or could have been. But it still is not firmly and finally settled. There remain many arguments over the exact mechanism of evolution, and furthermore there are many scientists who are dissatisfied with some aspects of evolution that most other scientists accept. There are always minority views among scientists in every respect, but virtually no scientist denies the fact of evolution. It is as though we were all arguing about just exactly what makes a car go even though nobody denies that cars go.

Kurtz: What about the metaphorical interpretations? When I was growing up, the general view was that we should accept creationism and that it is not incompatible with evolution but is to be interpreted metaphorically or allegorically in terms of stages.

Asimov: There is always that temptation. I am perfectly willing, for instance, to interpret the Bible allegorically and to speak of the days of creation as representing eons of indefinite length. Clarence Darrow badgered William Jennings Bryan into admitting that the days could have been very long. This horrified Bryan's followers, as it would horrify creationists today. You can say that the entire first chapter of Genesis is a magnificent poem representing a view of creation as transcending the silly humanoid gods of the Babylonians and presenting a great abstract deity who by his word alone brings the universe into existence. You can compare this with the Big Bang. You can say that God said "Let there be light" and then there was the Big Bang; and one could then follow with all sorts of parallels and similarities if one wished. I have no objection to that.

Kurtz: But aren't the stages wrong, even if it is interpreted metaphorically? You said earlier that, according to the Bible, God created the earth before the heavenly bodies.

Asimov: Yes. Some of the stages are wrong. But you could say that, when the Bible says "In the beginning God created the heaven and the earth," what was really meant was the universe. We could say that, at the time the first chapter of Genesis was written, when people spoke of the earth they meant everything there was. But as our vision and perspective expanded we saw that what was really meant was the universe. Thus, if necessary, we can modify the words. But the creationists won't do this; they insist on the literal interpretation of the creation story. When it says "earth" they want it to mean *Earth;* when it says on the first "day" they want it to mean a twenty-four-hour day.

Kurtz: When the Bible says, "And God made the firmament," what does it mean? Isn't that odd?

Asimov: Well, if you trace the word *firmament* back to its original meaning, it is a thin, beaten layer of metal. It is like the top you put on a platter in a restaurant. It is like the lid of a dish. The earth is a dish and the firmament comes down upon it on all sides. It is a material object that separates things. There are waters above the firmament and waters below. In fact, in the Book of Revelation, which was written about 100 C.E., centuries after Genesis was written, the writer describes the firmament as folding up like a scroll. It was still viewed as a thin metal plate. But we know as surely as we can know anything at all that there is no firmament up there—there's no thin metal layer—there's only an atmosphere, and beyond it a vacuum, an empty space, except where there are planets, stars, and other objects. The blueness of it is an illusion due to the scattering of light, and the blackness of night is due to the absence of any light that we can see, and so on.

Kurtz: In a metaphorical interpretation, how would you interpret "the waters above and the waters below"? Does that make any sense?

Asimov: Not to me. Obviously the people who first wrote about the waters above the firmament were thinking of rain. The rain supposedly came down through the windows in the firmament. There were little holes, as in a shower head, and the rain drizzled through. I don't blame them for not understanding. I don't criticize the ancients for not knowing what we know. It took centuries to work up this knowledge, and the ancients contributed their share. They were every bit as intelligent as we are and every bit as much seekers after the truth. I'm willing to admit that. But the fact is that they didn't know as much as we know now.

Kurtz: They were limited by the prevailing scientific and philosophical views of the day.

Asimov: And by the little that had been learned up to that time. So this seemed a logical explanation of the rain. They didn't know the nature of the evaporation from the ocean. They didn't understand what the clouds really were and that is why they spoke of the waters above the firmament and below, but there is no reason that we should speak of it that way.

Kurtz: If you take Genesis metaphorically, you can believe in the theory of evolution as the Big Bang and also that everything evolved, so this need not be a threat to science necessarily?

Asimov: No, if you are willing to say that the universe began fifteen billion years ago—the exact number of billions of years is under dispute—as a tiny object that expanded rapidly and dropped in temperature, and all the other things that scientists believe happened, then you can say that God created it, and the laws of nature that controlled it, and that he then sat back and watched it develop. I would be content to have people say that. Frankly, I don't believe it, but there's no way one can disprove it.

Kurtz: You don't believe it? You don't think there is sufficient evidence that there was a cosmic egg that shattered and that God created this cosmic egg?

Asimov: I believe there's enough evidence for us to think that a big bang took place. But there is no evidence whatsoever to suppose that a superhuman being said, "Let it be." However, neither is there any evidence against it; so, if a person feels comfortable believing that, I am willing to have him believe it.

Kurtz: As an article of faith?

Asimov: Yes, as an article of faith. I have articles of faith, too. I have an article of faith that says the universe makes sense. Now there's no way you can prove that the universe makes sense, but there's just no fun in living in the universe if it doesn't make sense.

Kurtz: The universe is intelligible because you can formulate hypotheses and make predictions and there are regularities.

Asimov: Yes, and my belief is that no matter how far we go we will always find that the universe makes sense. We will never get to the point where it suddenly stops making sense. But that is just an assumption on my part.

Kurtz: Religion then postulates and brings in God.

Asimov: Except it tends to retreat. At the very start you had rain gods and sun gods. You had a god for every single natural phenomenon. Nothing took place without some minor deity personally arranging it. In the Middle Ages some people thought the planets revolved around the earth because there were angels pushing them, because they didn't know about the Galilean notion that the planets didn't require a constant impetus to keep moving. Well, if people want to accept a God as initiating the big bang, let them. But the creationists won't do that.

Kurtz: Are you fearful that this development of a literal interpretation of the Bible is anti-science and can undermine rationality in this country and in the rest of the world?

Asimov: I don't believe it can actually stop sensible people from thinking sensibly, but it can create a situation whereby there are laws against allowing sensible people to think sensibly in the open. Right now the fight is over creation and evolution. In the long run, in any fight between evolutionists and creationists, evolution will win as long as human beings have sense. But there are laws now in Louisiana and Arkansas, and other legislatures are considering similar laws.

Kurtz: It was struck down in Arkansas.

Asimov: Fortunately! But wherever the law exists, school teachers must teach creationism if they mention evolution. This is a dreadful precedent. In the United States a state can say: "This is scientific. This is what you must teach in science." Whereas in many nations that have had an established church—nations we may have looked upon as backward—they nevertheless understood that within the subsystem of science it is science that decides what is scientific. It is scientists who make the decision. It is in the scientific marketplace that ideas win or lose. If they want to teach religion, they can teach it outside of science, and they can say that all of science is wicked and atheistic. But to force their way into science and to dictate what scientists must declare science to be destroys the meaning of all of science. It is an absolutely impossible situation and scientists should not permit it without a fight to the very end.

Kurtz: I fully share your concern. What about religion itself? Should religion be a subject for free inquiry? Should examination of the Bible be openly discussed in American society?

Asimov: I don't see why not. I think nothing is sacred, at least in a country that considers itself intellectually free. We can study the political process all we want. We can examine the reasoning behind communism, fascism, and Nazism. We can consider the Ku Klux Klan and what they believe. There is nothing that we should not be able to examine.

Kurtz: And your examination of the Bible indicates that it is contradicted in many places by modern science?

Asimov: Yes. Now this does not automatically mean that science is correct and the Bible is wrong, although I think it is. People should examine it. One thing we cannot do is to say without examination that the Bible is right.

Kurtz: Isaac, how would you describe your own position? Agnostic, atheist, rationalist, humanist?

Asimov: I am an atheist, out and out. It took me a long time to say it. I've been an atheist for years and years, but somehow I felt it was intellectually unrespectable to say one was an atheist, because it assumed knowledge that one didn't have. Somehow it was better to say one was a humanist or an agnostic. I finally decided that I'm a creature of emotion as well as of reason. Emotionally I am an atheist. I don't have the evidence to prove that God doesn't exist, but I so strongly suspect he doesn't that I don't want to waste my time.

Kurtz: But the burden of proof is on the person who claims God exists. You don't believe in Santa Claus, but you can't disprove his existence. The burden of proof is upon those who maintain the claim.

Asimov: Yes. In any case, I am an atheist.

Kurtz: You have no doubt reflected a good deal on this. Can people live without the God myth, without religion? You don't need it presumably. Does man need it?

Asimov: Well, individual human beings may. There's a certain comfort, I suppose, in thinking that you will be with all of your loved ones again after death, that death is not the end, that you'll live again in some kind of never-never land with great happiness. Maybe some people even get a great deal of comfort out of knowing that all the people they they don't like are going to go straight to hell. These are all comforts. Personally, they don't comfort me. I'm not interested in having anyone suffer eternally in hell, because I don't believe that any crime is so nearly infinite in magnitude as to deserve infinite punishment. I feel that I couldn't bring myself to condemn anyone to eternal punishment. I am opposed to punishment.

Kurtz: The height of wickedness, is it not?

Asimov: Yes. I feel if I can't do it, then God, who presumably is a much more noble being than I am, could certainly not do it. Furthermore, I can't help but believe that eternal happiness would eventually be boring. I cannot grasp the notion of eternal anything. My own way of thinking is that after death there is nothingness. Nothingness is the only thing that I think is worth accepting.

Kurtz: Do you think that one can lead a moral life, that life is meaningful, and that one can be just and noble without a belief in God?

Asimov: Well, as easily as with a belief in God. I don't feel that people who believe in God will automatically be noble, but neither do I think they will automatically be wicked. I don't think those who don't believe in God will be automatically noble or automatically wicked either. I think this is a choice for every human being, and frankly I think that perhaps if you don't believe in God this puts a greater strain on you, in the sense that you have to live up to your own feelings of ethics. But, if you do believe in God, you also believe in forgiveness. There is no one to forgive me.

Kurtz: No escape hatch.

Asimov: That's right. If I do something wrong, I have to face myself and I may not be able to figure out a way of forgiving myself. But, if you believe in God, there are usually rituals whereby you may express contrition and be forgiven, and so on. So it seems to me that many people can feel free to sin and repent afterward. I don't. In my way of life, there may be repentance but it doesn't make up for the sin.

Kurtz: Of course a lot of people who are humanists say that, if ethics is based upon either fear of God or love of God and his punishment and reward, then one is not really ethical, that ethics must grow out of human experience.

Asimov: Well, I said the same thing in an argument about what I called the Reagan doctrine. Early in what I already consider his disastrous administration, Reagan said that one couldn't believe anything the Soviets said because they didn't believe in God. In my view, maybe you can't believe anything the Soviets say, but not for that reason. If you are ethical only because you believe in God, you are buying your ticket to heaven or trying to tear up your ticket to hell. In either case, you are just being a shrewd profiteer, nothing else. The idea of being ethical is to be ethical for no reason except that that is the way to be if you want the world to run smoothly. I think that people who say virtue is its own reward or honesty is the best policy have the right idea.

Kurtz: Are you suggesting that morality is autonomous, that you learn by living and that one doesn't need an independent religious support for moral choice?

Asimov: Yes. If a group of people are living together in a community where there is a lot of lying and stealing going on, it is an unpleasant way to live. But if everyone tells the truth and is honest and thoughtful of his neighbor, it is a good way to live. You don't need to go any further than that.

Kurtz: Is there one value that you have always felt is the most important—one moral principle?

Asimov: I am scrupulously honest, financially speaking, but I have never really had a serious temptation to be otherwise. I long for a temptation so that I can prove to myself that I am really scrupulously honest, you see.

Kurtz: I thought you were going to say that you were committed to truth and knowledge!

Asimov: When I think of being committed to truth and knowledge, that seems to be such a natural sort of thing. How can anyone be anything else? I give myself no credit for that. I don't see how it is possible to be tempted away from it, and if you can't be tempted away from it then there is no point in even considering it a virtue. It is like saying that it is a virtue to breathe. But when I think of truth, I wonder about telling those little social lies we tell for our own convenience, such as telling someone you have another appointment when you don't want to go out some evening. I don't have much occasion to do that, but I guess I am as prone to it as almost anyone is. Although I am apt to call someone up and say, "Gee, I meant to call you yesterday but I forgot." I probably shouldn't say that. I should say that I was busy all day long.

Kurtz: These are not great moral dilemmas. Have you never been tested or challenged morally? You are a man of great courage, but perhaps you are old enough that you don't have to worry.

Asimov: There's no such thing as not having to worry. I suppose that if people wanted to make a big fuss about my atheism it could conceivably reflect itself in the sales of my books so that my economic security would suffer. I figure, what the hell! There is a certain amount of insistence inside me to prevent me from bartering my feelings, opinions, or views for the sake of a few extra dollars.

Kurtz: So you have the courage of your convictions?

Asimov: I suppose so, or it may be just a desire to avoid the unpleasantness of shame! Unfortunately, many people define wickedness not according to what a person does but according to what a person believes. So an atheist who lives an upright and noble life, let us say, is nevertheless considered wicked. Indeed, a religious believer might argue that an upright and noble atheist is far more wicked than an atheist who happens to be a murderer or a crook.

Kurtz: Is this because the atheist lacks faith in God, and that is considered the ultimate "sin"?

Asimov: Yes. The atheist who is a murderer or a crook gives a bad example for atheism and persuades everyone else not to be atheistic. But a noble and upright atheist, so the believer fears, causes people to doubt the existence of God by the mere fact that a person who does not believe in God can still be upright and noble. Religious believers might argue that way, but I think that is a horrible perversion of thought and of morality.

(Spring 1982)

B. F. Skinner on Humanism, Freedom, and the Future of the Human Species

Paul Kurtz: In what sense do you consider yourself a humanist?

B. F. Skinner: In the sense of one who puts the present and future well-being of the human species above all other things. Everyone is a humanist who acts to preserve the resources of the world, prevent its pollution, keep the population within bounds, and make a nuclear holocaust impossible.

Kurtz: Would you add the term *secular?*

Skinner: By all means. I do not believe that the inhabitants of one of the smaller planets of a small sun will ever fully understand this enormous universe—how it began or what will happen to it. It does not help me to suppose that it was created according to plan by a god, nor do I believe that any god has ever revealed to us any such action or plan. Moreover, I think we know enough about human behavior to know why all cultures have invented gods, usually in the image of a ruler or father to turn to for help and to thank for good fortune, as well as to administer supposed rewards and punishments for social purposes.

Kurtz: There are humanist critics of your viewpoint, particularly of the idea of freedom (e.g., Thomas Szasz, Eric Fromm, Karl Popper). Can we clarify in what sense you believe in freedom? We are not talking about determinism vs. free will but, given alternative political and social systems, whether you believe in democracy.

Skinner: Note that I said that my first and ultimate concern was for the present and *future* well-being of the human species. I would almost be willing to say simply *future.* Certainly the future is more important in terms of quantity. Those of us alive on the earth today are presumably only a small sample of the species. I believe a genuine humanism must look to the future.

The trouble is, the future doesn't exist. We deal with it only as a prediction, and hence ineffectively. To make matters worse, action that is likely to promote a future tends to conflict with current interests. For example, there are many reasons why the earth is overpopulated: sex is highly reinforcing, in many parts of the world children are important economically, governments and religions often assess their power in terms of the sheer number of constituents, and so on. Those are current reasons, and they conflict with any effort to reduce the population of the earth in order to prevent its ultimate destruction.

My book *Beyond Freedom and Dignity* was a defense of the future of the species against present personal satisfactions. I was not saying "Down with freedom and dignity"; I was saying that something lay beyond them. The gains that have come from the historical struggle for freedom are very real and should be preserved in a continuing defense of personal rights, but the process can go too far. I recently prepared a paper for an international congress on the environmental future in which I drew a parallel between our current concern for rights and the disease *anorexia nervosa*. In a typical case, an overweight woman starts to reduce, passes through a satisfactory weight, and proceeds to become extremely emaciated. I suggested that a similar illness might be called *libertas nervosa*. We reach a stage in which the individual is freed from unreasonable control by the group and then pass on to a demand for lesser "rights" that do not contribute to the future of the species. Indeed, the "right to be let alone," to breed, consume, pollute the world, and construct weapons that could destroy all life on the earth may prove to be a lethal trait.

Another illness might be called *caritas nervosa*. A culture is strong if it gives help to those who need it—among them the very young, the severely ill, the aged, and the impoverished—but a culture actually grows weaker when it gives help to those who do not need it. A wise god would not help those who help themselves; he would not deny them the satisfaction of achievement. In a world in which it is too easy to get help, we lack incentives. Very few reasons for doing anything survive, and we turn, as the leisure classes have always turned, to alcohol and drugs, gambling, extremes of sexual gratification, and vicarious violence, as in professional sports.

Western civilization is suffering from both *libertas nervosa* and *caritas nervosa*. Technology has freed us from starvation, extremes of heat and cold, and many illnesses, but it has gone on to gratify our slightest wishes. (Watch the advertisements on television if you want proof.) And all in the name of rights. None of this is any longer working for the welfare of the species. It is, in fact, a threat. Thomas Szasz has a bad case of *libertas nervosa* and Eric Fromm was suffering from *caritas nervosa*.

Kurtz: What about those critics who maintain that you do not appreciate pluralism, dissent, and the open society?

Skinner: I believe that it has been a good thing to challenge, weaken, and destroy central autocratic forms of power. To date, a relatively unplanned pluralistic society has probably done more for the future of the species than any closed plan. But that is not so much evidence of the success of an open society as of the failure of all other plans to date. Can anyone accept the world today as proof of the ultimate value of *any* past or present form of government, religion, or economic system? I think we should look for better forms, and they will necessarily be planned. Placing the good of the species above the individual is not placing the state above the individual. A good plan would certainly preserve diversity and remain "open" to change in the light of experience. In particular, it would sample and respond to satisfactions and dissatisfactions much more accurately than does democracy in America today. I believe that the traditional aggrandizement of the individual in governmental, religious, and economic philosophies is responsible for much of our present trouble and for the present very real threat to the species.

There was a deeper significance to the argument in *Beyond Freedom and Dignity,* which I elaborated shortly after the book was published in a lecture at the Poetry Society in New York. The lecture was called "On 'Having' a Poem," and in it I drew a parallel between a poet and a mother. The mother has a baby. It is *her* baby, but she is not responsible for any of its features. She gave it half its genes, but she got those from her own father and mother. She simply nourished and protected the developing organism during a critical phase. I suggested that the same thing could be said of poets. If we knew all the reasons they write poems, we should not give them credit, any more than we give mothers credit for any feature of *their* products.

At the turn of the century, Samuel Butler made the point that a hen is simply an egg's way of making more eggs. Geneticists put it a different way today: the organism is the servant of the gene. The human mother is the way in which human genes make more human genes. The poet is the way in which a literary tradition makes more of a literary tradition. Much the same can be said of science, philosophy, and all the other fields of human endeavor. The person is, of course, the locus of variation as well as the agent of transmission. I have just completed the third and last volume of my autobiography, to be published under the title *A Matter of Consequences.* In it I tried to use my own life to make that point.

The individual does not *originate* anything. Darwin replaced the creation of Genesis with natural selection, and in a modern analysis the origin of behavior is explained as Darwin explained the origin of species. The role of the individual is diminished, but the role of the species is aggrandized.

Kurtz: Do you prefer some kind of society in which the behavioral scientists play a strong role? Would it be only advisory or would they have power? How does it differ from Plato's philosophical kings?

Skinner: I believe, as Lincoln did, in the control of the people by the people for the people, but I would prefer a society in which there were no strong personal controllers at all—as in *Walden Two.* I should like to see behavioral science used in the design of a world in which people naturally behave in the ways needed to support and advance that world. Behavioral scientists would participate in such a design, but no one would be in the position of Plato's philosophical king. In *Walden Two* it is the world in which people live that induces them to do the things they need to do to perpetuate and improve that world. People respond to people—with commendation and censure—but only for reasons of the moment. No one *controls* the behavior of anyone else.

Kurtz: How influential do you think behaviorism is today in psychology and the social sciences, in comparison with ten or twenty years ago, say?

Skinner: Psychology is, I think, in disarray. For economic reasons the national society has become almost wholly professional rather than scientific. The experimental analysis of behavior seems to me to be the only field that has maintained an earlier commitment to science. (I regard ethology, pharmacology, neurology—including the study of sense organs—separate sciences. Cognitive psychology is, I think, a fad, spurred on by its mistake in taking the computer as a model of the human organism.)

Kurtz: What do you think is the most important issue in the world today?

Skinner: If we are really concerned about the future of the species, rather than the aggrandizement of the individual, we should:

1. Dismantle all nuclear arms, giving complete freedom of inspection to a large, well-financed international agency.

2. Reduce the number of people in the world—by devising better methods of birth control and sex education, by ameliorating the economic conditions that cause families to have many children, and by strongly opposing the political and religious encouragement of breeding.

3. Reduce the consumption of all resources and the pollution of the environment—at first with governmental and economic measures, but eventually and primarily through education.

To do all this we must improve out understanding of human behavior. To me that means better behavioral science, and humanism. As I said several years ago when I received the Humanist of the Year Award, behaviorism is *effective* humanism.

(Winter 1983/84)

Steve Allen and Jayne Meadows
on the Frailty of Reason

Tim Madigan: I'm sure you're often asked why you are so open with your political and philosophical views. One would think such openness might offend a certain portion of your potential audience.

Steve Allen: It does. It's quite risky, actually, for people who work in television to be extremely outspoken. It's easier if you work in motion pictures; they almost can't touch you. Jane Fonda can say anything she wants. In today's world I don't know *what* scandalous behavior would result in your being forced out of the motion picture industry. It probably would increase the price of your next film, in fact. We now have what I call "stars of scandal"—the more divorces, the more public fights in saloons, whatever, the more they seem to get respect and/or notoriety. But that, I repeat, does not apply to television performers. There's not the slightest question that Ed Asner's show was yanked out from under him when he began to speak out politically.

Madigan: I have no idea where David Letterman, for example, stands politically.

Allen: I don't think anyone does.

Madigan: He obviously keeps his views to himself.

Allen: Yes. Johnny Carson will never speak out on an issue.

Madigan: And yet, you were debating William F. Buckley back in 1963 on the policies of the Kennedy administration, at a time when the Goldwater-types were hungering for power (rather than being *in* power, as they are now).

Allen: Well, why human beings do whatever they do, for good or for evil, remains partly mysterious. I just feel strongly about certain issues. There is a certain responsibility that comes with prominence or fame. You should never confuse your personal opinions with automatic wisdom. If you're going to speak out on any issue you'd better do your homework. But once you've fulfilled that requirement, then it seems to me that an entertainer has as much right as anyone else to express an opinion.

Madigan: Was there a point early in your career when you decided, "To hell with it, I'm not going to just play it cool"?

Allen: No, not really. You should never cast caution to the wind. You must recognize the realities of your society. And that is true, of course, of the history of ideas. There was a time in Europe, not so terribly long ago on the scale of history, when even the most courageous thinkers put their works out under pseudonyms.

Madigan: Or, as David Hume did, had their more controversial works published posthumously.

Allen: Yes, there was a lot of that, too. Even those elements in society that see themselves, occasionally with some justification, as "the good guys"—the decent, law-abiding, honest folks—can be moved to vicious extremes when they hear an opinion that contradicts something to which they feel a loyalty. They don't behave like the good guys in those instances. So there is always a risk involved when one expresses an opinion not generally held.

Madigan: There is a quote in your introduction to the first volume of your book *Meeting of Minds* that I found very interesting: "I perceive myself as occupying a middle ground between scholars and people. At the moment, however, the middle ground seems very thinly populated. It might be likened to a no-man's land, a barrier, which prevents rather than facilitates communication between the Academy and the streets." I think that one of the great triumphs of your television series "Meeting of Minds" was that you were able to get across great philosophical ideas in an exciting, provocative manner. If somebody heard the same ideas in a philosophy class he would probably get nothing out of it.

Allen: Yes, he could hear exactly the same merchandise, so to speak, and not buy it, whereas coming from a popular entertainer he would be more likely to pay attention. There's something dumb about that, but since it does exist, the sensible thing to do is to make good use of it. And the "Meeting of Minds" project was, by and large, successful. We'll never know how many millions of people were enlightened or inspired by it. When I say "it," I don't mean anything I did; I mean the ideas of the important thinkers and doers who were "guests" on the program. As far as I know, we never attributed to any of them a view he or she did not in fact hold.

Madigan: Obviously the series was viewed by people who had written biographies or who considered themselves experts on certain of the figures portrayed. Did you ever receive any objections from them?

Allen: We had an academic advisor on every one of the shows. One of them finally withdrew after being with the series for a few years. He said, "I haven't found any mistakes yet, but I live in fear that someday, in my professional capacity, I'm going to hear from one of my colleagues, 'You let Steve Allen say that Louis

XIV was eight feet tall? Don't you know, you dope, he was only seven feet tall!' "

Madigan: After seeing the Marquis de Sade portrayed on your show, I read some of his works. It is amazing how well you were able to capture his basic beliefs about humankind.

Allen: As far as accuracy and reliability, I think we did a damned good job. That reminds me of an instance that happened after the pair of shows in which Martin Luther appeared. We received six or seven letters saying, in effect, "You've finally come a cropper, Mr. Allen! I cannot believe that Martin Luther said many of the things you put into his mouth." Yet these were almost all direct quotes. He probably had more direct quotes than most other guests. No one knows, for instance, what Attila the Hun actually said—there are no direct quotes of any kind—but in the case of Luther, we had enough to do a forty-week series.

Madigan: He said some pretty scatological things in his time.

Allen: Yes, he was also an anti-Semite and a bit of a lout, for all his greatness. So the next day when we opened the mail there was a letter from a Luther scholar named Jaroslav Pelikan, congratulating us on the presentation of Luther. I simply made photocopies of his letter and sent them to people who'd complained.

Madigan: How did you decide which famous people to have on the show?

Allen: The first name in any grouping could be more or less taken out of a hat. Any important person from history would obviously make a great guest. Then it came to putting two or three other people at the table with this first choice. The primary consideration was that we wanted to present ideas in conflict. If we had four guests at the table who agreed that capital punishment was terrible, that would have been comforting to those of us who hold that opinion, but it'd be very dull dramatically. The essence of all good drama, and even of all third-rate drama, is conflict.

Margaret Sanger, for instance, was in favor of birth control, so we wanted to put somebody at the table who was opposed to it—Gandhi was a dramatic choice for a number of reasons. First of all, if there's any nation that needs birth control, it's India, and the fact that this almost saintly, heroic figure was on what many would consider to be the wrong side of the issue made for great drama. He was very puritanical about sex. His view was very close to the old Catholic position—there is absolutely no justification for sex unless it is your intention to create a child. He felt that sex for pleasure was decadent and sinful. Again, you can criticize him for that, but for our show it was terrific.

I got the idea to use the Marquis de Sade, by the way, from Clare Booth Luce. I had to select someone who would be critical of him. That wasn't too tough, since almost any intelligent person would be outraged by many of his views.

Madigan: Why did Luce suggest you use him?

Allen: At first I chuckled when she suggested him, since it was like saying, "Why don't you have Hitler as a guest?" She said, "No, I'm quite serious. Sick as his opinions were, I see them as very influential in today's decadent society."

Madigan: Some people claim that de Sade's views were actually the end result of the Enlightenment, the dark side of Locke and Jefferson.

Allen: You mean because he said that if you destroy the religious safeguards, then anything goes?

Madigan: Yes. Also, if all men are created equal, then why can't you do whatever you want? What's to stop you? I don't believe this is a valid philosophy, by the way.

Allen: This is an ancient and important question. If it were to be discovered, let us say, that there is no personal god, or if there is a god but people lose their faith in him, then what is to prevent them from killing or raping or stealing?

I suggest that we step away from dealing with that question in a purely abstract, theoretical sense and look at how people actually behave when they have formally decided that there is no God. What often happens is that they become even more puritanical. The Soviet Union and China, for instance, have both tried to remake human beings and to change human behavior, but of course every religious leader and every reformer of whatever stripe tries to do that and never with much success. The point is, far from encouraging licentiousness, these societies permit much less. It is our society— a free society—that is sicko with sex, depravity, child abuse, drugs, and violence. That of course leads into the ancient debate about the proper balance between two highly esteemed values, freedom on the one hand and law and order on the other.

Madigan: I recently taught a course at a local prison on the Philosophy of Religion. All but one guy said they were religious. One would think that if removing the religious safeguards led to licentiousness, the prisons would be filled with atheists. But this was an example of just the opposite.

Allen: The first person I ever encountered who pointed that out was Joseph McCabe. He checked out some prisons, and something like 99 percent of the inmates were religious. McCabe was very effective, since he was knowledgeable about history. He was a former priest, and very bitter about the church. I don't harbor any hatred for the church; my relations are cordial. I haven't been a Catholic since the moment I got married for the second time and was automatically excommunicated.

Madigan: That'll do it. Getting back to "Meeting of Minds," it seems that, aside from a few shows, television is generally a vast wasteland. There's so much that could be done but is not.

Allen: Well, the reaction to the twenty-four shows of "Meeting of Minds" far exceeded my expectations. I thought we would take a lot of heat, and I was quite prepared for that. But it got almost no negative criticism. It not only pleased, but thrilled all major philosophical camps. Conservatives loved it, liberals loved it, atheists, Marxists, anti-Marxists. I never got a single letter of basic criticism. I thought, "Can I really get away with having every ancient verity questioned?"— though they were also defended, of course. I wouldn't load the dice either way. I thought a lot of people wouldn't hold still for that. I think they approved because they perceived the attempt to be fair.

Madigan: That came across very well in the series. I remember the first show, where Thomas Aquinas debated Cleopatra on women's rights.

Allen: It was remarkable how modern some of the arguments sounded. In one instance we totally lucked out. It was one of the shows with Theodore Roosevelt and there was a fairly extensive conversation about his role in taking over the Panama Canal. As luck would have it, a week before the airing, there was a big scuffle about the Canal treaty.

Madigan: It seems that the *raison d'etre* of "Meeting of Minds" was this clash of ideas.

Allen: Yes. It grew out of my having concluded, a good many years earlier, that the gap between what is reasonably possible in education in this country, and what in fact actually occurs, is enormous. I had no way of knowing, after this insight first occurred to me, that this situation would seriously deteriorate year by year. For the last five years or so I've been working on a book. The original title was *How to Think*. The title at the moment is *Dumbth and Seventy-Seven Things to Do About It*. I give seventy-seven specific suggestions on how to think better. If by show time I think of eighty-seven, we'll just change the number in the title. The idea of "Meeting of Minds" grew out of such considerations. We've never had such means of education, and yet people are getting dumber all the time.

Madigan: What do you think of such recent works as *Cultural Illiteracy* and *The Closing of the American Mind,* which seem to be blaming liberal education for this state of affairs?

Allen: Those people beat me to the punch by getting their books published before mine. I think when anything is that seriously wrong it's likely to have dozens of causative factors, rather than anything as simplistic as "liberal education" or John Dewey. Clearly, the kind of education most Americans have been getting in the past twenty-five years is inferior. But it does not automatically follow that the cause is as simple as "They don't teach as much Latin or math as they used to." Such factors are relevant but they are certainly not at the heart of the explanation or the solution. Television is on that list of causative factors. During the years in which Americans are formally educated, from about the age of five to about the age of twenty, they spend more time watching television than they do reading or getting educated. That's scary, it's wrong, it's a pity, and it's one of the reasons Americans are getting dumber.

I cannot open a magazine of substance without encountering new evidence. A recent issue of *Time,* devoted to America's youth, gave some disturbing examples. We may be down the tube of history already if the five lives described by *Time*'s researchers are typical, and I'm afraid they are. In that same issue I came across something totally consistent with what I've been observing for the last twenty years—the now almost total lack of knowledge about geography among Americans of high-school or college age. Some scary percentage of them don't know where

France is on a map of Europe. Jayne and I were watching a newscast one evening—a professor at the University of Miami had just announced some tests he'd given to his students. Six percent of them did not know where Miami was.

Jayne Meadows (entering the room): And they were going to school there!

Allen: That was the worst thing, but the rest of his findings were almost as bad.

Madigan: What is your conception of humanism? What do you think it can offer to a world filled with troubles?

Allen: It's a question on which there is much debate among humanists themselves. It's obviously not as clearly defined a philosophy or movement as, say, Mormonism or Orthodox Judaism, but I take that as a plus. It is left to the conscience, or the intelligence, of the individual whether he thinks the universe just happened or it was created by some previously existing entity. One may hold either view, I take it, and still be a humanist in regard to a great many other questions.

Humanism puts its primary concentration on humankind as far as changing the world is concerned. Naturally, in a free society one is perfectly at liberty to pray to superhuman creatures for material things, but the material things we actually get in fact come from other humans or from our own efforts. A deity has never yet created an orphanage, a hospital, a convent or other religious institution. So humanists, for the most part, simply leave the question of divine inspiration to one side, and approach things from a more practical point of view.

I was impressed with the United Nations' "Universal Declaration of Human Rights," which was distributed to all participants in the Tenth Humanist World Congress. The classical ideals of human rights are consistent with the great majority of religious philosophies or philosophical schools of thought. The U.N. Declaration is harmonious with humanism and its ideals, and I think that, with the exception of authoritarian Marxists or fascists, most people would agree with it. Who could oppose freedom or argue against the dignity of the human being?

I address all kinds of groups—Catholic, Protestant, Left, Right—and I'm interested in observing to what extent they share these ideals. Everyone wants peace, everyone wants law, justice, compassion, and courage. They differ chiefly in regard to the means for bringing those ideals closer to realization.

Meadows: It's easier for kids today in the United States. Why should they study? There's no ambition at all. I think the young people in America today, with few exceptions, are geared toward pleasure. They don't realize that that's the worst way of life.

Why do kids go on drugs or become alcoholics? Why do they do all these self-destructive things? Because nothing is exciting to them. What we need is a few people in important positions who will show them the excitement of achievement.

There was an excitement during the Kennedy period—lately we've had an old man in power who's deaf and half asleep. He's put the whole country to sleep. And there hasn't been such a corrupt administration since Ulysses S. Grant's.

Allen: And Reagan came in preaching morality.

Meadows: And look who were his sponsors—many of the most prominent evangelists. The seeds I see being sown in America are like those sown before the fall of Rome and Greece.

Madigan: That's an interesting point. The intellectuals are up on high, and everyone else pays no attention to them.

Meadows: I portrayed Margaret Sanger on "Meeting of Minds," and received a beautiful letter from her son, complimenting me on my performance. But he said, "Did you have to tell all those personal stories about my mother? I wish you had known her. You would have loved her." *Of course* I would have loved her.

Madigan: You wanted to portray her truthfully, warts and all.

Meadows: Absolutely.

Allen: That was an important element of the show. There's one section we had to cut from the script because of time limitations, but it is in the book. I discovered that Aquinas was not only an advocate of capital punishment— that can't be held against him, since everyone was for it in those days—he not only thought it was permissible, but that it was *virtuous* to burn heretics at the stake. There's no pain more hideous than that caused by fire. I dealt with that on the show with Galileo. That was the punishment he most feared. At a certain point in the discussion, he asked me to hold my index finger over the flame. I recoiled, the pain was excruciating. "Now you have a little better appreciation of what we were talking about when we use the dry phrase 'burned at the stake.' " Aquinas thought heretics should be burned alive, like a piece of bacon. For me, that's not such a heroic thing to have believed.

Madigan: The theme of the Tenth Humanist Congress was "Building A World Community." Coincidentally, Billy Graham was in town at the same time, leading a Christian Crusade. I attended his press conference. He said that he'd traveled all over the world, to nearly every country, and "there is only one family of man." He, too, recognizes the commonality of human beings, and the urge to help our fellow humans. We may differ on the means to do this, but the urge is the same.

Allen: Yes. Many people were moved to Marxism by a thirst for social justice. In fact, many current leaders who are now conservative were dedicated Marxists in their youth. A passionate concern with the injustice that is the common mode of human existence often leads people to espouse a certain cause. Justice is a rarity, injustice is the norm, and you don't have to be compassionate to the point of sanctity to be outraged by that. The chief problem with communists is that, though they often start with better intentions than some Christians have started with, they become so dogmatically convinced of not only the rightness of their cause but also the wisdom of the means of bringing about their desired ends, that they make the tragic mistake of becoming authoritarian and *ordering* virtue among the people. Virtue can be encouraged by example or by very careful moral argumentation, but you can never order people to be virtuous. Whenever this happens in history, either by forces of Islam, Catholicism, communism, or anything else, overwhelmingly tragic results follow.

Madigan: Paul Kurtz told me that during his student days at New York University and at Columbia, both before and after the Second World War, ideas really meant something to the students. Many of them were committed Marxists, but they became Marxists out of good intentions. They really wanted to do something about the injustices of society.

Allen: They had just witnessed, and in many cases suffered through, a little thing called the Great Depression, which involved the collapse of capitalism— not for all times, but the thousand-and-one tragic results of the stock-market crash represented literally a failure of the capitalist economy. You can't see people going hungry for too long without saying "Goddamn it, there's gotta be a better way than this." It turned out that the Marxist solution was not that better way, but nobody went into it knowing that. They went into it because they assumed it *might* be a better way.

Madigan: That's a crucial point.

Meadows: Communists or not, these were young people who had a cause. They had something that inspired them, whether it turned out to be right or wrong.

Madigan: Something greater than themselves.

Meadows: Exactly.

Allen: They wouldn't have had to be inspired had they not witnessed injustice, suffering, poverty.

Meadows: The point was, they knew that many people were enormously wealthy, while the majority of the population was poor and some were starving or selling apples on the street corners. But communism rarely survives in democratic countries with a strong middle class.

Allen: The American Depression did more to encourage Marxism in this country than any twenty-seven Marxist college professors. Look at Latin America. The Latin American people and the world jury that observes them will not sit idly by forever and let the right-wing dictators and the few families who own the countries continue to create even more injustice than they already have. Many Catholic clergy, when they get down there and see the reality of what they've only known through reading, start out by trying to improve things. But they quickly realize that the Latin American elite won't *let* them improve anything, and so it is these capitalists in Latin America who are turning our best young priests and nuns—among others—into some kind of Marxists.

Meadows: I think one of the wonderful things about the Catholic church today is that it's one of the first times in history when it has stood up against the un-Christian governments of these countries. It used to be hand in hand with them, but not today.

Madigan: Steve, you've used the phrase "the frailty of human reason" in some of your writings. I was wondering what you think can be done to bolster reason, as best one can, in the onslaught of all this irrationalism.

Allen: My approach is to try first to get the American people to recognize the deterioration of simple intelligence itself. This is a real problem. We must keep talking about it, organizing about it, until people realize it's an issue. Thank God, in the last ten years word has finally begun to take root. In 1983 Ronald Reagan finally woke up and referred to it as a matter for public concern. His solution was simplistic; he said there should be better teachers. Nobody can argue with that—nobody's in favor of *worse* teachers. But there's a hell of a lot more to it than that. Most people think that they're in pretty good shape but that other people are dumb. I think we should borrow something from Alcoholics Anonymous: just as they preach that your case is hopeless until you have the courage to stand up and say "I am an Alcoholic," the average person is highly unlikely to get much more intelligent until he says, "I am ignorant."

Madigan: It's the same as Socrates being considered the wisest man in Athens because he realized how little he really knew about anything.

Allen: Yes. But there's a sense in which the problem has no solution, because there are limitations in the brain. Even an Einstein may know a great deal about his specialty but probably no more than the rest of us about Ping-Pong, making an apple pie, or solving the economic problems of Poland. The world is simply too enormous for even the brightest people to keep total track of. That's a given. Still, we must begin to move closer to our potential. Now we're marching fast as hell in the opposite direction, getting less intelligent every year.

Meadows: If young people had a cause, something that inspired them, they wouldn't be in such a mess.

Allen: Even their patriotism is suspect. Some of it is the belligerence of ignoramuses, the Rambo mentality.

Madigan: It's an attitude that goes completely against John Kennedy's statement: They *are* asking, "What can my country do for me?"

Allen: "What can Reagan and his tax advisors do to make me richer?"

Meadows: "Everybody owes me a living."

Madigan: I think that's why Reagan captured most of the young vote. Not because they love the man, but because they figured they would do better economically.

Meadows: If you think in terms of what we vote for, every country suffers from the same thing. We vote for image. Carter had no charisma. And along comes a second-rate B-picture actor who has that charming manner. That's what too many Americans vote for.

Allen: Of course, it can also work for the good. A lot of people voted for Jack Kennedy because he was a good-looking man, a fine public speaker, witty, charming, sophisticated, whereas Nixon looked like the crook he turned out to be.

Madigan: You've raised the point that specialists know their own fields and nothing else. I think it is crucial that we encourage what you call "the people in the middle ground," the people who may not be experts in astronomy or economics or political science, but who can understand what the experts are saying, and can get this across to people who are interested.

Allen: One of the stupidest forms of criticism involves attacking the "popularizers of science." We must *encourage* the popularizers, because many of the scientists themselves are poor teachers, and even those who are great teachers are so busy doing their work that they don't have time to teach. The man in the street is not going to learn much about science from the world's leading scientists—they're too busy, and we'd better keep them busy. The solution is *more* popularizing of science, more use of television to instruct about science, more articles in popular journals. We must stop this nonsense of criticizing those who provide this needed service. The same criticism was leveled against Will and Ariel Durant and their books on "The Story of Civilization." When you see those books on the library shelves and realize the monumental achievement of their work, and the value of the writing, you must realize that those are excellent history books. I don't care whether they were "popularizers of history." But if they were, I love them all the more. We need ten thousand Will and Ariel Durants today.

Meadows: The very first letter we got about "Meeting of Minds" was a congratulatory one from Will Durant.

Allen: I'm glad to be a popularizer. I know how to communicate, partly as a natural gift and partly as the result of forty-five years of experience in radio and television. I'm glad to be of public service in that modest connection.

Madigan: I think that both of you should be commended for your efforts in getting these important ideas across.

(Winter 1988/89)

E. O. Wilson on Sociobiology and Religion

Jeffrey Saver: Let me begin by noting that your writings suggest that you feel that the topic of religion is in many ways a special one, that religion plays a particularly important role in human life and offers tremendous promise to sociobiology as a phenomenon to be explained. You have even written that, "the sacred rituals are the most distinctively human." Why did you say that?

E. O. Wilson: I said that because sacred rituals are among the cultural universals and are generally regarded in most cultures as of overriding importance, taking precedence over almost anything else. And because they are affective—that is, they produce such powerful emotions so readily. It is a common experience to observe people go through startling mental transformations in connection with ritual or tribal religion. And sacred rituals typically entail the most complicated domain of culture in each separate society. These features together indicate to me that there is a very powerful, emotive force built into human beings that strongly influences them to produce affective and elaborate religious systems.

Saver: Nonetheless you have argued that scientific materialism is now in a position to deal a final blow to religion. You have suggested that the increasing power of sociobiological accounts of the evolutionary sources of religious belief will undermine the religious position. However, Hume, Freud, and many others in the past have advanced plausible, even compelling, explanations of the behavioral basis of religion, and religious belief survived these earlier attacks on much the same front as the one you hold is crucial now. How would you respond to the suggestion that you were falling prey to what you yourself have called "the humanist's touching faith in the power of knowledge and the idea of evolutionary progress over the minds of men"?

Wilson: I argued that scientific materialism is currently posing a new challenge to religious belief because up to this time no one has thought through the full implications for religion of the Darwinian evolution of the mind. Consider, for example, what Charles Lumsden and I called, in our book *Genes, Mind and*

Culture, "the epigenetic rules." These are the features by which the mind is assembled. In some instances they are very strict, narrow procedures, in others much more subtle and flexible; but all are nevertheless rules materialistically based on physical brain mechanisms. Very few people have thought carefully about the implications for religion of this conception of how the mind originated and focused genetic evolution in individual mental development. And the more we know about the neurobiology of the brain and mind—a subject that is expanding exponentially fast—and the more we understand from population biology and sociobiology about the origins of social patterns during Darwinian evolution, the more likely it is that before very long we will have a much fuller, and maybe intellectually fully satisfying, account of the origin of religion in Darwinian terms. And if that is the case, then we—we the materialist, humanist scientists—have not simply proposed explanations of phenomena around us that compete with the traditional, mythological religious explanations, but we have set out to explain religion itself as a materialistic phenomenon. This is a distinction that I believe gives humanism the decisive edge over religion.

But of course no one expects that the realization by neurobiologists and philosophers of the biological meaning of religion and their resulting rejection of most traditional religious claims will result in a tidal wave of materialism that sweeps around the world. Materialism is still largely an upper-middle-class, educated, elite phenomenon because it requires the possession of so much information. It also requires a certain amount of material security, so that the mind is not being repeatedly staggered by the threats to its survival for which evolution has had literally hundreds of thousands of years to prepare it via the shortcut of religion. So you can't expect more than a tiny fraction of the population to see the import sociobiology has for religion, not right away. What the new sociobiology does seem likely to threaten is theology. It will threaten the Hans Kungs and the Billy Grahams of this world, within the seminaries and academic halls, not the religious pulse itself. The Averrhoist dictum holds firm: philosophy for the philosophers, religion for the rest.

Yet, I believe a time will come when scientists will be far more interested in religion, mainly as a phenomenon for analysis, and the schizoid character of intellectual life, particularly scientific intellectual life, will tend to yield to a more monistic view of the universe. At the moment there are a large number of philosophers, scientists, and others who maintain a pure, natural scientific approach to the large scientific problems they are dealing with, but in matters of ethics and personal belief they are able to be religious, or to concede that part of the universe to the theologian. I don't believe that honesty will permit us to continue this easy compromise much longer.

Saver: Do you think that this affluent elite who are able to take on the materialist view should seek to expand its following? Should they proselytize it at all?

Wilson: Yes, I think they should. That's something I worry about a lot. As you know, humanism right now is a dirty word around the country. I was really surprised to see that happen, frankly—that the fundamentalists, the New Right, would take as their target something called "secular humanism." And, to put a lighter touch on the matter, I'm disappointed that *On Human Nature* has not been a major target by the right wing. It would have made my life at Harvard much more comfortable to be targeted by the New Right and its allies instead of just the New Left. But I do think that, faced with this kind of challenge, and with the real dangers that organized fundamental, dogmatic religion presents around the world, a more powerful counterforce has to be mounted.

Religion is a great deal more than just the opiate of the people, the happy pill for people to take during rites of passage—death, marriage, and so on. If it were only that, it would be fine. I'm willing to swallow that pill myself. If it really did simply provide personal comfort, I think most scientists and materialist philosophers would say, "Indeed, religion for the rest and we won't worry about it." But it is much more than that.

The emotional power of religion is too easily captured by nationalism and madmen's fantasies. Parts of the Muslim world now are a perfect example of this—religion has become the substance in a new sea of fanaticism. It has been adopted by people who are quite capable of leading their followers to suicidal actions. In the newspaper this morning I read Khomeini's latest pronouncement. He said, "What is a dictatorship? A dictatorship is that movement which opposes the will of the Muslim Council." You have madness like this that is predicated . . .

Saver: Such doublespeak . . .

Wilson: . . . It's obvious doublespeak and its powered by the authority people are able to surround themselves with in the name of religion. Elsewhere in the world we can see how in other cultures religion or religionlike fervor produces fanatical political movements. I would include here many of the world's revolutionary Marxist movements.

But remember too that a large part of the leadership in many places does consist of upper-middle-class, educated people. It doesn't really matter if the population of the state of Tennessee believes in the literal interpretation of the Bible if enough of its leaders are educated enough—have been reached by enough training and experience, including science training— to know what the score is.

Saver: What do you think of the threat to biology posed by the creationists in the United States? Will the creationist movement sputter or is it here for some time?

Wilson: I couldn't predict. As I said, I was taken by surprise at its revival, so I don't consider myself a very good social prophet. I would say it's a menace and hope it's just a passing movement.

Remember, it's easy to exaggerate the power of groups like this. One could get the impression from part of the New Right and some organized religious groups that to end abortion is the overwhelming will of the American people— and of course, as always, God. Not at all. I don't have the exact figures, but something like 60 to 70 percent of the American people are in favor of abortion. A substantial percentage of that, probably a majority of the American people, would favor some kind of governmental support for abortion, at least for people who are disadvantaged or victims of rape. So the absolutists constitute a minority group that may wear out its welcome in a few years.

Saver: Do you think that, in the contest for adherents, scientific materialism has any competitive advantages over the various religious faiths or other intellectual frameworks?

Wilson: Well, scientific materialism does have a unique advantage in that no competing scientific materialisms exist. There have supposedly been about 100,000 religions in the history of man, but only one scientific materialism. The church of scientific materialism is kept united and pure because its assumptions and conclusions are always being tested. Any found impure—a theory that doesn't work, a fact that turns out to be incorrect when double-checked—are banished.

But as to how well it can compete with the religions, that's hard to say, because, as I pointed out in *On Human Nature,* it doesn't have their emotional punch. It does not have the capacity to trigger those deep limbic responses that give you such satisfaction when you hear a beautiful Haydn mass or watch a parade on the Fourth of July. You just don't have that with scientific materialism, and that's its great disadvantage. In this case, enlightenment really does short-circuit and circumvent the elaborate biological reinforcing mechanisms that have made us a group-oriented, religious species.

Saver: Would you oppose a Positivist, Comtean scheme to elaborate rituals around scientific materialism?

Wilson: Yes, absolutely. Let me say I'm a great believer in rituals, but the pathetic example of Robespierre and Comte in the history of this subject suggests caution in any attempt to ritualize scientific materialism itself. I think it was Robespierre who, shortly before he was arrested and deposed, wanted to change all the churches in France to Cathedrals of Reason, with pomp and ceremony devoted to the god Reason. His fate and that of the revolution do not speak very well for the impulse. And Comte, as you mentioned, wanted to do much the same thing: enthrone reason and materialism.

I think the way out is not to enthrone materialism, but to employ it as a cleansing fire through which all our assumptions and decisions about ourselves, our meaning, and our ethics and morals are passed. And that will come about increasingly, I believe, as the social sciences get a firmer underpinning—when they finally give up this ridiculous resistance to biology and accept it as what it is, a powerful potential ally. When we start bringing neurobiology, genetics, and evolutionary theory together to build a much stronger social science, then we can finally begin to put our basic assumptions and procedures through purifying tests to evaluate their truthfulness and effectiveness.

And, also, I *am* a great believer in ritual and ceremony of a secular nature when it is connected with real events in life. I don't know if the Harvard Commencement (the oldest truly American ceremony) moves you the way it does me, but for most people it's a reaffirmation and an uplifting experience, in the same way that religion is. One can surround the rites of passage—birth, assumption to adulthood, marriage, death—with beautiful ritual and in so doing draw on the whole history of the species and human social institutions in a way that provides the kind of deep satisfaction that religion also provides. Combine this with a more realistic and scientific view of the world and ultimately we could satisfy both parts of the brain.

Saver: The "second dilemma" you stated in *On Human Nature* asked on what grounds and in what direction we shall decide to aim our energies once a more powerful biology of social behavior has revealed to us the evolutionary sources of our basic drives and goals. This concern calls to mind similar questions raised by thinkers like William James in *The Moral Equivalent of War* and Konrad Lorenz in *On Aggression.* Both of these men recommended that mankind undertake a commitment to tame and overcome nature as a way to beneficially redirect the aggressive biological drives that lead to conflict and warfare in modern society. You seem to offer instead an ideal of scientific discovery as a higher goal to which we might commit ourselves. This raised in my mind two questions. First, why did you not suggest the ideal of taming nature?

Wilson: Because I'm a biologist. In particular, I'm an evolutionary biologist and a naturalist, and that makes an enormous difference in the way I view the world. Typically, the grand scientific thinkers have not been trained in natural history. That may sound strange to say about Konrad Lorenz because he is naturalistic in his approach, yet he knows only a very small number of animals. When you have been trained in the tradition of natural history, particularly in the tropics, you have a better appreciation of the staggering complexity of the biosphere. You acquire a sense of true awe at the astounding range of species diversity that has stretched across billions of years of history.

I like to say that you can scoop almost anywhere two handfuls of earth and have enough in your hand to occupy you for a lifetime, be able to embark on a kind of Magellanic voyage through inches of soil. It's not generally appreciated, but there's more complexity in such a fistful of life on earth than there is on the entire surface of all the other planets put together. One ant contains genetic information that, if measured in bits and then transformed into words, would just about fill all the editions of the *Encyclopaedia Britannica,* from the first one published in 1768. If we could turn inward, not narcissistically to ourselves and the human species, but inward to the biosphere, and recognize its special character, we'd have an almost unlimited scope for discovery, exploration, and appreciation.

Sure, tame nature to the extent necessary for human welfare. Convert that arable portion of the earth necessary for food production to maximum productivity. But look forward to gaining almost unlimited satisfaction for the human mind from scientific exploration of the living world we have inherited. In terms of what could be known, despite the fascinating information we've already gathered, we must count ourselves at the dawn of biology and naturalism. This exploration would also include a study of ourselves, the history of our own species and how the human mind works. To me, that's an outward-looking, potentially almost endlessly satisfying enterprise to offer the world.

Saver: You may have just touched upon an answer to my second question, but let me nevertheless ask it. How would you reply to the charge that—unlike the ideal of conquering nature, which would require the efforts of people on all levels of society, galvanizing individuals at every intellectual level—your future would unleash the energies of only a scientific, intellectual elite?

Wilson: I would disagree. To discover doesn't entail being first to make an important abstract generalization. It includes that of course, but it also can mean discovering in the sense of the gardener or the amateur naturalist. Even the average person today could be transported to the Amazon or Costa Rica and within a week be seeing things that no other person has ever seen, or at least rediscovering known phenomena for themselves in new places and new contexts. And as education gets better, this sort of personal exploration can really become much more advanced than it is now. I don't think this is an exclusionary, elitist view of the world at all.

In fact I see it as by far the best, most human way to view the world. Otherwise, without any kind of appreciation of the biosphere for its own sake, without the joy of exploring it and knowing it that you can transmit to people so readily, you are in danger of having the mass of people defining themselves with reference to inherently inferior artifacts. I don't think the human mind evolved hundreds of thousands of years to live in a steel and concrete cage. It evolved in a way that tends to open it out toward exploration, especially the exploration of life.

People do have a strong tendency to appreciate and love life. I use the word *biophilia* to stress this natural human impulse to affiliate with and even to love living things. It's no coincidence, for example, that most science fiction entails life, either at the fairly crude level of a transference of human life, politics, or social existence to some distant imagined place, or at the more speculative level of envisioning contact with other forms of life. Very little sci-fi entails the real substance of physics and chemistry. How compelling is it in the end to know what lies one kilometer below the surface of Jupiter? But people become truly excited when writers start talking about the prospect of making contact with extraterrestrial life. Then unlimited possibilities seem to open.

Saver: You have offered a majestic evolutionary epic of the mind as scientific materialism's "mythopoeic" vision of the beginning, but I haven't seen you discuss scientific materialism's rather less attractive vision of the end—that is, the running down of the universe according to the second law of thermodynamics with all its nihilistic implications. Do you see any way to successfully integrate this element of the scientific world-view into an attractive scientific materialism?

Wilson: Each person uses a personal timescale to reflect on the meaning of life. Some, hedonists, live on essentially a weekly timescale. The average person tends to live on a timescale of years or decades. Young adults think in terms of at most ten to twenty years. As they age they tend to extend the scale a bit, thinking about the span of time that remains until the day of their death. Evolutionary biologists are a bit different—they are trained to reason in terms of generations or thousands of years, but still not on a scale of millions of years.

Perhaps some physicists feel an anxiety about proton decay over billions of years, but I don't think on that scale. Such a cosmic projection is meaningless not just for our generation but literally for millions of generations stretching as far into the future as one can reasonably conceive. It's a problem that one puts out of mind.

Saver: You have written that "all religions are probably oppressive to some degree." Would a mythopoeic scientific materialism be oppressive, and, if so, in what ways?

Wilson: Well, that's an interesting question. It may be that it could become oppressive. It is likely that materialism will gain increasing influence over our thinking, in social planning, in technology, in everyday life. If so, then the need for scientific training and thinking in the scientific mode will grow correspondingly intense, to the extent that young people might be captured by it and virtually forced into a much more scientific education, à la the Soviet Union, which now has its whole population taking two years of calculus. In the wrong hands or with poor planning, the trend could lead to a withering of certain of the creative enterprises—art, music, poetry—that are more prominent in our present culture. Surely there is a powerful call at the moment for *more* science in education. The humanities are on the retreat. Science is on the march. I don't think that it must necessarily work this way, but it is possible that science and scientific materialism could become so overwhelmingly important in everyday life and education that it would be oppressive in this narrow sense. And certainly there is a feeling among humanistic scholars that science is becoming oppressive.

Saver: Let me ask you about the charge that some critics have advanced that sociobiologists sometimes fall prey to the naturalistic fallacy—violating the categories of logic by trying to derive moral values from scientific facts. In contrast, you have argued that we can no longer naively go about deriving "oughts" without any reference at all to what "is," that all our ethical decisions must be informed by scientific information . . .

Wilson: I have attempted to weaken the naturalistic fallacy or, more precisely, to rework the naturalistic fallacy into less of a fallacy. Yes.

Saver: But your argument seems to leave behind an important residual issue. Even if social planners make full use of scientific knowledge, you seem to envision that they could still be confronted by several different "oughts" to choose between, several different possible and desirable biological-social patterns.

Wilson: I think that will always be the case.

Saver: Now is there any way that a "biologized ethics," such as the one you have called for, could help us make a final choice among competing societal goals in addition to telling us what the cost and benefits of choosing each would be?

Wilson: That's a profound question, and at the moment I can't answer it. It's just as simple as that. In *On Human Nature,* I felt satisfied to get as far as offering a means of performing the cost-benefit analysis. Even there we're still on shaky ground, though our recent work is moving in the direction of making such evaluations more feasible. Also, I tried to identify those present injustices that are clearly due to outdated religious dogma about what is natural in human behavior, as opposed to modern biological understanding, which I consider to be much closer to the truth.

But aside from that, I don't have any prescriptions. This is a fundamental philosophical issue that has yet to be properly addressed by philosophers. Peter Singer did try to deal with it in *The Expanding Circle,* but to my mind not very successfully. He reaches the point you described, accepting the main premises of sociobiology but then asking, "Where do we go from here?" His answer is to propose that humanity continue to allow the circle of its concern to expand, insofar as we are able in practical terms and consistent with our nature. As an ethical precept, that's hard to argue with, and at the moment I don't have any additions or newer ideas on how to handle the implications. But I don't think it is grounded solidly enough to be a really satisfying solution.

Saver: In *On Human Nature* you wrote, "I also believe that it will soon be within our power to identify many of the genes that influence behavior." How close do you think we are?

Wilson: We've come much closer since I wrote that. The number of genes actually identified in the four years after I wrote *On Human Nature* jumped 50 percent, thanks to the new techniques being developed in molecular biology, and quite a few of those have been associated with behavior. Since that time, for example, investigators have identified genes that alter reactions to particular odors and other genes that differentially affect performances on four of an array of fifteen standard cognitive tests. The chances of actually specifying the genes affecting schizophrenia, or the rate of certain mental processes, or fluctuations in temperament, are now much more likely. We know that much of mood and mental activity is based on neurohormones and neurotransmitters. Such molecules are being chemically defined at a rapid pace. They are used increasingly in psychiatry to diagnose and correct certain conditions, and the evidence has become quite strong that their levels of production are under genetic control. So I would say that the odds are very high that within ten years—twenty on the outside—a number of genes will have been identified whose effects can be traced through the actual production of particular chemicals in the brain to measurable properties of temperament, mood, and even cognitive ability.

Saver: This progress in specifying the genetic basis of behavior makes even more urgent the "third dilemma" that you raised at the end of *On Human Nature:* the issue of taking charge of our own evolution through eugenics or genetic engineering. It seemed to me that there you shirked trying to solve this dilemma, even though you had not hesitated to at least grapple with the similar second dilemma, which also demanded that we choose a future course by selecting among the component elements of human nature, albeit culturally and not genetically. Do you now have any feeling about how to approach the third dilemma?

Wilson: You're right, I side-stepped the third dilemma, in part because I already had enough controversy on my hands in that book. At the time *On*

Human Nature was written, genetic engineering was still quite a controversial subject on its own. Now that has abated somewhat. Attitudes among scientists and the educated public have visibly shifted in the past several years, and people are a lot more sensible. Not only has much of the fear of recombinant techniques and genetic engineering in bacteria dissipated, but medical scientists have been able to talk seriously about such topics as genetic surgery, using advanced techniques to modify the most defective human genes, the ones that cause sickness and death.

And you're correct in observing that the second and third dilemmas are basically similar. In one we merely have the difficulty of deciding which of these limbic satisfactions we want to cultivate and which we must find a detour around, and in the other we actually have the option of engineering the genes at a more basic level so that we can permanently wipe out a drive or enhance another drive. At first the two sound different, but they are fundamentally the same moral problem.

I had thought when I wrote the book that the time when we would have to confront the dilemma was sufficiently far ahead of us that we could concentrate on the first two, and on the biology of the mind and the problems of ethics. I didn't expect the pace of technological development to accelerate so quickly. So I was surprised when Matthew Meselson, a molecular biologist very much involved in biotechnology, stated at a recent meeting of the American Academy of Arts and Sciences that the advent of genetic engineering of human beings is possibly closer than we had ever dreamed. He said that we are going to have to soon start thinking about the biological basis of our own humanity, in order to make decisions about what we wish to tamper with and what not. He even went so far as to cite sociobiology as a possible means of getting at the fundamental problem.

So the experiment is probably now worth talking about. How could we change our basic nature with genetic intervention? With more knowledge of the genetic assembly of the mind, you could tinker with the strength of the sex bond, or the pleasure we get from children. It still sounds like science fiction to me, but it is possible that in a couple of generations human beings can actually be created who respond to the world very differently from the way you and I do, people who take deep pleasure in rural communes or space colonies— human nature could go in any of a great many directions.

Saver: Do you think that we should indeed desire to tamper with our basic nature? Leaving aside the matter of which direction we might move in, do you think that we should intervene at all?

Wilson: Again, that's a question I can't answer. Suppose we really could do it. Should we? And, if so, what direction would we choose? How might we go about making such a momentous decision? There may well be something within us that will prevent us from making *any* changes. In the end we could say, "All right, fellow hominids, we are sad, mixed-up monsters, but we are what we are, and this is the way we would like to remain. That is our basic humanity, and there is something fundamentally wrong with changing basic humanity. Let's improve our life without leaving home."

The artificial intelligence (AI) people are coming at this problem from a fascinating and entirely different direction that is nevertheless converging on sociobiology. They are talking realistically now about the actual duplication of human intelligence in machines. They have started to add to AI devices not just the capacity to solve problems but also the capacity to formulate them. And they might soon supplement rationality with a limited form of emotive feelings, building in rewards for going in certain directions and not others. In short, they are creating machines that are increasingly human in at least a few rudimentary features. The most adventurous are also beginning to pose a troublesome question: "What will be left to human beings? If machines can perform most of our reasoning, even seek *new* problems to solve for us, what does that leave us?"

One possible answer is that it leaves human beings with their limbic system. It leaves us with all the nuances of altruism, jealousy, sex bonding, exhilaration, tribal lore, and other mostly primate traits that we inherited and do so relish on a day-to-day basis. Maybe it's these that we will try to preserve. Of course we will continue to train our reasoning faculties and be better educated than we are now. But we will not try to advance with AI to the point of being able to actually produce a fully human-primate brain in a machine. And, for the same reasons, we will decide not to alter mankind genetically so that we ourselves become more like machines. We will refuse to start tampering with the limbic controls and become cool, rational superdrones. Instead we will choose, I believe, to live in symbiosis with artificial intelligence. We will have the emotional limbic system; it will have a still indeterminately larger part of the rational cortex.

Saver: In suggesting that evolutionary pressures have selected for an inherent indoctrinability in man, you wrote: "In support of this simple biological hypothesis is the fact that the blinding force of religious allegiance can operate in the absence of theology." Does it operate in the dedication of scientists?

Wilson: Yes, I think, a great deal. Scientists work with very variable motivations. Most scientists are not excessively bright—and this includes university professors. Some of the most successful are essentially supertechnicians. They're very bright people, remarkable, and have done extraordinary things, but if you looked inside them you'd find basically business people—success-oriented careerists with great fascination for a certain kind of problem solving. They may well devote their lives to being the first to isolate a particular hormone to develop a certain technique. And that's it, finis. Many of them go home to their families in the evening without ever thinking about the evolutionary biosocial significance of their families; some attend church without being bothered by the incongruities between prayers and science.

For those who do think beyond these confines, who have philosophical ambitions or unsatisfied needs in growth of spirit, I would say that scientific materialism is very much of a belief system and can be blinding in terms of its effects on attitudes and ways of thinking. However, I believe that this effect is likely to be lessened in the future as the social sciences, sociobiology, and neurobiology become more sophisticated. Then when we ask, "What is the meaning of man?" or "What is religion?" there will be more ready answers available in textbooks and the popular press. It won't be so much a matter of blind faith, but instead a domain of intellectual inquiry open to everyone.

Saver: In your own textbook, *Life on Earth,* you call the evolutionary struggle for survival "the ultimate existential game," and in *Sociobiology* you sympathetically quote Camus. How would you distinguish scientific materialism from a competing atheism, existentialism?

Wilson: What I like most about Camus is the poetry in his prose, the way he vividly captures the existentialist attitude. As much distaste as I have for most French philosophy I've read, I have an almost unnatural attraction for that common French style of writing that is polemical, heated, and tends to cut to the center of things quickly.

As I understand the original French version, existentialism is a relatively uninformed and attitudinal approach to the meaning of human life. Its central pronouncement is that man is alone and that he makes himself, that each individual must create himself in life. Now that of course is not incompatible with a full-fledged scientific materialism. The difference is that the latter is informed. It recognizes that in shaping ourselves we make choices among different biological channels of development along which we naturally tend to move. We have certain epigenetic rules of mental development that guide us with varying strengths in the different categories of behavior. Certain activities give us deep satisfaction innately and hence require a very small amount of learning and effort; others are acquired only with great difficulty but may eventually be very rewarding, while still others automatically repel us. So I look on sociobiology as a development that is not incompatible with existentialism, but which provides a program for acquiring information toward a rational reconstruction of humanity. It can expand the spirit in a way that is a great deal more comforting, efficient, and hopeful than the original existentialism.

Saver: This hopefulness runs counter to what seemed to me to be an apocalyptic element in some of your writings. You have suggested that at some point, roughly one hundred years from now, man will subscribe to a fully materialistic view of behavior and so be deprived of the support of all religious "illusions," be facing momentous decisions about where to aim his evolutionary future, and, having overcome the problem of supplying his material needs, be confronting his residual spiritual emptiness. You often seem very happy that you can say that all this is one hundred years away, that it's not for our generation to confront. But do you have any words that you think would be of help to those who will be living at that critical time, if it indeed comes to pass?

Wilson: Yes. Your question is drawn, I think, from the wistful note with which I ended *Sociobiology.* I was thinking very much in terms of sociobiology's contrast with dogmatic religion, with all the pleasures and, as Camus said, the "illusions and lights" of unexamined beliefs that compel us to feel awe and mystery and sustain us over a lifetime, if we are somehow able to remain committed to mysticism. I was enthusiastic about neurobiology and sociobiology and envisioned that one hundred years would be enough to produce an exact social science and a pretty complete understanding of how the mind works, where it came from, and what the meaning of it is. And I concluded that this knowledge will take away the illusions and the lights that most of humanity so conspicuously enjoys—but that we still have a century before that really takes hold.

My thinking brightened somewhat as I wrote *On Human Nature*. I now feel that, once we have achieved that understanding, we will have opened up endlessly branching new avenues of exploration in the examination of life and mind. Once you know how the violin is constructed, you can still compose and produce original melodies of unimagined beauty, and perhaps with even greater frequency. And then there will be the rest of the world, the rest of life, which a fuller materialistic view will free us to explore in an unhampered and more satisfying manner. I'm not sure if I've answered your question, but it is true that from the somewhat gloomy, fatalistic position at the close of *Sociobiology* I've moved to a more open, optimistic way of looking at the future.

Saver: I'd like to ask you a more personal question. One cannot help but be struck by the impression that, despite being an opponent of dogmatic religion, you have a genuine sensitivity to the religious viewpoint and a very real sense of what it is the atheist has lost. Does this knowledge spring from a source in your upbringing and religious background?

Wilson: Yes, it does. I was raised a Southern Baptist in Alabama and Florida, and had a traditional Baptist upbringing, including baptism and being born again at the age of seventeen. I was immersed, literally immersed in the chapel water tank, in a strong evangelical tradition. One holdover to which I readily admit is the delight I take in constructing a good sermon, and I suppose *On Human Nature* reflects this. In a recent *Time* article, the writer was uncomfortably close to the truth when he called me "the chief preacher of sociobiology."

I abandoned the doctrines of my religious background rather early, in the traditional manner of an emancipated young college student and intellectual. Yet I remained very sensitive to the deep religious needs of people that I had perceived so vividly when I was growing up. Mine was not the experience of a young wealthy New York Episcopalian or secular upper-middle-class Jew with a certain ethnic affiliation blended with rational detachment. I saw the power of the charismatic religion all around me, in my family and the people I lived with, and therefore could appreciate the strength of the need that people have for some kind of satisfaction of the religious impulse. Probably a major motivation in my later research, particularly now that I've become more involved in philosophical and other generalizing scholarship, has been an attempt to recapture that religious feeling, but in a more sustainable form.

Saver: My last question is this. You've said that the cosmological God is a last, unassailable redoubt of theology, that science will never be able to disprove the concept of God as creator of the universe. You have also said this concept of God cannot alone sustain organized religion, for by itself it is unable to unleash the deep emotions and allegiances of man's biological religious impulse. However,

I've never seen you discuss whether you yourself believe in the cosmological God. Do you?

Wilson: I am at this point uncommitted. I won't say that I'm an agnostic, since agnosticism maintains that one *cannot* know. But I'm not averse to the idea of some intelligence or organizing force that set the initial conditions of the universe in such a way that ultimately generated stars, planets, and life. Physicists tell us that the physical constants and certain parameters of the known physical laws had to fall within a limited range in order to permit the evolution of molecules and aggregate matter. If they had been set otherwise, you would have had a universe that was eternally composed entirely of energy or low-level subatomic particles. But in fact the variables are adjusted and do exist within the limits required for atomic build-up, planetary bodies, and the potential for life to develop. And that's worth pondering.

(Spring 1985)

X.

The New Ethics

Humanist ethics—some would call this an oxymoron. For how can a person lead a moral, upstanding life without adhering to some form of religious belief? Indeed, is not religion the very *basis* for ethical standards? Without the threats of eternal punishment that religions exact for wrongdoing, would not all moral restraint immediately disappear? Secular humanists are quite familiar with the famous statement made by Dostoyevsky: "Without God, everything is permitted."

As the following articles show, *Free Inquiry* has always been concerned about the popular conception that religion and morality go hand in hand. After all, such a conception immediately puts the nonreligious on the defensive. "How can you be moral without being religious?" they are challenged. However, as Joe Edward Barnhart demonstrates in his article "The Relativity of Biblical Ethics," religious beliefs in and of themselves do not always provide clear-cut guidelines to ethical behavior, and certain sacred texts would seem to actually condone behavior such as lying and killing, which are usually considered to be highly immoral. The point is, one must evaluate the various commandments found in the Bible, the Talmud, the Koran, the Book of Mormon and other holy works, before one follows them. A humanist, who uses reason and evidence to test truth claims, can rightly counter the above challenge by asking, "How can *you* be moral by blindly adhering to religious tenets?"

The relationship between religion and morality is by no means as clear-cut as it seems. The argument over whether or not religion is the basis of morality dates back to at least the time of Plato, who deals with it in his dialogue *The Euthyphro*. The title character of the dialogue is a callow know-it-all bent upon prosecuting his own father for murder—not because he's particularly upset by the action itself (the victim was his father's slave) but because to commit murder is to go against the will of the gods. Socrates meets Euthyphro outside of the Athenian courtroom, where he himself will soon be sentenced for the crime of impiety, and he questions him on the nature of reverence to the gods. Is it not the case, he asks, that it is often very difficult to ascertain just what constitutes proper reverence for the gods? And is it not often almost impossible to understand just what it is they want us to do? Also, are there not times when actions such as murder, usually thought to go against the gods' wishes, are nonetheless excusable—for instance, when one engages in acts of self-defense? Euthyphro grows more and more uncomfortable with Socrates' interrogation. It becomes clear that he has no real explanation as to why the gods decree certain actions to be permissible and others forbidden. Socrates then asks him the all-important question: Is an action right because the gods say it is, or do the gods concur with it because it is right? Such a question cuts to the very heart of all divinely sanctioned ethical systems. Euthyphro has no real response, and he quickly goes on his merry way to continue his paternal prosecution.

Do *humanists* have a real response to Socrates' question? The articles in this section attempt to spell out the humanist position on ethical behavior. Sidney Hook shows that moral virtues and religious belief are not synonymous, that the existence of a supreme deity is irrelevant in evaluating the moral worth of an individual.

Tom Franczyk's article dispels the old canard that secular humanists are an evil and pernicious influence upon society. In fact, it is humanists who are the upholders of the long and noble tradition that human beings must rely upon their own abilities and good will to better their existence and the existence of those around them.

But Marvin Kohl leaves us with another point worth considering. Even if we grant that religions are not the basis for morality, they still play a powerful role in enforcing moral duties. "Thou shalt not" is a useful tool for keeping people in line. Does humanism, which places its reliance upon self-determination and reason-ableness, have an adequate enforcement factor of its own? Or might Dostoyevsky have been right after all?

It is helpful at this point to recall the words of Bertrand Russell's "The Faith of a Rationalist," which closes with the following statement:

> Men tend to have the beliefs that suit their passions. Cruel men believe in a cruel god and use their belief to excuse cruelty. Only kindly men believe in a kindly god, and they would be kindly in any case. . . . More and more people are becoming unable to accept traditional beliefs. If they think that, apart from these beliefs, there is no reason for kindly behavior, the results may be needlessly unfortunate. This is why it is important to show no supernatural reasons are needed to make men kind and to prove that only through kindness can the human race achieve happiness.

Free Inquiry has been in the forefront of the battle for personal freedoms and self-autonomy. It devoted an issue to "The Case for Active Euthanasia" because it strongly holds that it is up to each individual to determine his or her own quality of life. The statement contained in this section was drafted by Gerald Larue, president emeritus of the Hemlock Society, a national organization devoted to advocating the right to die with dignity.

Ethics will continue to be a subject much debated in *Free Inquiry*. Humanism, with its commitment to moral excellence and its view that human beings have both the ability and the inclination to better the world they live in, *does* have a powerful ethical code. Far from being an oxymoron, humanist ethics is quite a harmonious phrase.

—T.M.

The Relativity of Biblical Ethics
Joe Edward Barnhart

It is an axiom among fundamentalists and evangelicals that theology is the foundation of ethics and morality in North American culture. Without this foundation, they fear, ethics would fragment into total relativism or dissolve into whim, arbitrariness, and chaos. I would like to contest that view by showing how some organized religions are parasitical to the body of ethics and how the Bible itself exemplifies moral relativism.

Various theologians of the Middle Ages raised the interesting question of whether right and wrong are whatever God decrees them to be. For example, if God had commanded "Thou shall rape thrice daily," would it have been morally right to carry out the command and wrong to disobey it? If divine decree is not only the source but the *ultimate criterion* of right and wrong, is there any basis for trusting the Supreme Being who concocts the meaning of right and wrong? Indeed, were this putative Being to trick his creatures by scrambling the consequences of commands and prohibitions, it would be irrational to call him evil; he is the Cosmic Existentialist who invents right and wrong *ex nihilo*. If he should lie, deceive, order Joshua to slaughter the Canaanites, or command rape, he could do all this and still label himself as perfectly good.

Apparently having second thoughts about a Supreme Being unrestrained by moral principles, in the year of his death C. S. Lewis wrote: "The real danger is of coming to believe such dreadful things about Him. The conclusion I dread is not 'So there's no God after all,' but 'So this is what God is really like. Deceive yourself no longer.' "[1] Only four months before his death, Lewis wrote in a letter to an American philosopher that there were dangers in judging God by moral standards. However, he maintained, that "the dangers of believing in a God whom we cannot but regard as evil, and then, in mere terrified flattery calling Him 'good' and worshipping Him, is a still greater danger."[2] Lewis was responding specifically to the question of Joshua's slaughter of the Canaanites by divine decree and Peter's striking Ananias and Sapphira dead. Knowing that the evangelical doctrine of the Bible's infallibility required him to approve of "the attrocities (and treacheries) of Joshua," Lewis made this surprising concession: "The ultimate question is whether the doctrine of the goodness of God or that of the inerrancy of Scripture is to prevail when they conflict. I think the doctrine of the goodness of God is the more certain of the two. Indeed, only that doctrine renders this worship of Him obligatory or even permissible."[3]

In short, Lewis came close to saying that the Supreme Might must live up to moral standards if he is to be regarded as God and not as some cosmic sadist unworthy of worship.

In his letter to the philosopher, Lewis expresses the realization that he could not wholly relativize and trivialize the concept of goodness for the Supreme Being he envisioned:

> To this some will reply "ah, but we are fallen and don't recognize good when we see it." But God Himself does not say that we are as fallen as all that. He constantly, in Scripture, appeals to our conscience: "Why do ye not *of yourselves* judge what is right?"—"What fault hath my people found in Me?" And so on. Socrates' answer to Euthyphro is used in Christian form by Hooker. Things are not good because God commands them; God commands certain things because he sees them to be good. (In other words, the Divine Will is the obedient servant of the Divine Reason.) The opposite view (Ockham's, Paley's) leads to an absurdity. If "good" means "what God wills" then to say "God is good" can mean only "God wills what he wills." Which is equally true of you or me or Judas or Satan.[4]

Lewis was not always consistent in his attempt to find a foundation for morality. In some of his earlier books he suggests that God's goodness is compatible with whatever happens, which, instead of giving theism any advantage over atheism, does little more than make Cosmic Might the personification of moral randomness, of relativism gone out of control.

Recently, I asked a fundamentalist author and apologist who had labeled abortion as murder to tell me whether the killing of pregnant Canaanite women by putative divine decree and Joshua's sword was murder. He replied that the unborn babies killed by Joshua went straight to heaven—which of course does not answer the question of whether God commanded *murder* or whether God is above (or below) moral standards. The point here is not to determine whether the fetus is a person but to call attention to the fact that there is considerable moral and ethical relativism in theology and the Bible. Consider this passage from Deuteronomy:

> He whose testicles are crushed or whose male member is cut off shall not enter the assembly of the Lord.
>
> No bastard shall enter the assembly of the Lord; even to the tenth generation none of his descendants shall enter the assembly of the Lord.

> No Ammorite or Moabite shall enter the assembly of the Lord; even to the tenth generation none belonging to them shall enter the assembly of the Lord for ever. [Deut. 23:1-2 (RSV)]

Whatever the circumstances prompting these prohibitions, it is noteworthy that fundamentalist and evangelical apologists find it necessary to call upon their own version of situation ethics in order to make it clear that not all moral injunctions in the scriptures are moral absolutes. Evangelical scholar G. T. Manley in *The New Bible Commentary,* tries to justify the morally inferior outlook found in Deuteronomy by noting that it belongs to "the Mosaic age, and [is] quite different from that of the later monarchy."[5]

Unfortunately, to cast the biblical material in historical context (as doubtless it should be) serves only to emphasize the historical relativism of so-called biblical morality. Indeed, the very notion of a complete and self-consistent biblical morality is problematic. The attempt by some evangelicals to borrow the "progressive revelation" principle in order to make the claim that the later revelation (i.e., the New Testament) stands on a higher plane than the earlier revelation (the Old Testament) collapses when one considers the rage against, and hatred of, most of the human race exemplified in the Book of Revelation. And certainly the threat found in Hebrews 6:4-6—which proclaims that God will never forgive a repentant apostate—is more, not less, vicious than anything found in the Old Testament. When theologians try to justify the vendetta that the Book of Revelation describes in lurid detail, they demonstrate just how perverse the human mind can sometimes become.

Those who believe that the Bible presents its readers moral absolutes have failed to acknowledge the staggering diversity of its moral perspectives. These differing perspectives are often grounded in the political and evangelical experiences of the early Christian church. Professor Daniel Fuller, noted evangelical scholar and former president of Fuller Seminary, pointed out to me, for example, that the apostle Paul had three major problems to face in the early Christian churches: (1) the wall separating Jew and gentile, (2) the wall separating male and female, and (3) the wall separating slave from free citizen. According to Fuller, Paul, whose theological interpretation of Christ's teachings formed the foundation of the church, felt that he had to make a practical decision to concentrate on the problem of the ethnic and religious relationship between Judaism and Christianity to the exclusion of the other two problems. Fuller's point is that, while racism and sexism are *in principle* undermined by the Christian gospel ("Love thy neighbor as thyself"), Paul was forced to leave to later generations the application of this subversive Christian insight to the problems of racism and sexism. For Paul, getting the church off the ground was the key thing; to try to implement total Christian justice would have scared most potential converts away. I take this to be an example of situation ethics. Whether Paul utilized situation ethics in order to advance the *agape* principle of 1 Corinthians 13 more effectively is a question open for debate. As Morton Smith ably demonstrated in *Free Inquiry*

(Spring 1987) there is much in the Bible that contributed to the institution of slavery and little that in actual practice moved against it. Even the Golden Rule of the New Testament, because of its abstractness and adaptability, has throughout history often failed to override the deep-seated racial bigotry of the Book of Genesis.

The doctrine of election accepted by the Puritans did not incline them to gentleness in their dealing with inferior races. The savage Negroes and the savage Indians were accursed peoples whom it was quite proper to destroy or enslave. "We know not when or how these Indians first became the inhabitants of this mighty continent," says Cotton Mather, "yet we may guess that probably the Devil decoyed these miserable savages hither, in hope that the gospel of the Lord Jesus Christ would never come to destroy or disturb this absolute empire over them."[6]

To be sure, the Bible gives conflicting messages regarding the assimilation of strange peoples. Compare, for example, the books of Ruth and Ezra. The moving and humanistic story of Ruth in the Old Testament is viewed by some scholars as a moral challenge to the Deuteronomic injunction to bar Moabites from the Lord's assembly. The book tells the story of an Israelite man who, because of famine in Israel, chose to move to Moab, taking his wife Naomi with him. The man died, leaving Naomi with two sons, one of whom married Ruth, a Moabite. In time, the two Israelite sons living in Moab died, leaving Naomi with two widowed daughters-in-law. According to this tightly woven story, when the famine in Israel passed and Naomi returned to her homeland, Ruth the Moabitess moved with her, asserting, "Your people shall be my people, and your God my God" (Ruth 1:16 RSV).

The author of the Book of Ruth remarks again and again that Ruth was the Moabitess; she even calls herself "a foreigner." Despite this, Boaz (of Bethlehem in Judah) takes Ruth for his wife. He marries her in part because of the goodness she has shown her mother-in-law, Naomi. Boaz declares that "all my fellow townsmen know that you are a woman of worth" (3:11 RSV).

The story closes with a telling blow against racial bigotry: Ruth has a son, Obed, who in time becomes the grandfather of none other than David himself. So, the Moabitess is the great-grandmother of Israel's most beloved king.

The moral conclusion of the book of Ezra is less savory. According to Ezra 9 and 10 the Israelite exiles returning from captivity had brought a curse on themselves. God had sent a heavy rain to the land as punishment for their sin of marrying foreign women and bringing them back to pollute the land of Israel. Ezra's solution was simple. Those Israelite men who had foreign (even Moabite) wives should demonstrate their faithfulness to God by putting all these wives away. If the story of Ezra 10 reflects an actual historical period, we must believe that there was wholesale divorce in the land of Israel during Ezra's time. Indeed, Ezra destroyed more than the marriages. Upon his command, and in the name of God, the men who had married foreign women were forced to separate themselves from their children as well.

It is interesting to see how this kind of moral relativism is perpetuated by evangelical commentaries. In *The New Bible Commentary*, evangelical scholar J. Stafford Wright claims that Ezra's morality should be accorded the status of a norm, the biblical story of Ruth merely an exception to the rule. This strange piece of gerrymandering becomes even more strange when set against the background of the apostle Paul's instruction, which is the opposite of Ezra's. Paul advises the Christian woman who is married to an unbeliever to remain with him as long as he consents to the marriage. Paul then says that the children will greatly benefit by the marriage being kept intact. Ezra's justification for commanding divorce is that the mixed marriage is a pollution or defilement. Paul's justification for advising against divorce is twofold: to provide the Christian with opportunities in marriage to spiritually redeem her or his spouse, and to prevent the children from becoming "unclean" (1 Cor. 7:12–16).

Those who think that the Bible is above situation ethics might find the following worth pondering. In 1 Corinthians 7:20–31, Paul appears to believe that the end of the world is around the corner. In the context of that conviction, the following advice is given: "Every one should remain in the state in which he was called" (1 Cor. 7:20 RSV). Paul elaborates:

> I think that in view of the impending distress it is well for a person to remain as he is. Are you bound to a wife? Do not seek to be free. Are you free from a wife? Do not seek marriage. But if you marry, you do not sin. Yet those who marry will have worldly troubles, and I would spare you that. I mean, brethren, the appointed time has grown very short; from now on, let those who have wives live as thou they had none . . . and those who mourn as though they were not mourning, and those who rejoice as though they were not rejoicing, and those who buy as though they had no goods, and those who deal with the world as though they had no dealings with it. For the form of this world is passing away. [1 Cor. 7:26–31]

It turned out that Paul's judgment of the historical situation was in error. The end was not around the corner, and this miscalculation made his situational advice less than useful. Human miscalculation is one of the weaknesses of situation ethics; but it is a weakness inherent in finite human nature—and it is finite human nature that pervades biblical thought.

My criticism, however, is not of situation ethics. Rather, I criticize those theologians who tell people that biblical ethics advances moral absolutes. In fact, so-called biblical ethics is situation ethics that often sets itself up as immutable divine decree. The unfortunate consequence of this tactic is that moral positions taken in the Bible are denied the useful process of criticism and refinement, a process that is essential if ethics is to escape the brutalizing effects of dogmatism.

Notes

1. C. S. Lewis, *A Grief Observed* (New York: Seabury Press, 1963), pp. 9–10.

2. July 3, 1963, letter from C. S. Lewis to John Beversluis. Letter quoted in full in John Beversluis, *C. S. Lewis and the Search for Rational Religion* (Grand Rapids: Eerdmans, 1985), pp. 156f.

3. Ibid., p. 157. Italics added.

4. Ibid., p. 157.

5. G. T. Manley, in *The New Bible Commentary,* 2nd ed., F. Davidson, ed. (Grand Rapids: Eerdmans, 1954), p. 215.

6. Thomas J. Wertenbaker, *The First Americans, 1607–1690* (Chicago: Quadrangle Books, 1971), pp. 231f.

7. J. Stafford Wright, in *The New Bible Commentary,* op. cit., p. 371.

(Summer 1987)

God and Morality

Sidney Hook

The relation between religion and morality, public and private, has so many facets that a brief treatment can only suggest lines for development. Although we continually hear that the validity of a moral judgment presupposes the existence of God or some transcendental power, it is demonstrable that no one can derive a judgment of what is good or right from the alleged fact of a divine command without antecedently claiming to know the meaning of good and bad, right and wrong. This is a Platonic and Kantian commonplace.

Similarly, whether "a person led a good life and significantly contributed to society without the benefit of religious belief" is not a problematic question. Everyone is acquainted with someone or has read about someone like Socrates, Spinoza, Mill, or Dewey who, without belief in the gods of religious faith, led a life that would be universally considered a good life.

The genuine problem that seems to recur whenever there is a periodic outbreak of criminality or anti-social conduct that results in social disorder is whether, despite the autonomy of moral judgment, human behavior in the large will conform to the standards of morality in the absence of mass belief in some form of organized religion. Those who maintain that public and private morality ultimately depends upon sincere religious belief and religious practices admit that here and there atheists and agnostics can live the good life of men and women and perform all the duties of good citizens. Usually it is said that these worthy citizens are living on the moral capital, so to speak, of past religious belief, as assertion that clearly begs the question and reverts to the demonstably false belief that unless we believed in God we would not know the meaning of good and bad, right and wrong. But, in the end, those who argue for the necessity of undergirding moral behavior by religious belief assert as a matter of empirical fact that, despite the presence of some secular saints or moral, law-abiding atheists, no society can survive for long as a morally good society if religious belief and practice have been eroded. Sooner or later, if religious belief and practice fall into desuetude, the norms of public and private morality that have been internalized as a result of religious training are themselves gradually undermined. Everything then seems morally permissible. Only the exercise or threat of police power keeps people in line.

The view that religious belief and practice were indispensable for the preservation of social order, not only between classes, but within classes, seems to have been held by leading statesmen like Napolean and Metternich, who were not themselves noteworthy for their religious piety. Some members of elite groups in Western society who cite themselves as illustrations of the possiblility of living by a morality without religion are dubious about the same being true for the commonality of mankind. Whatever may be the case for the enlightened thinker, "we need religion for the masses."

The great difficulty with the position that, regardless of its intellectual validity, belief in God and instructional practices associated with that belief are required for the preservation of morality is the historical record itself from antiquity to the present. Until very recently, all Western societies have been religious societies in which divine worship and church attendance were normal modes of behavior. Why is it that these religious societies have become secularized, and why have religious education and belief failed to sustain modes of ethical behavior different from the current mores often deplored by the pious as "a breakdown in moral behavior"? If faith in religion is required to sustain the standards of a moral society and our present-day society is regarded as immoral, what justification is there for believing that a return to religion would lead to an improvement in moral behavior? Obviously it cannot be a return to "the good old-fashioned religion of the past." For that did not do what was expected of it. Must we find a new religious outlook?

If there is a return to religious faith in order to safeguard the foundations of moral behavior, what measures will be adopted to prevent the leaching out of that faith and the spread of the skeptical outlook that led to the secularization of society and the demise of "old-fashioned religion" in the first place? Surely it is not being proposed in the interests of a new religious faith to curb the progress of scientific research, whose Copernican and Darwinian revolutions did so much to call the religious dogmas of the past into question. And if the new religion is prepared to leave the catalogue of the furniture of heaven and earth to the discoveries of scientific cosmology, how does it differ from the religion of Ethical Culture except in its colorful pageantry?

There is a further difficulty in reading the historical record as it concerns the moral behavior of religious societies. Despite the common religious beliefs of Western societies, there are marked variations in the public and private moralities of these societies reflected, for example, in the reports written by foreign travelers on the way they have been treated or mistreated. And within any particular religious society there are marked differences in behavior considered acceptable and unacceptable, as in Puritan and Restoration England. Can these variations in moral behavior plausibly be correlated with different intensities of religious faith? Does transcendental religious dogma of any kind uniquely determine a pattern of ethical behavior or judgment? If a person calls himself or herself a Christian, will he or she subscribe to the moral values of Torquemada or Tolstoy, Aimee Semple McPherson or Mother Teresa?

Finally, there seems to be good reason to believe that the moral behavior of individuals does not depend so much on ratiocination as on early education. If, according to Matthew Arnold, conduct is nine-tenths of morality, habit, according to John Dewey, is ninety-nine one-hundredths of morality. The moral virtues—honesty, thoughtfulness, truthfulness, etc.—to be operative must become habits long before children can understand the justification for them. The moral situation arises in human experience when values conflict. Even if the child is taught that violations of moral value will be punished by God or hellfire, this by itself does not determine the specific action that is morally desirable in the situation. Here is where reflective morality begins and with it responsibility for the consequences of actions taken or not taken. There is a need for improving the quality of moral education in our schools to supplement and sometimes to modify the moral education children receive at home, if they receive any. A good case can be made on reflective grounds for the existence and recognition of rules and laws as in general law-abiding behavior. Although it is not the best and should not be the only reason, fear of the law is sometimes a good reason for obeying the law. If law enforcement becomes capricious, uncertain, or lax, this may be a contributing factor to the decline of public morality.

There are great many problems and difficulties in developing and implementing a program of moral education in our schools and homes. But, if our aim is to develop reflective men and women who are prepared to accept responsibility for the moral choices they make, at no point will the injection of religious faith facilitate the process.

*   *   *

As far as my own personal history goes, it was my moral judgment that undermined my religious belief. Shortly before my confirmation, I discovered the problem of evil. I could not reconcile divine omnipotence with the sufferings of the innocent and the affluence of the wicked. Neither my rabbi nor my parents could allay my doubts. Nor in the course of a long life have I found anyone who could. This creates a difficulty for those who by some variation of the argument from design have convinced themselves that the world has a rational designer. The conclusion is not logically impossible but has a low degree of probability. But if there is a rational designer he is more like a Devil than like an all-loving God. And that could hardly serve as a premise for human morality.

I do not believe there is empirical evidence that large ideas about the existence of God, freedom, and immortality have a direct bearing on human behavior and that the erosion of transcendental beliefs gets expressed in immoral conduct. Man is more a creature of habit than of sudden impulse inspired by belief or loss of belief. If we were to be told that all laws were suddenly to be suspended and that we were free to do what we pleased without let or hindrance, most human beings would continue on their round of duties. The patterns of habit, the weight of peer pressure, family, and public opinion would still operate. It is true, of course, that in the absence of any physical sanctions for a sustained period of time or the breakdown of law and order, there would be an increase in immoral and criminal behavior among those few who had lived up to the demands of the law primarily out of fear of the law, and then among others who were influenced by the spectacle of others violating the traditionally accepted canons of law-abiding behavior with impunity.

But does this not vindicate the position of those who plead the social necessity of religion? No, because fear of the Lord and hellfire is certainly not the same as fear of the law. Whatever may have been the case in the primitive religious societies of the past is certainly no longer true in modern secular cultures. Some religious thinkers who believe in the total depravity of man may resign themselves to the belief that only fear of the Lord and his terrible punishments can keep the feet of man on the path of virtue. Most religionist today would not regard very highly moral behavior inspired only by fear of being caught out. They, too, admit that there are other causes well as grounds of moral behavior independent of speculative fancies and fears of otherworldly creatures.

There are some who postulate the existence of God and an afterlife in order to achieve cosmic harmony of justice in which the wicked who prosper at the expense of the virtuous in this world and the virtuous who suffer at the hands of the wicked get their deserts. But such a postulate is obviously question-begging since it assumes that the cosmic order is a moral order. There is no evidence for such an assumption. The ways of the cosmos, the order of things, are indifferent to human weal and woe, to good and evil. There is no point in wailing about this or hurling romantic defiance against nature. It is sufficient that the cosmos make possible the organization of a good society and the pursuit of a good life or one better than what we have known in the past.

A pious friend once told me that such a view of the world required more courage than was available to most people he knew. Perhaps he was alluding to the fact that it had no rational place for prayer or, since prayer can take many different forms, prayers for intercession into the natural order. It may very well be that human beings cannot live without belief in some vital illusions. But even if true, this does not require belief in the illusions of supernaturalism.

(Winter 1986/87)

Are Secular Humanists Evil?

Tom Franczyk

The classic but unfounded argument against secular humanism, nonbelief in the supernatural, and atheism states that there can be no morality or goodness without belief and faith in one god or another and that ethics can only have a meaningful basis in religion. (I use a definition of religion that includes belief in God or some other supernatural concept.) We hear these assertions from American pulpits, we read them in the op-ed pages, and even the president of the United States repeats them more often than we care to hear. Humanists have been called "evil," "pernicious," "the new barbarians," and some things I won't repeat here; and these accusations are spread nationwide.

In one editorial that crossed my desk, a clergyman claimed that "a godless system of education . . . will only enhance to create a generation of monsters and criminals in the society." The fundamentalists, the orthodox, and even religious "liberals" generally concur with that sentiment, although all would not choose the same language. Yet no evidence—that is, real evidence and not conjecture—is offered to support their assumptions. Could it be just wishful thinking on their part? Is all of this name-calling employed because religion would have no purpose, other than social, unless these allegations were valid?

I will not argue here why I consider morality based on nonbelief more solid than morality based on God or why taking responsibility for one's actions is better than shrugging it off on a deity. But there is a way to check this with some degree of veracity: compare the number of felons confined in our penal institutions who believe in a god with the number who don't believe. If the argument stated above is valid, one would expect nonbelievers to constitute a *vastly* inordinate proportion when compared with their relative numbers in society as a whole.

A study published in the *Sociology and Research Journal* (May-June 1949) found that 0.5 percent of 85,000 convicts polled were nonbelievers. There is no reason to believe that this dated study is not valid today. Since 85 percent of today's convicts are listed as Christians or Jews, according to some surveys, the other 15 percent must include members of all other religions, unaffiliated theists, and nonbelievers. It is generally accepted that nonbelievers constitute at least 7 percent of the population in the United States. It would seem apparent that secular humanists are not crowding our prisons.

Those who take the Bible literally should know where good and evil—morality and immorality—come from: "I make peace and create evil: I the Lord do all these things" (Isaiah 45:7 [KJV]). It is absurd for *them* to blame secular humanists for all that they perceive as wrong with the world. If one arbitrarily equates evil with nonbelief, there is no sense in further rational discussion.

(Spring 1987)

Morality Without Religion
Marvin Kohl

Secular humanists and their opponents are fond of debating the vague question, Can one be moral and not believe in God? The question is vague because it is glaringly unclear. As a rule, it leads to senseless dispute. If the question is interpreted (as secular humanists would be inclined to interpret it) to mean 'Is it possible for a person to follow, in general, the principles or precepts of justice, veracity, beneficence, and not believe in a theist-type god?' then the answer, based on evidence of the behavior of some agnostics and atheists, is in the affirmative. On the other hand, if the question is interpreted to mean (as most theists are likely to interpret it) 'Is it possible for a person to be moral (i.e., to believe in God *and* generally follow his commandments) and, at the same time, not believe in God?' then the answer, for reasons of logic, is in the negative.

There are, I agree, a few intellectuals who would be content with this kind of standoff. But many would not. The secularist probably would reject the identification of morality with belief in God and following his commandments. He would insist that, even if one admitted that God exists and commands only what is good, one has to know independently what is good in order to know what God commands. The theist, on the other hand, probably would insist, and I think correctly so, that one of the basic issues here is not what exceptional persons can or cannot do but whether or not ordinary men and women can be moral without belief in God. He argues that the exception does not make the rule. The fact that some men can run the four-minute mile or can be moral without an explicit commitment to God does not mean that men generally can do either of these things.

The secularist, of course, rejects the latter move and quickly takes up the gauntlet. He argues that ordinary people can be taught morality and that this in no way entails religious belief. He maintains that with proper education, especially in early childhood, men can be trained to be moral and that this can be accomplished without any appeal to religious belief. "Early religious teaching," writes Mill, "has owed its power over mankind rather to its being early than its being religious."[1]

> When . . . any rule of life and duty, whether grounded or not on religion, has conspicuously received the general assent, it obtains a hold on the belief of every individual, stronger than it would have even if he had arrived at it by the inherent force of his own understanding. . . . And, as it cannot be imagined that the commands of God are to young children anything more than the commands of their parents, it is reasonable to think that any system of social duty which mankind might adopt, even though divorced from religion, would have the same advantage of being inculcated from childhood. . . .[2]

Indeed, it is tempting to conclude that Mill and the secular humanists are right. For if the original question is interpreted to mean 'Can ordinary men and women be educated to believe in and generally follow the principles of justice, veracity, and beneficence and not believe in God?' then it would appear that the available evidence clearly supports the secular-humanist contention. Given a kindly environment and proper moral training at an early age, it seems to be true that individuals so educated generally will behave in a moral manner.

I have two worries. The first, the lesser one, is that this conclusion is only likely to appeal to those who advocate soft theism, that is, those who believe that, although God exists and is the source of morality, morality can be learned and effectively practiced without commitment to a deity. It is improbable that it will appeal to, or in any significant way alter, the beliefs of the advocates of hard theism, that is, those who claim that in order to be moral a person must explicitly believe in God and follow his commandments. Contrary to what the secular humanist often likes to believe, the hard theist maintains, first, that both the goodness and justice of God can be derived from his existence and, second, that morality therefore demands a commitment to his existence. In other words, the claim is that God's existence entails his goodness, that morality thereby requires a commitment to Him (and not merely a belief that He exists), and that this is known to be true. My point is a simple one. I am not suggesting that what the theist claims is known to be true or that the teleological argument is viable. Quite the contrary. I believe that a formidable case can be made for igtheism (the claim that we know that we have no knowledge about God) and against the teleological argument. What I wish to suggest is that if the purpose of raising the God-morality question is to convince the hard theist, and if there is no common ground for doing so, as appears to be the case, then the undertaking has little point.

My second worry raises a complex and difficult question, one that has been relatively neglected in the literature. The question is, 'Can ordinary people be moral without an enforcement factor and is belief in God a sufficient enforcement factor?'[3] Any general answer to this question is likely to be too simple; but I suspect that one reason people are inclined to identify morality with belief in God is that they reject the notion that holding people to be praiseworthy, or blameworthy, is sufficient, sufficient to prevent self-interest, in moments of serious conflict, from overruling the commands of morality. They maintain that, without an enforcement factor (in this case the threat of God's judgment and punishment), people will behave morally only when it is convenient. In short, the claim is that, while morality can be taught, the effectiveness of this teaching is roughly proportionate to the power of those beliefs or their correlates to control behavior and that a deep commitment to God is effective because it does accomplish that control; that without God, without an effective enforcement factor, moral etiquette may be taught, but not morality per se.

It may be objected that the history of religion has not been exactly the history of morality; but if this is to be taken to imply that the history of religion has been a history of a deep commitment to God, I think that it is false. What may be true is that we have failed to make ordinary men and women, as well as common clergy, truly religious. But since this is an end that there is no sufficient reason to regard as generally obtainable, and which, when attempted, nurtures a sinister form of totalitarianism, it should be rejected by all who are guided by knowledge and inspired by a genuine love for mankind.

There is another objection, which seems to strike closer to the mark. What if the theist charges that humanist morality—a morality largely based upon the sentiments of praise and blame being the only moral sanction—is, and probably must be, *less effective* than a theist morality based upon the ideal of being truly religious? And what if such an ideal is limited to classical ethical Judaism or the ethics of the Sermon on the Mount? Now it is the fashion in secular circles to mock religious claims. But these questions give rise not to a religious or metaphysical claim but to an empirical one. The general claim is that religion may be morally useful without being otherwise intellectually sustainable. The specific claim is that morality (in contrast to moral etiquette) requires an effective enforcement factor and that, with proper limits, the traditional theist grounding of morality provides a *better* enforcement factor than humanist theories.

As for myself, I share the conviction that morality, if it is to be effective, must have an adequate enforcement factor; that theories in which the sentiments of praise and blame are the sole factor are, in this respect, inadequate; and that, because of the necessity of having to couple adequate moral principles and precepts with an enforcement factor, some theist theories may be better than some humanist ones. However, I would also maintain that humanist theories need not have timid enforcement factors and, therefore, need not become extensionally equivalent with egoism. Where basic human rights are consistent with social justice and are conceived of as claims (or their like), there is no need to surrender oneself to the authority of reactionary humanism or to the illusions of religion.

Notes

1. J. S. Mill, "Utility of Religion," in *Three Essays on Religion* (New York: Henry Holt, 1874), p. 83.

2. Ibid., pp. 79–81.

3. An enforcement factor may be partially defined as something in, or intimately associated with, a theory or moral code that has the power of causing men to act morally when they would have acted otherwise.

(Winter 1980/81)

The Case for Active Voluntary Euthanasia
Drafted by Gerald A. Larue

We, the undersigned, declare our support for the decriminalization of medically induced active euthanasia when requested by the terminally ill.

We acknowledge that techniques developed by modern medicine have been beneficial in improving the quality of life and increasing longevity, but they have sometimes been accompanied by harmful and dehumanizing effects. We are aware that many terminally ill persons have been kept alive against their will by advanced medical technologies, and that terminally ill patients have been denied assistance in dying. In attempting to terminate their suffering by ending their lives themselves or with the help of loved ones not trained in medicine, some patients have botched their suicides and brought further suffering on themselves and those around them. We believe that the time is now for society to rise above the archaic prohibitions of the past and to recognize that terminally ill individuals have the right to choose the time, place, and manner of their own death.

We respect the opinions of those who declare that only the deity should determine the moment of death, or who find some spiritual merit in suffering, but we reject their arguments. We align ourselves with those who are committed to the defense of human rights, human dignity, and human self-determination: this includes the right to die with dignity. An underlying motive is compassion for those who wish to end their suffering by hastening their moment of death.

There are those who would make a distinction between "active" and "passive" euthanasia; they would support the abandonment of "heroic" efforts to sustain life while opposing any positive act to hasten death by increasing dosage of drugs or administering a lethal injection. We point out, however, that both passive and active euthanasia involve the intention of ending a person's life.

We support only *voluntary* euthanasia. We believe that once an adult has signed a living will expressing his or her personal wishes concerning treatment during a terminal illness and/or has signed a durable power of attorney for health care statement enabling another to act on his or her behalf, the individual's wishes should be respected. Because most persons lack professional knowledge concerning methods of inducing death, we believe that only a cooperating medical doctor should be the one to administer the life-taking potion or injection to the patient who has requested it and that the doctor should be able to fulfill the patient's request without fear or threat of prosecution.

We respect the doctor's and the hospital's right to refuse to participate in administering such terminal medications. We would urge the medical profession to make clear the patient's right to change doctors and hospitals should his or her wishes for aid in dying be refused. We would urge that every effort be made to honor the terminally ill person's wishes in regard to the time and place of death, and that if the patient desires family members to be present to give comfort, these requests will be respected.

We recognize that there may be some who would exploit the right to active voluntary euthanasia and take advantage of the ill and suffering. But we believe that protective laws can, and indeed must, be enacted to discourage and punish such action.

We respect the right of terminally ill individuals who do not wish to utilize euthanasia or hasten the moment of death. But we affirm that the wishes of those who believe in the right to die with dignity should be respected and that to do so involves the highest expression of moral compassion and beneficence.

(Winter 1988/89)

Notes on the Contributors

The late **John M. Allegro** was the first British representative on the international team called together in 1953 to edit a newly discovered cache of Dead Sea Scroll fragments. In 1961 he was appointed by H. M. King Hussein as honorary advisor on the scrolls to the Jordanian government. His many books include *The Dead Sea Scrolls and the Christian Myth* and *Physician, Heal Thyself.*

Steve Allen, humorist, songwriter, and author, created and hosted numerous television programs, including "Meeting of Minds" and the "Tonight Show."

Isaac Asimov is perhaps the world's most prolific writer, certainly on issues of science. His more recent books include *The Tyrannosaurus Prescription* and *Past, Present, and Future.*

William Sims Bainbridge, professor of sociology at the University of Washington, is the author of *Dimensions of Science Fiction, Satan's Power,* and other books.

Joe Edward Barnhart is professor of philosophy at North Texas State University. A member of the Committee for the Scientific Examination of Religion, Barnhart is the author of *Jim and Tammy: Charismatic Intrigue Inside PTL* and *The Southern Baptist Holy War,* among many other books.

Robert Basil is the former executive editor of *Free Inquiry* magazine and editor of the anthology *Not Necessarily the New Age: Critical Essays.*

The late **Paul H. Beattie** was president of the Fellowship of Religious Humanists and coeditor of the magazine *Religious Humanism.*

Daniel Boorstin is emeritus Librarian of Congress and the author of numerous works, including *The Discoverers*.

Art Buchwald is an author and a columnist for the Los Angeles Times Syndicate.

L. Sprague de Camp is the author of more than thirty books on science and science fiction, including *The Ragged Edge of Science* and *The Fringe of the Unknown*.

Director of the Institute for Rational-Emotive Therapy in New York City, **Albert Ellis**'s most recent book is *Why Some Therapies Don't Work*.

The late **Sam J. Ervin, Jr.**, served in the United States Senate from 1946 to 1974 and played a central role in the Watergate hearings.

Paul Feyerabend is a professor at the University of California, Berkeley, whose works include *Against Method* and *Science in a Free Society*.

Joseph Fletcher is a theologian and former professor of medical ethics at the University of Virginia Medical School. Widely known as the founder of "situation ethics," he is the author of *The Ethics of Genetic Control: Ending Reproductive Roulette* and *Humanhood: Essays in Biomedical Ethics*.

Thomas Flynn is coeditor of the *Secular Humanist Bulletin*.

Tom Franczyk is coeditor of the *Secular Humanist Bulletin*.

Martin Gardner is a prolific author whose books include *The New Age: Notes of a Fringe-Watcher; Science: Good, Bad and Bogus;* and *The Annotated Alice*.

Mary Beth Gehrman is managing editor of *Free Inquiry* magazine.

Adolf Grünbaum is Andrew Mellon Professor of Philosophy at the University of Pittsburgh. His critique of Freud, *The Foundations of Psychoanalysis,* was extensively debated in *Free Inquiry,* Fall 1985.

R. Joseph Hoffmann is professor of humanities at California State University at Sacramento and chairman of the Biblical Criticism Research Project. He has written and edited many books of biblical criticism, including *Jesus Outside the Gospels* and *The Origins of Christianity*.

The late **Sidney Hook,** one of this century's most persuasive critics of totalitarianism, was professor of philosophy at New York University and a senior research fellow at Stanford University's Hoover Institution. His autobiography, *Out of Step,* was published in 1987.

Marvin Kohl is professor of philosophy at the State University of New York College at Fredonia and the author of *Beneficent Euthanasia* and *The Morality of Killing.*

Paul Kurtz, professor of philosophy at the State University of New York at Buffalo, has written more than 500 articles and twenty-five books, including *The Transcendental Temptation, Forbidden Fruit: The Ethics of Humanism,* and *Eupraxophy: Living Without Religion.* He is the founding editor of *Free Inquiry* magazine.

"Laura Lage" is the pseudonym of a former Jehovah's Witness who now lives in Arizona.

Gerald A. Larue is emeritus professor of religion and adjunct professor of gerontology at the University of Southern California at Los Angeles. He is the president of the Committee for the Scientific Examination of Religion.

Tim Madigan is executive editor of *Free Inquiry* magazine and national coordinator of the magazine's local secular humanist groups.

Jayne Meadows is an accomplished actress who often appeared on "Meeting of Minds," hosted by her husband, Steve Allen.

The late **Sir Karl Popper** was professor emeritus of logic and scientific method at the University of London.

James Randi is a professional conjuror and lecturer who has been investigating claims of psychic phenomena for thirty years. He is a consultant to the Committee for the Scientific Examination of Religion and has written many books, including *Flim-Flam!* and *The Faith Healers.* In 1986 he was awarded a MacArthur Fellowship for his work in exposing the fraud behind psychic surgeons and many televangelists.

Jeffrey Saver is a medical doctor who lives in Boston, Massachusetts.

B. F. Skinner, the world's preeminent behavioral psychologist, is professor emeritus of psychology at Harvard University and author of *Walden Two* and *Beyond Freedom and Dignity.*

George Smith is president of Signature Books, which publishes the works of authors in the Mormon community. He has written for *Dialogue* and *Sunstone,* two intellectual Mormon magazines.

Morton Smith, professor of history at Columbia University, is the author of many works on biblical history, including *Jesus the Magician* and *The Secret Gospel,* and coeditor of *What the Bible Really Says.* Professor Smith is a member of the Biblical Criticism Research Project and the Committee for the Scientific Examination of Religion.

Gordon Stein is the editor of the *Encyclopedia of Unbelief.*

Rita Swan, a former member of the Christian Science church, is the founder and president of Children's Healthcare Is a Legal Duty, Inc. (CHILD) and adjunct professor of English at Morningside College in Sioux City, Iowa.

Thomas Szasz is professor of psychiatry at the Upstate Medical Center, Syracuse University, and the author of *Psychiatric Slavery, The Myth of Mental Illness, The Therapeutic State,* and many other books.

Lowell P. Weicker, Jr., former United States Senator from Connecticut, was a key figure in the 97th Congress in defending religious liberty and the separation of church and state.

E. O. Wilson is Frank B. Baird, Jr., Professor of Science at Harvard University and the author of numerous books, including *The Insect Societies, Sociobiology: The New Synthesis,* and *On Human Nature.*